D0571311

ATM
User-Network
Interface
Specification

Version 3.0

PTR Prentice Hall
Englewood Cliffs, New Jersey 07632

Production editor: *Camille Trentacoste*
Production coordinator: *Alexis Heydt*
Cover design: *Design Solutions*
Cover photo: *Letraset USA, Phototone Image*
Acquisitions editor: *Mary Franz*
Editorial assistant: *Noreen Regina*

© 1993 by The ATM Forum
Published by PTR Prentice Hall
Prentice-Hall, Inc.
A Paramount Communications Company
Englewood Cliffs, New Jersey 07632

The publishers offers discounts on this book when ordered in bulk quantities.
For more information, contact:

Corporate Sales Department
PTR Prentice Hall
113 Sylvan Avenue
Englewood Cliffs, NJ 07632

Phone: 201-592-2863
FAX: 201-592-224

Printed in the United States of America

10 9 8 7 6 5 4 3 2 1

ISBN 0-13-225863-3

Prentice-Hall International (UK) Limited, *London*
Prentice-Hall of Australia Pty. Limited, *Sydney*
Prentice-Hall Canada Inc., *Toronto*
Prentice-Hall Hispanoamericana, S.A., *Mexico*
Prentice-Hall of India Private Limited, *New Delhi*
Prentice-Hall of Japan, Inc., *Tokyo*
Simon & Schuster Asia Pte. Ltd., *Singapore*
Editora Prentice-Hall do Brasil, Ltda., *Rio de Janeiro*

ATM User-Network Interface Specification
Version 3.0
September 10, 1993

The information in this publication is believed to be accurate as of its publication date. Such information is subject to change without notice and the ATM Forum is not responsible for any errors. The ATM Forum does not assume any responsibility to update or correct any information in this publication. Notwithstanding anything to the contrary, neither The ATM Forum nor the publisher make any representation or warranty, expressed or implied, concerning the completeness, accuracy, or applicability of any information contained in this publication. No liability of any kind shall be assumed by The ATM Forum or the publisher as a result of reliance upon any information contained in this publication.

The receipt or any use of this document or its contents does not in any way create by implication or otherwise:

- Any express or implied license or right to or under any ATM Forum member company's patent, copyright, trademark or trade secret rights which are or may be associated with the ideas, techniques, concepts or expressions contained herein; nor

- Any warranty or representation that any ATM Forum member companies will announce any product(s) and/or service(s) related thereto, or if such announcements are made, that such announced product(s) and/or service(s) embody any or all of the ideas, technologies, or concepts contained herein; nor

- Any form of relationship between any ATM Forum member companies and the recipient or user of this document.

Implementation or use of specific ATM standards or recommendations and ATM Forum specifications will be voluntary, and no company shall agree or be obliged to implement them by virtue of participation in the ATM Forum.

The ATM Forum is a non-profit international organization accelerating industry cooperation on ATM technology. The ATM Forum does not, expressly or otherwise, endorse or promote any specific products or services.

Acknowledgements

The Technical Committee of the ATM Forum was able to expeditiously complete this implementation agreement because of the solid base of work done in regional and international standardization groups. Numerous individuals made significant technical contributions. Explicit thanks are due to the editorial team led by Jim Grace. Team members included Richard Breault, John Jaeger, and Lou Wojnaroski.

Glenn Estes
Chairman
The ATM Forum Technical Committee

Foreword

Asynchronous Transfer Mode (ATM) is rapidly becoming acknowledged as the base technology for the next generation of global communications, spanning diverse applications, and a variety of interface speeds and distances. Originally conceived as the base switching technology for the Broadband ISDN concept, ATM now has taken on a wider use for immediate deployment in local and wide area networks of all types. This User-Network Interface provides the primary specification on which a number of new products and services will be based.

The ATM Forum is a non-profit international industry consortium whose charter is to accelerate rapid convergence on interoperability specifications based on international standards and to promote industry cooperation. The ATM Forum began in November of 1991 with 4 member companies. As of this writing, the Forum has grown to a global membership of over 370 organizations.

The importance of ATM goes beyond the pure technology. It is one of the few networks that can provide the real time and quality of service guarantees required for new multimedia data types. There has rarely been so much consensus across the spectrum of industry participants and users behind a communications technology in such an early stage of development as there has been with ATM. Wide acceptance of ATM and its eventual ubiquitous deployment will allow users to stop focusing on infrastructure issues and instead concentrate on the overlying services and applications.

ATM has become synonymous with communications in the information age.

The coming of the information revolution has been predicted for many years. In fact, in many ways ATM was designed to support the needs and requirements of users and applications in that future revolution. Along with that came the original predictions that ATM would only be deployed and be successful as a technology *after* the need for real time data transport arose from the demands of new multimedia applications.

However, we are finding that the inverse may actually be true. ATM deployment may become an *enabler* for the information age, and not just a result of new transmission requirements. In addition to wide area companies and equipment providers, a number of computer manufacturers, local area network, routing, and equipment providers are looking for ATM to solve problems with existing networks carrying traditional packet data. Wide deployment of ATM to solve today's problems will provide the installed base for future networks carrying the real time data of tomorrow. The high speed transmission and low cost switching of ATM may be the technology that heralds the information age.

The technical content of this specification is based on the work of international standards organizations. Completion of the document is due to the active participation of member companies and individuals who often gave up much of their personal time to accomplish the work. I would particularly like to acknowledge the work of Glenn Estes and Steve Agard, the Chair and Vice Chair of the ATM Forum Technical Committee, and Steve Walters, ATM Forum Vice President of Committee Management, for their leadership in developing the work plan and guiding our diverse and ever-growing committee to final agreement.

Fred Sammartino
President and Chairman of the Board
The ATM Forum

Table of Contents

List of Figures

List of Tables

Section 1:

Introduction

In the emerging field of high speed virtual networking, Asynchronous Transfer Mode (ATM) is a key component. ATM is a telecommunications concept defined by ANSI and ITU (formally CCITT) standards for carriage of a complete range of user traffic, including voice, data, and video signals, on any User-to-Network Interface (UNI). As such, ATM is extremely well suited to high speed networking in the 1990s. ATM technology can be used to aggregate user traffic from existing applications onto a single UNI (e.g. PBX tie trunks, host-to-host private lines, video conference circuits), and to facilitate multi-media networking between high speed devices (e.g. workstations, supercomputers, routers or bridges) at multi-megabit speeds (e.g. 150 Mbit/s).

On the basis of its numerous strengths, ATM has been chosen by standards committees (e.g. ANSI T1, ITU SG XIII) as an underlying transport technology within many Broadband Integrated Services Digital Network (B-ISDN) protocol stacks. In this context, "transport" refers to the use of ATM switching and multiplexing techniques at the data link layer (i.e., OSI Layer 2) to convey end-user traffic from source to destination within a network.

While B-ISDN is a definition for public networks, ATM can also be used within private networking products. In recognition of this fact, and for clarity, this document defines two distinct forms of ATM UNI:

1. <u>Public UNI</u> - which will typically be used to interconnect an ATM user with an ATM switch deployed in a public service provider's network,

2. <u>Private UNI</u> - which will typically be used to interconnect an ATM user with an ATM switch that is managed as part of the same corporate network (e.g., MIS department responsible for the user device is also responsible for the private ATM switch).

The primary distinction between these two classes of UNI is physical reach. There are also some functionality differences between the public and private UNI due to the applicable requirements associated with each of these interfaces. Both UNIs share an ATM layer specification, but may utilize different physical media. Facilities that connect users to switches in public central offices must be capable of spanning long distances. In contrast, private switching equipment can often be located in the same room as the user device (e.g. computer, PBX), and hence can use limited distance technologies.

The term "ATM user" represents any device that makes use of an ATM network, via an ATM UNI, as illustrated in Figure 1-1.

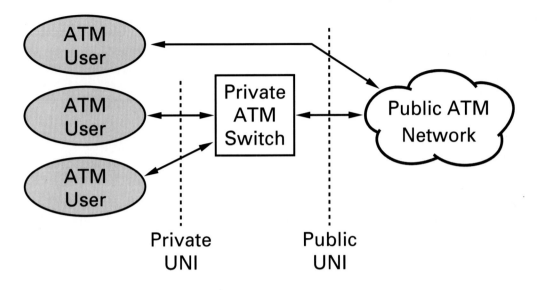

Figure 1-1 Implementations of the ATM UNI

For example, an ATM user device may be either of the following:

- An Intermediate System (IS), such as an IP router, that encapsulates data into ATM cells, and then forwards the cells across an ATM UNI to a switch (either privately owned, or within a public network),

- A private network ATM switch, which uses a public network ATM service for the transfer of ATM cells (between public network UNIs) to connect to other ATM user devices.

The carriage of user information within ATM format cells is defined in standards as the "ATM Bearer Service". Implementation of an ATM bearer service involves the specification of both an ATM protocol layer (Layer 2) and a compatible physical media (Layer 1).

1.1 Purpose of Document

This document is a specification of the interface(s) to be used between:

- ATM user devices and private ATM network equipment (operating as Customer Premises Equipment (CPE)
- ATM user devices and public ATM network equipment
- Private ATM network equipment and public ATM network equipment.

It defines "standards based" (when possible) Layer 1 and Layer 2 protocols needed for early interoperability. Layer 3 protocol is also defined for UNI signalling.

This document does not specify upper layer protocols to ensure multi-vendor compatibility of end-user devices[1] (e.g. method of encapsulating application data within network layer PDUs, choice of ATM adaptation layer for segmenting application PDUs into ATM format cells).

1.2 Scope of Document

The scope of the document includes the following:

- Background information on ATM technology and protocols used for broadband networking.

- The initial service attributes defined at the User-Network Interface.

- The set of physical layer specifications supported for the carriage of ATM cells.

- The ATM Layer specification which is common for all the physical layer interfaces specified.

- The Interim Local Management Interface (ILMI) specification.

- The signalling protocols and procedures used across the UNI for call control.

1.3 Structure of Document

This document is structured as follows:

- Section 1 constitutes the Introduction. It first describes the purpose, scope and structure of this document. It also introduces some basic ATM network concepts and provides a description of the initial service capabilities offered at the User-Network interfaces. Finally it describes the equipment configuration and protocol layers involved at the interfaces.

- Section 2 provides the specification of the physical layer interfaces for connecting ATM equipment (user or network).

- Section 3 specifies the ATM layer requirements common to all physical layer interfaces.

- Section 4 contains the Interim Local Management Interface (ILMI) specification.

- Section 5 contains the UNI Signalling specification.

- Annexes A through E contains additional signalling requirements.

- Appendix A contains the Quality of Service guidelines.

---

[1] Except to support ILMI across the UNI.

- Appendix B contains the Conformance Examples in a Traffic Contract

- Appendix C contains explanatory information for multipoint signalling state machines.

- Appendix D contains examples of signalling codlings.

- Appendix E contains a listing of differences with draft recommendation Q.93B.

- Appendix F is a glossary of terms and acronyms.

1.4 Terminology

In the context of this document, the term "UNI" is used generically to indicate interfaces to both public or private ATM networks. In the same manner, the generic term "ATM switch" refers to public or private switches. The terms "private ATM switch" and "public ATM switch" are used when a specific requirement or definition applies to only a private or public ATM switch. The definitions of "ATM user", "Public UNI", and "Private UNI" are as provided in the Introduction (Section 1). Additionally, two more terms are defined as follows:

- <u>Public Network Interface</u>, which is synonymous with "Public UNI"

- <u>Private Local Interface</u>, which is synonymous with "Private UNI"

This document uses three levels for indicating the degree of compliance necessary for specific functions/procedures/coding associated with the UNI:

- **Requirement (R)** : functions, procedures and coding necessary for operational compatibility.

- **Conditional Requirement (CR)** : functions, procedures and coding necessary providing the specified optional function is implemented.

- **Option (O)** : functions, procedures and coding that may be useful, but are not necessary for operational compatibility.

This document also uses the term "byte" (8-bit byte) which is synonymous with "octet".

1.5 ATM Bearer Service Overview

The concept of service as described in this section mainly applies to the Public Network Interface. However, in most cases the same service attributes are available at the Private Local Interface too.

The ATM bearer service, as defined by ANSI and ITU standards, provides a sequence-preserving, connection-oriented cell transfer service between source and destination with an agreed Quality of Service (QoS) and throughput. The ATM bearer service[2] involves at a minimum the two lower protocol layers (ATM, Physical) of the B-ISDN protocol stack as described in section 1.7. These two layers are service-independent and contain functions applicable to all upper layer protocols (i.e. they are independent of user applications). Additionally, the ATM bearer service may involve the C-Plane adaptation layer and signalling protocol for SVC service. U-Plane adaptation layers, which reside above the ATM layer, have been defined in standards to adapt the ATM bearer service to provide several networking classes of service including Constant Bit-Rate (CBR) and Variable Bit-Rate (VBR) services.

An ATM bearer service at a Public UNI is defined in this document to offer point-to-point, bi-directional or point-to-multipoint uni-directional virtual connections at either a virtual path (VP) level and/or a virtual channel (VC) level. Networks can provide either a VP or VC (or combined VP and VC) level service. For ATM users that desire only a VP service from the network, the user will be able to allocate individual VCs (which are not reserved or allocated for ILMI) within the VP connection (VPC) as long as none of the VCs is required to have a higher QoS than the VP connection. QoS of a VPC can be either explicitly specified at subscription time or implicitly specified (through a variety of mechanisms) and is selected to accommodate the most demanding QoS of any VC to be carried within that VPC. For VC level service at the UNI, the QoS and throughput are configured for each virtual channel connection (VCC) individually. The virtual connection (VPC or VCC) will be established or released via the signalling protocol or on a subscription basis.

The ATM bearer service attributes to be supported by network equipment conforming to this UNI specification are shown in Figure 1-2. Figure 1-2 indicates implementation requirements and does not imply services provided.

---

[2]   Also referred to as the B-ISDN Class X service.

ATM Bearer Service Attribute	Private UNI	Public UNI
Support for point-to-point VPCs	Optional	Optional
Support for point-to-point VCCs	Required	Required[1]
Support for point-to-multipoint VPCs	Optional	Optional
Support for point-to-multipoint VCCs, SVC	Required	Required[1]
Support for point-to-multipoint VCCs, PVC	Optional	Optional
Support of Permanent Virtual Connection	Required[2]	Required[2]
Support of Switched Virtual Connection	Required[2]	Required[2]
Support of Specified QoS Classes	Optional	Required[3]
Support of an Unspecified QoS Class	Optional	Optional
Multiple Bandwidth Granularites for ATM Connections	Optional	Required
Peak Rate Traffic Enforcement via UPC	Optional	Required
Sustainable Cell Rate Traffic Enforcement via UPC	Optional	Optional
Traffic Shaping	Optional	Optional
ATM Layer Fault Management	Optional	Required
Interim Local Management Interface	Required	Required

Note 1: Public ATM network equipment conforming to this interface specification shall be capable of providing ATM users with either a VPC service, or VCC service, or combined VPC/VCC service.

Note 2: ATM network equipment conforming to this interface specification shall be capable of providing ATM users with either support for PVC or SVC capability or both.

Note 3: Only one of the specified QoS connection categories is required at the Public UNI (see §4.1).

Figure 1-2 ATM Bearer Service Attributes

Two categories of QoS classes are defined initially, Specified QoS classes and an Unspecified QoS class. The specified QoS classes are initially aligned with the types of service defined for the ATM Adaptation Layers. The detailed definitions of the QoS classes are given in section 4 of Appendix A.

1.6 User-Network Interface Configuration

Figure 1-3 illustrates how equipment at both the Private UNI and Public UNI, as defined in this document, map into the B-ISDN access reference configuration shown in standards. The B-ISDN access configuration and interface definition at each reference point as well as the complete description of the functional entities can be found in ANSI T1E1.2/92-020, CCITT Recommendation I.413.

The Public UNI is modeled after the B-ISDN User-Network interface defined in ITU Recommendations and ANSI Standards. It embraces the physical characteristics corresponding to both U_B and T_B reference points. The Public UNI defined in this document specifies the criteria for connecting Customer Premises Equipment (e.g. ATM end-points and private ATM switch) to a public service provider's ATM switch.

The Private UNI is an interface that is optimized for local campus or "on premises" applications. It provides an alternative physical layer interface for short distance links with reduced operation and management complexity. The Private UNI, defined in this document, specifies criteria for connecting User equipment (e.g. workstation, router) to a private (on-premises) ATM switch.

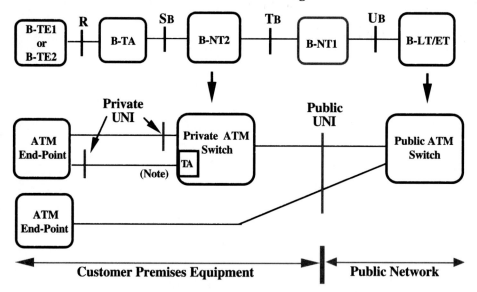

B-ISDN Access Reference Configuration

Note: The "R" reference point indicates a non-B-ISDN standard interface
(e.g. Both block coded interfaces). In this case, the TA functionality is
limited to physical layer conversion.

Figure 1-3 User-Network Interfaces Configuration

1.7 User-Network Interface Protocol Architecture

The B-ISDN protocol reference model defined in CCITT Recommendation I.121 is shown in Figure 1-4. The reference model is divided into multiple planes as follows:

U-plane: The User plane provides for the transfer of user application information. It contains Physical Layer, ATM Layer and multiple ATM Adaptation Layers required for different service users (e.g. CBR service, VBR service).

C-plane: The Control plane protocols deal with call establishment and release and other connection control functions necessary for providing switched services. The C-plane structure shares the Physical and ATM layers with the U-plane as shown in Figure 1-4. It also includes ATM adaptation layer (AAL) procedures and higher layer signalling protocols.

M-plane: The Management plane provides management functions and the capability to exchange information between U-plane and C-plane. The M-plane contains two sections: Layer Management and Plane Management. The Layer Management performs layer-specific management functions while the Plane Management performs management and coordination functions related to the complete system.

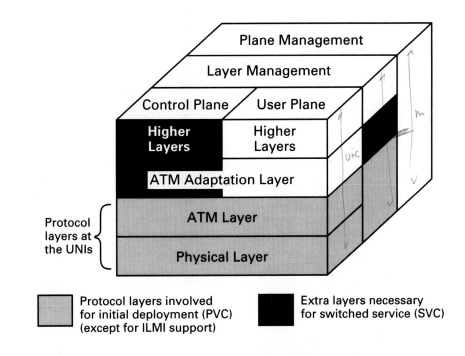

Figure 1-4 B-ISDN Protocol Reference Model

9

The UNI specification involves those protocols which are either terminated or manipulated at the user-network interfaces. Based on the ATM bearer service capabilities defined in Section 1.5, the protocol layers involved at both UNIs are limited to the Physical and ATM layers, C-plane higher protocol layers for SVC support and other protocols required for UNI management. Many physical layers (e.g. SONET, DS-3) can be specified at both the private or public User-Network Interfaces. Additional physical layers (e.g. block-coded) are specified for the private UNI. The applicability of any physical layer at a given interface will depend on technology limitations (e.g. maximum reach) or cost effectiveness (e.g. complexity). The UNIs may also contain Physical Layer Management functions (e.g. SONET-OAM) and ATM Layer Management functions. Since the initial ATM bearer service will support PVC only, no C-plane protocol layers are involved at the UNI.

Section 2:

Physical Layer Interfaces Specification

2 Physical Layer Interfaces Specification

This section provides specifications for physical layer ATM interfaces for the public and private User-Network Interface (UNI). Currently 44.736 Mbps, 100 Mbps and two 155.52 Mbps interfaces are specified. It is expected that other interface bit rates and physical media characteristics will be defined in the future.

An implementation is compliant if it supports any non-null subset of the interfaces specified in this section.

Given that SONET/SDH is an international standard, it is expected that SONET hierarchy-based interfaces will be a means for attaining interoperability in the long term for both the public and private UNI. However, for various availability and/or economic reasons, other physical layers are specified to accelerate the deployment of interoperable[1] ATM equipment.

2.1 SONET STS-3c Physical Layer Interface

This section specifies the physical layer for a 155.52 Mbps STS-3c frame applicable at both the public and private User-Network Interface (UNI). The transmission system is based on the Synchronous Optical Network (SONET) standards which provides, through a framing structure, the payload envelope necessary for the transport of ATM cells. SONET also includes overhead bytes for the carriage of OAM information. The SONET OAM functions residing in the physical layer management (M-plane) are covered in section 2.1.2. The functions of the physical layer (U-plane) are grouped into the Physical Media Dependent (PMD) sublayer and the Transmission Convergence (TC) sublayer (see Figure 2-1).

---

[1]   Interoperability can only be achieved if both ATM systems implement the same physical layer.

Transmission Convergence Sublayer	HEC generation/verification	B-ISDN specific functions
	Cell scrambling/descrambling	
	Cell delineation (HEC)	
	Path signal identification (C2)	
	Frequency justification/Pointer processing	Synchronous Digital Hierarchy (SDH) or SONET
	Multiplexing	
	Scrambling/descrambling	
	Transmission frame generation/recovery	
Physical Media Dependent Sublayer	Bit timing, Line coding	
	Physical medium	

Figure 2-1 Physical Layer Functions (U-plane)

2.1.1 Physical Layer U-plane Specification

2.1.1.1 Physical Media Dependent (PMD) Specification

The Physical Media Dependent (PMD) sublayer deals with aspects which are dependent on the transmission medium selected. The PMD sublayer specifies physical medium and transmission (e.g. bit timing, line coding) characteristics and does not include framing or overhead information.

2.1.1.1.1 Physical Medium Characteristics at 155.52 Mbps

The physical characteristics of the UNI at the UB, TB and SB reference points are defined in ANSI T1E1.2/93-020R1 and TR-NWT-000253 Issue 2 (e.g., OC-3 SMF, OC-3 MMF). Other SONET physical medium specifications could be defined in the future.

(R) The physical medium characteristics at the UNI shall be compliant with the SONET PMD criteria specified in T1E1.2/93-020R1.

2.1.1.2 Transmission Convergence (TC) Sublayer Specification

The Transmission Convergence (TC) sublayer deals with physical layer aspects which are independent of the transmission medium characteristics. Most of the functions comprising the TC sublayer are involved with generating and processing some overhead bytes contained in the SONET STS-3c frame. The description of SONET STS-3c frame format and overhead bytes involved at the UNI will be covered in section 2.1.1.3

2.1.1.2.1 B-ISDN Independent TC Sublayer Functions

The B-ISDN independent TC sublayer functions and procedures involved at the UNI are defined in the relevant sections of TA-NWT-000253 Issue 6, ANSI T1.105-1991 and T1E1.2/93-020R1.

(R) Equipment supporting the UNI shall process and generate all mandatory active overhead bytes (see section 2.1.1.3) listed inT1E1.2/93-020R1 and in accordance with TR-NWT-000253 Issue 2.

(R) Equipment supporting the UNI shall perform the SONET procedures related to STS-1 signal concatenation, STS-3c frame scrambling, timing and framing as defined in T1E1.2/93-020R1.

2.1.1.2.2 B-ISDN Specific TC Sublayer Functions

The B-ISDN specific TC sublayer contains functions necessary to adapt the service offered by the SONET physical layer to the service required by the ATM layer. As shown in Figure 2-1, some of these functions are not specified within SONET, but are required at the UNI. The B-ISDN specific physical layer functions listed in Figure 2-1 are described in the following sections.

2.1.1.2.2.1 HEC Generation/Verification

The entire header (including the HEC byte) is protected by the Header Error Control (HEC) sequence. The HEC code is contained in the last octet of the ATM cell header (ref. section 3.3).

The HEC sequence code is capable of:
- single-bit error correction
- multiple-bit error detection

At the transmission side, the HEC is computed based on a specified polynomial. At the receiver two modes of operation are defined: correction mode and detection mode. In correction mode only a single-bit error can be corrected while detection mode provides for multiple-bit error detection. In "detection mode" all cells with detected errors in the header are discarded.

(R) Equipment supporting the UNI shall implement error detection as defined in CCITT Recommendation I.432.

(O) Equipment supporting the UNI may also implement single bit error correction in addition to error detection. In this case, the two modes of operation shall interact in accordance to the procedure defined in CCITT Recommendation I.432 and T1E1.2/93-020R1.

(R) Equipment supporting the UNI shall generate the HEC byte as described in CCITT Recommendation I.432.

(R) The generator polynomial, coset used and the HEC sequence generation procedure shall be in accordance with CCITT Recommendation I.432.

2.1.1.2.2.2 Cell Scrambling and Descrambling

Cell scrambling/descrambling permits the randomization of the cell payload to avoid continuous non-variable bit patterns and improve the efficiency of the cell delineation algorithm.

(R) Equipment supporting the UNI shall implement the self synchronizing scrambler polynomial and procedures as defined in CCITT Recommendation I.432.

2.1.1.2.2.3 Cell Mapping

The mapping of ATM cells is performed by aligning by row, the byte structure of every cell with the byte structure of the SONET STS-3c payload capacity (Synchronous Payload Envelope). The entire STS-3c payload capacity is filled with cells, yielding a transfer capacity for ATM cells of 149.760 Mbps. Because the STS-3c payload capacity is not an integer multiple of the cell length, a cell may cross an SPE boundary.

(R) Equipment supporting the UNI shall map ATM cells into the SONET STS-3c SPE as specified in T1E1.2/93-020R1 and T1.105-1991 (see also CCITT recommendations I.432 and G.709).

2.1.1.2.2.4 Cell Delineation

The cell delineation function permits the identification of cell boundaries in the payload. It uses the Header Error Control (HEC) field in the cell header.

(R) Equipment supporting the UNI shall perform cell delineation using the HEC based algorithm described in I.432.

(O) Equipment supporting the UNI may implement the cell delineation state-machine in conformance with the following state transition timing requirements:

- The time to declare "Hunt state" once cell delineation is lost shall be less than 7 cell times.

- The time to declare "Sync state" once "Pre-Sync state" is obtained (i.e. one valid HEC) shall be less than 6 cell times.

2.1.1.2.2.5 ATM Payload Construction Indication

The construction of the STS-3c SPE loaded with ATM cells is indicated through the STS path signal label (C2) byte in the STS Path Overhead (STS POH).

(R) Equipment supporting the UNI shall set the C2 byte of the STS-3c POH to value 00010011 as defined in T1E1.2/93-020R1.

2.1.1.3 SONET STS-3c Frame at the UNI

The format of the STS-3c frame used at the 155.52 Mbps B-ISDN User-Network interface is given in Figure 2-2 . The description of the overhead bytes that must be activated at the UNI is given in Figure 2-3. A more detailed description on the STS-3c frame construction and overhead bytes is given in TR-NWT-000253 Issue 2.

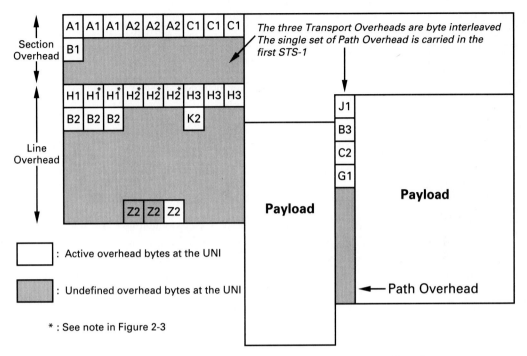

Overhead bytes: A1, A2, C1, H1, H2, H3, B2 are replicated
Overhead bytes: B1, K2, Z2 are not replicated

Figure 2-2 SONET STS-3c at the UNI

(R) Transmitting equipment supporting the UNI shall encode all undefined overhead bytes/ bits to zero patterns before scrambling and transmission.

(R) Receiving equipment supporting the UNI shall ignore all overhead bytes/bits undefined at the UNI (including the Data Communications Channels).

Overhead	Coding	Definition
A1, A2	A1: 11110110, A2: 00101000	Framing Bytes (note 3)
C1	00000001-00000010-00000011	STS-1 Identifiers (note 3)
B1	BIP-8	Section Error Monitoring (previous STS-3c)
B2	BIP-24 (STS-3c)	Line Error Monitoring
H1 (1-4)	0110 (norm) ,1001 (act)	New Data Flag (indicates change in pointer value)
H1-H2 (7-16)	0000000000-1100001110	Pointer Value (note 1)
H1*, H2*	10010011, 11111111	Concatenation Indication (note 1)
H3		Pointer Action (note 3)
K2 (6-8)	111, 110, any non 110 values	Line AIS, Line RDI, Removal of Line RDI
3rd Z2 byte(2-8)	B2 Error Count	Line FEBE (up to [(8 times 3) +1] values for STS-3c)
J1		STS Path Trace
B3	BIP-8	Path Error Monitoring (previous SPE)
C2	00010011	Path Signal Level Indicator
G1 (1-4)	B3 Error Count	Path FEBE (up to 9 legal values)
G1 (5)	0 or 1	Path RDI (note 2)

* note 1: Bits of H1,H2 bytes are set to all 1's for Path AIS
note 2: Also used to indicate loss of cell delineation
note 3: For all replicated overhead bytes (see Figure 2-2)

Figure 2-3 SONET Overhead Bytes at the UNI

2.1.2 Physical Layer Operation and Maintenance Specification (M-plane)

This section identifies the physical layer OAM[2] functions and procedures involved over the UNI. These functions are defined in standards documents and are grouped into three categories for illustrative purposes: Performance monitoring, Fault Management and Facility Testing as shown in Figure 2-4.

Functions		SONET overhead bytes	
Performance Monitoring	Cell Header error monitoring	Error type (corrected/ uncorrectable)	B-ISDN specific functions
	Line Error Monitoring	B2, Z2(18-24)	
	Path Error Monitoring	B3, G1(1-4)	Synchronous Digital Hierarchy (SDH) or SONET
	Section Error Monitoring	B1	
Fault Management	STS Path AIS	H1, H2, H3	
	STS Path RDI	G1(5)	
	Loss of cell delineation/ Path RDI	G1(5) (note 1)	
	Line Alarm Indication Signal (AIS) and Remote Defect Indicator (RDI)	K2(6-8)	
Facility Testing	Connectivity Verification Trace (Path)	J1	

Note 1: Loss of cell delineation generates a "STS-Path RDI" to alert the upstream SONET PTE about the failure detected downstream.

Figure 2-4 Physical Layer Management at the UNI

- Performance Monitoring includes functions that gather information about the network and network element behavior in order to evaluate and report on their performance.

---

[2]   The Administration (A) part of the OAM functions is not covered within this document.

- Fault Management functions provide detection, isolation and correction of failure conditions in the network.

- Facility Testing (Path Trace) permits verification of the connection continuity between two Path Terminating Equipments.

Figure 2-5a shows the OAM flows defined for the exchange of operations information between nodes in the network access (including customer premises nodes). At the physical layer (F1, F2, F3 flows), the exchange of information is done via well defined overhead bytes within the SONET framing structure (see section 2.1.1.3). The ATM layer information flows will be carried via OAM cells at the F4, F5 level (see ATM Layer Management section). Figure 2-5b gives an example of equipment configuration and the associated OAM flow at the UNI. A detailed explanation of OAM layers and information flows is given in CCITT I.610.

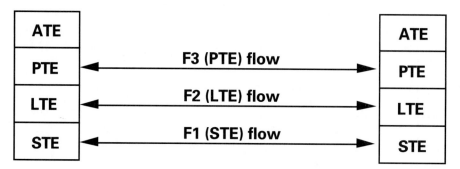

ATE: ATM Terminating Equipment
PTE: SONET Path Terminating Equipment
LTE: SONET Line Terminating Equipment
STE: SONET Section Terminating Equipment

Figure 2-5a SONET Physical Layer OAM flow

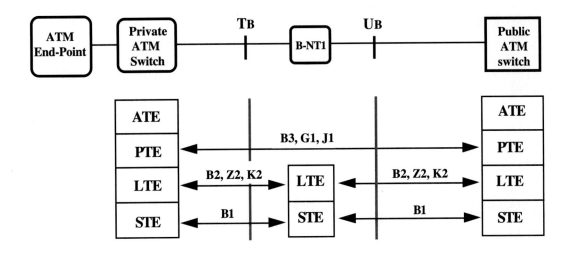

Figure 2-5b Example of OAM flow at the UNI

2.1.2.1 B-ISDN Independent Operation and Maintenance Functions

The B-ISDN independent Operation and Maintenance functions at the UNI are performed by SONET Section, Line and Path terminating equipment involved at the UNI. The following sub-sections define the subset (with some minor modification) of the Operation and maintenance functions defined in TR-NWT-000253 Issue 2.

2.1.2.1.1 Performance Monitoring

Performance Monitoring at the SONET level mainly involves detecting Coding Violations by using the B1 byte at the section level, B2, Z2 bytes at the line level and B3 byte, G1(1-4) bits at the path level. Monitoring is performed across the UNI by calculating the section BIP-8, line BIP-24 and Path BIP-8 of the incoming signal and comparing the values obtained with the one encoded in the proper bytes by the transmitting end. The Line and Path Far End Block Error (FEBE) signals are used to convey back to the upstream equipment the number of BIP errors detected by the Line or Path terminating equipment.

(R) Equipment supporting the UNI shall perform the Performance Monitoring functions included in T1E1.2/93-020R1 in accordance with the procedures described in TR-NWT-000253 Issue 2.

Note: A modified Line Transmission Performance Monitoring procedure has been defined for use at the UNI. It is described in section 2.1.2.2.1.

21

2.1.2.1.2 Fault Management

Fault management actions at the UNI can be triggered by incoming signal failures, equipment failures, detection or removal of Alarm Indication Signal (AIS) or Remote Defect Indicator (RDI) signal. The failures detected on the incoming signal are: Loss of Signal (LOS), Loss of Frame (LOF), Loss of Pointer (LOP), and Signal Label Mismatch.

(R) Equipment supporting the UNI shall perform the Fault Management functions (Alarm Surveillance) included in T1E1.2/93-020R1 in accordance with the procedures described in TR-NWT-000253 Issue 2.

(O) Equipment supporting the UNI shall perform the Signal Label Mismatch Fault Management Function in accordance with the procedures described in TR-NWT-000253 Issue 2.

2.1.2.1.3 Facility testing

(O) Equipment supporting the UNI can perform facility testing by repetitively sending the appropriate 64 byte code in the J1 POH byte as defined in T1E1.2/93-020R1 and TR-NWT-000253 Issue 2.

2.1.2.2 B-ISDN Specific Operation and Maintenance Functions

The B-ISDN specific Operation and Maintenance functions at the UNI include:

- Modified or extended SONET functions for the UNI

- Additional functions included at the Transmission Convergence (TC) sublayer to meet the ATM based UNI specific needs.

2.1.2.2.1 Line Error Monitoring

A modified Line Performance Monitoring procedure is defined to permit a receiving LTE to convey the error count and alert the far end (originating) LTE about its transmission performance on its outgoing link. The Z2 byte of the third STS-1 is used to carry the Far End Block Error (FEBE) count.

(R) Equipment supporting the UNI shall implement the Line Performance Monitoring function (including the line FEBE function) as defined in T1E1.2/93-020R1 and TR-NWT-000253 Issue 2.

2.1.2.2.2 Loss of Cell Delineation

The Loss of Cell Delineation event generates a SONET "Path RDI" alarm to alert the upstream SONET PTE of the failure detected downstream.

(R) Equipment supporting the UNI shall detect the out-of-cell Delineation (OCD) anomaly when the HEC coding rule is determined to be incorrect alpha consecutive times for the incoming signal (e.g., alpha = 7). An LOC state shall be declared after persistence of the OCD anomaly for a time period, at which time the "Path RDI" shall be generated.

The OCD persistence time period for LOC state entrance and LOC state exit requirements are under study in standards. Target values are expected to be in the 4 ms range.

2.2 DS3 Physical Layer Interface

This section is based upon T1S1/92-623. The functions of the DS3 physical layer are grouped into the Physical Media Dependent (PMD) sublayer and the Transmission Convergence (TC) sublayer as shown in Figure 2-6.

Transmission Convergence Sublayer	*HEC generation/verification* *PLCP Framing and Cell Delineation* *Path Overhead utilization* *PLCP Timing (125 usec clock recovery)* *Nibble Stuffing*
Physical Media Dependent Sublayer	*Bit timing, Line coding* *Physical medium*

Figure 2-6 Physical Layer Functions

2.2.1 Format at 44.736 Mbps

The 44.736 Mbps interface, if used, shall comply with the specifications in this section.

The interface format at the physical layer is based on asynchronous DS3 using the C-Bit Parity application (CCITT G.703, ANSI T1.107, ANSI T1.107a, and Bellcore TR-TSY-000499). Use of the C-Bit Parity application is the default mode of operation. However, if equipment supporting C-Bit Parity interfaces with equipment that does not support C-Bit Parity, then the equipment supporting C-Bit Parity must be capable of "dropping back" into a clear channel mode of operation.

To carry ATM traffic over existing DS3 44.736 Mbps communication facilities, a Physical Layer Convergence Protocol (PLCP) for DS3 is defined. This PLCP is a subset of the PLCP defined in IEEE P802.6 and Bellcore TR-TSV-000773. Mapping of ATM cells into the DS3 is accomplished by inserting the 53 byte ATM cells into the DS3 PLCP (Figure 2-7). The PLCP is then mapped into the DS3 information payload.

Extraction of ATM cells from the DS3 operates in the analogous reverse procedure, i.e. by framing on the PLCP and then simply extracting the ATM cells directly.

(R) Equipment supporting C-Bit Parity interfacing with equipment that does not support C-Bit Parity shall be capable of "dropping back" into a clear channel mode of operation.

PLCP Framing		POI	POH	PLCP Payload	
A1	A2	P11	Z6	First ATM Cell	
A1	A2	P10	Z5	ATM Cell	
A1	A2	P9	Z4	ATM Cell	
A1	A2	P8	Z3	ATM Cell	
A1	A2	P7	Z2	ATM Cell	
A1	A2	P6	Z1	ATM Cell	
A1	A2	P5	X	ATM Cell	
A1	A2	P4	B1	ATM Cell	
A1	A2	P3	G1	ATM Cell	
A1	A2	P2	X	ATM Cell	
A1	A2	P1	X	ATM Cell	
A1	A2	P0	C1	Twelfth ATM Cell	Trailer
1 Octet	1 Octet	1 Octet	1 Octet	53 Octets	13 or 14 Nibbles

Object of BIP-8 Calculation

POI = Path overhead Indicator
POH = Path Overhead
BIP-8 = Bit Interleaved Parity - 8
X = Unassigned - Receiver required to ignore

Figure 2-7 DS3 PLCP Frame (125 us)

2.2.1.1 PLCP Format

The ATM Physical Layer Convergence Protocol (PLCP) for DS3 defines the mapping of ATM cells onto existing DS3 facilities.

The DS3 PLCP consists of a 125 us frame within a standard DS3 payload. Note that there is no fixed relationship between the DS3 PLCP frame and the DS3 frame, i.e. the DS3 PLCP may begin anywhere inside the DS3 payload. The DS3 PLCP frame, Figure 2-7, consists of 12 rows of ATM cells, each preceded by 4 octets of overhead. Although the DS3 PLCP is not aligned to the DS3 framing bits, the octets in the DS3 PLCP frame are nibble aligned to the DS3 payload envelope. Nibble[3] stuffing is required after the twelfth cell to frequency justify the 125 μs PLCP frame. Nibbles begin after the control bits (F, X, P, C or M) of the DS3 frame. Note that the stuff bits are never used in the DS3, i.e. the payload is always inserted. Octets comprising the DS3 PLCP frame are described in the following sections.

Order of transmission of all PLCP bits, shown in Figure 2-7, is from left to right and top to bottom. The figures represent the most significant bit (MSB) on the left and the least significant bit (LSB) on the right.

2.2.1.2 PLCP Overhead Utilization

(R) The following PLCP overhead bytes/nibbles are required to support the coding/functions (as defined) across the UNI:

- A1 - Frame Alignment
- A2 - Frame Alignment
- B1 - Bit Interleaved Parity
- C1 - Cycle/Stuff Counter
- G1 - PLCP Path Status
- Px - Path Overhead Identifier
- Zx - Growth Octets
- Trailer Nibbles

2.2.1.2.1 Framing Octets (A1, A2)

The PLCP framing octets use the same framing pattern used in SONET and SDH.

(R) These octets are defined as A1=11110110, A2=00101000.

2.2.1.2.2 Bit Interleaved Parity - 8 (B1)

The Bit Interleaved Parity - 8 (BIP-8) field supports path error monitoring.

---

[3]   A nibble is 4 bits.

(R) The BIP-8 shall be calculated over a 12 x 54 octet structure consisting of the Path Overhead (POH) field and the associated ATM cells (648 octets) of the previous PLCP frame. It is an 8 bit code in which the nth bit of the BIP-8 code calculates the even parity of the nth bit of each octet covered by the BIP-8. Thus, it provides for 8 separate even parity calculations.

2.2.1.2.3 Cycle/Stuff Counter (C1)

The Cycle/Stuff Counter provides a nibble stuffing opportunity cycle and length indicator for the PLCP frame. A stuffing opportunity occurs every third frame of a 3 frame (375 µs) stuffing cycle. The value of the C1 code is used as an indication of the phase of the 375 µs stuffing opportunity cycle (see Figure 2-8).

(R) A trailer containing 13 nibbles shall be used in the first frame of the 375 µs stuffing opportunity cycle. A Trailer of 14 nibbles shall be used in the second frame. The third frame provides a nibble stuffing opportunity. A Trailer containing 14 nibbles shall be used in the third frame if a stuff occurs. If not, the Trailer shall contain 13 nibbles.

C1 Code	Frame Phase of Cycle	Trailer Length
11111111	1	13
00000000	2	14
01100110	3 (no stuff)	13
10011001	3 (stuff)	14

Figure 2-8 Cycle/Stuff Counter Definition

2.2.1.2.4 PLCP Path Status (G1)

Figure 2-9 illustrates the G1 octet subfields: a 4-bit Far End Block Error (FEBE), a 1-bit RAI (Yellow), and 3 X bits (X bits are ignored).

Far End Block Error (FEBE)	RAI (Yellow)	X - X - X
4 Bits	1 Bit	3 Bits

Figure 2-9 PLCP Path Status (G1) Definition

(R) FEBE shall provide a count of 0 to 8 BIP-8 errors received in the previous frame, i. e., G1 (FEBE)=0000 through G1 (FEBE)=1000. If not implemented, G1 (FEBE) shall be set to 1111. Any other value of G1 than described above, would be caused by other errors and is interpreted as 0 errors.

(R) RAI (Yellow) shall alert the transmitting PLCP that a received failure indication has been declared along the path. When an incoming failure condition is detected which persists for a "soaking period" (typically 2 - 10 seconds), an RAI shall be sent to the far end by setting G1 (RAI)=1. The RAI shall be detected when G1 (RAI)=1 for 10 consecutive PLCP frames. The indication is cleared by setting G1 (RAI)=0 when the incoming failure has ceased for 15 ± 5 seconds. At the receiving end, removal of the RAI signal is recognized by detecting G1 (RAI)=0 for 10 consecutive PLCP frames.

2.2.1.2.5 Path Overhead Identifier (P0-P11)

The Path Overhead Identifier (POI) indexes the adjacent Path Overhead (POH) octet of the DS3 PLCP. Figure 2-10 provides the coding for each of the POI octets.

POI	POI Code	Associated POH
P11	00101100	Z6
P10	00101001	Z5
P9	00100101	Z4
P8	00100000	Z3
P7	00011100	Z2
P6	00011001	Z1
P5	00010101	X
P4	00010000	B1
P3	00001101	G1
P2	00001000	X
P1	00000100	X
P0	00000001	C1

X - Receiver Ignores

Figure 2-10 POI Code Definition

(R) The POI coding in Figure 2-10 shall be supported.

2.2.1.2.6 Growth Octets (Z1-Z6)

The Growth Octets are reserved for future use.

(R) The growth octets shall be set to Zi=00000000, by the transmitter (i=1, 2..., 6). The receiver shall be capable of ignoring the value contained in these fields.

2.2.1.2.7 Trailer Nibbles

(R) The contents of each of the 13/14 Trailer nibbles shall be 1100.

2.2.2 ATM Transfer Capability

Because of the overhead induced by the PLCP, the nominal bit rate available for the transport of ATM cells in the DS3 PLCP shall be 40.704 Mbps.

2.2.3 Timing

(R) The PLCP frame from the network equipment to the customer shall have timing traceable to a Primary Reference Source (PRS).

(R) The incoming PLCP frame from the customer to the network equipment shall be traceable to a PRS. The customer may use the clock recovered from the PLCP or other source traceable to a PRS.

2.2.4 Cell Payload Scrambling

For some DS3 physical links, cell scrambling can provide a solution to some transmission equipment unexpected behavior sensitive to bit patterns in the ATM cell payload (e.g., "101010..." or "00000000..." patterns). Another solution to this problem would be to disable alarm monitoring/reporting on transmission equipment. Alarm disablement however, reduces alarm visibility and fault isolation capability.

(R) Equipment supporting the DS3 based UNI shall implement the Cell Payload Scrambler (self synchronizing) as defined in ITU-TS I.432. This scrambler shall have the capability of being enabled or disabled.

(R) As a default mode, the Cell Payload Scrambler shall be disabled for the DS3 based UNI.

(O) As a configurable option, the Cell Payload Scrambler may be enabled for the DS3 based UNI.

> **Note 1:** The use of scrambling/descrambling may increase the bit error rate through error multiplication.

2.2.5 Cell Delineation

Because the cells are in predetermined locations within the PLCP, framing on the DS3 and then on the PLCP is sufficient to delineate cells.

2.2.6 HEC Generation/Verification

The Header Error Control (HEC) covers the entire cell header. Support of bit error detection based on the HEC field is mandatory.

The transmitter calculates the HEC value for the first four octets of the cell header, and inserts the results into the HEC field, the last octet of the header. The HEC field shall be an 8-bit sequence [11]. It shall be the remainder of the division (modulo 2) by the generator polynomial x^8+x^2+x+1 of the polynomial x^8 multiplied by the content of the header excluding the HEC field. The pattern 01010101 is XORed with the 8-bit remainder before being inserted in the last octet of the header [12].

(R) Equipment supporting the UNI shall implement HEC error detection as defined in CCITT Recommendation I.432.

(O) Equipment supporting the UNI may also implement single bit error correction in addition to error detection. In this case, the two modes of operation shall interact in accordance to the procedure defined in CCITT Recommendation I.432 and T1E1.2/93-020R1.

(R) Equipment supporting the UNI shall generate the HEC byte as described in CCITT Recommendation I.432.

(R) The generator polynomial and coset used shall be in accordance with CCITT Recommendation I.432.

2.3 Physical Layer for 100 Mbps Multimode Fiber Interface

This section specifies the physical layer for the 100 Mbps multimode fiber for the private UNI. The private UNI does not need the operation and maintenance complexity or link distance provided by telecom lines (e.g. SONET). The physical layer OAM functions performed over the local fiber link are provided by the Interim local Management Interface (ILMI) specification (see chapter 4). The functions of the physical layer (U-plane) are grouped into the Physical Media Dependent (PMD) sublayer and the Transmission Convergence (TC) sublayer as shown in Figure 2-11.

Transmission Convergence Sublayer	*Cell delineation* *HEC generation/verification*
Physical Media Dependent Sublayer	*Bit timing, Line coding* *Physical medium*

Figure 2-11 Physical Layer Functions (U-plane)

The private UNI connects customer premises equipment, such as computers, bridges, routers, and workstations, to a port on an ATM switch. For the purposes of this specification, the Network Interface Unit (NIU) in conjunction with user equipment provides frame segmentation and reassembly functions and includes the Local Fiber Link Interface (see Figure 2-12). The links are full duplex point to point.

The private UNI could potentially use several different link speeds and technologies. This section specifies the rate, format, and function of the 100M fiber interface. The fiber interface is based on the FDDI physical layer.

The bit rate used throughout this document refers to the logical information rate, before line coding. The term *line rate* will be used when referring to the rate after line coding (e.g. a 100 Mbps bit rate results in a 125 Mbaud line rate if using 4B/5B coding).

This Physical Layer carries 53 byte ATM cells with no physical layer framing structure. Fields inside cells are used by the ATM layer and described in section 3.1.1.

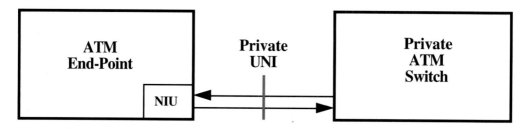

Figure 2-12 Local Fiber Link

2.3.1 Physical Media Dependent (PMD) Specification

The Physical Media Dependent (PMD) sublayer deals with aspects which are dependent on the transmission medium selected. The PMD sublayer specifies physical medium and transmission (bit timing, line coding) characteristics and does not include framing or overhead information. This section specifies the 100 Mbps multimode fiber interface.

2.3.1.1 Physical Medium Characteristics

This Physical Layer follows the FDDI PMD specification. The link uses 62.5 micron multimode fiber at 100 Mbps (125 Mbaud line rate). The optical transmitter and fiber bandwidth should adhere to the specification ISO DIS 9314-3 such that a 5 ms exit response time is achieved after 2 km of fiber.

The fiber connector is the MIC duplex connector specified for FDDI. This allows single connector attachment and keying if desired. FDDI transceivers with integrated MIC connectors may be used. The transmit and receive cables cannot be accidentally swapped with a duplex connector.

(R) The fiber connector used shall be the MIC duplex connector specified for FDDI in ISO DIS 9314-3.

(R) The local physical interface shall meet the FDDI PMD specification as defined in ISO DIS 9314-3.

2.3.1.2 Line Coding

The fiber link encoding scheme is based on the ANSI X3T9.5 (FDDI) committee 4 bit/5 bit (4B/5B) code. An ANSI X3T9.5 system uses an 8-bit parallel data pattern. This pattern is divided into two 4-bit nibbles which are each encoded into a 5-bit symbol. Of the thirty two patterns possible with these five bits, sixteen are chosen to represent the sixteen input data patterns. Some of the others are used as command symbols. Control codes are formed with various combinations of FDDI control symbol pairs. For example, the SR control code is formed by the combination of the FDDI S and R symbols.

Figure 2-13 shows the defined control codes for the 100 Mbps local link.

Mnemonic	Definition
JK (Sync)	Idle
II	Reserved
TT	Start of cell
TS	Reserved
IH	Not recommended
TR	Reserved
SR	Reserved
SS	Unused
HH	Not recommended
HI	Not recommended
HQ	Not recommended
RR	Unused
RS	Reserved
QH	Not recommended
QI	Not recommended
QQ	Loss of signal

Note: The codes labelled "Reserved" are reserved for future definition. Link receivers recognizing a "Reserved", "Not recommended" or "Unused line codes are not required to take any further action.

Figure 2-13 ATM Access Link Control Code Summary

(R) This Physical Layer shall use the 4B/5B coding as described above.

Owing to the use of an error multiplying block coding scheme, this interface may impose a service limitation. This error multiplication may impact the cell discard rate.

2.3.1.3 Line Rates and Bit Timing

The ATM link operates at 100 Mbps, which is 125 Mbaud line rate, the same rate used for FDDI. Timing on the full duplex link uses the same base frequency in each direction, but with no phase relationship. The link operates as two simplex links at the same nominal frequency. The NIU may generate its transmit clock locally, or loop time the network clock with an appropriate smoothing PLL. There is no requirement for the NIU to loop time the network clock.

(R) This Physical Layer shall operate at 125 Mbaud line rate.

2.3.2 Transmission Convergence (TC) Sublayer Specification

The Transmission Convergence (TC) sublayer deals with physical layer aspects which are independent of the transmission medium characteristics. Most of the functions comprising the TC sublayer are involved with generating and processing of some overhead bytes contained in the transmission format overhead and ATM cell header.

2.3.2.1 Idle Line

While idle, the line contains continuous idle codes. The idle code for ATM links is the JK sync code. The line is at idle unless cells are actively being sent. The FDDI idle line pattern is not used.

(R) When data or control codes are not being sent (Idle state), the "JK" sync code shall be transmitted continuously

2.3.2.2 Cell Delineation

Cell boundaries are asynchronous i.e. they can occur any time the line is idle. This physical layer provides a noncontinuous stream of assigned cells to the ATM layer. Each cell is preceded with the TT code, followed by the 53 byte cell. The TT code denotes the start of cell at the receiver. The 54 bytes (53 bytes of cell plus start of cell code) must be contiguous on the line.

Since the idle (JK sync) code is used to gain byte alignment, there must be a minimum density of idle codes on the line. Noise bursts can knock the receiver out of byte alignment; alignment will be regained upon reception of the next idle code. Therefore having an idle code between every cell ensures the loss of at most one cell per sync loss. If higher losses are acceptable, fewer idle codes can be used. When the link is first connected, the receiver will not sync up until at least one idle code is received.

Data bytes are sent as 4B/5B symbol pairs with a serial bit order defined as follows. Serial bits are shifted out with MSB of the most significant nibble coming out first.

(R) Each cell transmitted shall be preceded by a "TT" (start of cell) code.

(R) There must be a minimum of 1 JK symbol pair transmitted on the link every 0.5 second.

(R) The 54 bytes (53 bytes of cell plus start of cell code) shall be contiguous on the line.

2.3.2.3 HEC Generation/Verification

The Header Error Control (HEC) covers the entire cell header. For the private environment, only the detection of bit errors is described. Support of bit error detection based on the HEC field is mandatory.

The transmitter calculates the HEC value for the first four octets of the cell header, and inserts the results into the HEC field, the last octet of the header. The HEC field shall be an 8-bit sequence [11]. It shall be the remainder of the division (modulo 2) by the generator polynomial x^8+x^2+x+1 of the polynomial x^8 multiplied by the content of the header excluding the HEC field. The pattern 01010101 is XORed with the 8-bit remainder before being inserted in the last octet of the header [12].

(R) Equipment supporting this private UNI shall implement HEC error detection as defined in CCITT Recommendation I.432.

(R) Equipment supporting this private UNI shall generate the HEC byte as described CCITT Recommendation I.432.

(R) The generator polynomial and coset used shall be in accordance with CCITT Recommendation I.432.

Figure 2-14 depicts the HEC verification flow on the receive side. The TC will not forward any cell to the ATM layer which has an incorrect HEC value.

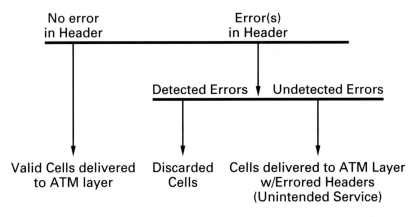

Figure 2-14 HEC Verification Flow

The HEC code is capable of:
- single-bit error correction
- multiple-bit error detection

Since the 4B/5B block code causes multiple bit errors per corrupted code bit, error correction must not be attempted; only error detection should be performed.

(R) On detection of a header error, the cell shall be discarded.

2.4 Physical Layer for 155 Mbps Interface

This section specifies the Physical Layer for a 155.52 Mbps private UNI. The functions of the Physical Layer (U-plane) are grouped into the Physical Media Dependent (PMD) sublayer and the Transmission Convergence (TC) sublayer as shown in Figure 2-15. The transmission system is based on a framing structure which provides the transport of ATM cells which exactly matches the cell payload rate of CCITT Recommendation I.432. It also provides overhead bytes for the carriage of OAM information.

Transmission Convergence Sublayer	*Cell delineation* *125 usec clock recovery* *HEC generation/verification*
Physical Media Dependent Sublayer	*Bit timing, Line coding* *Physical medium*

Figure 2-15 Physical Layer Functions (U-plane)

2.4.1 Fiber Physical Medium Dependent Specification

The PMD provides the digital baseband point-to-point communication between stations and switches in the ATM LAN. The PMD shall provide all the services required to transport a suitably coded digital bit stream across the link segment.

This PMD specification outlines the requirements for a 155 Mbps (194.4 MBaud) 1300 nm multimode fiber interface. This provides for a physical interface between the switch and the host which is a full duplex, fiber optic connection. A 62.5/125 micron, graded index, multimode fiber, with a minimum modal bandwidth of 500 MHz-km, shall be used as the communication link. Alternatively, a 50 micron core fiber may be supported as the communication link. The interface should be able to operate up to 2 km maximum with the 62.5/125 micron fiber, at a wavelength of 1300 nm. The maximum link length may be shortened when 50 micron fiber is incorporated.

The PMD specified in this section has the following general characteristics:

- Provide a means of coupling the TC to the fiber optic segment by way of the Active Interface.
- Provide for driving up to 2 km of fiber optic cable between two fiber optic interfaces.
- Meet the topology and distance requirements of the building and wiring standard, EIA/TIA 568.

2.4.1.1 Line Rates and Bit Timing

The non-encoded line frequency is 155.52 Mbps, which is identical to the SONET STS-3 rate described in [12]. This rate is derived from the insertion of one Physical Layer unit for every 26 data cells. With the 8B/10B block code described below, the resultant media transmission rate is 194.40 Mbaud.

(R) The encoded line rate shall be 194.40 Mbaud.

A receiver must first acquire bit synchronization, before attempting to align received bytes. This time is measured from the receipt of a valid input to the time the receiver is synchronized to the bit stream and delivering valid re-timed data within the BER objective of the system.

(R) Bit synchronization shall occur in not more than 1 ms.

2.4.1.2 Fiber Optic Medium Characteristics.

The fiber optic medium consists of one or more sections of fiber optic cable containing one or more optical fibers as specified below along with any intermediate connectors required to connect sections together and terminated at each end in the optical connector plug as specified in 2.4.1.3. The optical fibers are interconnected to provide two continuous light paths which are connected to the port pair at each end. Each light path connects to a transmit port at one end and a receive port at the other end.

(R) The optical medium requirements are satisfied by the 62.5/125 micrometer nominal diameter fiber specified in IEC 793-2, type A1b with the exceptions noted below. The system can operate, subject to certain restrictions, with a variety of optical fibers. However, performance to this specification and interoperability between different vendors' equipment is assured only through the use of the optical fiber specified in this section.

This specification was developed on the basis of an attenuation value of less than or equal to 1.5 dB/km, when measured at a wavelength of 1300 nm. Higher loss fiber may be used for shorter fiber pair lengths.

(R) Each optical fiber shall have a modal bandwidth-length product of not less than 500 MHz-km at a wavelength of 1300 nm.

(R) Each optical fiber shall have a zero dispersion wavelength in the range 1295 nm to 1365 nm and a dispersion slope not exceeding 0.110 ps/nm^2-km. Each optical fiber shall have a dispersion characteristic in the range shown in Figure 2-16.

Zero Dispersion Wavelength Lambda (0); nm	Maximum Dispersion Slope $S_{0;}$ ps/nm^2-km
1295 - 1300	[Lambda(0) - 1190] / 1000
1300 - 1348	0.110
1348 - 1365	[1458 - Lambda(0)] / 1000

Figure 2-16 Chromatic Dispersion Requirements

2.4.1.3 Optical Medium Connector Plug and Socket.

(R) Each end of the fiber optic cable shall be terminated in BFOC/2.5 connector plugs (one per fiber), as specified in IEC 86B (Secretariat) 127. The corresponding mating connector sockets shall be used on all network elements covered by this specification to which the fiber optic cable attaches. In-line or patch panel connectors may be of other types, provided they meet the connector loss requirement below.

The use of the SC connector as an alternative to the BFOC/2.5 is under review in TR-41.8.1.

(R) Optical Connector Loss is assumed to have a maximum insertion loss of 1.0 dB (see Note below). Connectors with different loss characteristics may be used as long as any additional loss is compensated for elsewhere in the fiber loss budget.

> Note: Per test method EIA/TIA 455/34, Method A (Factory Testing) or EIA/TIA-455-59 (Field Testing).

2.4.1.4 Optical Characteristics

(R) The transmit (Active Output Interface [AOI]) and receive (Active Input Interface [AII]) parameters for the 155 Mbps Multimode Fiber interface are summarized in Figure 2-17 and 2-19. The parameters must be met over the temperature, voltage, and lifetime range of the system. Optical measurements shall be made with the Active Output Interface (AOI) terminated with the optical connector specified in 2.4.1.3. and the optical fiber specified in section 2.4.1.2. Fiber length shall be sufficient to ensure equilibrium mode distribution.

Note: Transmit and receive optical parameters refer to optical power in the respective fiber. Typically fibers require 1 to 5 meters to establish equilibrium mode distribution.

Parameter	Units	Value
Nominal baud	Mbaud	194.40
Baud Rate Tolerance	ppm	100
Optical Transmit Average Power Range - Min.	dBm	-20
- Max.	dBm	-14
Center Wavelength - Min.	nm	1270
- Max.	nm	1380
Spectral Width (FWHM)	nm	<200
Optical Extinction Ratio	%	<10
Optical Transmit Pulse Rise and Fall Times (10% to 90%) - Min.	ns	0.6
- Max.	ns	2.5
Optical Transmit Pulse -Overshoot	%	10
-Undershoot	%	10
Optical Transmit Data Dependent Jitter	ns	± 0.5
Optical Transmit Pulse Duty Cycle Distortion	ns	± 0.5
Optical Transmit Pulse Random Jitter	ns	± 0.5

Figure 2-17 AOI Optical Transmit Parameters

(R) The transmit optical output shall fit within the boundaries of the Eye Diagram shown in Figure 2-18. The value of X1, X2 and Y1 are 0.15, 0.35 and 0.1 respectively.

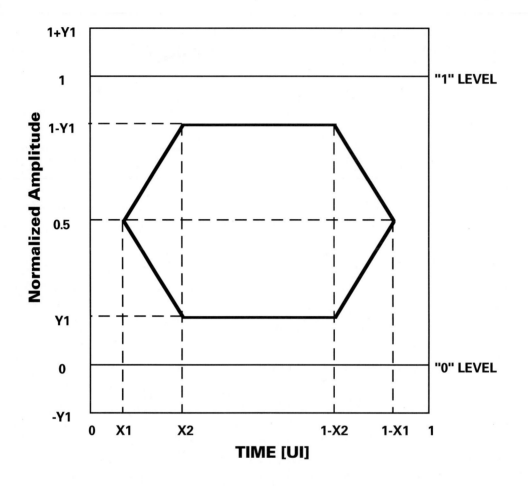

Figure 2-18 MMF Eye Diagram for the Transmitter

(R) The BER shall be less than one part in 10^{10}, when measured between end-points on the UNI physical layer[4] , for all combinations of valid optical transmit parameters, valid optical receive parameters, and allowable media.

---

[4] Including bit timing recovery.

Parameter		Units	Value
Nominal baud		Mbaud	194.40
Baud Rate Tolerance		ppm	100
Optical Receive Average Power Range			
	- Min.	dBm	-29
	- Max.	dBm	-14
Center Wavelength	- Min.	nm	1270
	- Max.	nm	1380
Optical Receive Pulse Rise and Fall Times			
(10% to 90%)	- Min.	ns	0.6
	- Max.	ns	3.0
All Optical Receive Data Dependent Jitter		ns	± 1.0
Optical Receive Pulse Duty Cycle Distortion		ns	± 0.5
Optical Receive Pulse Random Jitter		ns	± 0.5

Figure 2-19 All Optical Receive Parameters

2.4.2 STP Physical Medium Dependent Specification

The PMD provides the digital baseband point-to-point communication between stations and switches in the ATM LAN. The PMD shall provide all the services required to transport a suitably coded digital bit stream across the link segment.

This PMD specification outlines the requirements for a 155 Mbps (194.4 MBaud) shielded twisted pair interface. This provides for a physical interface between the switch and the host which is a full duplex, 150Ω shielded twisted pair cable connection. The interface operates over 100 m maximum with either Type 1 or Type 2 cable (reference ANSI/IEEE 802.5).

The PMD specified in this section has the following general characteristics and guidelines:

- Provides a means of coupling the TC to the shielded twisted pair segment by way of the Active Interface.
- Provides for driving up to 100 m of shielded twisted pair between two STP interfaces.
- Use of the installed 150 ohm cable plant including connectors as currently used for IEEE 802.5 Token Ring networks, e.g., Types 1 and 2. Type 6 may be used for short patch cables.
- Meets the topology and distance requirements of the building and wiring standard, EIA/TIA 568.

2.4.2.1 Line Rates and Bit Timing

The non-encoded line frequency is 155.52 Mbps, which is identical to the SONET STS-3 rate described in [12]. This rate is derived from the insertion of one Physical Layer unit for every 26 data cells. With the 8B/10B block code described below, the resultant media transmission rate is 194.4 Mbaud.

(R) The encoded line rate shall be 194.4 Mbaud.

A receiver must first acquire bit synchronization, before attempting to align received bytes. This time is measured from receipt of a valid input to the time the receiver is synchronized to the bit stream and delivering valid re-timed date within the BER objective of the system.

(R) Bit synchronization shall occur in not more than 1 ms.

2.4.2.2 Electrical Medium Characteristics

The copper medium consists of one or more sections of shielded twisted pair cable containing one or more pairs along with intermediate connectors required to connect sections together and terminated at each end in the electrical data connector as specified in 2.4.2.3. The cable is interconnected to provide two continuous electrical paths which are connected to the interface port at each end.

(R) The copper medium requirements are satisfied by the 150 ohm shielded twisted pair cable as specified in EIA/TIA 568, Commercial Building and Telecommunications Wiring Standard, July 1991. Examples of this cable type are Type 1 and Type 2 cables. The following requirements are typically met with 100 m of Type 1 or Type 2. Type 6 cable may be used for short patch cables. The system can operate with a variety of STP cable, however, performance to this specification and interoperability between different vendors' equipment is assured only through the use of the STP cable specified in this section.

This specification was developed on the basis of an attenuation value of less than 124 dB/km at 100 MHz. Higher loss cable may be used for shorter segment lengths.

(R) The STP cable attenuation shall be less than 124 dB/km at 100 MHz.

(R) With the maximum transmit level specified in Figure 2-2, the near end crosstalk (NEXT) shall be no greater than -38.5 dB at 100 MHz.

2.4.2.3 Electrical Medium Connector Plug and Socket

(R) Each end of the STP link shall be terminated in the shielded 9 pin D connector. The plug connector (male receptacle) shall be used on the ATM Switch and the jack (female receptacle) on the ATM End Point (e.g., ATM workstation attachment or an intermediate system such as a router). The data connector and pin out is depicted (for informational use only) in Figure 2-20.

(R) The electrical data connector loss is assumed to have a maximum insertion loss of 0.25 dB at 100 MHz (see note below).

(R) The near-end crosstalk of any pair within the data connector shall not exceed -46.5 dB at 100 MHz (see note below).

Note: All measurements shall be made in accordance with the methods described in ANSI/IEEE 802.5.

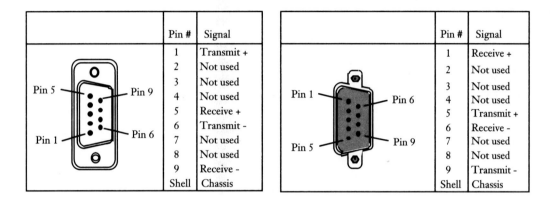

**Figure 2-20 Pin Assignment and Data Connector Detail
(Plug and Jack respectively)**

2.4.2.4 Electrical Characteristics

(R) The transmit (Active Output Interface [AOI]) and receive (Active Input Interface [AII]) parameters for the 155 Mbps STP interface are summarized in Figures 2-21 and 2-23. The parameters must be met over the temperature, voltage and lifetime range of the system. Electrical measurements shall be made with the AOI terminated with the connector specified in 2.4.2.3 into a 150 ohm resistive termination.

Parameter		Units	Value
Nominal baud rate		Mbaud	194.40
Baud Rate Tolerance		ppm	100
Differential Output Voltage	-Min.	V	1.0
	- Max.		1.6
Transmit Pulse Rise & Fall Times (10 to 90%)			
	- Min.	ns	0.6
	- Max.	ns	2.0
Transmit Pulse	-Overshoot	%	15
	- Undershoot		15
Total AOI Output Jitter, peak-to-peak		ns	1.0

Figure 2-21 AOI Electrical Transmit Parameters

(R) The transmit electrical output shall fit within the boundaries of the pulse envelope shown in Figure 2-22 when sending a continuous stream of K28.7s.

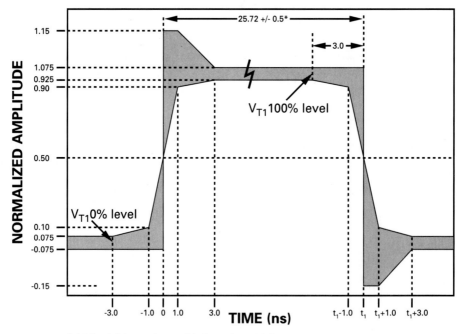

*+/- 0.5 ns (=1.0 ns peak-to-peak) is the total transmit jitter.

Figure 2-22 AOI Electrical Transmit Pulse Envelope

(R) The BER shall be less than one part in 10^{10}, when measured between end-points on the UNI physical layer, for all combinations of valid electrical transmit parameters, valid electrical receive parameters and allowable media.

Parameter		Units	Value
Nominal baud rate		Mbaud	194.40
Baud Rate Tolerance		ppm	100
Differential Input Voltage	- Min.	V	0.17
	- Max.		1.6

Figure 2-23 All Electrical Receive Parameters

2.4.3 Transmission Convergence (TC) Specification

The Transmission Convergence (TC) sublayer deals with physical layer aspects which are independent of the physical media characteristics. Most of the functions comprising the TC sublayer are involved with generating and processing of some of the overhead bytes contained in the transmission format overhead and ATM cell header.

2.4.3.1 Line Coding

(R) The 8B/10B transmission code specified in the Fibre Channel Physical Layer document [19], sections 10.1 and 10.2, shall be the encoding protocol utilized in the Physical Layer. Other than the K28.2, K28.5 and K28.7 special characters described below, use of other valid special characters is for further study.

Owing to the use of an error multiplying block coding scheme, this interface may impose a service limitation. This error multiplication may impact the cell discard rate.

(R) The byte alignment pattern shall be the K28.5 of the 8B/10B code. The receiver shall present a properly aligned byte stream after the receipt of two K28.5 special characters within a 5 byte window. The first byte received after the second K28.5 shall have valid byte alignment.

2.4.3.2 Transmission Frame Structure

The maximum transfer rate for ATM layer data is 149.760 Mbps. This rate has been chosen to exactly match the cell payload described in [12]. The transmission frame structure is used to transport cells from the ATM Layer and to provide 125 microsecond synchronization.

(R) Figure 2-24 describes the sequence of cells in a Physical Layer frame. Each set consists of a sequence equivalent to 27 cells of 53 octets. The first 53 octets is the Physical Layer Overhead Unit which provides byte synchronization, frame synchronization and Physical Layer OAM. This is followed by 26 ATM layer cells. Cell rate decoupling is performed by adding unassigned cells to the data stream. The unassigned cell header is as defined in CCITT Recommendation I.361 [13]. The payload transmission rate for data cells is exactly 149.76 Mbps (155.52 * 26/27 = 149.76).

43

Physical Layer Overhead Unit		Cell 1-26
Frame Delimiter 5 bytes	PL OAM 48 bytes	Data Cells 53 bytes/cell

Figure 2-24 Physical Layer Frame Format

The Frame Delimiter field is used to place special codes to provide byte and frame synchronization. These are described in Section 2.4.3.3. The Physical Layer Overhead Unit is used to signal PL-OAM at the UNI. The 6th byte in the Overhead Unit contains the PL-OAM bits which are currently defined in section 2.4.4. This byte is depicted below in Figure 2-25. Unused bytes within the Physical Layer Overhead Unit shall be Hex 00 with other values for further study.

Bit 8	Bit 7	Bit 6	Bit 5	Bit 4	Bit 3	Bit 2	Bit 1
0	0	0	0	0	AIS	EFI	FERF

Figure 2-25 Byte 6 Definition

(R) The TC only passes valid, non-Physical Layer cells to the ATM Layer. Physical Layer cells and cells with invalid HEC are not forwarded to the ATM layer.

2.4.3.3 Frame and Cell Delineation

Cell boundaries are synchronous with respect to frame structure. The K28.5/K28.7 ordered pair provides positive frame synchronization; the first byte of the first data cell follows the K28.7 symbol by 49 data bytes.

(R) Figure 2-26 describes the synchronization sequence used in the first five symbols of the transmission frame. The structure of the Physical Layer Overhead Unit (PL-OU) header consists of 4 K28.5 special characters followed by a K28.7 special character.

Symbol 0	Symbol 1	Symbol 2	Symbol 3	Symbol 4
K28.5	K28.5	K28.5	K28.5	K28.7

Figure 2-26 Synchronization Symbols

2.4.3.4 125 μsec Clock recovery

This 125 μsec Strobe and 125 μsec Reserved symbols provide a mechanism to deliver a 125 μsec clock across the transmission link. It is normally used in one direction across the UNI. The 125 μsec reference clock may be derived from any source, be it local to the switch, recovered from a SONET input or from any other mechanism. The K28.2 special character is placed in the data stream to explicitly realize the 125 μsec Strobe. It may be inserted between any two symbols of the data stream, and is considered part of the transmission frame (PL-OU and 26 ATM cells) which contains the symbol that precedes it. The first symbol location in the Physical Layer Overhead Unit is the 125 μsec Reserved Symbol. Normally, the 125 μsec Reserved Symbol (a K28.5 special character) is transmitted along with the rest of the PL-OU. If a 125 usec Strobe was transmitted in the previous transmission frame, the 125 μsec Reserved Symbol is deleted.

(O) The K28.2 special character [16] is transmitted to explicitly realize the 125 μsec Strobe anywhere in the data stream. It may be inserted between any two symbols of the data stream, and is considered part of the transmission frame which contains the symbol that precedes it. The 125 μsec Reserved Symbol (K28.5) from the PL-OU is removed if the 125 μsec Strobe was transmitted in the previous transmission frame.

(O) The first byte of the first data cell in the transmission frame follows the K28.7 special character by 49 non-Strobe symbols.

(R) All receivers must terminate the 125 μsec Strobe. The K28.7 special character is used as the reference marker for the frame, and the K28.2 special character is ignored for all frame synchronization purposes.

2.4.3.5 HEC Generation/Verification

The Header Error Control (HEC) covers the entire cell header. For the private UNI, only the detection of bit errors is described. Support of bit error detection based on the HEC field is mandatory.

The transmitter calculates the HEC value for the first four octets of the cell header, and inserts the results into the HEC field, the last octet of the header. The HEC field shall be an 8-bit sequence [11]. It shall be the remainder of the division (modulo 2) by the generator polynomial x^8+x^2+x+1 of the polynomial x^8 multiplied by the content of the header excluding the HEC field. The pattern 01010101 is XORed with the 8-bit remainder before being inserted in the last octet of the header [12].

(R) Equipment supporting the UNI shall implement HEC error detection as defined in CCITT Recommendation I.432.

(R) Equipment supporting the UNI shall generate the HEC byte as described in CCITT Recommendation I.432.

(R) The generator polynomial and coset used shall be in accordance with CCITT Recommendation I.432.

Figure 2-27 depicts the HEC verification flow on the receive side. The TC will not forward any cell to the ATM layer which has an incorrect HEC value.

(R) On detection of a header error, the cell shall be discarded.

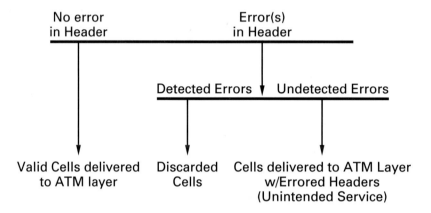

Figure 2-27 HEC Verification Flow

2.4.4 Physical Layer Operation and Maintenance Specification (M-plane)

The following PL-OAM functions associated with the 155 Mbps UNI have been identified and are described below. These functions provide for transmission and reception of maintenance signals and low level link performance monitoring. This PL-OAM information is carried in the Physical Layer Overhead Unit described in section 2.4.3.2.

Maintenance signals are defined for the physical layer to indicate the detection and location of a transmission failure. These signals are:

(R) Far End Receive Failure (FERF): FERF is used to alert the associated upstream termination point that a failure has been detected downstream. FERF is signalled upon the loss of frame synchronization or loss of the incoming signal. This failure is continuously indicated by a logical 1 in the Physical Layer Overhead Unit until frame synchronization has been achieved.

A link transmission performance monitoring signal is defined for the physical layer to detect and report link transmission errors. This signal is used to provide a low level indication of degraded link error performance and is defined as follows:

(R) Errored Frame Indicator (EFI): EFI is used to alert the associated upstream termination point that a frame has been received that contained an 8B/10B code rule violation.[5] An EFI

---

[5]   No other action is required for code rule violation.

flag is set upon the reception of one or more code rule violations within an incoming frame and is signalled to the upstream termination point by a logical 1 in the next available Physical Layer Overhead Unit in the outgoing frame.

(R) Alarm Indication Signal (AIS): AIS is used to alert the associated downstream termination point that a failure has been detected upstream. AIS is signalled upon the loss of frame synchronization or loss of the incoming signal. This failure is continuously indicated by a logical 1 in bit three of byte six in the Physical Layer Overhead Unit until frame synchronization has been achieved. Logical 0 in this position indicates normal operation.

The number of consecutive AIS assertions to indicate an alarm condition needs further definition.

2.5 E3 Physical Layer Interface

This section will specify a physical layer for a 34 368 kbps interface. It will be based upon section 8 of CCITT Recommendation G.703 and the mapping of ATM cells will be based upon section 6 of ITU-TS Draft Recommendation G.804.

2.6 E4 Physical Layer Interface

This section will specify a physical layer for a 139 264 kbps interface. It will be based upon section 9 of CCITT Recommendation G.703 and the mapping of ATM cells will be based upon section 9 of ITU-TS Draft Recommendation G.804.

Section 3:

ATM Layer Specification

3.1 ATM Layer Services

The ATM layer provides for the transparent transfer of fixed size ATM layer Service Data Units (ATM-SDUs) between communicating upper layer entities (e.g., AAL-entities). This transfer occurs on a pre-established ATM connection according to a traffic contract. A traffic contract is comprised of a QoS class, a vector of traffic parameters, a conformance definition and other items as specified in section 3.6. Each ATM end-point is expected to generate traffic which conforms to these parameters. Enforcement of the traffic contract is optional at the Private UNI. The Public Network is expected to monitor the offered load and enforce the traffic contract.

Two levels of virtual connections can be supported at the UNI:

- A point-to-point or point-to-multipoint Virtual Channel Connection (VCC) which consists of a single connection established between two ATM VCC end-points.
- A point-to-point or point-to-multipoint Virtual Path Connection (VPC) which consist of a bundle of VCCs carried transparently between two ATM VPC end-points.

Note: For VPC at the Public UNI, traffic monitoring and throughput enforcement will be performed across all cells carried on the same VPI independently of the VCI values.

(R) From a single source the relay of cells within a VPC/VCC must preserve cell sequence integrity.

No retransmission of lost or corrupted information is performed by this layer. Flow control over ATM connections is for further study. The ATM layer also provides its users with the capability to indicate the loss priority of the data carried in each cell. The information exchanged between the ATM layer and the upper layer (e.g., the AAL) across the ATM-SAP includes the following primitives:

Primitive	Request	Indicate	Confirm	Respond
ATM-DATA	X	X		

Figure 3-1 ATM Service Access Point (SAP) Primitives

These primitives make use of the following parameters:

Parameter	Associated Primitives	Meaning	Valid values
ATM-SDU	ATM-DATA.request ATM-DATA.indication	48 byte pattern for transport	Any 48 byte pattern
SDU-type	ATM-DATA.request ATM-DATA.indication	End-to-end cell type indicator	0 or 1
Submitted Loss-priority	ATM-DATA.request	Requested Cell Loss-priority	High or Low priority
Received Loss-priority	ATM-DATA.indication	Received Cell Loss Priority	High or Low priority
Congestion-experienced	ATM-DATA.indication	EFCN indication	True or False

Figure 3-2 ATM-SAP Parameters

The primitives provide the following services:

ATM-DATA.request: Initiates the transfer of an ATM-SDU and its associated SDU-type to its peer entity over an existing connection. The loss priority parameter and the SDU-type parameter are used to assign the proper CLP and PTI fields to the corresponding ATM-PDU generated at the ATM layer.

ATM-DATA.indication: Indicates the arrival of an ATM-SDU over an existing connection, along with a congestion indication and the received ATM-SDU type. In the absence of errors, the ATM-SDU is the same as the ATM-SDU sent by the corresponding remote peer upper layer entity in an ATM-DATA.request.

The following parameters are passed within one or more of the previous primitives:

ATM-SDU: This parameter contains 48 bytes of ATM layer user data to be transferred by the ATM layer between peer communicating upper layer entities.

Submitted Loss Priority: This parameter indicates the relative importance of the requested transport for the information carried in the ATM-SDU. It can take only two values, one for high priority and the other for low priority.

Received Loss Priority: This parameter indicates the relative importance of the transport given to the information carried in the ATM-SDU. It can take only two values, one for high priority and the other for low priority.

Congestion indication: This parameter indicates that the received ATM-SDU has passed through one or more network nodes experiencing congestion.

SDU-type: This parameter is only used by the ATM layer user to differentiate two types of ATM-SDUs associated with an ATM connection.

3.2 Service Expected from the Physical Layer

The ATM layer expects the Physical layer to provide for the transport of ATM cells between communicating ATM-entities. The information exchanged between the ATM layer and the Physical layer across the PHY-SAP includes the following primitives:

Primitive	Request	Indicate	Confirm	Respond
PHY-UNITDATA [1]	X	X		

1: The ATM-entity passes one cell per PHY-UNITDATA.request and accepts one cell per PHY-UNITDATA.indicate.

Figure 3-3 PHY-SAP Services Required by the ATM Layer

3.3 ATM Cell Structure and Encoding at the UNI

(R) Equipment supporting the UNI shall encode and transmit cells according to the structure and field encoding convention defined in T1 LB310 [7]. (see Figure 3-4 and Figure 3-5)

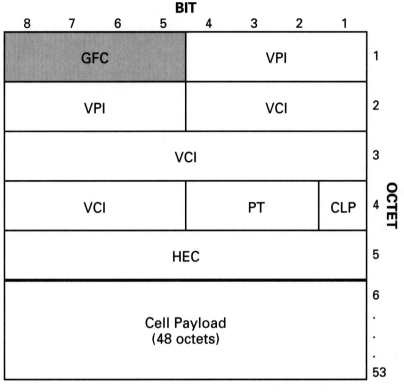

GFC: General Flow Control   VPI: Virtual Path Identifier
VCI: Virtual Channel Identifier PT: Payload Type
CLP: Cell Loss Priority   HEC: Header Error Check

Figure 3-4 ATM Cell Structure at the UNI

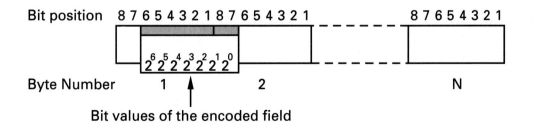

Figure 3-5 ATM Field Encoding Covention

The structure of the ATM cell is shown in Figure 3-4. It contains the following fields:

Generic Flow Control (GFC): This field has local significance only and can be use to provide standardized local functions (e.g. flow control) on the customer site. The value encoded in the GFC is not carried end-to-end and will be overwritten by the ATM switches.

Two modes of operation have been defined for operation of the GFC field. These are "uncontrolled access" and "controlled access". The "uncontrolled access" mode of operation is used in early ATM environment. This mode has no impact on the traffic which a host generates. Each host transmits the GFC field set to all zeros (0000). In order to avoid unwanted interactions between this mode and the "controlled access" mode where hosts are expected to modify their transmissions according to the activity of the GFC field, it is required that all CPE and public network equipment monitor the GFC field to ensure the attached equipment is operating in "uncontrolled mode". A count of the number of non-zero GFC fields should be measured for non-overlapping intervals of 30,000 +/- 10,000 cell times. If ten (10) or more non-zero values are received within this interval, an error is indicated to Layer Management.

(R) CPE at the UNI shall encode the GFC value to all zeros (0000).

(R) Public network equipment at the public UNI shall encode the GFC value to all zeros (0000).

(O) CPE shall inform Layer Management if a count of the non-zero GFC fields measured for non-overlapping intervals of 30,000 +/- 10,000 cell times reaches ten (10) or more.

(O) Public network equipment shall inform Layer Management if a count of the non-zero GFC fields measured for non-overlapping intervals of 30,000 +/- 10,000 cell times reaches ten (10) or more.

Virtual Path/Virtual Channel (VPI/VCI) Identifier: The actual number of routing bits in the VPI and VCI subfields use for routing is negotiated between the user and the network, e.g. on a subscription basis. This number is determined on the basis of the lower requirement of the user or the network.

> Note: The number of VCI routing bits used in a user-to-user VP is negotiated between the users of the VP.

(R) The bits within the VPI and VCI fields used for routing are allocated using the following rules:

- The allocated bits of the VPI subfield shall be contiguous;

- The allocated bits of the VPI subfield shall be the least significant bits of the VPI subfield, beginning at bit 5 of octet 2;

- The allocated bits of the VCI subfield shall be contiguous;

- The allocated bits of the VCI subfield shall be the least significant bits of the VCI subfield, beginning at bit 5 of octet 4;

(R) Any bits of the VPI subfield that are not allocated are set to 0. For a given VP, any bits of the VCI subfield that are not allocated are set to 0.

Payload Type (PT): This is a 3-bit field used to indicate whether the cell contains user information or Connection Associated Layer Management information (F5 flow). It is also used to indicate a network congestion state or for network resource management. The detailed coding and use of the PT field will be described in section 3.4.4

Cell Loss Priority (CLP): This is a 1-bit field which allows the user or the network to optionally indicate the explicit loss priority of the cell. More details on the use of the CLP bit are given in section 3.4.5.

Header Error Control (HEC): The HEC field is used by the physical layer for detection/correction of bit errors in the cell header. It may also be used for cell delineation.

3.4 ATM Layer Functions Involved at the UNI (U-plane)

This section describes ATM layer functions that need to be supported at the User-Network Interfaces (see Figure 3-6). It does not cover those ATM functions that are described in standards but have no impact on the UNI specification.

Functions	Parameters
Multiplexing among different ATM connections	VPI/VCI
Cell rate decoupling (unassigned cells)	Pre-assigned header field values
Cell discrimination based on pre-defined header field values	Pre-assigned header field values
Payload type discrimination	PT field
Loss priority indication and Selective cell discarding	CLP field, Network congestion state
Traffic shaping	Traffic descriptor

Figure 3-6 Functions supported at the UNI (U-plane)

3.4.1 Multiplexing among different ATM connections

This function multiplexes ATM connections with different QoS requirements. ATM connections may have either a specified or the unspecified QoS class as defined in section 4 of Appendix A.

The QoS class is the same for all cells belonging to the same connection, and remains unchanged for the duration of the connection.

(R) Network equipment supporting the public UNI shall support at least the Specified QoS Class 1 as defined in section 4.1 of Appendix A.

(O) Network Equipment supporting the public UNI may support the unspecified QoS class defined in section 4.2 of Appendix A.

(O) Network equipment supporting the private UNI may support either one or more specified QoS classes and/or the unspecified QoS class.

3.4.2 Cell rate decoupling

The cell rate decoupling[1] function at the sending entity adds unassigned cells to the assigned cell stream (cells with valid payload) to be transmitted, transforming a non-continuous stream of assigned cells into a continuous stream of assigned and unassigned cells. At the receiving entity the opposite operation is performed for both unassigned and invalid cells. The rate at which the unassigned cell are inserted/extracted depends on the bit rate (rate variation) of assigned cell and/or the physical layer transmission rate. The unassigned and invalid cells are recognized by specific header patterns which are shown in Figure 3-7.

Physical layers that have synchronous cell time slots generally require cell rate decoupling (e.g. SONET, DS3 and 8B/10B block-coded interfaces) whereas physical layers that have asynchronous cell times slots do not require this function (e.g. 4B/5B block-coded interface) since no continuous flow of cells needs to be provided. Therefore the requirements in this section only apply to physical layers that require continuous cell streams at the Physical-ATM layers boundary.

(R) Equipment supporting the UNI shall generate unassigned cells in the flow of cells passed to the physical layer in order to adjust to the cell rate required by the payload capacity of the physical layer.

(R) Equipment supporting the UNI shall encode the header fields of unassigned cells in accordance with the pre-assigned header field values defined in T1LB310 [7] and CCITT Recommendation I.361.

---

[1] The term "cell rate decoupling" has a different meaning within ITU-TS and refers to a physical layer process involving physical layer cells (e.g. idle cells) [12]. Further, the term "invalid" when applied to a cell or pattern refers to the illegal appearance of a physical layer cell at the ATM layer. The E3 and E4 interfaces may apply the ITU-TS definition of the cell rate decoupling.

(R) The receiving ATM entity shall extract and discard the unassigned and invalid cells from the flow of cells coming from the physical layer.

Note: The cell rate governing the flow between physical and ATM layer will be extracted from Physical layer (e.g. SONET) timing information if required.

3.4.3 Cells discrimination based on pre-defined header field values

The pre-defined header field values defined at the UNI are given in Figure 3-7 (Ref. T1 LB310).

Use	Value [1,2,3,4]			
	Octet 1	Octet 2	Octet 3	Octet 4
Unassigned cell indication	00000000	00000000	00000000	0000xxx0
Meta-signalling (default) [5,7]	00000000	00000000	00000000	00010a0c
Meta-signalling [6,7]	0000yyyy	yyyy0000	00000000	00010a0c
General Broadcast signalling (default) [5]	00000000	00000000	00000000	00100aac
General broadcast signalling [6]	0000yyyy	yyyy0000	00000000	00100aac
Point-to-point signalling (default) [5]	00000000	00000000	00000000	01010aac
Point-to-point signalling [6]	0000yyyy	yyyy0000	00000000	01010aac
Invalid Pattern	xxxx0000	00000000	00000000	0000xxx1
Segment OAM F4 flow cell [7]	0000aaaa	aaaa0000	00000000	00110a0a
End-to-End OAM F4 flow cell [7]	0000aaaa	aaaa0000	00000000	01000a0a

1: "a" indicates that the bit is available for use by the appropriate ATM layer function
2: "x" indicates "don't care" bits
3: "y" indicates any VPI value other than 00000000
4: "c" indicates that the originating signalling entity shall set the CLP bit to 0. The network may change the value of the CLP bit
5: Reserved for user signalling with the local exchange
6: Reserved for signalling with other signalling entities (e.g. other users or remote networks)
7: The transmitting ATM entity shall set bit 2 of octet 4 to zero. The receiving ATM entity shall ignore bit 2 of octet 4.

Figure 3-7 Pre-Defined Header Field Values

Meta-signalling cells are used by the meta-signalling protocol for establishing and releasing signalling virtual channel connections. For virtual channels allocated permanently (PVC), meta-signalling is not used.

(R) Equipment not supporting meta-signalling protocol at the UNI shall discard any cells received with VCI value = 1.

General broadcast signalling cells are used by the ATM network to broadcast signalling information independent of service profiles. For permanent virtual channel (PVC) service, the general broadcast signalling channel is not used since there is no control-plane process involved above the ATM layer.

(R) Equipment not supporting general broadcast signalling at the UNI shall discard any cells received with VCI value = 2.

The Virtual Path Connection (VPC) operation flow (F4 flow) is carried via specially designated OAM cells. F4 flow OAM cells have the same VPI value as the user-data cell transported by the VPC but are identified by two unique pre-assigned virtual channels within this VPC. At the UNI, the virtual channel identified by a VCI value = 3 is used for VP level management functions between ATM nodes on both sides of the UNI (i.e., single VP link segment) while the virtual channel identified by a VCI value = 4 can be used for VP level end-to-end (User <-> User) management functions.

The detailed layer management procedures making use of the F4 flow OAM cells at the UNI and the specific OAM cells format will be covered in section 3.5.

(R) Equipment supporting VP level management functions at the UNI shall encode the VCI field of the F4 flow OAM cells with the appropriate values as defined in T1 LB310 and shown in Figure 3-7.

(R) Equipment supporting VP level management functions at the UNI shall have the capability to identify F4 flow OAM cells within each VPC.

(R) Equipment not supporting VP level management functions at the UNI shall not transmit cells with VCI values 3 and 4 and shall discard any cells received with VCI value = 3 or 4.

A default header field value has been defined for the carriage of ILMI messages across the UNI. The specific encoding is shown in Figure 3-8.

Use	Value [1]			
	Octet 1	Octet 2	Octet 3	Octet 4
Carriage of ILMI message [2]	00000000	00000000	00000001	0000aaa0

1: "a" indicates that the bit is available for use by the appropriate ATM layer function

2: The transmitting ATM entity shall set the CLP bit to 0. The receiving ATM entity shall process ILMI cells with CLP=1 as ILMI cells and as any other CLP=1 cell.

Figure 3-8 Default Header Field Value

(R) Equipment supporting the UNI shall support VPI = 0 and VCI = 16 as the default values for the carriage of ILMI messages across the UNI.

3.4.4 Cell discrimination based on Payload Type (PT) Identifier field values

The main purpose of the PT Identifier is to discriminate between user cells (i.e., cell carrying user information) from non-user cells (see Figure 3-9). Code points 0 to 3 are used to indicate user cells. Within these code points, values 2 and 3 are used to indicate that congestion has been experienced in the network (see §3.6). Code points 4 and 5 are used for VCC level management functions. The PT value of 4 is used for identifying OAM cells communicated within the bounds of a VCC segment (i.e., single link segment across the UNI) while the PT value of 5 is used for identifying end-to-end OAM cells

The detailed layer management procedures making use of the F5 flow of OAM cells at the UNI and the specific OAM cells format is covered in section 3.5.

PTI Coding (MSB first)	Interpretation
000	User data cell, congestion not experienced, SDU-type = 0
001	User data cell, congestion not experienced, SDU-type = 1
010	User data cell, congestion experienced, SDU-type = 0
011	User data cell, congestion experienced, SDU-type = 1
100	Segment OAM F5 flow related cell
101	End-to-end OAM F5 flow related cell
110	Reserved for future traffic control and resource management
111	Reserved for future functions

Figure 3-9 Payload Type Indicator Encoding

(R) Equipment supporting VC level management functions at the UNI shall encode the PT field of the F5 flow OAM cells with the appropriate code points as defined in T1 LB310 [7].

(R) Equipment supporting VC level management functions at the UNI shall have the capability to identify F5 flow OAM cells within each VC.

(R) Equipment not supporting VC level management functions,via OAM cells, at the UNI shall ignore PT code points 100, 101.

3.4.5 Loss priority indication and selective cell discarding

The CLP field may be used for loss priority indication by the ATM end point and for selective cell discarding in network equipment. In a given ATM connection and for each user-data cell in the connection, the ATM equipment that first emits the cell can set the CLP bit equal to zero or one. The CLP bit is used to distinguish between cells of an ATM connection: A CLP bit equal to zero indicates a higher priority cell and a CLP bit equal to one indicates a lower priority cell. Upon entering the network, a cell with CLP value = 1 may be subject to discard depending on network traffic conditions.

The treatment of cells with CLP bit set (low priority cells) by the network traffic management functions is covered in section 3.6.

(O) User equipment supporting the UNI may use the CLP header field to indicate lower priority traffic (cells).

(O) ATM switches may tag CLP=0 cells detected by the UPC to be in violation of the Traffic Contract by changing the CLP bit from 0 to 1 (see 3.6).

3.4.6 Traffic Shaping

Traffic Shaping is expected to be an important function of ATM end-points in order to acheive the desired QoS. Traffic Shaping is covered in section 3.6.3.2.5

3.5 ATM Layer Management Specification (M-plane)

This section identifies the ATM Layer Management functions and procedures at the User Network Interface. Management functions at the UNI require some level of cooperation between customer premises equipment and network equipment. To minimize the coupling required between equipment on both sides of the UNI, the functional requirements have been reduced to a minimal set. The ATM Layer Management functions supported at the UNI are grouped into the following categories (see Figure 3-10):

Functions	Parameters
Fault Management • *Alarm surveillance (VP)* • *Connectivity Verification (VP,VC)* • *Invalid VPI/VCI detection*	**OAM cells** **OAM cells** **VPI/VCI**

Figure 3-10 ATM Layer Management Functions at the UNI

- Fault Management contains Alarm Surveillance and Connectivity Verification functions. OAM cells are used for exchanging related operation information. ATM cells with invalid VPI/VCI values are discarded and Layer Management is informed.

3.5.1 ATM Layer Management Information Flows

Figure 3-11 shows the OAM flows defined for the exchange of operations information between nodes (including customer premises equipment). At the ATM layer, the F4-F5 flows will be carried via OAM cells. The OAM cell flow used for end-to-end management functions may be carried transparently through the private ATM switch and made available to the user. The F4 flow is used for segment[2] or end-to-end (VP termination) management at the VP level using VCI values 3 and 4. The F5 flow is used for segment[3] or end-to-end (VC termination) management at the VC level using PT code points 4 and 5. A detailed explanation on OAM cell flow mechanism is given in T1S1.5/92-029R3, CCITT Recommendation. I.610.

---

[2] In this case, the segment is defined as the link between the ATM nodes on either side of the UNI.

[3] In this case, the segment is defined as the link between the ATM nodes on either side of the UNI.

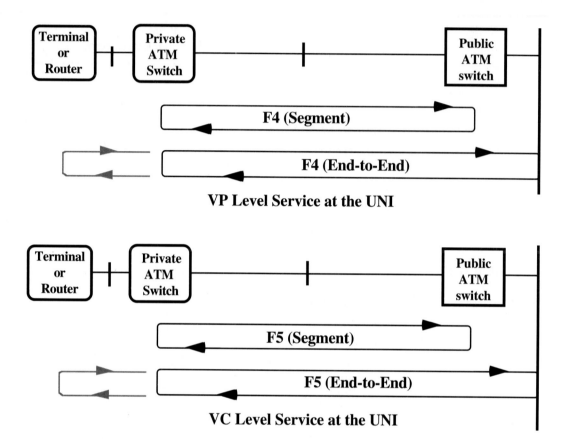

Figure 3-11 ATM Layer OAM flows at the UNI

In case of only Virtual Path (VP) visibility (i.e., VPC service at the Public Network Interface) the OAM operation information exchange will be limited to the F4 flow. Under this scenario, any VC level OAM functions and information exchange (F5 flow) are user-specific and ignored by the network. It is however possible to have VP level service at the Public UNI while maintaining VC visibility at the Private UNI. In this case, the private ATM switch would terminate the F4 flow but could carry transparently the user end-to-end F5 flow. For Virtual Channel (VC) visibility (VCC service), the OAM operation information exchange specified at the Public UNI could be limited to the F5 flow or could invoke both F4 and F5 flows.

(R) Equipment requiring/offering VP level service at the UNI shall support the F4 management flow as defined in T1S1.5/92-029R3 and CCITT Recommendation I.610 for the functions defined in 3.5.3. Equipment should also be capable of transparently passing/carrying the F5 management flow.

(R) Equipment requiring/offering VC level service at the UNI shall support the F5 management flow as defined in T1S1.5/92-029R3 and CCITT Rec. I.610 for the required functions defined in 3.5.3.

(R) Equipment requiring/offering VC level service only at a UNI shall either 1) process the F4 flow in accordance with T1S1.5/920029R3 and ITU-T Recommendation I.610, or 2) discard any F4 flow cells (i.e., cells with VCI = 3 and VCI = 4 are considered as cells with invalid VCI value).

The definition of "zero bandwidth" for a particular direction of any connection does not prohibit the transmission of OAM cells (ref. 3.6.3.2.3.7).

(R) For a point-to-multi-point connection, the only allowed use of F4 and F5 OAM flows is segment flows. Neither the user nor the network shall send end-to-end OAM cells.

3.5.2 ATM OAM Cell Format

The virtual path connection (VPC) operational information is carried via the F4 flow OAM cells. These cells have the same VPI value as the user-data cells but are identified by pre-assigned VCI values. Two unique VCI values are used for every VPC as shown in Figure 3-12a. The VCI value = 3 is used to identify the connection between ATM layer management entities (LMEs) on both sides of the UNI (i.e., single link segment) and VCI value = 4 is used to identify connection between end-to-end ATM LMEs.

The virtual channel connection (VCC) operation information is carried via the F5 flow OAM cells. These cells have the same VPI/VCI values as the user-data cells but are identified by pre-assigned code points of the Payload Type (PT) field. Two unique PT values are used for every VCC as shown in Figure 3-12a. The PT value = "100" (4) is used to identify the connection between ATM layer management entities (LMEs) on both sides of the UNI (i.e., single link segment) while the PT value = "101" (5) is used to identify connection between end-to-end ATM LMEs.

End-to-end OAM cells must be passed unmodified by all intermediate nodes. The contents of these cells may be monitored by any node in the path. These cells are only to be removed by the endpoint of the VPC (F4 flow) or VCC (F5 flow). Segment OAM cells shall be removed at the end of a segment where, for the purposes of this specification, segment is defined as a single VP or VC link across the UNI.

The format of the Functions-Specific fields of the Fault Management OAM cell is defined in T1S1.5/92-029R3 and CCITT Rec. I.610 and shown in Figure 3-12b.

(R) Equipment supporting the F4 and/or F5 flow at the UNI shall encode /interpret the OAM cells according to the format and encoding rules defined in T1S1.5/92-029R1 and CCITT Rec. I.610 for the functions defined in 3.5.3.

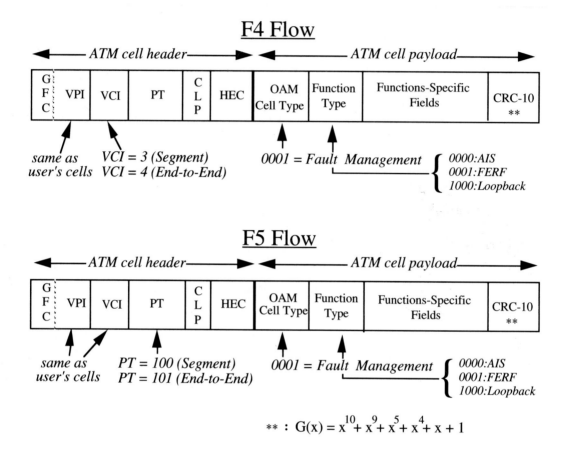

$$** : G(x) = x^{10} + x^9 + x^5 + x^4 + x + 1$$

Figure 3-12a Common OAM Cell Format

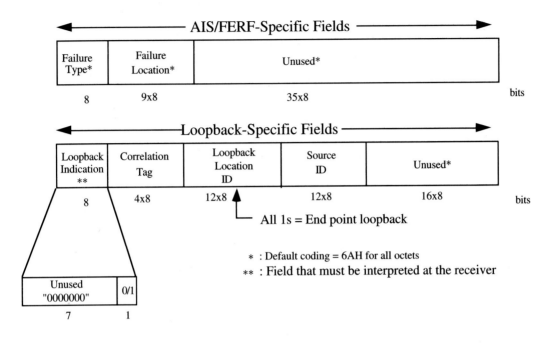

Figure 3-12b OAM Cell Fault Management-Specific Fields

Note: OAM Fault Management functions and cell formats may continue to evolve and software implementations may be advisable.

3.5.3 ATM Fault Management functions at the UNI

The Fault Management functions at the UNI are grouped in two categories: Alarm Surveillance and Connectivity Verification.

3.5.3.1 Alarm Surveillance

Alarm surveillance at the public UNI involves detection, generation and propagation of VPC/VCC failures (failure indications). In analogy with SONET physical layer, the failure indication signals are of two types: Alarm Indication Signal (AIS) and Far End Receive Failure (FERF). These signals are carried via OAM cells as defined in section 3.5.2. The VP/VC Alarm Indication Signal (VP-AIS/VC-AIS) is generated by a VPC/VCC node at a connecting point to alert the downstream VPC/VCC nodes that a failure has been detected upstream. The VP-AIS/VC-AIS can be caused by the detection of a VPC/VCC failure or by the notification of a physical layer failure. Upon receiving a VP-AIS/VC-AIS, the VPC/VCC end-point at the public UNI will return a VP-FERF/VC-FERF to alert the upstream nodes that a failure has been detected downstream. VP-AIS and VP-FERF are always carried on VCI = 4. VC-AIS and VC-FERF are always carried over cells with PT = 101.

(R) ATM End-Point at the public UNI shall detect all incoming VP-AIS and generate a VP-FERF in the upstream direction (toward the public network) to alert the ATM nodes about the failure.

(R) Public network equipment supporting the UNI, acting as VP intermediate node, shall generate VP-AIS upon detection of a VPC failure or upon receiving a physical layer failure notification.

(O) End-Point of VCCs traversing the public network may detect an incoming VC-AIS and generate a VC-FERF in the upstream direction (toward the public network).

(O) Public network equipment supporting the UNI may generate VC-AIS upon detection of a VCC failure or upon receiving a physical layer failure notification.

Equipment inserting Alarm Surveillance cells will do so at a rate low enough to insure that Alarm Surveillance cells amount to less than one percent of the capacity of any link in the connection.

The duration of the condition and the rate associated with the generation and removal of alarm signals (VP-AIS, VP-FERF) is to be defined.

3.5.3.2 Connectivity Verification

Connectivity verification is supported by the use of the OAM loopback capability for both VP and VC connections. More complete details on this loopback function can be found in the modified text of I.610 [37]. The VCC or VPC being checked can remain in service while this loopback function is being performed. The OAM Cell Loopback function supported at the UNI uses the following three fields:

- Loopback indication - This eight-bit field identifier for the end point receiving the OAM cell, whether the incoming cell is to be looped back. A value of (00000001) indicates that the cell should be looped back. All other values indicate that the cell is to be discarded. Before the cell is looped back, the end point should decrement the value of the loopback indication field.

- Correlation Tag - At any given time multiple OAM Fault Management cells may be inserted in the same virtual connection. As a result, the OAM cell loopback mechanism requires a means of correlating transmitted OAM cells with received OAM cells. The node inserting the OAM cell may put any value in this 32-bit field and the endpoint looping back the cell shall not modify it.

- Loopback Location ID (optional) - This 96-bit field identifies the point(s) along a virtual connection where the loopback is to occur. The default value of all ones is used by the transmitter to indicate the end point. The receiver is not required to decode this field.

- Source ID (optional) - This 96-bit field can be used to identify the originator of the Loopback cell so the originator can identify the looped back cell when it returns. This may be encoded any way that enables the originating point to be certain that it has received the cell it transmitted. The default value is all ones.

(R) Endpoints receiving OAM cells with a loopback indication value other than (00000001) and Function Type = 1000 shall discard the cell.

(R) Endpoints receiving OAM cells with a loopback indication value of (00000001) and Function Type = 1000 shall decrement the loopback indication value and then loopback the cell within one second.

For connections that do not terminate in the public network, public network equipment will only insert end to end loopback cells when attempting to verify or isolate a fault. Equipment inserting loopback cells will do so at a rate low enough to insure that loopback cells amount to less than one percent of the capacity of any link in the connection. No requirement should be made that loopback cells support delay measurement.

3.5.3.2.1 End to End Loopback

End to end loopback cells are only looped back by the end point of a VPC or VCC. These cells may be inserted by any node in the connection (intermediate or end point) and may be monitored by any node. However, only end points may remove these cells. End to end loopback cells are indicated by a Payload Type value of (101) for VCCs and a VCI value of (4) for VPCs. An example of how the end to end loopback cell is used is shown in Figure 3-13.

3.5.3.2.2 UNI Loopback

UNI loopback is performed using segment loopback cells which are looped back by the end point of a VPC or VCC segment. The segment is defined as the link between the ATM nodes on either side of the UNI. Segment end points must either remove these cells or loop them back depending on the value in the loopback indication field. That is, these cells must not travel beyond the segment in which they are generated. UNI loopback cells are indicated by a Payload Type value of (100) for VCCs and a VCI value of (3) for VPCs. An example of how the segment loopback cell is used is shown in Figure 3-13.

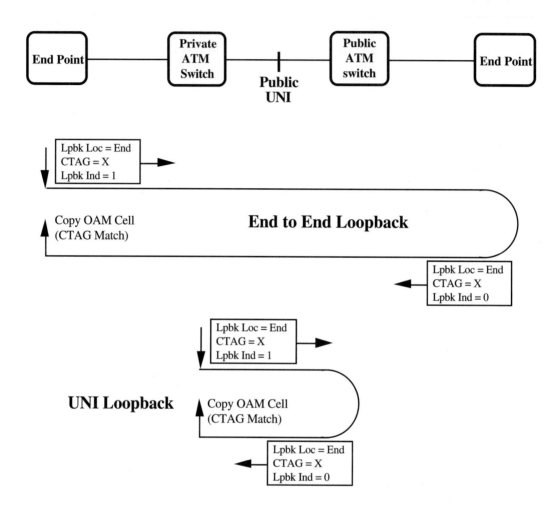

Figure 3-13 Loopback Function

3.6 Traffic Control and Congestion Control

3.6.1 Introduction

The B-ISDN, which is based on the ATM technique, is designed to transport a wide variety of traffic classes satisfying a range of transfer capacity needs and Network Performance objectives.

This section describes aspects of the Traffic Control and Congestion Control procedures relevant to the UNI specification.

In B-ISDN, ATM Layer congestion is defined as a state of Network Elements (e.g. switches, concentrators, cross-connects, and transmission links) in which the network is not able to meet the negotiated Network Performance objectives for the already established connections.

Congestion at the connection/call level is not considered in detail in this version of the specification.

In general, ATM Layer congestion can be caused by:

- unpredictable statistical fluctuation of traffic flows,
- fault conditions within the network.

ATM Layer congestion is to be distinguished from the state where buffer overflow is causing cell losses, but still meets the negotiated Quality of Service.

ATM Layer Traffic Control refers to the set of actions taken by the network to avoid congested conditions.

ATM Layer Congestion Control refers to the set of actions taken by the network to minimize the intensity, spread and duration of congestion. These actions are triggered by congestion in one or more Network Elements.

3.6.1.1 Objectives

The primary role of Traffic Control and Congestion Control parameters and procedures is to protect the network and the user in order to achieve Network Performance objectives. An additional role is to optimize the use of network resources.

The uncertainties of broadband traffic patterns and the complexity of Traffic Control and Congestion Control suggest a step-wise approach for defining traffic parameters and network Traffic Control and Congestion Control mechanisms. This document defines a restricted initial set of Traffic Control and Congestion Control capabilities aiming at simple mechanisms and realistic network efficiency.

It may subsequently be appropriate to consider additional sets of such capabilities, for which additional traffic control mechanisms will be used to achieve increased network efficiency.

The objectives of ATM Layer Traffic Control and Congestion Control for B-ISDN are as follows:

- ATM Layer Traffic Control and Congestion Control should support a set of ATM Layer Quality of Service (QoS) classes sufficient for all foreseeable B-ISDN services; the specification of these QoS classes should be consistent with Appendix A "ATM Bearer Service Quality of Service Objectives".

- ATM Layer Traffic Control and Congestion Control should not rely on AAL protocols which are B-ISDN service specific, nor on higher layer protocols which are application specific. Protocol layers above the ATM Layer may make use of information which may be provided by the ATM Layer to improve the utility those protocols can derive from the network.

- The design of an optimum set of ATM Layer Traffic Controls and Congestion Controls should minimize network and end-system complexity while maximizing network utilization.

3.6.1.2 Generic Functions

To meet these objectives, the following functions form a framework for managing and controlling traffic and congestion in ATM networks and may be used in appropriate combinations.

- Network Resource Management (NRM): Provisioning may be used to allocate network resources in order to separate traffic flows according to service characteristics.

- Connection Admission Control (CAC) is defined as the set of actions taken by the network during the call set-up phase (or during call re-negotiations phase) in order to determine whether a virtual channel/virtual path connection request can be accepted or should be rejected (or whether a request for re-allocation can be accommodated). Routing is part of CAC actions.

- Feedback controls are defined as the set of actions taken by the network and by the users to regulate the traffic submitted on ATM connections according to the state of Network Elements.

- Usage Parameter Control (UPC) is defined as the set of actions taken by the network to monitor and control traffic, in terms of traffic offered and validity of the ATM connection, at the user access. Its main purpose is to protect network resources from malicious as well as unintentional misbehavior, which can affect the QoS of other already established connections, by detecting violations of negotiated parameters and taking appropriate actions.

- Priority Control: the user may generate different priority traffic flows by using the Cell Loss Priority bit. A Network Element may selectively discard cells with low priority if necessary to protect as far as possible the Network Performance for cells with high priority.

- Traffic Shaping: traffic shaping mechanisms may be used to achieve a desired modification of the traffic characteristics.

- Other control functions are for further study.

All of these functions can make use of information that passes across the UNI. As a general requirement, it is desirable that a high level of consistency be achieved between the above traffic control capabilities.

3.6.1.3 QoS, Network Performance and Cell Loss Priority

The ATM Layer Quality of Service is defined by a set of parameters such as delay and delay variation, cell loss ratio, etc. Other QoS parameters are for further study.

For a complete list of QoS parameters defined in this document, refer to Appendix A.

A user requests one ATM Layer QoS class for each direction of an ATM layer connection. For each direction of an ATM Layer connection, a user requests a specific ATM Layer QoS from the QoS classes that a network provides. These requested QoS classes are a part of the Traffic Contract. The network commits to meet the requested Quality of Service as long as the user complies with the Traffic Contract (see §3.6.2.2).

A requested QoS class may be the "Unspecified QoS class" or may be one of the "Specified QoS classes," see Appendix A, Section 4. A specified QoS class may contain at most two cell loss ratio objectives. If a specified QoS class does contain two cell loss ratio objectives, then one objective is for the CLP=0 cells and the other objective is for the CLP=1 cells of the ATM connection.

Network Performance objectives at the ATM Layer Service Access Point are intended to capture the network's ability to meet the requested ATM Layer Quality of Service. It is the role of the upper layers, including the ATM Adaptation Layer, to translate this ATM Layer QoS to any specific application requested QoS.

3.6.1.4 Relation with other Standard documents

Section 3.6 of this UNI Specification is largely based on the ITU-T Recommendation I.371(Formerly CCITT Recommendation I.371)[41]. Progress has been made in the ATM Forum on some of the issues that were left for further study in I.371. In addition, some modifications have been made to the text taken from I.371. Main additions, omissions and modifications to I.371 are as follows:

- Recommendation I.371 states that "The use of UPC function is recommended." However, in this specification, the UPC function is required at the Public UNI (§3.6.3.2.3.3).

- In this specification, in addition to the Peak Cell Rate definition of I.371, two new traffic parameters (namely Sustainable Cell Rate (SCR) and Burst Tolerance) have been defined which are to be used jointly. These are optional traffic parameters which are defined by a Generic Cell Rate Algorithm (GCRA) which is the generalized version of the Peak Cell Rate monitoring algorithm described in Annex 1/I.371.

- I.371 states that when a traffic contract uses the CLP capability, the traffic parameters should be specified in terms of CLP=0 and CLP=0+1 traffic flows of the ATM connection (see section 2.3.2/I.371). This is intended to apply not only for Peak Cell Rate currently defined in I.371, but for any future traffic parameter as well.

  The ATM Forum specification conforms to I.371 for the Peak Cell Rate. However, this specification allows that the SCR and Burst Tolerance Traffic Parameters of an ATM Layer connection can also be specified in terms of CLP=0 and CLP=1 traffic flows. This is mainly due to the need for additional flexibility for mapping the traffic parameter definitions of some existing services, such as the Frame Relay service (see Appendix B, Figure B-2).

- In section 1.5/I.371, it is stated that "A user may request at most two different QoS classes for a single ATM connection, which differ with respect to Cell Loss Ratio objectives. The Cell Loss Priority bit of the ATM cell header allows for two Cell Loss Ratio objectives for a given ATM connection." Furthermore, in section 2.3.2/I.371, it is stated that "As indicated in section 1.5, the network provides an ATM Layer QoS for each of the components (CLP=0 and CLP=0+1) of an ATM connection. The traffic contract specifies the particular QoS choice (from those offered by the network operator) for each of the ATM connection components. There may be a limited offering of QoS specifications for the CLP=1 component."

  The text in section 1.5/I.371 is not consistent with sections 3.4.2.1 and 3.4.2.2 of I.150, moreover the text in section 2.3.2/I.371 is open to different interpretations. In an effort to provide a consistent interpretation of the above basic concept, in this specification, the QoS classes have been divided into two categories: Specified QoS class, and Unspecified QoS Class (see Appendix A, Section 4). For each direction of an ATM Layer connection, a user requests one QoS class at connection setup or subscription time. A specified QoS class may contain two cell loss ratio objectives, one for the CLP=0 cells and the other for the CLP=1 cells.

- Fast Resource Management functions are not included in this specification.

- This specification concentrates on Traffic Management and Quality of Service issues involved at the UNI, and therefore does not include these issues at the NNI.

3.6.2 User-Network Traffic Contract

3.6.2.1 Traffic Parameters and Descriptors

Traffic parameters describe traffic characteristics of an ATM connection. For a given ATM connection, Traffic Parameters are grouped into a Source Traffic Descriptor, which in turn is a component of a Connection Traffic Descriptor. These terms are defined below.

Definition: Traffic Parameters

A traffic parameter is a specification of a particular traffic aspect. It may be quantitative or qualitative. Traffic parameters may for example describe Peak Cell Rate, Sustainable Cell Rate, Burst Tolerance, and/or source type (e.g., telephone, video phone).

Definition: ATM Traffic Descriptor

The ATM Traffic Descriptor is the generic list of traffic parameters that can be used to capture the traffic characteristics of an ATM connection.

Definition: Source Traffic Descriptor

A Source Traffic Descriptor is a subset of traffic parameters belonging to the ATM Traffic Descriptor. It is used during the connection set-up to capture the intrinsic traffic characteristics of the connection requested by a particular source. The set of Traffic Parameters in a Source Traffic Descriptor can vary from connection to connection.

Definition: Connection Traffic Descriptor

The Connection Traffic Descriptor specifies the traffic characteristics of the ATM Connection at the Public or Private UNI. The Connection Traffic Descriptor is the set of traffic parameters in the Source Traffic Descriptor, the Cell Delay Variation (CDV) Tolerance and the Conformance Definition that is used to unambiguously specify the conforming cells of the ATM connection. Connection Admission Control procedures will use the Connection Traffic Descriptor to allocate resources and to derive parameter values for the operation of the UPC. The Connection Traffic Descriptor contains the necessary information for conformance testing of cells of the ATM connection at the UNI.

Any traffic parameter and the CDV Tolerance in a Connection Traffic Descriptor should fulfill the following requirements:

- be understandable by the user or terminal equipment; conformance testing should be possible as defined in §3.6.2.2;

- be useful in resource allocation schemes meeting Network Performance requirements described in §3.6.3.2.2;

- be enforceable by the UPC as specified in §3.6.3.2.3.

These criteria should be respected since users may have to provide these traffic parameters and CDV Tolerance at connection set-up. In addition, these traffic parameters and CDV Tolerance should be useful to the CAC procedure so that Network Performance objectives can be maintained once the connection has been accepted. Finally, they should be enforceable by the UPC in case of non-compliant usage in order to maintain Network Performance.

3.6.2.2 Traffic Contract Specification

A Traffic Contract specifies the negotiated characteristics of an ATM Layer Connection at a Private or Public UNI.

(R) The Traffic Contract at the Public UNI shall consist of a Connection Traffic Descriptor and a requested QoS class for each direction of the ATM Layer connection and shall include the definition of a compliant connection.

(O) The Private UNI may optionally support the same traffic contract as the Public UNI or a different traffic contract from the Public UNI.

The Connection Traffic Descriptor consists of all parameters and the Conformance Definition used to specify unambiguously the conforming cells of the ATM connection, i.e.:

- the Source Traffic Descriptor (e.g. Peak Cell Rate, Sustainable Cell Rate and Burst Tolerance),

- the CDV Tolerance,

- the Conformance Definition based on one or more applications of the Generic Cell Rate Algorithm (GCRA). See §3.6.2.4.1 for details on the GCRA.

The Conformance Definition based on the GCRA is used to specify unambiguously the conforming cells of an ATM Connection at the UNI. See §3.6.2.4 for further details on the GCRA and conformance definition. Examples on conformance definitions using the GCRA are provided in Appendix B.

The UNI Specification places no restrictions on the possible combinations that a user may request for (1) QoS class and (2) parameters in the Connection Traffic Descriptor.

The Conformance Definition should not be interpreted as the UPC algorithm. Although traffic conformance at the UNI is defined by the Conformance Definition based on the GCRA, the network provider may use any UPC as long as the operation of the UPC does not violate the QoS objectives of compliant connections.

The values of the traffic contract parameters can be specified either explicitly or implicitly as summarized in Figure 3-14. A parameter value is explicitly specified when it is specified by the user via signalling for SVCs or when it is specified via Network Management System (NMS) for PVCs. A parameter value specified at subscription time is also considered explicitly specified. A parameter value is implicitly specified when its value is assigned by the network operator using default rules, which, in turn, can depend on the information explicitly specified by the user. A default rule is the rule used by a network to assign a value to a traffic contract parameter that is not explicitly specified. In this version no default rules are specified, hence default rules are network-specific.

explicitly specified parameters		*implicitly specified parameters*
parameter values set at circuit-setup time	parameter values specified at subscription time	parameter values set using default rules
requested by user/NMS	assigned by network operator	

SVC	signalling	by subscription	network-operator default rules
PVC	NMS	by subscription	network-operator default rules

Figure 3-14 Procedures Used to Set Values of Traffic Contract Parameters

(R) For switched or permanent ATM connections, traffic contract parameters shall be either explicitly specified or implicitly specified in accordance with the requirements listed in Section 3.6.2.4.

The CAC and UPC procedures are operator specific and should take into account the knowledge of the specified traffic contract to operate efficiently.

(R) In order to accommodate additional, experimental traffic parameters at either the Private or Public UNI, signalling messages shall have the capability to encode proprietary manufacturer or network operator information elements corresponding to the experimental traffic parameters.

(O) Experimental traffic parameters may be supported by the network equipment and the end user device across the UNI (either the Private UNI or the Public UNI) via mutual agreement.

3.6.2.3 Cell Conformance and Connection Compliance

Conformance applies to the cells as they pass the UNI and are in principle tested according to some combination of GCRA algorithms. The first cell of the connection initializes the algorithm and from then on each cell is either conforming or not conforming. As in all likelihood even with the best of intentions a cell or two may be non-conforming, it is inappropriate for the network operator to only commit to the QoS objectives for connections all of whose cells are conforming. Thus, the term "compliant", which is not precisely defined, is used for connections in which some of the cells may be non-conforming.

(R) The precise definition of a compliant connection is left to the network operator. For any definition of a compliant connection, a connection for which all cells are conforming shall be identified as compliant.

Based on actions of the UPC function the network may decide whether a connection is compliant or not. The commitment by the network operator is to support the QoS for all connections that are compliant. The precise phrasing of the commitment is stated below.

(R) For compliant connections, at the Public UNI, the agreed QoS class shall be supported for at least the number of cells equal to the conforming cells according to the Conformance Definition.

For non-compliant connections, the network need not respect the agreed QoS class.

The Conformance Definition that defines conformity at the public UNI of the cells of the ATM connection uses a GCRA configuration in multiple instances to apply to particular combinations of the CLP=0 and CLP=0+1 cell streams with regard to the Peak Cell Rate and to particular combinations of CLP=0, CLP=1 and CLP=0+1 cell streams with regard to the Sustainable Cell Rate and Burst Tolerance. For example, the Conformance Definition may use the GCRA twice, once for Peak Cell Rate of the aggregate (CLP=0+1) cell stream and once for the Sustainable Cell Rate of the CLP=0 cell stream. Appendix B provides more details and further examples of the Conformance Definition that defines conformity of the cells of the ATM connection. The network operator may offer a limited set of alternative Conformance Definitions (all based on the GCRA) from which the user may choose for a given ATM connection. The minimum set of conformance definitions for early interoperability is defined in §3.6.2.5.

3.6.2.4 Traffic Contract Parameter Specification

(R) Peak Cell Rate for CLP=0+1 is a mandatory traffic parameter in any Source Traffic Descriptor.

(R) For switched ATM Layer connections, the Peak Cell Rate for CLP=0+1 and the QoS class must be explicitly specified for each direction in the connection-establishment SETUP message.

(R) The Cell Delay Variation Tolerance is a mandatory parameter in any Connection Traffic Descriptor.

(R) The Cell Delay Variation Tolerance shall be either explicitly specified at subscription time or implicitly specified.

Explicit specification of the CDV Tolerance within the signalling message is for further study.

(O) Sustainable Cell Rate and Burst Tolerance is an optional traffic parameter set in the Source Traffic Descriptor.

If either Sustainable Cell Rate or Burst Tolerance is specified then the other must be specified within the relevant Traffic Contract.

The Best-Effort-Capability is the label for a parameter in the ATM-User-Cell-Rate information element (see Section 5.4.5.6). The Best-Effort-Capability is used with the Unspecified QoS class (see Section A.4.2) with the only traffic parameter specified being the Peak Cell Rate specified for CLP=0+1.

If the Best-Effort-Capability is selected in the connection-establishment message then the connection admission-control procedures will not reject the call simply because the signalled Peak Cell Rate is greater than the rate of a link in the path (or is greater than the available bandwidth). The user need not conform to the signalled PCR and the network may enforce a PCR different than the signalled PCR. However, the network operator may reject the call request for other reasons, such as the number of such connections already established on a Network Element is at a chosen threshold, or the network operator simply does not support such connections that request the Best-Effort-Capability. The Best-Effort-Capability will be used to support those user terminals that are capable of and adapting to the time-variable available resources.

In future versions of this specification, traffic parameter negotiation, user notification of assigned traffic parameters, flow control mechanisms and further uses of the Best-Effort-Capability label may be defined.

Introduction of additional parameters to enhance the network resource management procedures or to capture traffic characteristics of a new type of connection is left open for further study.

3.6.2.4.1 Generic Cell Rate Algorithm (GCRA)

The Generic Cell Rate Algorithm (GCRA) is a Virtual Scheduling Algorithm or a continuous-state Leaky Bucket Algorithm as defined by the flowchart in Figure 3-15. The GCRA is used to define, in an operational manner, relationship between PCR and the "Cell Delay Variation tolerance" and relationship between SCR and the "Burst Tolerance", see respectively §3.6.2.4.2.4 and §3.6.2.4.3.3. In addition, for the cell flow of an ATM connection, the GCRA is used to specify the conformance at the public or private UNI to declared values of the above two tolerances, as well as declared values of the Traffic Parameters "Peak Cell Rate" and "Sustainable Cell Rate and Burst Tolerance", see respectively §3.6.2.4.2.2 and §3.6.2.4.3.2.

For each cell arrival, the GCRA determines whether the cell is conforming with the Traffic Contract of the connection, and thus the GCRA is used to provide the formal definition of traffic conformance to the Traffic Contract. Although traffic conformance is defined in terms of the GCRA, the network provider is not obligated to use this algorithm (or this algorithm with the same parameter values) for the Usage Parameter Control (UPC). Rather, the network provider may use any UPC as long as the operation of the UPC does not violate the QoS objectives of a compliant connection.

The GCRA depends only on two parameters: the increment I and the Limit L. These parameters have been denoted by T and τ respectively in Annex 1 of I.371, but have been given more generic labels herein since the GCRA will be used in multiple instances. The notation "GCRA(I, L)" means the Generic Cell Rate Algorithm with the value of the increment parameter set equal to I and the value of the limit parameter set equal to L.

The GCRA is formally defined in Figure 3-15. Figure 3-15 is a generic version of Figure 1 in Annex 1 of I.371. The two algorithms in Figure 3-15 are equivalent in the sense that for any sequence of cell arrival times, $\{t_a(k), k >= 1\}$ the two algorithms determine the same cells to be conforming and thus the same cells to be non-conforming. The two algorithms are easily compared if one notices that at each arrival epoch, $t_a(k)$, and after the algorithms have been executed, TAT = X + LCT, see Figure 3-15. An explanation of each algorithm follows.

The virtual scheduling algorithm updates a Theoretical Arrival Time (TAT), which is the "nominal" arrival time of the cell assuming equally spaced cells when the source is active. If the actual arrival time of a cell is not "too" early relative to the TAT, in particular if the actual arrival time is after TAT - L, then the cell is conforming, otherwise the cell is non-conforming.

Tracing the steps of the virtual scheduling algorithm in Figure 3-15, at the arrival time of the first cell $t_a(1)$, the theoretical arrival time TAT is initialized to the current time, $t_a(1)$. For subsequent cells, if the arrival time of the kth cell, $t_a(k)$, is actually after the current value of the TAT then the cell is conforming and TAT is updated to the current time $t_a(k)$, plus the increment I. If the arrival time of the kth cell is greater than or equal to TAT - L but less than TAT (i.e., as expressed in Figure 3-15, if TAT is less than or equal to $t_a(k) + L$), then again the cell is conforming, and the TAT is increased by the increment I. Lastly, if the arrival time of the kth cell is less than TAT -L (i.e., if TAT is greater than $t_a(k) + L$), then the cell is non-conforming and the TAT is unchanged.

The continuous-state leaky bucket algorithm can be viewed as a finite-capacity bucket whose real-valued content drains out at a continuous rate of 1 unit of content per time-unit and whose content is increased by the increment I for each conforming cell. Equivalently, it can be viewed as the work load in a finite-capacity queue or as a real-valued counter. If at a cell arrival the content of the bucket is less than or equal to the limit value, L, then the cell is conforming, otherwise the cell is non-conforming. The capacity of the bucket (the upper bound on the counter) is L + I.

Tracing the steps of the continuous-state leaky bucket algorithm in Figure 3-15, at the arrival time of the first cell $t_a(1)$, the content of bucket, X, is set to zero and the last conformance time (LCT) is set to $t_a(1)$. At the arrival time of the kth cell, $t_a(k)$, first the content of the bucket is provisionally updated to the value X', which equals the content of the bucket, X, after the arrival of the last conforming cell minus the amount the bucket has drained since that arrival, where the content of the bucket is constrained to be non-negative. Second, if X' is less than or equal to the limit value L, then the cell is conforming, and the bucket content X is set to X' plus the increment I for the current cell, and the last conformance time LCT, is set to the current time $t_a(k)$. If, on the other hand, X' is greater than the limit value L, then the cell is non-conforming and the values of X and LCT are not changed.

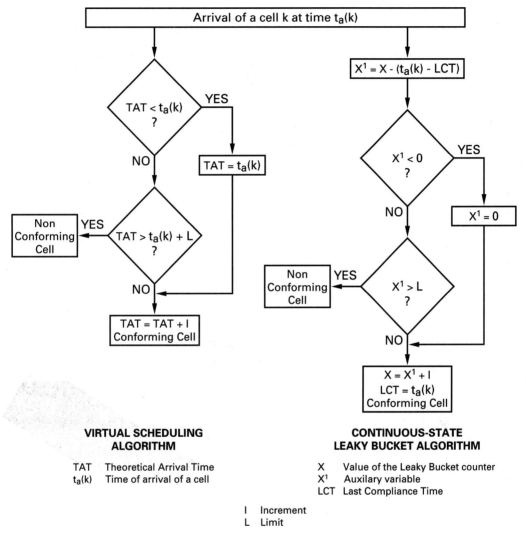

VIRTUAL SCHEDULING ALGORITHM

TAT	Theoretical Arrival Time
$t_a(k)$	Time of arrival of a cell

CONTINUOUS-STATE LEAKY BUCKET ALGORITHM

X	Value of the Leaky Bucket counter
X^1	Auxilary variable
LCT	Last Compliance Time

I	Increment
L	Limit

At the time of arrival ta of the first cell of the connection, TAT = $t_a(1)$

At the time of arrival ta of the first cell of the connection, X = 0 and LCT = $t_a(K)$

Figure 3-15 Equivalent versions of the Generic Cell Rate Algorithm

3.6.2.4.2 Peak Cell Rate

The Peak Cell Rate (PCR) traffic parameter specifies an upper bound on the traffic that can be submitted on an ATM connection. Enforcement of this bound by the UPC allows the network operator to allocate sufficient resources to ensure that the Network Performance objectives (e.g., for Cell Loss Ratio) can be achieved.

3.6.2.4.2.1 Peak Cell Rate Reference Model

The Equivalent Terminal configuration is given in Figure 3-16. Traffic sources, the multiplexer and the shaper define the Equivalent Terminal. This is only a model and does not preclude any particular implementation of the CPE or of the Terminal Equipment.

All traffic sources (AALs, FRM, etc.) offering cells to a connection are put together in the Equivalent Terminal. Each source generates Requests to send ATM cells at its own rate. All Requests are multiplexed in a Multiplexer (MUX in Figure 3-16) on a single link before entering the Virtual Shaper.

The Virtual Shaper is intended to reflect some smoothness in the cell flow offered to the ATM connection: at the PHY_SAP, the minimal inter arrival time between two consecutive Requests is greater than or equal to T which is called the Peak Emission Interval of the Connection. The output of the Virtual Shaper at the PHY_SAP of the Equivalent Terminal conforms to GCRA(T, 0). This conformity cannot be required at the Private or Public UNIs since CDV is allowed in the CPE as well as in the Terminal Equipment (TE). The output of the Virtual Shaper is affected by functions in the Equivalent Terminal that cause CDV characterized by τ^*. The value of τ^* is chosen such that the output cell flow conforms to GCRA(T, τ^*)

The output of the Equivalent Terminal is affected by functions in other CPE which may modify the CDV at the Public UNI characterized by τ. The value of τ is chosen such that the output cell flow is conforms to GCRA(T, τ)

The value of the Peak Emission Interval T is left to the discretion of the user to allow for intelligent multiplexing within the Customer and Terminal Equipment. For instance, AALs producing sporadic traffic may be synchronized to share the same transmission capacity. In other cases, T may be set to account for the combined activity of all traffic sources, e.g. the PCR of a VPC may be the sum of the PCRs of the VCCs contained in the VPC.

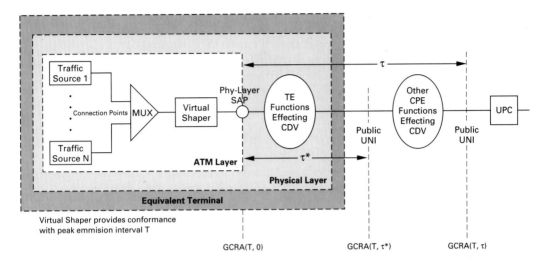

Figure 3-16 PCR Reference Model

The PCR traffic parameter is defined at the PHY_SAP within an Equivalent Terminal. The CDV Tolerance specified at the private UNI (τ^*) that directly connects an end system to a private network accounts for the cell clumping introduced by the end system. The CDV Tolerance specified at the public UNI (τ) that connects an end system to a public network through a private ATM network via a private UNI accounts for the cell clumping introduced by the end system and the private ATM network.

3.6.2.4.2.2 Peak Cell Rate Parameter Definition

The following definition applies to ATM connections supporting both CBR and VBR services.

The PCR definition for a VPC/VCC is as follows:

Location: At the Physical Layer SAP in an Equivalent Terminal representing the VPC/VCC (this is only a reference configuration; see Figure 3-16).

Basic Event: Request to send an ATM_PDU in the Equivalent Terminal.

Definition: The PCR (R_p) of the ATM connection is the inverse of the minimum inter-arrival time T between two basic events above. T is called the Peak Emission Interval of the ATM connection.

In the signalling message, the PCR is coded as cells per second. The granularity supported by the signalling message is 1 cell/s. The defined coding for the Peak Cell Rate in the signalling message does not imply that any UPC mechanism has to support the same linear granularity for the PCR across the complete defined cell rate range.

3.6.2.4.2.3 Interpretation of the Definition of Peak Cell Rate and Equivalent Terminal

A "natural" or "intuitive" definition for Peak Cell Rate is the reciprocal of the minimum spacing of cells of an ATM connection on a transmission link. This intuitive definition is a rough approximation of the definition given in the previous section; however, this intuitive definition has technical flaws. These flaws are resolved by the above Equivalent-Terminal definition, at the possible expense of some obtuseness.

A simple, technical flaw of the "intuitive" definition is that for a slotted transmission medium, it constrains the possible values of Peak Cell Rate to be the reciprocal of an integral number of cell slot times. For example and using round numbers, if 150Mb/s is provided to the ATM layer, then the next possible peak rate below 150Mb/s is 75Mb/s and the next possible one below that is 50Mb/s, and so on. This granularity is too coarse.

Note that the equivalent-terminal is a conceptual model (or reference configuration). The definition does not imply that the real Customer Premises Equipment must do the shaping. The shaping by the Equivalent-Terminal may be viewed as a "thought experiment". The fact that the source may not have shaped the traffic does not imply that the traffic is non-conforming since the criterion for conformance is at the UNI and is defined in terms of the GCRA.

Lastly, note that a definition of Peak Cell Rate does not tell the user the proper choice for the rate that meets the specific needs of the user. In particular, for VBR traffic sources, the equivalent-terminal model does not uniquely determine the value the user should pick for T. In the equivalent terminal, T must be chosen so that the queue in the buffer ("mux") behind the shaper is stable. This allows T to be chosen so that its reciprocal is any value greater than the sustainable rate, up to the link rate.

3.6.2.4.2.4 Cell Delay Variation Tolerance

ATM Layer functions (e.g. cell multiplexing) may alter the traffic characteristics of ATM connections by introducing Cell Delay Variation as illustrated in Figure 3-16. When cells from two or more ATM connections are multiplexed, cells of a given ATM connection may be delayed while cells of another ATM connection are being inserted at the output of the multiplexer. Similarly, some cells may be delayed while physical layer overhead or OAM cells are inserted. Consequently with reference to the Peak Emission Interval T (i.e., the inverse of the contracted PCR R_p), some randomness may affect the inter-arrival time between consecutive VPC/VCC cells (i.e., the inverse of the contracted PCR) as monitored at the UNI (public or private). The upper bound on the "clumping" measure is called CDV Tolerance.

The CDV Tolerance allocated to a particular VPC/VCC at the private UNI(denoted by the symbol τ^*) represents at this interface a bound on the VPC/VCC cell clumping phenomenon due to the slotted nature of the ATM, the physical layer overhead and the ATM Layer Functions, i.e., cell multiplexing performed within the source terminal equipment. The CDV Tolerance allocated to a particular VPC/VCC at the public UNI (denoted by the symbol τ) represents at this interface a bound on the VPC/VCC cell clumping phenomenon due to the slotted nature of the ATM, the physical layer overhead, and the ATM layer functions performed within the Customer Premises Network before the public UNI.

The CDV Tolerance is defined in relation to the Peak Cell Rate according to the GCRA. In particular, the CDV Tolerance at the public UNI, τ, is defined in relation to the PCR according to the algorithm GCRA(T, τ), where T is the inverse of R_p (the PCR). Likewise, the CDV Tolerance at the private UNI, τ^*, is defined in relation to the PCR according to the algorithm GCRA(T, τ^*).

Figures 3-17 - 3-20 show a few examples that illustrate the potential cell clumping allowed at the Public UNI for a given value of τ and for a given value of T (the inverse of the contracted PCR) of an ATM connection according to the GCRA (T, τ). In all these examples, it is assumed that T = 4.5δ, where δ is the time required to send 53 octets at the ATM layer data rate of 150 Mb/s (i.e., a peak bit rate of 33.3 Mb/s, including the cell header, is assumed). The notation in Figures 3-17 - 3-20 is defined in §3.6.2.4.1, where it is noted that "X + LCT" equals the "TAT" at each cell arrival time and after the GCRA has been executed.

From Figure 3-17, it can be observed that the minimum value of τ to be accommodated at the UNI is 0.5δ. From Figures 3-18 to 3-20, we observe that as τ increases, the minimum inter arrival time between conforming cells decreases. When τ is greater than or equal to T - δ, the maximum number N of conforming back-to-back cells, i.e., at the full link rate, equals:

$$N = \left\lfloor 1 + \frac{\tau}{T - \delta} \right\rfloor \quad \text{For T > } \delta \text{ where } \lfloor x \rfloor \text{ stands for the integer part of x.}$$

This result of back-to-back cell clumping is illustrated in Figures 3-19 and 3-20.

The value of the CDV Tolerance may have an impact on the allocation of network resources for a particular VPC/VCC. It is therefore recommended that the CDV Tolerance (at both private and public UNI) be upper bounded, as a function of the PCR.

(R) A user shall explicitly or implicitly select a value for the CDV Tolerance at the public UNI for an ATM connection from a set of values supported by the network. Whether the set of values is to be standardized or to be determined by the network operator is for further study.

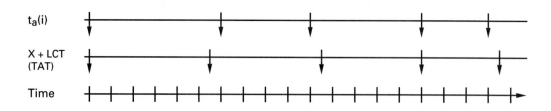

Figure 3-17 Ideal Cell Arrival at the Public UNI ($\tau = 0.5\delta$)

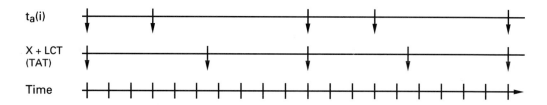

Figure 3-18 Possible Cell Arrival at the Public UNI ($\tau = 1.5\delta$)

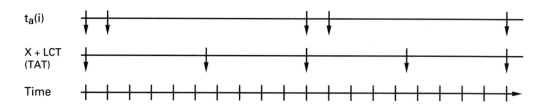

Figure 3-19 Possible Cell Arrival at the Public UNI ($\tau = 3.5\delta$)

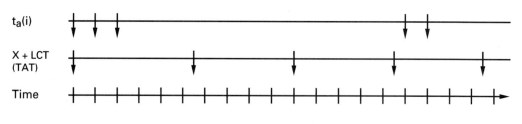

Figure 3-20 Possible Cell Arrival at the Public UNI ($\tau = 7\delta$)

3.6.2.4.3 Sustainable Cell Rate and Burst Tolerance

The Sustainable Cell Rate is an upper bound on the conforming average rate of an ATM connection. Enforcement of this bound by the UPC could allow the network operator to allocate sufficient resources, but less than those based on the Peak Cell Rate, and still ensure that the performance objectives (e.g., for Cell Loss Ratio) can be achieved.

3.6.2.4.3.1 Sustainable Cell Rate and Burst Tolerance Reference Model

The Sustainable Cell Rate (SCR) Reference Model is defined with reference to Figure 3-21.

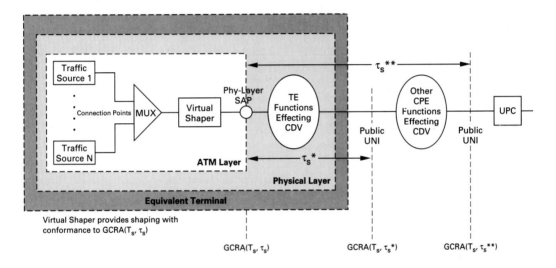

Figure 3-21 SCR and Burst Tolerance Reference Model

The SCR and Burst Tolerance traffic parameters are defined at the PHY_SAP within an Equivalent Terminal.

3.6.2.4.3.2 Sustainable Cell Rate and Burst Tolerance Parameter Definitions

The following definition applies to ATM connections supporting VBR services. The SCR and Burst Tolerance parameters for a VPC/VCC are defined according to the GCRA (§3.6.2.4.1) as follows:

Location: At the Physical Layer SAP in an Equivalent Terminal representing the VPC/VCC (this is only a reference configuration; see Figure 3-21.)

Basic Event: Request to send an ATM_PDU in the Equivalent Terminal.

Definition: The SCR, denoted as R_s, and the Burst Tolerance denoted as τ_s, of the ATM connection are defined by the GCRA(T_s, τ_s) based on the arrivals of the Basic Event above. R_s is the inverse of T_s, the increment parameter of the GCRA and τ_s is the limit parameter of the GCRA.

In the signalling message, the SCR is coded as cells per second. The granularity supported by the signalling message is 1 cell/s. The defined coding for the Sustainable Cell Rate in the signalling message does not imply that any UPC mechanism has to support the same linear granularity for the SCR across the complete defined cell rate range.

3.6.2.4.3.3 Interpretation of the Definition of Sustainable Cell Rate and Burst Tolerance in Conjunction with Peak Cell Rate

The SCR is an upper bound on the possible conforming "average rate" of an ATM connection, where "average rate" is the number of cells transmitted divided by the "duration of the connection"; where in this case, the "duration of the connection" is the time from the emission of the first cell until the state of the GCRA for the SCR returns to zero after the emission of the last cell of the connection. Relative to the Peak Cell Rate parameter, T_s is greater than T.

The SCR and Burst Tolerance traffic parameters are optional traffic parameters a user may choose to declare jointly, if the user can upper bound the realized average cell rate of the ATM connection to a value below the PCR. Note that as specified in §3.6.2.4 the PCR must be specified for every connection. To be useful to the network provider, the value of the SCR must be less than the PCR. For CBR connections, the user would not declare a SCR and would only declare a PCR.

The SCR and Burst Tolerance traffic parameters enable the end-user/terminal to describe the future cell flow of an ATM connection in greater detail than just the PCR. If an end-user/terminal is able to specify the future cell flow in greater detail than just the PCR, then the network provider may be able to more efficiently utilize the network resources. This directly benefits the network provider whether public or private, and in the case of public ATM networks, benefits the end-user with possible reduced charges for the connection.

If the source wants to submit traffic that conforms to the SCR ($R_s = 1/T_s$) and the Burst Tolerance (τ_s) and the Peak Cell Rate (1/T) at the PHY-SAP of the equivalent terminal, then it offers traffic that is conforming to the GCRA(T_s, τ_s) and the peak emission interval T (i.e., GCRA(T, 0)).

The Burst Tolerance together with the SCR and the GCRA determine the maximum burst size (MBS) that may be transmitted at the peak rate and still be in conformance with the GCRA(T_s, τ_s). The maximum burst size in number of cells is given by

$$MBS = \left\lfloor 1 + \frac{\tau_s}{T_s - T} \right\rfloor$$

where $\lfloor x \rfloor$ stands for the integer part of x.

In the signalling message, the Burst Tolerance is conveyed through the MBS which is coded in number of cells. The granularity supported by the signalling message is 1 cell. The MBS is used to derive the value of τ_s. The MBS and τ_s apply at the PHY_SAP of the Equivalent Terminal. Note that in order to determine τ_s from the MBS, the Peak Cell Rate also needs to be specified. By convention, the peak rate used in the calculation of τ_s is the Peak Cell Rate of the CLP=0+1 cell flow. This convention holds whether τ_s is associated with the SCR for the CLP=0, or the CLP=1, or the CLP=0+1 cell flow of the connection. Also, given the MBS, T, and T_s, then τ_s is not uniquely determined, but can be any value in the half-closed interval:

$[\,(MBS - 1)(T_s - T),\ MBS(T_s - T)\,]$.

Hence, in order for all parties to derive a common value for τ_s, by convention, the minimum possible value is used. Thus, given the MBS, T, and T_s, then τ_s is set equal to:

$\tau_s = (MBS - 1)(T_s - T)$

Note that over any closed time interval of length t, the number of cells, N(t), that can be emitted with spacing no less than T and still be in conformance with GCRA(T_s, τ_s) is bounded by:

$$N(t) \le \min\left(\left\lfloor 1 + \frac{t + \tau_s}{T_s} \right\rfloor, \left\lfloor 1 + \frac{t}{T} \right\rfloor \right)$$

Observe that if t is greater than or equal to the MBS $\times$ T, then the first term of the above equation applies; otherwise, the second term applies.

Note that the maximum conforming burst size, defined above, does not imply that bursts of this size with arbitrary spacing between the bursts would be conforming with the GCRA(T_s, τ_s). Rather, in order for a burst this large to be conforming, the cell stream needs to be idle long enough for the state of the GCRA associated with SCR to become zero (i.e., long enough for the continuous-state leaky bucket to become empty) prior to the burst.

If a user chooses to specify a value for the SCR and Burst Tolerance traffic parameters and wishes to emit conforming bursts at the peak rate, then the appropriate choice of T_s and τ_s depends on the minimum spacing between bursts as well as the burst size. For a cell flow of an ATM connection, if the minimum spacing between bursts at the equivalent terminal is T_I

and if the maximum burst size (with inter-cell spacing T) is B, then the cell flow is conforming with GCRA(T_s, τ_s), if T_s, τ_s are chosen at least large enough to satisfy the following equation:

$$B = 1 + \left\lfloor \frac{\min (T_I - T_s, \tau_s)}{T_s - T} \right\rfloor$$

where $\lfloor x \rfloor$ stands for the integer part of x.

The traffic pattern conforming with the GCRA(T_s, τ_s) is in general not unique. Two traffic patterns are equivalent in relationship with the GCRA(T_s, τ_s) if they both conform at the PHY-SAP with the GCRA(T_s, τ_s) within the equivalent terminal. Therefore, any cell stream that complies with the GCRA(T, 0) and GCRA(T_s, τ_s) at the PHY_SAP has a Peak Cell Rate of $R_p = 1/T$, a mean cell rate which is bounded by $R_s = 1/T_s$ and a burst length which is bounded by B. Note that the bounds R_s and B are achievable. For example, a periodic cell stream with period B * T_s which transmits B cells at the peak rate with inter burst spacing $T_I = B * (T_s - T) + T$ has Peak Cell Rate R_p, mean cell rate R_s and burst length B, and is compliant with both GCRAs.

3.6.2.4.3.4 Relationship of CDV Tolerance, SCR and Burst Tolerance

ATM Layer functions (e.g. cell multiplexing) may alter the characteristics of a connection's cell flow between the Equivalent Terminal and the public or private UNI. Thus, as with the Peak Cell Rate, some tolerance for Cell Delay Variation may need to be considered in order that cells conforming to the GCRA(T_s, τ_s) at the Equivalent Terminal are also conforming at the public UNI.

It can be shown that if a terminal emits cells such that the emission epochs are conforming with GCRA(T_s, τ_s) and if the cells pass through a customer premises ATM network that introduces a random delay, but which is within the interval [d_{min}, d_{max}], then the cell arrival process at the public UNI is conforming with GCRA(T_s, $\tau_s + d_{max} - d_{min}$). Thus if τ, the CDV Tolerance parameter for the Peak Cell Rate is chosen to be $d_{max} - d_{min}$ (or is chosen to be a small quantile, e.g. 10^{-9}, of the possible delay variation), then τ could be used for the CDV Tolerance for the SCR as well. Thus, for simplicity, in the present UNI Specification, the same value for CDV Tolerance is used for the Peak Cell Rate and for the Sustainable Cell Rate of an ATM connection. Note that although a user may choose to select the CDV Tolerance from the set of values supported by the network to be greater than or equal to $d_{max} - d_{min}$, there is no requirement to do so.

In analogy with the PCR, the criterion for conformance to the SCR and the Burst Tolerance is specified at the UNI (both public and private). At the public UNI, the criterion for conformance is specified in terms of the Generic Cell Rate Algorithm with the argument T_s and $\tau_s + \tau$, GCRA(T_s, $\tau_s + \tau$).

With regard to conformance to the SCR at the public UNI, note that conformance depends on τ_s and on τ only via their sum. Thus, the constraint of a common CDV Tolerance τ for both Peak Cell Rate and SCR is not unduly restrictive as a user still has freedom in the choice of τ_s (by the choice of MBS), and thus can choose τ_s so that $\tau_s + \tau$ has the desired value. However, note that a negative consequence of choosing τ_s dependent on τ is that it violates the modeling principle that traffic parameters in the Source Traffic Descriptor are chosen based solely on the characteristics of the source and do not consider the equipment and traffic between the source and the UNI. For example, Peak Cell Rate is a traffic parameter, but CDV Tolerance is not a traffic parameter. Thus, although Burst Tolerance is defined herein as a traffic parameter, if the user chooses its value based on factors besides the source traffic, then the modeling principle for source traffic descriptors is violated. This matter will be revisited in the next edition of the UNI Specification.

Also note that to apply the equations for "MBS", "N(t)" and "B" in the previous section to burst sizes at the public UNI, as opposed to at the equivalent terminal, one simply needs to replace the "τ_s" with "$\tau_s + \tau$."

The text in this section is also applicable to the private UNI, one simply needs to replace τ with τ^*.

3.6.2.5 Conformance Definitions Supported at the Public UNI

The conformity of cells of an ATM connection at the public UNI is defined according to the GCRA algorithm in relation to the corresponding parameters specified in the Connection Traffic Descriptor. This Conformance Definition is specified in the Traffic Contract. The set of Conformance Definitions that will be supported at the public UNI is the network provider's choice.

The Conformance Definitions include only traffic parameters for user data traffic of an ATM connection. For specification of OAM traffic see §3.6.3.2.3.7.

(R) For switched connections the signalling message shall be capable of conveying information that identifies at least the following set of Conformance Definitions. For permanent connections the Conformance Definition shall be explicitly identified at subscription time.

3.6.2.5.1 Conformance Definition for PCR

The following is a Conformance Definition for a Source Traffic Descriptor that specifies PCR for the CLP=0 cell stream and PCR for the CLP=0+1 cell stream:

Conformance Definition:

1. One GCRA(T_{0+1}, τ) defining the CDV tolerance in relation to the PCR of the CLP=0+1 cell stream.

2. One GCRA(T_0, τ) defining the CDV tolerance in relation to the PCR of the CLP=0 cell stream.

A CLP=0 cell that is conforming to both GCRAs (1) and (2) above is said to be conforming to the Connection Traffic Descriptor. A CLP=1 cell that is conforming to GCRA (1) above is said to be conforming to the Connection Traffic Descriptor. If the user requests tagging and if tagging is supported by the network, a CLP=0 cell that is not conforming to GRCA (2) above but is conforming to GCRA (1) above is considered to have the CLP bit changed to 1 and said to be conforming to the Connection Traffic Descriptor.

For networks that handle cells of the connection independent of the value of the CLP bit, the above Conformance Definition reduces to GCRA (1). The tagging option is not applicable to this Conformance Definition.

If the same value is specified for both PCR of the CLP=0 cell stream and PCR of the CLP=0+1 cell stream, this Conformance Definition could be used by a connection that only wants to send CLP=0 cells at its PCR (e.g. the example 3 given in Appendix B, the Constant Bit Rate Services). If the PCR of CLP=0 cell stream is set to zero, this Conformance Definition could be used by a connection that only wants to send CLP=1 cells at its PCR. Proper specification of the values of the PCRs allow this Conformance Definition to be used to accommodate all traffic mixes of a connection that only uses PCR traffic parameter.

3.6.2.5.2 Conformance Definition for PCR CLP=0+1 and SCR CLP=0

The following is a Conformance Definition for a Source Traffic Descriptor that specifies PCR for the CLP=0+1 cell stream and SCR for the CLP=0 cell stream:

Conformance Definition:

1. One $GCRA(T_{0+1}, \tau)$ defining the CDV tolerance in relation to the PCR of the CLP=0+1 cell stream.

2. One $GCRA(T_{s0}, \tau_{s0}+\tau)$ defining the sum of the CDV tolerance and the Burst Tolerance in relation to the SCR of the CLP=0 cell stream.

A CLP=0 cell that is conforming to both GCRAs (1) and (2) above is said to be conforming to the Connection Traffic Descriptor. A CLP=1 cell that is conforming to GCRA (1) above is said to be conforming to the Connection Traffic Descriptor. If the user requests tagging and if tagging is supported by the network, a CLP=0 cell that is not conforming to GRCA (2) above but is conforming to GCRA (1) above is considered to have the CLP bit changed to 1 and said to be conforming to the Connection Traffic Descriptor.

This conformance definition allows a connection to send CLP=1 cells at a PCR equal to the specified PCR of the CLP=0+1 cell stream.

3.6.2.5.3 Conformance Definition for PCR CLP=0+1 and SCR CLP=0+1

The following is a Conformance Definition for a Source Traffic Descriptor that specifies PCR for the CLP=0+1 cell stream and SCR for the CLP=0+1 cell stream:

Conformance Definition:

1. One GCRA(T_{0+1}, t) defining the CDV tolerance in relation to the PCR of the CLP=0+1 cell stream.

2. One GCRA(T_{s0+1}, t_{s0+1}+t) defining the sum of the CDV tolerance and the Burst Tolerance in relation to the SCR of the CLP=0+1 cell stream.

A cell that is conforming to both GCRAs (1) and(2) above is said to be conforming to the Connection Traffic Descriptor. The tagging option is not applicable to this Conformance Definition.

3.6.3 Functions and Procedures for Traffic Control and Congestion Control at the UNI

3.6.3.1 Introduction

Generic Traffic Control and Congestion Control functions are defined as the set of actions taken by the network in all the relevant Network Elements.

Under normal operation, i.e., when no network failures occur, functions referred to as traffic control functions in this Specification are intended to avoid network congestion.

However, congestion may occur, e.g. because of malfunctioning traffic control functions caused by unpredictable statistical fluctuations of traffic flows or by network failures. Therefore, additionally, functions referred to as congestion control functions in this Specification are intended to react to network congestion in order to minimize its intensity, spread and duration.

A range of traffic and congestion control functions will be used in the B-ISDN to maintain the QoS of ATM connections. The following functions are described in this Specification:

Traffic Control Functions:

i   Network Resource Management (§3.6.3.2.1)

ii   Connection Admission Control (§3.6.3.2.2)

iii   Usage Parameter Control (§3.6.3.2.3)

iv   Selective Cell Discarding (§3.6.3.2.4)

v   Traffic Shaping (§3.6.3.2.5)

vi   Explicit Forward Congestion Indication (§3.6.3.2.6)

Congestion Control Functions:

vii   Selective Cell Discarding (§3.6.3.3.1)

viii   Explicit Forward Congestion Indication (§3.6.3.2.6)

Additional Control Functions:

Possible useful techniques that require further study to determine details are:

ix   Connection Admission Control that reacts to and takes account of the measured load on the network

x   Variation of usage monitored parameters by the network. For example, reduction of the peak rate available to the user.

xi   Other traffic control techniques (e.g. re-routing, connection release, OAM functions) are for further study.

xii   Fast Resource Management.

The impact on standardization of the use of these additional techniques (e.g. the impact on the ATM layer management, user-network signalling and control plane) requires further study.

Different levels of Network Performance may be provided on ATM connections by proper routing, Traffic Shaping, Priority Control and Resource Allocation to meet the required ATM Layer QoS for these connections.

3.6.3.2 Traffic Control Functions

3.6.3.2.1 Network Resource Management

The section on Network Resource Management of I.371 is included in the UNI Specification because Virtual Paths may be used at the UNI, even though the underlying structures are created and managed in the Network.

The use of Virtual Paths is described below. Other networking techniques are for further study.

Use of Virtual Paths

Virtual Paths are an important component of Traffic Control and Resource Management in the B-ISDN. With relation to Traffic Control, VPCs can be used to:

- simplify CAC,

- implement a form of priority control by segregating traffic types requiring different QoS,

- efficiently distribute messages for the operation of traffic control schemes (for example to indicate congestion in the network by distributing a single message for all VCCs comprising a VPC),

- aggregate user-to-user services such that the UPC can be applied to the traffic aggregate.

VPCs also play a key role in Network Resource Management. By reserving capacity on VPCs, the processing required to establish individual VCCs is reduced. Individual VCCs can be established by making simple connection admission decisions at nodes where VPCs are terminated. Strategies for the reservation of capacity on VPCs will be determined by the trade-off between increased capacity costs and reduced control costs. These strategies are left to the decision of network operators.

The peer-to-peer Network Performance on a given VCC depends on the performances of the consecutive VPCs used by this VCC and on how it is handled in Virtual Channel Connection Related Functions (CRF(VC)s). See Figure 3-22. A Connection Related Function may be a switch, concentrator or other network equipment.

If handled similarly by CRF(VC)s, different VCCs routed through the same sequence of VPCs experience similar expected Network Performance - e.g. in terms of Cell Loss Ratio, Cell Transfer Delay and Cell Delay Variation - along this route.

When VCCs within a VPC require a range of QoS, the VPC performance objective should be set suitably for the most demanding VCC carried. The impact on resource allocation is for further study.

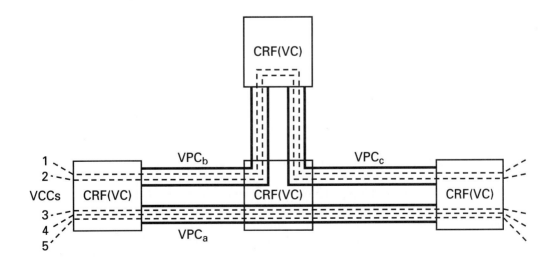

Figure 3-22 Mapping Cell Loss Ratios for VCC and VPC

Notes:

- VCCs 1 and 2 experience a Network Performance which depends on Network Performance on VPCs b and c and on how these VCCs are handled by Cell Relay Function CRF(VC)s. It may differ from Network Performance experienced by VCCs 3, 4 and 5, at least due to different Network Performances provided by VPCs.

- VCCs 3, 4 and 5 experience similar Network Performances in terms of Cell Delay and Cell Delay Variation if handled similarly by CRF(VC)s.

- On a user-to-user VPC, the QoS experienced by individual VCCs depends on CPE traffic handling capabilities.

On the basis of the applications of VPCs contained in ITU-T document I.311 [35] see §2.3.2, namely:

A) User-user application: the VPC extends between a pair of UNIs,

B) User-network application: the VPC extends between a UNI and a network node,

C) Network-Network application: the VPC extends between network nodes.

The above implies:

In case A: because the network has no knowledge of the QoS of the VCCs within the VPC, it is the user's responsibility to determine in accordance with the network capabilities the necessary QoS for the VPC.

In case B and C: the network is aware of the QoS of the VCCs carried within the VPC and has to accommodate them.

Statistical multiplexing of VC links within a VPC, where the aggregate peak of all VC links may exceed the Virtual Path Connection capacity, is only possible when all Virtual Channel links within the Virtual Path Connection can tolerate the QoS that results from this statistical multiplexing. The way this is managed is for further study.

As a consequence, when statistical multiplexing of Virtual Channel links is applied by the network operator, Virtual Path Connections may be used in order to separate traffic thereby preventing statistical multiplexing with other types of traffic. This requirement for separation implies that more than one Virtual Path connection may be necessary between network origination/destination pairs to carry a full range of QoS between them. Further implications of this are for further study.

3.6.3.2.2 Connection Admission Control

Connection Admission Control is defined as the set of actions taken by the network at the call set up phase (or during call re-negotiation phase) in order to establish whether a Virtual Channel Connection or a Virtual Path Connection can be accepted or should be rejected.

(R) The information contained in the Traffic Contract (§3.6.2.2) shall be accessible to the CAC function.

On the basis of Connection Admission Control in an ATM based network, a connection request is accepted only when sufficient resources are available to establish the connection through the whole network at its required Quality of Service (QoS) and to maintain the agreed QoS of existing connections. This applies as well to re-negotiation of connection parameters within a given call.

For each connection request the CAC function shall be able to derive the following information from the Traffic Contract (See §3.6.2.2):

- Values of parameters in the Source Traffic Descriptor (§3.6.2.1);

- the requested QoS class (§3.6.1.3);

- the value of the CDV Tolerance (§3.6.2.4.2.3);

- the requested Conformance Definition (§3.6.2.5).

Connection Admission Control makes use of the derived information and the network operator's defintion of a compliant connection to determine:

- whether the connection can be accepted or not;

- traffic parameters needed by usage parameter control;

- routing and allocation of network resources.

Different strategies of network resource allocation may be applied for CLP=0 and CLP=1 traffic flows. If tagging is not requested, the network may still tag non-conforming cells, therefore CAC may accept a call even if tagging is not requested. In addition, information such as the measured network load may be used when performing CAC. This may allow a network operator to achieve higher network utilization while still meeting the Network Performance objectives.

Resource allocation schemes are currently left to network operator's decision.

3.6.3.2.3 Usage Parameter Control

Recommendation I.371 states that "The use of UPC function is recommended." However, in this specification, the UPC function is required at the Public UNI (§3.6.3.2.3.3).

(R) The UPC function shall be provided at the Public UNI.

3.6.3.2.3.1 UPC Functions

Usage Parameter Control is defined as the set of actions taken by the network to monitor and control traffic in terms of traffic offered and validity of the ATM connection, at the user access. Its main purpose is to protect network resources from malicious as well as unintentional misbehavior which can affect the QoS of other already established connections by detecting violations of negotiated parameters and taking appropriate actions.

Connection monitoring encompasses all connections crossing the Public UNI. Usage Parameter Control applies to both user VCCs/VPCs and signalling virtual channels. Methods for monitoring meta-signalling channels and OAM flows are for further study.

The monitoring task for usage parameter control is performed for VCCs and VPCs respectively by the following two actions:

1. checking the validity of VPI and VCI (i.e., whether or not VPI/VCI values are associated with active VCCs) and monitoring the traffic entering the network from active VCCs in order to ensure that parameters agreed upon are not violated;

2. checking the validity of VPI (i.e., whether or not VPI values are associated with active VPCs), and monitoring the traffic entering the network from active VPCs in order to ensure that parameters agreed upon are not violated.

3.6.3.2.3.2 UPC Requirements

(R) The operation of the UPC mechanism, utilized by a network operator, shall not violate the QoS objectives of a compliant connections, see §3.6.2.2.

A number of desirable features of the UPC algorithm can be identified as follows:

- capability of detecting any non-compliant traffic situation;

- selectivity over the range of checked parameters (i.e., the algorithm could determine whether the user's behavior is within an acceptance region);

- rapid response time to parameter violations;

- simplicity of implementation.

There are two sets of requirements relating to the UPC:

- those which relate to the quality of service impairments the UPC might directly cause to the user cell flow;

- those which relate to the resource the operator should allocate to a given connection and the way the network intends to protect those resources against misbehavior from the user side (due to fault conditions or maliciousness).

Two performance parameters are identified that could be considered when assessing the performance of UPC mechanisms. Methods for evaluating UPC performance and the need to standardize these methods are for further study.

- Response time: the time to detect a given non-compliant situation on a VPC/VCC under given reference conditions.

- Transparency: for given reference conditions, the accuracy with which the UPC initiates appropriate control actions on a non-compliant connection and avoids inappropriate control actions on a compliant connection.

Additional UPC performance parameters are for further study.

A specific UPC mechanism may commit errors by taking policing actions on a compliant connection, e.g. the number of discarded cells of a compliant connection is more than the number of non-conforming cells according to the Traffic Contract. The UPC can also fail to take the appropriate policing actions on a non-compliant connection.

Excessive policing actions of the UPC on a compliant connection are part of the overall Network Performance degradation. Safety margins may be provisioned depending upon the UPC algorithm to limit the degradation introduced by the UPC.

Policing actions performed on the excess traffic in case of Traffic Contract conformance violation are not to be included in the Network Performance degradation allocated to the UPC.

Impact of UPC on cell delay should also be considered. Cell Delay and Cell Delay Variation introduced by the UPC is also part of the delay and delay variation allocated to the network.

Performance of UPC

A method to determine whether a traffic flow is conforming to a negotiated PCR at a given interface is currently considered for Network Performance purposes. Non-conformance is measurable by a 1-point measurement process in terms of the ratio γ_M between the number of cells exceeding the traffic contract and the total number of submitted cells.

An ideal UPC implementing the 1 point-measurement process would just take policing actions on a number of cells according to this ratio. Although the process allows for a cell-based decision, it is not possible to predict which particular cells of a connection with non-conforming cells will suffer from the policing action (this is because of measurement phasing).

According to the definition of the conformance of a traffic flow to a PCR, the transparency of a UPC mechanism can be defined by the accuracy with which this mechanism approaches the ideal mechanism, i.e., the difference between the reference policing ratio γ_M and the actual policing ratio γ_p. A positive difference means that the UPC is taking less policing action than allowed. A negative difference means that policing action are unduly taken by the UPC.

The above discussion can also be applied to the SCR and the Burst Tolerance traffic parameters. The exact way of measuring the transparency of a given mechanism for the UPC and its dependence on time requires further study.

3.6.3.2.3.3 UPC location

Usage parameter control is performed on VCCs or VPCs at the point where the first VP or VC links are terminated within the network. Three possibilities are shown in Figure 3-23.

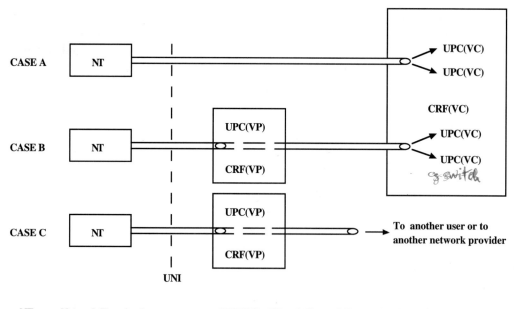

NT :   Network Termination   CRF(VC) : Virtual Channel Connection Related Function
CRF :   Connection Related Function   CRF(VP) : Virtual Path Connection Related Function

Figure 3-23 Location of the UPC Functions

Notes:

- In case A, the VPI value does not identify a negotiated VPC.

- Provision of UPC at other locations is for further study.

In the following, CRF(VC) stands for Virtual Channel Connection Related Function, and CRF(VP) stands for Virtual Path Connection Related Function. The following CRF(VC)s and CRF(VP)s refer to the first CRFs on the public network side of the Public UNI. A CRF(VC) or a CRF(VP) may respectively be a VC or VP concentrator.

(CR) If connected directly to CRF(VC) (CASE A of figure 3-23), the UPC function shall be performed within the CRF(VC) on VCCs before the switching function is executed (action 1, §3.6.3.2.3.1).

(CR) If connected directly to CRF(VC) via CRF(VP) (CASE B of figure 3-23), the UPC function shall be performed within the CRF(VP) on VPCs only (actions 2, §3.6.3.2.3.1) and within the CRF(VC) on VCCs only (action 1, §3.6.3.2.3.1).

(CR) If connected to user or to another network provider via CRF(VP) (CASE C of figure 3-23), the UPC function shall be performed within the CRF(VP) on VPCs only (action 2, §3.6.3.2.3.1).

In CASE C of figure 3-23, the VCC usage parameter control will be done by the first public network provider (if any) where CRF(VC) is present.

3.6.3.2.3.4 Traffic parameters subject to control at the UPC

Traffic Parameters that may be subject to control are those included in the Source Traffic Descriptor.

(R) The Peak Cell Rate of the CLP=0+1 cell flow shall be controlled for all types of connections at the Public UNI.

(O) Even when specified, control of Sustainable Cell Rate and Burst Tolerance is at the discretion of the network operator.

3.6.3.2.3.5 UPC actions

The UPC is intended to control the traffic offered by an ATM connection to ensure conformance with the negotiated Traffic Contract. The objective is that a user will never be able to exceed the Traffic Contract.

At the cell level, actions of the UPC function may be:

- cell passing;

- cell tagging (network operator's option); cell tagging operates on CLP=0 cells only, by overwriting the CLP bit to 1;

- cell discarding.

If the tagging option is used by the network operator, CLP=0 cells identified by the UPC function to be non-conforming to the CLP=0 cell stream are converted to CLP=1 cells. (For terminology, these cells with the converted CLP bit are called tagged cells). A tagged cell that is identified by the UPC function to be conforming is passed; otherwise, it is discarded. Likewise, a user submitted CLP=1 cell that is identified by the UPC function to be conforming is passed; otherwise, it is discarded.[4]

(R) Cell passing shall be performed on cells that are identified by the UPC as conforming. (For terminology, if the tagged cell is passed, then it is said to be conforming to the UPC function.)

(R) Cell discarding shall be performed on cells that are identified by the UPC as non-conforming.

(O) Following the UPC function, traffic shaping may be used to perform cell re-scheduling (e.g. to reduce cell clumping) on cells identified by the UPC as conforming.

Besides the above actions at the cell level, as an option, one other action performed at the connection level may be initiated by the UPC:

(O) At the option of the network provider, the UPC function may initiate the release of an identified non-compliant SVC connection.

3.6.3.2.3.6 Relationship between UPC, CLP and Network Performance

When an ATM connection utilizes the CLP capability on user request, network resources are allocated to CLP=0 and CLP=1 traffic flows as described in §3.6.3.2.2. By controlling the connection traffic flows, allocating adequate resources and suitably routing, a network operator may provide the requested QoS class for CLP=0 and CLP=1 cell flows.

When no additional network resource has been allocated for CLP=1 traffic flow (either on user request or due to network provisioning), CLP=0 cells identified by the UPC as non-conforming are discarded. In this case, tagging is not applicable.

---

[4]   Note that the in principle cell flow that is passed by the UPC with the tagging option is no greater than what might be passed by a UPC without the tagging option when the end terminal sets the CLP bit to 1 on those cells that would otherwise have been tagged under the tagging option.

Section 3.6.3.2.3.2 addresses undue UPC actions on compliant ATM connections. This is part of the Network Performance degradation allocated to the UPC and should remain of a very low probability.

When cells of the aggregate CLP=0+1 flow are non-conforming to the parameters negotiated for the aggregate stream, the UPC function performed on the aggregate flow may discard CLP=0 cells that would not be considered in excess by the UPC function performed on the CLP=0 cell stream.

3.6.3.2.3.7 Relationship Between UPC and OAM

For OAM cell flows across the UNI, the network may require from the user the knowledge of some traffic parameters such as the Peak Cell Rate and knowledge of some clumping tolerance t_{OAM} for the OAM traffic of an ATM connection. Regardless of whether a user explicitly or implicitly specifies the OAM cell stream, the network may police OAM cell flows separately from user data cell streams or may police OAM cell flows together with user data cell streams. However, the initial release of the user-network signalling protocol will not allow a user to explicitly specify traffic parameters of OAM flow. Traffic parameters for OAM cell flow across the UNI may be explicitly specified at subscription time, or implicitly by a default rule (see §3.6.2.2).

(R) OAM features for a VCC or a VPC shall be selected by the end user at service subscription from amongst the features supported by the public network.

(R) At the service subscription time, the network shall negotiate the upper limit on the OAM traffic as a function of the Connection Traffic Descriptor for the user data traffic of an ATM connection (VCC or VPC).

The function used to limit the OAM flow is determined by the network provider. The network may offer alternative limits from which the user may select. If the network polices the OAM cell flows together with user data cell flows the UPC parameters are adjusted to accommodate the OAM flow.

3.6.3.2.4 Selective Cell Discard

Network Elements may selectively discard cells of the CLP=1 flow while still meeting Network Performance objectives on both the CLP=0 and CLP=1 flows.

(R) For a given ATM connection the Cell Loss Ratio objective for CLP=1 cells shall be greater than or equal to the Cell Loss Ratio objective for CLP=0 cells.

3.6.3.2.5 Traffic Shaping (O)

When used in the source ATM end-point, traffic shaping is a mechanism that attains desired characteristics for the stream of cells emitted into a VCC or a VPC. When used in a private ATM Switch, traffic shaping is a mechanism that alters the traffic characteristics of a stream of cells on a VCC or a VPC to achieve a desired modification of those traffic characteristics. Traffic shaping must maintain cell sequence integrity on an ATM connection. Examples of traffic shaping are Peak Cell Rate reduction, burst length limiting and reduction of cell clumping due to CDV by suitably spacing cells in time.

(O) CPE may perform traffic shaping to be in conformance with the Connection Traffic Descriptor and associated parameter values that were negotiated with the public network.

Traffic shaping is an optional function. For example, an ATM end-point may choose to shape to the negotiated Peak Cell Rate for the aggregate cell stream of CLP=0 and CLP=1 cells and may choose not to shape to the negotiated Peak Cell Rate for the CLP=0 cell stream and instead to allow the network's UPC mechanism to tag as CLP=1 the non-conforming CLP=0 cells.

The algorithm used by the traffic shaping function is not specified. However, when used for conformance with negotiated parameters of a traffic descriptor, a natural choice for the algorithm is one that mimics the Conformance Definition (§3.6.2.2).

3.6.3.2.6 Explicit Forward Congestion Indication

The EFCI is a congestion notification mechanism that the ATM layer service user may make use of to improve the utility that can be derived from the ATM layer. Since the use of this mechanism by the CPE is optional, the network operator should not rely on this mechanism to control congestion.

A network element in an impending-congested state or a congested state may set an explicit forward congestion indication in the cell header so that this indication may be examined by the destination CPE. For example, the end user's CPE may use this indication to implement protocols that adaptively lower the cell rate of the connection during congestion or impending congestion. A network element that is not in a congested state or an impending congested state will not modify the value of this indication. An impending-congestion state is the state when a network equipment is operating around its engineered capacity level.

The mechanism by which a network element determines whether it is in an impending-congested or a congested state is an implementation issue and is not subject to standardization. The mechanism by which the congestion indication is used by the higher layer protocols in the CPE is for further study.

The impact of explicit forward congestion indication on the Traffic Control and Congestion Control functions requires further study.

3.6.3.3 Congestion Control Functions

For low priority traffic, some adaptive rate control facilities at the ATM layer or above may be used. Such cell-based reactive techniques are for further study.

The following congestion control functions have been identified. Other congestion control functions are for further study.

3.6.3.3.1 Selective Cell Discard

A congested Network Element may selectively discard cells explicitly identified as belonging to a non-compliant ATM connection and/or those cells with CLP=1. This is to primarily protect, as long as possible, CLP=0 flows.

3.6.3.3.2 Reaction to UPC failures

Due to equipment faults (e.g. in usage parameter control devices and/or other network elements) the controlled traffic characteristics at the UPC/NPC could be different from the values agreed to during the call set-up phase. To cope with these situations, specific procedures of the management plane should be designed (e.g. in order to isolate the faulty link). The impact of these malfunctioning situations on the usage parameter control needs further study.

Section 4:

Interim Local Management Interface Specification

Scope

Whereas the CCITT and ANSI standards committees have been working to define both C-plane and U-plane procedures for ATM, local network management procedures in the M-plane are in large part considered "for further study".

In the interim period until such standards are available, the Simple Network Management Protocol (SNMP) and an ATM UNI Management Information Base (MIB) will be required to provide any ATM user device with status and configuration information concerning the Virtual Path and Channel Connections available at its UNI. In addition, more global operations and network management information (e.g. status and operational measurement information for the public and private UNI as defined in this document) may also facilitate diagnostics procedures at the UNI.

The ILMI fits into the overall management model for an ATM device as illustrated in Figure 4-1 as clarified by the following principles and options.

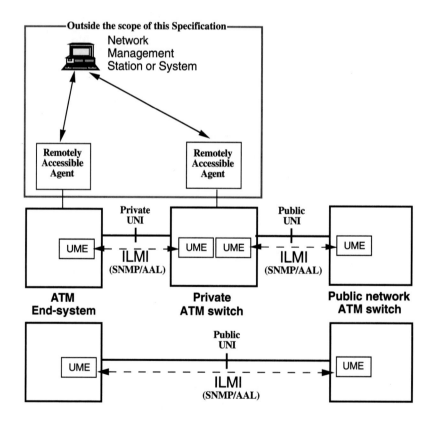

Figure 4-1 Definition and Context of ILMI

- Each ATM device shall support one or more UNIs.

- Interim Local Management Interface (ILMI) functions for a UNI provide status, configuration, and control information about link and physical layer parameters at the UNI.

- ILMI functions for a UNI also provide for address registration across the UNI. Further details on address registration are contained in section 5.8.

- There is a per-UNI set of managed objects, the UNI ILMI attributes, that is sufficient to support the ILMI functions for each UNI.

- The UNI ILMI attributes are organized in a standard MIB structure; there is one UNI ILMI MIB structure instance for each UNI.

- There is one MIB instance per ATM device, which contains one or more UNI ILMI MIB structures. This supports the need for general network management systems to have access to the information in the UNI ILMI MIB structures.

- For any ATM device, there is a UNI Management Entity (UME) associated with each UNI that supports the ILMI functions for that UNI, including coordination between the physical and ATM layer management entities associated with that UNI.

- When two ATM devices are connected across a *(point-to-point)* UNI, there are two UNI management entities (UMEs) associated with that UNI, one UME for each ATM device, and two such UMEs are defined as adjacent UMEs.

- The ILMI communication takes place between adjacent ATM UMEs.

- The ILMI communication protocol is an open management protocol (i.e., SNMP/AAL initially).

- A UNI Management Entity (UME) can access, via the ILMI communication protocol, the UNI ILMI MIB information associated with its adjacent UME.

- Whether access to additional information (beyond the adjacent UME's UNI ILMI MIB information) is available via the ILMI communication protocol is currently unspecified, and is regarded as a vendor implementation choice.

- Separation of the MIB structure from the access methods allows for the use of multiple access methods for management information. For the ILMI function, the access method is an open management protocol (i.e., SNMP/AAL) over a well known VPI/VCI value. For example, general network management applications (e.g., from a Network Management Station (NMS) performing generic Customer Network Management (CNM) functions) the access method is also an open management protocol (e.g., SNMP/UDP/IP/AAL) over a specific VPI/VCI value (or a completely separate communications method) allocated to support the general management applications. The peer entity in an ATM device that communicates directly with a NMS is a management agent, not a UME; however, since the management agent can access the MIB instance for the ATM device it can access all of the UNI ILMI MIB structure instances.

- This document pertains to the UNI ILMI MIB structure of the "Local UNI" (i.e., between adjacent UMEs) only.

The Simple Network Management Protocol (SNMP) without UDP and IP addressing along with an ATM UNI Management Information Base (MIB) were chosen for the ILMI.

4.1 Interim Local Management Interface (ILMI) Functions

An Interim Local Management Interface (ILMI) supports bi-directional exchange of management information between UNI Management Entities (UMEs) related to UNI ATM layer and physical layer parameters. The communication across the ILMI is protocol symmetric. In addition, each of the adjacent UMEs supporting ILMI will contain an agent application and may contain a management application. Unless otherwise stated for specific portions of the MIB, both of the adjacent UMEs contain the same Management Information Base (MIB). However, semantics of some MIB objects may be interpreted differently. As shown in Figure 4-2, an example list of the equipment that will use the ATM UNI ILMI include:

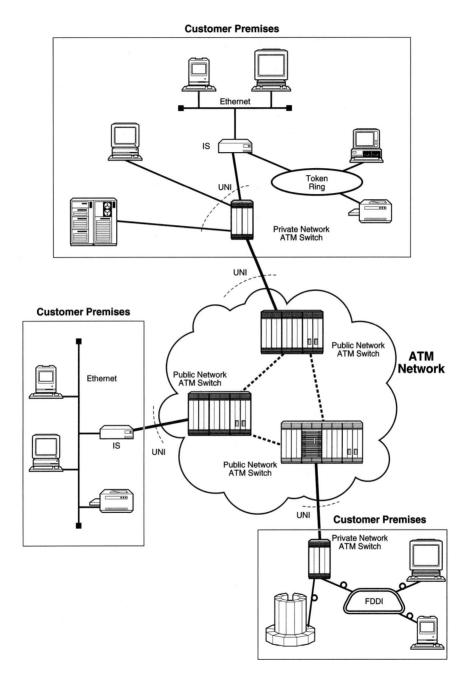

Figure 4-2 Examples of Equipment Implementing the ATM UNI ILMI

- Higher layer switches such as internet routers,frame relay switches, or LAN bridges, that transfer their frames within ATM cells and forward the cells across an ATM UNI to an ATM switch.

- Workstations and computers with ATM interfaces which send their data in ATM cells across an ATM UNI to an ATM switch.

- ATM Network switches which send ATM cells across an ATM UNI to other ATM devices.

4.2 ILMI Service Interface

The Interim Local Management Interface uses SNMP for monitoring and control operations of ATM management information across the UNI. The ATM UNI management information will be represented in a Management Information Base. The types of management information will be available in the ATM UNI MIB are as follows:

- Physical Layer
- ATM Layer
- ATM Layer Statistics
- Virtual Path (VP) Connections
- Virtual Channel (VC) Connections
- Address Registration Information

The tree structure of the ATM UNI ILMI MIB is depicted in Figure 4-3.

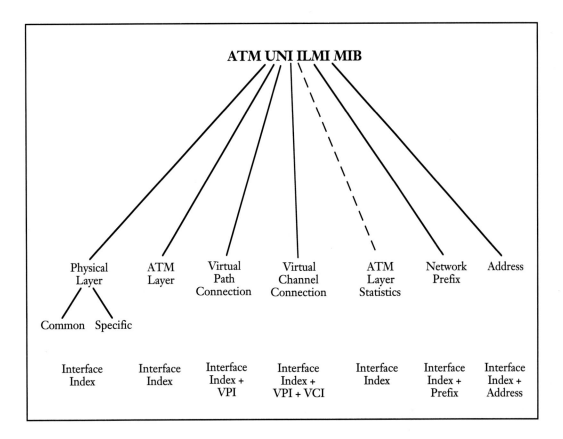

Figure 4-3 ILMI ATM UNI MIB Tree Structure

The ATM UNI MIB may be extended over time to allow for the addition of new items without requiring any changes to the management protocol or framework. In addition, vendors can define private ATM UNI MIB extensions to support additional or proprietary features of their products.

The following sections introduce the groups which categorize the management information. An entire tree group is either Optional **(O)**, Conditionally Required **(CR)** or Required **(R)**. If a group is Required, then every element in the group is Required. For a group which is Conditionally Required it follows that it every element in the group is required if implemented.

4.2.1 System (R)

The System group from RFC 1213 is included to define the following objects as defined in section 4.5.

4.2.2 Physical Layer (R)

The physical layer interfaces which the ILMI supports is identified as defined in section 2.

The physical media which the ILMI supports is identified as defined in section 2.

Each physical interface type has a set of specific attributes and information associated with it.

Status information reflects the state of the physical link connecting the adjacent UMEs.

4.2.3 ATM Layer (R)

The ILMI provides access to management information about the ATM Layer as defined in section 3.1.

There is one ATM layer per physical interface.

Certain attributes of the ATM layer are common across all Virtual Path Connections (VPCs) and Virtual Channel Connections (VCCs) at this UNI.

Configuration information at the ATM layer relates to the size of the VPI and VCI address fields in the ATM cell header, number of configured VPCs and VCCs, and maximum number of VPCs and VCCs allowed at this UNI.

4.2.4 ATM Layer Statistics (O)

Certain objects and attributes represent aggregate statistics across all VPCs and VCCs on the Local ATM UNI, accumulated over time.

4.2.5 Virtual Path Connections (R)

In the context of supporting ILMI functions, a point-to-point Virtual Path Connection (VPC) extends between two ATM User-Network Interfaces that terminate the VPC.

On the local ATM Layer interface the VPC is uniquely identified by the VPI value.

The status information indicates the UME's knowledge of the VPC status. The VPC status may be either end-to-end, local or unknown.

Configuration information relates to the QoS parameters for the VPC local end point.

4.2.6 Virtual Channel Connections (R)

In the context of supporting ILMI functions, a point-to-point Virtual Channel Connection (VCC) extends between two ATM User-Network Interfaces that terminate the VCC.

On the local ATM Layer interface the VCC is uniquely identified by the VPI and VCI value.

The status information indicates the UME's knowledge of the VCC status. The VCC status may be either end-to-end, local or unknown.

Configuration information relates to the QoS parameters for the VPC local end point.

4.3 Simple Network Management Protocol (SNMP)

The SNMP protocol as defined in RFC 1157 consists of four types of operations which are used to manipulate management information. These are:

Get   Used to retrieve specific management information.

Get-Next   Used to retrieve, via traversal of the MIB, management information.

Set   Used to alter management information.

Trap   Used to report extraordinary events.

4.4 Management Information Base (MIB) Model for ILMI Managed Objects

Information related to the operation of the ATM UNI is organized into a MIB in a hierarchical fashion as defined in section 4.2. Each ATM UNI corresponds to just one physical interface. Logically, the ATM UNI MIB accessed over the ILMI corresponds to the single ATM UNI/physical interface. Implementations of devices which have multiple physical interfaces (e.g., multiple interface end user devices, private switches and public switches) may implement a single ATM UNI MIB, indexed for each ATM UNI/physical interface.

The MIB attributes are used in the standard fashion: all attributes are by default read only across the ILMI, unless stated otherwise as readable and writeable across the ILMI for a specific UNI MIB variable.

The ILMI MIB for ATM devices is specified under the ATM Forum's node under the enterprises node of the standard SMI as defined in RFC 1212. This means it is prefixed by the following tree path or name, 1.3.6.1.4.1.353.

4.4.1 Per-System UNI MIB Attributes (R)

No per-system object is defined in the ILMI MIB. UMEs implementing the ILMI MIB are also expected to support the "system" group defined in MIB-II, see section 4.5.

4.4.2 Per-Physical Interface UNI MIB Attributes (R)

These attributes are located in the Physical Port Group (atmfPhysicalGroup). The physical interface is identified by the interface index (atmfPortIndex). MIB information at this level includes:

Common
- Interface Index
- Interface Address
- Transmission Type
- Media Type
- Operational Status

Transmission Type Specific Information

4.4.2.1 Common (R)

Certain objects and attributes are common to all transmission types.

4.4.2.1.1 Interface Index (R)

The interface index is used in the ATM Layer, VPC and VCC ATM UNI MIB subtrees to identify a particular physical interface on the ATM device.

When this object has the value zero, it implicitly identifies the physical interface over which ILMI messages are received. Only implicit identification is mandatory.

Optionally, one of many interfaces may be explicitly identified by an interface index unique to the ATM device.

4.4.2.1.2 Interface Address (O)

The Interface Address object specified in version 2.0 of the ATM Forum UNI Specification is deprecated. The Address Registration extensions, specified in section 5.8 of this specification, replaces the Interface Address object. The Interface Address object should not be implemented except as required for backward compatibility.

4.4.2.1.3 Transmission Type (R)

The following transmission types are currently supported, as defined in the indicated section

2.1 SONET STS-3c Physical Layer Interface

2.2 DS3 Physical Layer Interface

2.3 Physical Layer for 100 Mb/s Interface

2.4 Physical Layer for 155 Mb/s Interface

The Transmission Speed (in units of cells/second) is uniquely determined by the Transmission Type as defined in section 2.

4.4.2.1.4 Media Type (R)

Physical media types defined in the MIB currently are:

- Coaxial Cable
- Single Mode Fiber
- Multi-Mode Fiber
- Shielded Twisted Pair
- Unshielded Twisted Pair

4.4.2.1.5 Physical Layer Operational Status (R)

This object allows the adjacent UMEs to observe the operational state of the physical interface supported between them. Valid values are:

- In-Service
- Out-of-Service
- Loop Back Mode

If the Operational Status has the value of Out-of-Service, then the ILMI should not alarm on the physical interface. This capability is useful if equipment is to be disconnected, or for troubleshooting purposes.

The Loop Back Mode attribute indicates that a local loopback in place. For example C-Bit parity DS3 has a standard method of commanding a local interface loopback using physical layer signalling.

4.4.2.2 Transmission Type Specific Information (R)

This object is a reference to any additional management information which is available for the physical interaces and which is specific to the interface's transmission type.

4.4.2.2.1 SONET STS-3c Physical Layer Interface

Currently undefined.

4.4.2.2.2 DS3 Physical Layer Interface

This is defined as a reference to RFC 1407.

4.4.2.2.3 Physical Layer for 100 Mbps Interface

Currently undefined.

4.4.2.2.4 Physical Layer for 155 Mbps Interface

Currently undefined.

4.4.3 Per-ATM Layer Interface UNI MIB Attributes (R)

These attributes are located in the ATM Layer Group (atmfATMLayerGroup). The interface is identified by the interface index (atmfAtmLayerIndex). MIB information at this level includes:

Interface Index

Configuration Information
- Maximum Number of VPCs
- Maximum Number of VCCs
- VPI/VCI Address Width
- Number of Configured VPCs
- Number of Configured VCCs
- ATM UNI Port Type (Public/Private)

4.4.3.1 Interface Index (R)

The Interface Index is the same as that for the Physical interface as defined in section 4.4.2.1.

It is implicitly the local ATM UNI, unless the optional mode of explicit identification is supported.

4.4.3.2 Configuration Information (R)

Configuration information about the number of Virtual Path Connections (VPCs) and Virtual Channel Connections (VCCs) on the local interface is defined here.

4.4.3.2.1 Maximum Number of VPCs (R)

This is the maximum number of VPCs which the local interface can support.

4.4.3.2.2 Maximum Number of VCCs (R)

This is the maximum number of VCCs which the local interface can support.

4.4.3.2.3 Number of Configured VPCs (R)

This is the current number of VPCs for which the local interface is configured to process.

4.4.3.2.4 Number of Configured VCCs (R)

This is the current number of VCCs for which the local interface is configured to process.

4.4.3.2.5 Maximum Number of Active VPI bits (R)

This is the maximum number of VPI bits that can be active for this interface.

4.4.3.2.6 Maximum Number of Active VCI bits (R)

This is the maximum number of VCI bits that can be active for this interface.

4.4.3.2.7 ATM UNI Port Type (R)

This parameter indicates whether the ATM UNI is of the public or private type.

4.4.4 ATM Layer Statistics (O)

These attributes are located in the ATM Statistics Group (atmfStatisticsGroup). This group is indexed by the interface index (atmfAtmStatsIndex). MIB information at this level includes:

- Interface Index
- ATM Cells Received
- ATM Cells Dropped on the Receive Side
- ATM Cells Transmitted

Certain counters make sense only at the ATM Layer for an entire physical interface, while others are rolled up across all VPCs and VCCs at an interface. These counters are thus aggregated across the entire ATM UNI, and accumulated over time. All counters are 32 bits which wrap around.

The optional ATM layer statistics can be used for the following purposes.

- Identify problems that affect UNI performance, such as:
  - Loss due to bit errors, and/or
  - Unavailability of link connections.
- Aid in problem diagnosis and troubleshooting.
- Collect traffic engineering data.

4.4.4.1 ATM Cells Received (O)

This is a count of the number of ATM cells received across the ATM UNI which were assigned and not dropped.

4.4.4.2 ATM Cells Dropped on the Receive Side (O)

This is a count of the number of ATM cells received across the ATM UNI which were dropped for the following specific reasons. The reasons for which an ATM cell can increment this counter shall be:

The Header Error Control (HEC) processing either detected an error, or identified an uncorrectable error once cell delineation has been achieved.

An invalidly formatted cell header (as defined in section 3.4.3) was received.

This device was not configured to process the received VPI/VCI (i.e., it is unknown). For example, a switch translation table entry was not defined for the received VPI/VCI value.

4.4.4.3 ATM Cells Transmitted (O)

This is a count of the number of ATM cells transmitted across the ATM UNI which were assigned. This is a count of cells carrying actual user data across the ATM UNI.

4.4.5 Per-Virtual Path UNI MIB Attributes (R)

These attributes are located in the Virtual Path Group (atmfVpcGroup). This group is indexed by the interface index (atmfVpcPortIndex) and the VPI value (atmfVpcVpi). MIB information at this level includes:

- Interface Index
- VPI Value
- Transmit Traffic Descriptor
- Receive Traffic Descriptor
- Operational Status
- Transmit QoS Class
- Receive QoS Class

4.4.5.1 Interface Index (R)

The Interface Index is the same as that for the Physical interface as defined in section 4.4.2.1.1

It is implicitly the local ATM UNI, unless the optional mode of explicit identification is supported.

4.4.5.2 VPI (R)

This is the value of the Virtual Path Identifier (VPI) for this VPC.

4.4.5.3 Transmit Traffic Descriptor (R)

This is a specification of the conformance definition and associated source traffic descriptor parameter values described in section 3.6.2.5 that are applicable to the transmit side of this interface for this VPC.

4.4.5.4 Receive Traffic Descriptor (R)

This is a specification of the conformance definition and associated source traffic descriptor parameter values described in section 3.6.2.5 that are applicable to the receive side of this interface for this VPC.

4.4.5.5 Operational Status (R)

This object represents the state of the VPC as known by the local device. If the end-to-end status is known then a value of end2endUp(2) or end2endDown(3) is used. If only the local status is known then a value of localUpEnd2endUnknown(4) or localDown(5) is used.

4.4.5.6 Transmit (QoS) Class (R)

This is the QoS Class defined in section 4 of Appendix A, for the transmit side of this interface for thisVPC.

4.4.5.6 Receive (QoS) Class (R)

This is the QoS Class defined in section 4 of Appendix A, for the receive side of this interface for thisVPC.

4.4.6 Per-Virtual Channel UNI MIB Attributes (R)

These attributes are located in the Virtual Channel Group (atmfVccGroup). This group is indexed by the interface index (atmfVccPortIndex), VCC VPI value (atmfVccVpi) and VCC VCI value (atmfVccVci). MIB information at this level includes:

- Interface Index
- VPI/VCI Value
- Transmit Traffic Descriptor
- Receive Traffic Descriptor
- Operational Status
- Transmit QoS Class
- Receive QoS Class

4.4.6.1 Interface Index (R)

The Interface Index is the same as that for the Physical interface as defined in section 4.4.2.1.1. It is implicitly the local ATM UNI, unless the optional mode of explicit identification is supported.

4.4.6.2 VPI (R)

This is the value of the Virtual Path Identifier (VPI) for this VCC.

4.4.6.3 VCI (R)

This is the value of the Virtual Channel Identifier (VCI) for this VCC.

4.4.6.4 Transmit Traffic Descriptor (R)

This is a specification of the conformance definition and associated source traffic descriptor parameter values described in section 3.6.2.5 that are applicable to the transmit side of this interface for this VCC.

4.4.6.5 Recieve Traffic Descriptor (R)

This is a specification of the conformance definition and associated source traffic descriptor parameter values described in section 3.6.2.5 that are applicable to the receive side of this interface for this VCC.

4.4.6.6 Operational Status (R)

This object represents the state of the VCC as known by the local device. If the end-to-end status is known then a value of end2endUp(2) or end2endDown(3) is used. If only the local status is known then a value of localUpEnd2endUnknown(4) or localDown(5) is used.

4.4.6.7 Transmit (QoS) Class (R)

This is the QoS Class defined in section 4 of Appendix A, for the transmit side of this interface for thisVCC.

4.4.6.8 Receive (QoS) Class (R)

This is the QoS Class defined in section 4 of Appendix A, for the receive side of this interface for thisVCC.

4.5 Relationship to Other MIBs

It is required that an ATM device which implements the ILMI MIB will also implement the 'system' group defined in MIB-II.

4.5.1 Relationship to the 'system' group (R)

In MIB-II, the 'system' group is defined as being mandatory for all systems such that each managed entity contains one instance of each object in the 'system' group. Thus, those objects apply to the entity even if the entity's sole functionality is the forwarding of ATM cells.

RFC 1213 is the authoritative source for the definition of objects in the 'system' group. The group consists of the following 7 objects:

(For each textual object for which the device is not configured with a value, the object's value is a string of length 0.)

sysDescr   "A textual description of the entity. This value should include the full name and version identification of the system's hardware type, software operating-system, and networking software. It is mandatory that this only contain printable ASCII characters."

sysObjectID   "The vendor's authoritative identification of the network management subsystem contained in the entity. This value is allocated within the SMI enterprises subtree (1.3.6.1.4.1) and provides an easy and unambiguous means for determining 'what kind of box' is being managed. For example, if vendor 'Flintstones, Inc.' was assigned the subtree 1.3.6.1.4.1.4242, it could assign the identifier 1.3.6.1.4.1.4242.1.1 to its 'Fred Router'."

sysUpTime   "The time (in hundredths of a second) since the UME was last re-initialized."

sysContact   "The textual identification of the contact person for this managed node, together with information on how to contact this person."

sysName   "An administratively-assigned textual name for this managed node."

sysLocation   "A textual description of the physical location of this device (e.g., `telephone closet, 3rd floor')."

sysServices   "A value which indicates the set of services that this entity primarily offers. The value is a sum of individual values, each representing a particular switching function. The layers are:

layer	functionality
1	physical (e.g., repeaters)
2	datalink/subnetwork (e.g., bridges)
3	internet (e.g., IP routers)
4	end-to-end (e.g., IP hosts)
7	applications (e.g., mail relays)."

4.6 Actual MIB

4.6.1 Objects

Managed objects are accessed via a virtual information store, termed the Management Information Base or MIB. Objects in the MIB are defined using the subset of Abstract Syntax Notation One (ASN.1) [23] defined by the Structure of Management Information (SMI) [20]. In particular, each object has a name, a syntax, and an encoding. The name is an object identifier, an administratively assigned name, which specifies an object type. The object type together with an object instance serves to uniquely identify a specific instantiation of the object. For human convenience, we often use a textual string, termed the OBJECT DESCRIPTOR, to also refer to the object type.

The syntax of an object type defines the abstract data structure corresponding to that object type. The ASN.1 language is used for this purpose. However, the SMI purposely restricts the ASN.1 constructs which may be used. These restrictions are explicitly made for simplicity.

The encoding of an object type is simply how that object type is represented using the object type's syntax. Implicitly tied to the notion of an object type's syntax and encoding is how the object type is represented when being transmitted on the network.

The SMI specifies the use of the basic encoding rules of ASN.1 [24], subject to the additional requirements imposed by the SNMP [21].

4.6.1.1 Textual Conventions

Several data types are used as textual conventions in this document. These textual conventions have no effect on either the syntax nor the semantics of any managed object. Objects defined using these conventions are always encoded by means of the rules that define their primitive type. Hence, no changes to the SMI or the SNMP are necessary to accommodate these textual conventions which are adopted merely for the convenience of readers.

4.6.1.2 Use of Counters

This MIB defines all counter values using the standard SMI data type: Counter. This data type is defined [20] as representing a non-negative integer which monotonically increases until it reaches a maximum value of $2^{32}-1$ (4294967295 decimal), when it wraps around and starts increasing again from zero.

This definition disallows the clearing of Counter values, in order to prevent interference which would otherwise occur if two network managers were accessing the counters concurrently. Instead, interval values are obtained as the delta between a Counter's values at the beginning and end of a period.

4.6.1.3 Meaning of Transmit/Receive

The terms 'transmit' and 'receive' are used in the following MIB's object descriptors and textual descriptions. In each case, these terms are used from the perspective of the device local to the management information being defined.

4.6.2 Definitions

ATM-FORUM-MIB DEFINITIONS ::= BEGIN

IMPORTS
        enterprises, Counter   FROM RFC1155-SMI
        DisplayString   FROM RFC1213-MIB
        OBJECT-TYPE   FROM RFC-1212;

atmForum   OBJECT IDENTIFIER ::= { enterprises 353 }

                  -- a subtree for defining administrative
                  -- object identifiers
atmForumAdmin   OBJECT IDENTIFIER ::= { atmForum 1 }

                  -- a subtree for defining UNI MIB object types
atmForumUni   OBJECT IDENTIFIER ::= { atmForum 2 }

-- Textual Conventions

-- All representations of ATM addresses in this MIB Module use
-- the data type:

AtmAddress ::= OCTET STRING (SIZE (0 .. 32))

-- Note this data type is used only by the deprecated object
-- atmfPortAddress. Another definition (a refined one) is
-- specified in the separate MIB for Address Registration.

-- Object Identifier definitions

-- The following values are defined for use as possible values
-- of the atmfPortTransmissionType object.

atmfTransmissionTypes OBJECT IDENTIFIER ::= { atmForumAdmin 2 }
        -- unknown transmission type
atmfUnknownType
                OBJECT IDENTIFIER ::= { atmfTransmissionTypes 1}
        -- Sonet STS-3c physical layer at 155.52 Mbps
atmfSonetSTS3c
                OBJECT IDENTIFIER ::= { atmfTransmissionTypes 2 }
        -- DS3 physical layer at 44.736 Mbps
atmfDs3
                OBJECT IDENTIFIER ::= { atmfTransmissionTypes 3 }
        -- 4B/5B encoding physical layer at 100 Mbps
atmf4B5B
                OBJECT IDENTIFIER ::= { atmfTransmissionTypes 4 }
        -- 8B/10B encoding physical layer at 155.52 Mbps
atmf8B10B
                OBJECT IDENTIFIER ::= { atmfTransmissionTypes 5 }

-- The following values are defined for use as possible values
-- of the atmfPortMediaType object.

atmfMediaTypes OBJECT IDENTIFIER ::= { atmForumAdmin 3 }
    -- unknown media type
atmfMediaUnknownType
        OBJECT IDENTIFIER ::= { atmfMediaTypes 1 }
    -- Coaxial cable
atmfMediaCoaxCable
        OBJECT IDENTIFIER ::= { atmfMediaTypes 2 }
    -- Single Mode fiber
atmfMediaSingleMode
        OBJECT IDENTIFIER ::= { atmfMediaTypes 3 }
    -- Multi Mode fiber
atmfMediaMultiMode
        OBJECT IDENTIFIER ::= { atmfMediaTypes 4 }
    -- Shielded Twisted Pair
atmfMediaStp
        OBJECT IDENTIFIER ::= { atmfMediaTypes 5 }
    -- Unshielded Twisted Pair
atmfMediaUtp
        OBJECT IDENTIFIER ::= { atmfMediaTypes 6 }

-- The following values are defined for use as possible values
-- of the atmfVpcTransmitTrafficDescriptorType,
-- atmfVpcReceiveTrafficDescriptorType,
-- atmfVccTransmitTrafficDescriptorType and
-- atmfVccReceiveTrafficDescriptorType objects.

atmfTrafficDescrTypes OBJECT IDENTIFIER ::= { atmForumAdmin 4 }

    -- The "None" Traffic Descriptor Type
atmfNoDescriptor
        OBJECT IDENTIFIER ::= { atmfTrafficDescrTypes 1 }
--
atmfPeakRate
    OBJECT IDENTIFIER ::= { atmfTrafficDescrTypes 2 }
-- This type is no longer used

--

    -- The No CLP/No SCR Type
atmfNoClpNoScr
        OBJECT IDENTIFIER ::= { atmfTrafficDescrTypes 3 }
-- The use of the parameter vector for this type:
    -- Parameter #1 - peak cell rate in cells/second for CLP=0+1 traffic
    -- Parameters #2, #3, #4 and #5 are unused

```
--
        -- The CLP without Tagging/No SCR Type
atmfClpNoTaggingNoScr
                OBJECT IDENTIFIER ::= { atmfTrafficDescrTypes 4 }
-- The use of the parameter vector for this type:
        -- Parameter #1 - peak cell rate in cells/second for CLP=0+1 traffic
        -- Parameter #2 - peak cell rate in cells/second for CLP=0 traffic
        -- Parameters #3, #4 and #5 are unused


--
        -- The CLP with Tagging/No SCR Type
atmfClpTaggingNoScr
                OBJECT IDENTIFIER ::= { atmfTrafficDescrTypes 5 }
-- The use of the parameter vector for this type:
        -- Parameter #1 - peak cell rate in cells/second for CLP=0+1 traffic
        -- Parameter #2 - peak cell rate in cells/second for
        -- CLP=0 traffic, excess tagged as CLP=1
        -- Parameters #3, #4 and #5 are unused


--
        -- The SCR/No CLP Type
atmfNoClpScr
                OBJECT IDENTIFIER ::= { atmfTrafficDescrTypes 6 }
-- The use of the parameter vector for this type:
        -- Parameter #1 - peak cell rate in cells/second for CLP=0+1 traffic
        -- Parameter #2 - sustainable cell rate in cells/second for CLP=0+1 traffic
        -- Parameter #3 - maximum burst size in cells
        -- Parameters #4 and #5 are unused


--
        -- The CLP without Tagging/SCR Type
atmfClpNoTaggingScr
                OBJECT IDENTIFIER ::= { atmfTrafficDescrTypes 7 }
-- The use of the parameter vector for this type:
        -- Parameter #1 - peak cell rate in cells/second for CLP=0+1 traffic
        -- Parameter #2 - sustainable cell rate in cells/second for CLP=0 traffic
        -- Parameter #3 - maximum burst size in cells
        -- Parameters #4 and #5 are unused


--
        -- The CLP with Tagging/SCR Type
atmfClpTaggingScr
                OBJECT IDENTIFIER ::= { atmfTrafficDescrTypes 8 }
-- The use of the parameter vector for this type:
```

```
-- Parameter #1 - peak cell rate in cells/second for CLP=0+1 traffic
-- Parameter #2 - sustainable cell rate in cells/second for CLP=0
--          traffic, excess tagged as CLP=1
-- Parameter #3 - maximum burst size in cells
-- Parameters #4 and #5 are unused


--                      The MIB groups
atmfPhysicalGroup       OBJECT IDENTIFIER ::= { atmForumUni 1 }
atmfAtmLayerGroup       OBJECT IDENTIFIER ::= { atmForumUni 2 }
atmfAtmStatsGroup       OBJECT IDENTIFIER ::= { atmForumUni 3 }
atmfVpcGroup            OBJECT IDENTIFIER ::= { atmForumUni 4 }
atmfVccGroup            OBJECT IDENTIFIER ::= { atmForumUni 5 }


--                      The Physical Port Group
-- This group is mandatory for all UNI devices.
--
-- The Physical Port Table

atmfPortTable OBJECT-TYPE
        SYNTAX          SEQUENCE OF AtmfPortEntry
        ACCESS          not-accessible
        STATUS          mandatory
        DESCRIPTION
            "A table of physical layer status and parameter information for the UNI's
            physical interface."
        ::= { atmfPhysicalGroup 1 }

atmfPortEntry OBJECT-TYPE
        SYNTAX          AtmfPortEntry
        ACCESS          not-accessible
        STATUS          mandatory
        DESCRIPTION
            "An entry in the table, containing information about the physical layer of a
            UNI interface."
        INDEX { atmfPortIndex }
        ::= { atmfPortTable 1 }

AtmfPortEntry ::=
        SEQUENCE {
                atmfPortIndex
                        INTEGER,
                atmfPortAddress
                        AtmAddress,
                atmfPortTransmissionType
```

126

```
                    OBJECT IDENTIFIER,
          atmfPortMediaType
                    OBJECT IDENTIFIER,
          atmfPortOperStatus
                    INTEGER,
          atmfPortSpecific
                    OBJECT IDENTIFIER
      }
```

atmfPortIndex OBJECT-TYPE
      SYNTAX   INTEGER (0..2147483647)
      ACCESS   read-only
      STATUS   mandatory
      DESCRIPTION
            "A unique value which identifies this port. The value of 0 has the special meaning of identifying the local UNI."
      ::= { atmfPortEntry 1 }

atmfPortAddress OBJECT-TYPE
      SYNTAX   AtmAddress
      ACCESS   read-only
      STATUS   deprecated
      DESCRIPTION
            "This object should not be implemented except as required for backward compatibility with version 2.0 of the UNI specification. The Address Group, defined as part of the separate Address Registration MIB should be used instead."

      ::= { atmfPortEntry 2 }

atmfPortTransmissionType OBJECT-TYPE
      SYNTAX   OBJECT IDENTIFIER
      ACCESS   read-only
      STATUS   mandatory
      DESCRIPTION
            "The transmission type of this port. For example, for a port using the Sonet STS-3c physical layer at 155.52 Mbs, this object would have the Object Identifier value: atmfSonetSTS3c."
      ::= { atmfPortEntry 3 }

atmfPortMediaType OBJECT-TYPE
      SYNTAX   OBJECT IDENTIFIER
      ACCESS   read-only
      STATUS   mandatory

DESCRIPTION
"The type of media being used on this port. For example, for a port using coaxial cable, this object would have the Object Identifier value: atmfMediaCoaxCable."
::= { atmfPortEntry 4 }

atmfPortOperStatus OBJECT-TYPE
    SYNTAX   INTEGER {
                                other(1),
                                inService(2),
                                outOfService(3),
                                loopBack(4)
                            }
    ACCESS   read-only
    STATUS   mandatory
    DESCRIPTION
"The operational (i.e., actual) state of this port.

The ILMI should not alarm on a physical interface for when the value of this object is outOfService(3). This capability is useful if equipment is to be disconnected, or for troubleshooting purposes.

A value of loopBack(4) indicates that a local loopback is in place. "
::= { atmfPortEntry 5 }

atmfPortSpecific OBJECT-TYPE
    SYNTAX   OBJECT IDENTIFIER
    ACCESS   read-only
    STATUS   mandatory
    DESCRIPTION
"This object 'points' to additional transmission and/or media specific information relating to this port. In particular, this object's value is the name of a specific instance of the first columnar object of a MIB table with such additional information, where the specific instance is the one which corresponds to this port.

For example, for a DS3 interface, this object would contain the value, as defined in RFC 1407:
        dsx3LineIndex.i
where i would be the integer value uniquely identifying the DS3 interface corresponding to this port. If no additional transmission and/or media specific information is available, this object has the value { 0 0 }."
::= { atmfPortEntry 6 }

```
--                    The ATM Layer Group
-- This group is mandatory for all UNI devices.
--
-- ATM-layer specific information for the UNI interface
atmfAtmLayerTable OBJECT-TYPE
        SYNTAX              SEQUENCE OF AtmfAtmLayerEntry
        ACCESS              not-accessible
        STATUS              mandatory
        DESCRIPTION
                "A table of ATM layer status and parameter information for the UNI's
                physical interface."
        ::= { atmfAtmLayerGroup 1 }


atmfAtmLayerEntry OBJECT-TYPE
        SYNTAX              AtmfAtmLayerEntry
        ACCESS              not-accessible
        STATUS              mandatory
        DESCRIPTION
                "An entry in the table, containing information about the ATM layer of a
                UNI interface."
        INDEX { atmfAtmLayerIndex }
        ::= { atmfAtmLayerTable 1 }


AtmfAtmLayerEntry ::=
        SEQUENCE {
                atmfAtmLayerIndex
                        INTEGER,
                atmfAtmLayerMaxVPCs
                        INTEGER,
                atmfAtmLayerMaxVCCs
                        INTEGER,
                atmfAtmLayerConfiguredVPCs
                        INTEGER,
                atmfAtmLayerConfiguredVCCs
                        INTEGER,
                atmfAtmLayerMaxVpiBits
                        INTEGER,
                atmfAtmLayerMaxVciBits
                        INTEGER,
                atmfAtmLayerUniType
                        INTEGER
        }
atmfAtmLayerIndex OBJECT-TYPE
```

```
          SYNTAX              INTEGER (0..2147483647)
          ACCESS              read-only
          STATUS              mandatory
          DESCRIPTION
              "The unique value which identifies the UNI port. The value of 0 has the
              special meaning of identifying the local UNI."
          ::= { atmfAtmLayerEntry 1 }

atmfAtmLayerMaxVPCs OBJECT-TYPE
          SYNTAX              INTEGER (0..255)
          ACCESS              read-only
          STATUS              mandatory
          DESCRIPTION
              "The maximum number of VPCs supported on this UNI."
          ::= { atmfAtmLayerEntry 2 }

atmfAtmLayerMaxVCCs OBJECT-TYPE
          SYNTAX              INTEGER (0..16777215)
          ACCESS              read-only
          STATUS              mandatory
          DESCRIPTION
              "The maximum number of VCCs supported on this UNI."
          ::= { atmfAtmLayerEntry 3 }

atmfAtmLayerConfiguredVPCs OBJECT-TYPE
          SYNTAX              INTEGER (0..255)
          ACCESS              read-only
          STATUS              mandatory
          DESCRIPTION
              "The number of VPCs configured for use on this UNI."
          ::= { atmfAtmLayerEntry 4 }

atmfAtmLayerConfiguredVCCs OBJECT-TYPE
          SYNTAX              INTEGER (0..16777215)
          ACCESS              read-only
          STATUS              mandatory
          DESCRIPTION
              "The number of VCCs configured for use on this UNI."
          ::= { atmfAtmLayerEntry 5 }

atmfAtmLayerMaxVpiBits OBJECT-TYPE
          SYNTAX              INTEGER (0..8)
          ACCESS              read-only
          STATUS              mandatory
```

DESCRIPTION
    "The number of active VPI bits on this interface."
::= {atmfAtmLayerEntry 6 }

atmfAtmLayerMaxVciBits OBJECT-TYPE
    SYNTAX   INTEGER (0..16)
    ACCESS   read-only
    STATUS   mandatory
    DESCRIPTION
    "The number of active VCI bits on this interface."
::= {atmfAtmLayerEntry 7 }

atmfAtmLayerUniType OBJECT-TYPE
    SYNTAX   INTEGER {public(1), private(2)}
    ACCESS   read-only
    STATUS   mandatory
    DESCRIPTION
    "The type of the ATM UNI, either public or private."
::= { atmfAtmLayerEntry 8 }

--   The ATM Statistics Group
-- This group is optional. However, if any objects in this group
-- are supported, then all objects in the group must be supported.
--
-- ATM-layer statistics for the UNI interface

atmfAtmStatsTable OBJECT-TYPE
    SYNTAX   SEQUENCE OF AtmfAtmStatsEntry
    ACCESS   not-accessible
    STATUS   mandatory
    DESCRIPTION
    "A table of ATM layer statistics information for
    the UNI's physical interface."
::= { atmfAtmStatsGroup 1 }

atmfAtmStatsEntry OBJECT-TYPE
    SYNTAX   AtmfAtmStatsEntry
    ACCESS   not-accessible
    STATUS   mandatory
    DESCRIPTION
    "An entry in the table, containing statistics for the ATM layer of a UNI
    interface."
    INDEX { atmfAtmStatsIndex }
::= { atmfAtmStatsTable 1 }

```
AtmfAtmStatsEntry ::=
        SEQUENCE {
                atmfAtmStatsIndex
                        INTEGER,
                atmfAtmStatsReceivedCells
                        Counter,
                atmfAtmStatsDroppedReceivedCells
                        Counter,
                atmfAtmStatsTransmittedCells
                        Counter
        }
atmfAtmStatsIndex OBJECT-TYPE
        SYNTAX              INTEGER (0..2147483647)
        ACCESS              read-only
        STATUS              mandatory
        DESCRIPTION
                "The unique value which identifies the UNI port. The value of 0 has the
                special meaning of identifying the local UNI."
        ::= { atmfAtmStatsEntry 1 }


atmfAtmStatsReceivedCells OBJECT-TYPE
        SYNTAX              Counter
        ACCESS              read-only
        STATUS              mandatory
        DESCRIPTION
                "The accumulated number of ATM cells received on this UNI which were
                assigned and not dropped."
        ::= { atmfAtmStatsEntry 2 }


atmfAtmStatsDroppedReceivedCells OBJECT-TYPE
        SYNTAX              Counter
        ACCESS              read-only
        STATUS              mandatory
        DESCRIPTION
                "The accumulated number of ATM cells which were dropped for the
                reasons defined in section 4.4.4.2."
        ::= { atmfAtmStatsEntry 3 }


atmfAtmStatsTransmittedCells OBJECT-TYPE
        SYNTAX              Counter
        ACCESS              read-only
        STATUS              mandatory
        DESCRIPTION
```

"The accumulated number of assigned ATM cells which were transmitted across this interface."
::= { atmfAtmStatsEntry 4 }


```
--                      The Virtual Path Group
-- This group is mandatory for all UNI devices.
--
-- Information concerning Virtual Path Connections

atmfVpcTable OBJECT-TYPE
        SYNTAX                  SEQUENCE OF AtmfVpcEntry
        ACCESS                  not-accessible
        STATUS                  mandatory
        DESCRIPTION
                "A table of status and parameter information on the virtual path connections
                which cross this UNI."
        ::= { atmfVpcGroup 1 }

atmfVpcEntry OBJECT-TYPE
        SYNTAX                  AtmfVpcEntry
        ACCESS                  not-accessible
        STATUS                  mandatory
        DESCRIPTION
                "An entry in the table, containing information about a particular virtual path
                connection."
        INDEX { atmfVpcPortIndex, atmfVpcVpi }
        ::= { atmfVpcTable 1 }

AtmfVpcEntry ::=
        SEQUENCE {
                atmfVpcPortIndex
                        INTEGER,
                atmfVpcVpi
                        INTEGER,
                atmfVpcOperStatus
                        INTEGER,
                atmfVpcTransmitTrafficDescriptorType
                        OBJECT IDENTIFIER,
                atmfVpcTransmitTrafficDescriptorParam1
                        INTEGER,
                atmfVpcTransmitTrafficDescriptorParam2
                        INTEGER,
                atmfVpcTransmitTrafficDescriptorParam3
```

```
                        INTEGER,
        atmfVpcTransmitTrafficDescriptorParam4
                        INTEGER,
        atmfVpcTransmitTrafficDescriptorParam5
                        INTEGER,
        atmfVpcReceiveTrafficDescriptorType
                        OBJECT IDENTIFIER,
        atmfVpcReceiveTrafficDescriptorParam1
                        INTEGER,
        atmfVpcReceiveTrafficDescriptorParam2
                        INTEGER,
        atmfVpcReceiveTrafficDescriptorParam3
                        INTEGER,
        atmfVpcReceiveTrafficDescriptorParam4
                        INTEGER,
        atmfVpcReceiveTrafficDescriptorParam5
                        INTEGER,
        atmfVpcQoSCategory
                        INTEGER,
        atmfVpcTransmitQoSClass
                        INTEGER,
        atmfVpcReceiveQoSClass
                        INTEGER
    }
```

atmfVpcPortIndex OBJECT-TYPE
        SYNTAX   INTEGER (0..2147483647)
        ACCESS   read-only
        STATUS   mandatory
        DESCRIPTION
            "The unique value which identifies the UNI port. The value of 0 has the
            special meaning of identifying the local UNI."
        ::= { atmfVpcEntry 1 }

atmfVpcVpi OBJECT-TYPE
        SYNTAX   INTEGER (0..255)
        ACCESS   read-only
        STATUS   mandatory
        DESCRIPTION
            "The VPI value of this Virtual Path Connection at the local UNI."
        ::= { atmfVpcEntry 2 }

atmfVpcOperStatus OBJECT-TYPE
        SYNTAX INTEGER {

```
                              unknown(1),
                              end2endUp(2),
                              end2endDown(3),
                              localUpEnd2endUnknown(4),
                              localDown(5)
                    }
ACCESS              read-only
STATUS              mandatory
DESCRIPTION
       "The present actual operational status of the VPC.

       A value of end2endUp(2) or end2endDown(3) would be used if the end-to-
       end status is known. If only local status information is available, a value of
       localUpEnd2endUnknown(4) or localDown(5) would be used."

       ::= { atmfVpcEntry 3 }


atmfVpcTransmitTrafficDescriptorType OBJECT-TYPE
       SYNTAX              OBJECT IDENTIFIER
       ACCESS              read-only
       STATUS              mandatory
       DESCRIPTION
              "The type of traffic management, applicable to the transmit direction of this
              VPC. The type may indicate none, or a type with one or more parameters.
              These parameters are specified as a parameter vector, in the corresponding
              instances of the objects:
              atmfVpcTransmitTrafficDescriptorParam1,
              atmfVpcTransmitTrafficDescriptorParam2,
              atmfVpcTransmitTrafficDescriptorParam3,
              atmfVpcTransmitTrafficDescriptorParam4, and
              atmfVpcTransmitTrafficDescriptorParam5."
       ::= { atmfVpcEntry 4 }


atmfVpcTransmitTrafficDescriptorParam1 OBJECT-TYPE
       SYNTAX              INTEGER (0..2147483647)
       ACCESS              read-only
       STATUS              mandatory
       DESCRIPTION
              "The first parameter of the transmit parameter vector for this VPC, used
              according to the value of atmfVpcTransmitTrafficDescriptorType."
       ::= { atmfVpcEntry 5 }


atmfVpcTransmitTrafficDescriptorParam2 OBJECT-TYPE
       SYNTAX              INTEGER (0..2147483647)
```

ACCESS   read-only
STATUS   mandatory
DESCRIPTION
      "The second parameter of the transmit parameter vector for this VPC, used
      according to the value of atmfVpcTransmitTrafficDescriptorType."
::= { atmfVpcEntry 6 }

atmfVpcTransmitTrafficDescriptorParam3 OBJECT-TYPE
      SYNTAX   INTEGER (0..2147483647)
      ACCESS   read-only
      STATUS   mandatory
      DESCRIPTION
            "The third parameter of the transmit parameter vector for this VPC, used
            according to the value of atmfVpcTransmitTrafficDescriptorType."
      ::= { atmfVpcEntry 7 }

atmfVpcTransmitTrafficDescriptorParam4 OBJECT-TYPE
      SYNTAX   INTEGER (0..2147483647)
      ACCESS   read-only
      STATUS   mandatory
      DESCRIPTION
            "The fourth parameter of the transmit parameter vector for this VPC, used
            according to the value of atmfVpcTransmitTrafficDescriptorType."
      ::= { atmfVpcEntry 8 }

atmfVpcTransmitTrafficDescriptorParam5 OBJECT-TYPE
      SYNTAX   INTEGER (0..2147483647)
      ACCESS   read-only
      STATUS   mandatory
      DESCRIPTION
            "The fifth parameter of the transmit parameter vector for this VPC, used
            according to the value of atmfVpcTransmitTrafficDescriptorType."
      ::= { atmfVpcEntry 9 }

atmfVpcReceiveTrafficDescriptorType OBJECT-TYPE
      SYNTAX   OBJECT IDENTIFIER
      ACCESS   read-only
      STATUS   mandatory
      DESCRIPTION
            "The type of traffic management, applicable to the traffic in the receive
            direction of this VPC. The type may indicate none, or a type with one or
            more parameters. These parameters are specified as a parameter vector, in
            the corresponding instances of the objects:
            atmfVpcReceiveTrafficDescriptorParam1,

        atmfVpcReceiveTrafficDescriptorParam2,
        atmfVpcReceiveTrafficDescriptorParam3,
        atmfVpcReceiveTrafficDescriptorParam4, and
        atmfVpcReceiveTrafficDescriptorParam5."
    ::= { atmfVpcEntry 10 }

atmfVpcReceiveTrafficDescriptorParam1 OBJECT-TYPE
        SYNTAX   INTEGER (0..2147483647)
        ACCESS   read-only
        STATUS   mandatory
        DESCRIPTION
                "The first parameter of the receive parameter vector for this VPC, used
                according to the value of atmfVpcReceiveTrafficDescriptorType."
    ::= { atmfVpcEntry 11 }

atmfVpcReceiveTrafficDescriptorParam2 OBJECT-TYPE
        SYNTAX   INTEGER (0..2147483647)
        ACCESS   read-only
        STATUS   mandatory
        DESCRIPTION
                "The second parameter of the receive parameter vector for this VPC, used
                according to the value of atmfVpcReceiveTrafficDescriptorType."
    ::= { atmfVpcEntry 12 }

atmfVpcReceiveTrafficDescriptorParam3 OBJECT-TYPE
        SYNTAX   INTEGER (0..2147483647)
        ACCESS   read-only
        STATUS   mandatory
        DESCRIPTION
                "The third parameter of the receive parameter vector for this VPC, used
                according to the value of atmfVpcReceiveTrafficDescriptorType."
    ::= { atmfVpcEntry 13 }

atmfVpcReceiveTrafficDescriptorParam4 OBJECT-TYPE
        SYNTAX   INTEGER (0..2147483647)
        ACCESS   read-only
        STATUS   mandatory
        DESCRIPTION
                "The fourth parameter of the receive parameter vector for this VPC, used
                according to the value of atmfVpcReceiveTrafficDescriptorType."
    ::= { atmfVpcEntry 14 }

atmfVpcReceiveTrafficDescriptorParam5 OBJECT-TYPE
        SYNTAX   INTEGER (0..2147483647)

ACCESS   read-only
STATUS   mandatory
DESCRIPTION
     "The fifth parameter of the receive parameter vector for this VPC, used
     according to the value of atmfVpcReceiveTrafficDescriptorType."
::= { atmfVpcEntry 15 }

atmfVpcQoSCategory OBJECT-TYPE
    SYNTAX   INTEGER {
                      other(1),
                      deterministic (2),
                      statistical (3),
                      unspecified (4)
               }
    ACCESS   read-only
    STATUS   deprecated
    DESCRIPTION
         "This object should not be implemented except as required for backward
         compatibility with version 2.0 of the UNI specification."
    ::= { atmfVpcEntry 16 }

atmfVpcTransmitQoSClass OBJECT-TYPE
    SYNTAX   NTEGER (0..255)
    ACCESS   read-only
    STATUS   mandatory
    DESCRIPTION
         "The QoS Class, as defined in section 4 of Appendix A, for the transmit
         direction of this VPC connection at the local UNI."
    ::= { atmfVpcEntry 17 }

atmfVpcReceiveQoSClass OBJECT-TYPE
    SYNTAX   INTEGER (0..255)
    ACCESS   read-only
    STATUS   mandatory
    DESCRIPTION
         "The QoS Class, as defined in section 4 of Appendix A, for the receive
         direction of this VPC connection at the local UNI."
    ::= { atmfVpcEntry 18 }

--   The Virtual Channel Group
-- This group is mandatory for all UNI devices.
--
-- Information concerning Virtual Channel Connections
atmfVccTable OBJECT-TYPE

SYNTAX   SEQUENCE OF AtmfVccEntry
ACCESS   not-accessible
STATUS   mandatory
DESCRIPTION
          "A table of status and parameter information on the virtual channel connec-
          tions which are visible at this UNI."
     ::= { atmfVccGroup 1 }

atmfVccEntry OBJECT-TYPE
          SYNTAX   AtmfVccEntry
          ACCESS   not-accessible
          STATUS   mandatory
          DESCRIPTION
               "An entry in the table, containing information about a particular virtual
               channel connection."
          INDEX { atmfVccPortIndex, atmfVccVpi, atmfVccVci }
          ::= { atmfVccTable 1 }

AtmfVccEntry ::=
     SEQUENCE {
               atmfVccPortIndex
                    INTEGER,
               atmfVccVpi
                    INTEGER,
               atmfVccVci
                    INTEGER,
               atmfVccOperStatus
                    INTEGER,
               atmfVccTransmitTrafficDescriptorType
                    OBJECT IDENTIFIER,
               atmfVccTransmitTrafficDescriptorParam1
                    INTEGER,
               atmfVccTransmitTrafficDescriptorParam2
                    INTEGER,
               atmfVccTransmitTrafficDescriptorParam3
                    INTEGER,
               atmfVccTransmitTrafficDescriptorParam4
                    INTEGER,
               atmfVccTransmitTrafficDescriptorParam5
                    INTEGER,
               atmfVccReceiveTrafficDescriptorType
                    OBJECT IDENTIFIER,
               atmfVccReceiveTrafficDescriptorParam1
                    INTEGER,

```
                    atmfVccReceiveTrafficDescriptorParam2
                            INTEGER,
                    atmfVccReceiveTrafficDescriptorParam3
                            INTEGER,
                    atmfVccReceiveTrafficDescriptorParam4
                            INTEGER,
                    atmfVccReceiveTrafficDescriptorParam5
                            INTEGER,
                    atmfVccQoSCategory
                            INTEGER,
                    atmfVccTransmitQoSClass
                            INTEGER,
                    atmfVccReceiveQoSClass
                            INTEGER
            }
```

atmfVccPortIndex OBJECT-TYPE
        SYNTAX   INTEGER (0..2147483647)
        ACCESS   read-only
        STATUS   mandatory
        DESCRIPTION
                "The unique value which identifies the UNI port. The value of 0 has the
                special meaning of identifying the local UNI."
        ::= { atmfVccEntry 1 }

atmfVccVpi OBJECT-TYPE
        SYNTAX   INTEGER (0..255)
        ACCESS   read-only
        STATUS   mandatory
        DESCRIPTION
                "The VPI value of this Virtual Channel Connection at the local UNI."
        ::= { atmfVccEntry 2 }

atmfVccVci OBJECT-TYPE
        SYNTAX   INTEGER (0..65535)
        ACCESS   read-only
        STATUS   mandatory
        DESCRIPTION
                "The VCI value of this Virtual Channel Connection at the local UNI."
        ::= { atmfVccEntry 3 }

atmfVccOperStatus OBJECT-TYPE
        SYNTAX INTEGER {
                        unknown(1),

```
```

                        end2endUp(2),
                        end2endDown(3),
                        localUpEnd2endUnknown(4),
                        localDown(5)
                        }
        ACCESS   read-only
        STATUS   mandatory
        DESCRIPTION
                "The present actual operational status of the VCC. A value of
                end2endUp(2) or end2endUp(3) is used if the end to end status is known.

                If only local status is known a value of localUpEnd2endUnknown(4) or
                localDown(5) is used.

        ::= { atmfVccEntry 4 }

atmfVccTransmitTrafficDescriptorType OBJECT-TYPE
        SYNTAX   OBJECT IDENTIFIER
        ACCESS   read-only
        STATUS   mandatory
        DESCRIPTION
                "The type of traffic management, applicable to the transmit direction of this
                VCC. The type may indicate none, or a type with one or more parameters.
                These parameters are specified as a parameter vector, in the corresponding
                instances of the objects:
                atmfVccTransmitTrafficDescriptorParam1,
                atmfVccTransmitTrafficDescriptorParam2,
                atmfVccTransmitTrafficDescriptorParam3,
                atmfVccTransmitTrafficDescriptorParam4, and
                atmfVccTransmitTrafficDescriptorParam5."
        ::= { atmfVccEntry 5 }

atmfVccTransmitTrafficDescriptorParam1 OBJECT-TYPE
        SYNTAX   INTEGER (0..2147483647)
        ACCESS   read-only
        STATUS   mandatory
        DESCRIPTION
                "The first parameter of the transmit parameter vector for this VCC, used
                according to the value of atmfVccTransmitTrafficDescriptorType."
        ::= { atmfVccEntry 6 }

atmfVccTransmitTrafficDescriptorParam2 OBJECT-TYPE
        SYNTAX   INTEGER (0..2147483647)
        ACCESS   read-only

STATUS   mandatory
DESCRIPTION
          "The second parameter of the transmit parameter vector for this VCC, used
          according to the value of atmfVccTransmitTrafficDescriptorType."
     ::= { atmfVccEntry 7 }

atmfVccTransmitTrafficDescriptorParam3 OBJECT-TYPE
          SYNTAX   INTEGER (0..2147483647)
          ACCESS   read-only
          STATUS   mandatory
          DESCRIPTION
          "The third parameter of the transmit parameter vector for this VCC, used
          according to the value of atmfVccTransmitTrafficDescriptorType."
     ::= { atmfVccEntry 8 }

atmfVccTransmitTrafficDescriptorParam4 OBJECT-TYPE
          SYNTAX   INTEGER (0..2147483647)
          ACCESS   read-only
          STATUS   mandatory
          DESCRIPTION
          "The fourth parameter of the transmit parameter vector for this VCC, used
          according to the value of atmfVccTransmitTrafficDescriptorType."
     ::= { atmfVccEntry 9 }

atmfVccTransmitTrafficDescriptorParam5 OBJECT-TYPE
          SYNTAX   INTEGER (0..2147483647)
          ACCESS   read-only
          STATUS   mandatory
          DESCRIPTION
          "The fifth parameter of the transmit parameter vector for this VCC, used
          according to the value of atmfVccTransmitTrafficDescriptorType."
     ::= { atmfVccEntry 10 }

atmfVccReceiveTrafficDescriptorType OBJECT-TYPE
          SYNTAX   OBJECT IDENTIFIER
          ACCESS   read-only
          STATUS   mandatory
          DESCRIPTION
          "The type of traffic management, applicable to the traffic in the receive
          direction of this VCC. The type may indicate none, or a type with one or
          more parameters. These parameters are specified as a parameter vector, in
          the corresponding instances of the objects:
          atmfVccReceiveTrafficDescriptorParam1,
          atmfVccReceiveTrafficDescriptorParam2,

        atmfVccReceiveTrafficDescriptorParam3,
        atmfVccReceiveTrafficDescriptorParam4, and
        atmfVccReceiveTrafficDescriptorParam5."
    ::= { atmfVccEntry 11 }

atmfVccReceiveTrafficDescriptorParam1 OBJECT-TYPE
      SYNTAX   INTEGER (0..2147483647)
      ACCESS   read-only
      STATUS   mandatory
      DESCRIPTION
          "The first parameter of the receive parameter vector for this VCC, used
          according to the value of atmfVccReceiveTrafficDescriptorType."
    ::= { atmfVccEntry 12 }

atmfVccReceiveTrafficDescriptorParam2 OBJECT-TYPE
      SYNTAX   INTEGER (0..2147483647)
      ACCESS   read-only
      STATUS   mandatory
      DESCRIPTION
          "The second parameter of the receive parameter vector for this VCC, used
          according to the value of atmfVccReceiveTrafficDescriptorType."
    ::= { atmfVccEntry 13 }

atmfVccReceiveTrafficDescriptorParam3 OBJECT-TYPE
      SYNTAX   INTEGER (0..2147483647)
      ACCESS   read-only
      STATUS   mandatory
      DESCRIPTION
          "The third parameter of the receive parameter vector for this VCC, used
          according to the value of atmfVccReceiveTrafficDescriptorType."
    ::= { atmfVccEntry 14 }

atmfVccReceiveTrafficDescriptorParam4 OBJECT-TYPE
      SYNTAX   INTEGER (0..2147483647)
      ACCESS   read-only
      STATUS   mandatory
      DESCRIPTION
          "The fourth parameter of the receive parameter vector for this VCC, used
          according to the value of atmfVccReceiveTrafficDescriptorType."
    ::= { atmfVccEntry 15 }

atmfVccReceiveTrafficDescriptorParam5 OBJECT-TYPE
      SYNTAX   INTEGER (0..2147483647)
      ACCESS   read-only

STATUS   mandatory
DESCRIPTION
        "The fifth parameter of the receive parameter vector for this VCC, used
        according to the value of atmfVccReceiveTrafficDescriptorType."
    ::= { atmfVccEntry 16 }

atmfVccQoSCategory OBJECT-TYPE
        SYNTAX   INTEGER {
                                        other(1),
                                        deterministic (2),
                                        statistical (3),
                                        unspecified (4)
                                  }
        ACCESS   read-only
        STATUS   deprecated
        DESCRIPTION
        "This object should not be implemented except as required for backward
        compatibility with version 2.0 of the UNI specification."

    ::= { atmfVccEntry 17 }

atmfVccTransmitQoSClass OBJECT-TYPE
        SYNTAX   INTEGER (0..255)
        ACCESS   read-only
        STATUS   mandatory
        DESCRIPTION
        "The QoS Class, as defined in section 4 of Appendix A, for the transmit
        direction of this VCC connection at the local UNI."
    ::= { atmfVccEntry 18 }

atmfVccReceiveQoSClass OBJECT-TYPE
        SYNTAX   INTEGER (0..255)
        ACCESS   read-only
        STATUS   mandatory
        DESCRIPTION
        "The QoS Class, as defined in section 4 of Appendix A, for the receive
        direction of this VCC connection at the local UNI."
    ::= { atmfVccEntry 19 }

END

4.7 ILMI Protocol

The use of SNMP messages will be according to the following requirements.

4.7.1 Use of VCCs

One VCC will be used for sending AAL-encapsulated SNMP messages between adjacent UMEs. This VCC is used for requests, responses, and traps, differentiated according to the SNMP PDU type.

(R) Encapsulation of SNMP ILMI messages in AAL5 as defined in T1S1/92-283, [27], and T1S1/92-285, [28], is required.

(O) Encapsulation of SNMP ILMI messages in the common part of AAL3/AAL4 as defined in I.363 is an option.

(R) At all times one VCC will be provisioned for the ILMI. The default value for provisioning this VCC is VPI=0, VCI=16, however, the VPI/VCI value must be configurable.

(R) The cells carrying ILMI messages shall have cell loss priority (CLP = 0)

(R) The throughput of SNMP traffic on the ILMI VCC should be no.more than approximately one percent of the link bandwidth.

4.7.2 Message Format (R)

The message format specified in RFC 1157 will be used. That is, messages will be formatted according to SNMP version 1, not SNMP version 2. Any use of SMNP version 2 is for future study.

All SNMP messages will use the community name "ILMI", that is, the OCTET STRING value: '494C4D49'h.

In all SNMP Traps, the agent-addr field (which has syntax NetworkAddress), will always have the IpAddress value: 0.0.0.0.

In all SNMP Traps, the time-stamp field in the Trap-PDU will contain the value of the agent's sysUpTime MIB object at the time of trap generation (sysUpTime is defined in the system group of MIB-II).

In any standard SNMP Traps, (e.g., the coldStart Trap), the enterprise field in the Trap-PDU will contain the value of the agent's sysObjectID MIB object (sysObjectID is defined in the system group of MIB-II).

The supported traps are coldStart and enterpriseSpecific.

4.7.3 Message Sizes (R)

All UNI implementations will be able to accept SNMP messages of size up to and including 484 octets. Larger messages should not be sent unless the originator has information (e.g., via some out-of-band mechanism) that the receiver supports larger messages.

4.7.4 ILMI Traffic Requirements

The traffic requirements relating to the ATM connection used for ILMI communication are as follows:

(R) The VCC used for ILMI communication shall support a sustainable cell rate, R(s), no more than 1% of the UNI physical line rate and a peak cell rate, R(p), no more than 5% of the UNI physical line rate.

(R) The ILMI traffic burst length, L(b), shall be no more than 484 octets.

(R) The ILMI traffic bursts inter-arrival time, T(b), should be greater than or equal to (L(b)/(R(p) x 1%)), where L(b) and R(p) are respectively the ILMI burst length and the ILMI traffic peak rate.

4.7.5 Message Response Time

Response time refers to the elapsed time from the submission of an SNMP message (e.g., Get, Get-Next, or Set-Request message) by a UME across a UNI to the receipt of the corresponding SNMP message (e.g., Get-Response message) from the adjacent UME. An SNMP Get, Get-Next, or Set-Request message is defined in this context as a request concerning a single object. The following specifies ILMI response time requirements.

(R) The UME should support maximum Response Times of 1 second for 95% of all SNMP Get, GetNext or SetRequest requests containing a single object received from an adjacent UME independent of the UNI's physical line rate.

4.7.6 Object Value Data Currentness

Data currentness refers to the maximum elapsed time since an object value in the ATM UNI ILMI MIB was known to be current. The following specifies the requirements on the Data Currentness of the ILMI objects and the event notifications.

(R) The ATM UNI ILMI MIB objects should have the Data Currentness of a maximum of 30 seconds.

(R) The UME should support event notifications (i.e., SNMP Traps) for generic SNMP events (e.g., coldStart) within 2 seconds of the event detection by the UME.

4.7.7 Link Management Procedures

The network-side UME shall declare the UNI to be down either due to a physical layer failure or due to a loss of ILMI connectivity, but not due to any change in the status of the Signaling AAL. To detect loss of ILMI connectivity, the network-side UME issues periodic polls; that is, the network-side UME issues an ILMI request message every T seconds. The UNI is declared down when no ILMI response messages are received for K consecutive polls. The default values are K=4 and T=5; different values can be configured.

Link management procedures for the user-side UME are for further study.

Section 5:

UNI Signalling

5.1 General

This section specifies the procedures for dynamically establishing, maintaining and clearing ATM connections at the User-Network Interface. The procedures are defined in terms of messages and the information elements used to characterize the ATM connection and ensure interoperability.

5.1.1 Scope

This Implementation Agreement is based on a subset of the broadband signalling protocol standards that are currently under development (and currently identified as Q.93B [29]). Additions to this subset have been made where necessary to support capabilities identified by the ATM Forum as important for early deployment and interoperability of ATM equipment. The primary areas where the standard has been supplemented are to support point-to-multipoint connections, additional traffic descriptors, and private network addressing.

The procedures included in this Implementation Agreement apply to the interface between terminal or endpoint equipment and a public network, referred to as Public UNI, and terminal or endpoint equipment connected to a private network, referred to as Private UNI.

The term "Phase 1" is used to refer to the protocol as described in this document. This term is used to make an explicit distinction between the protocol as specified here and any future releases of this protocol.

> *Note 1* - The subsections of §5 and the annexes of this document are numbered, where both practical and useful, to follow the section numbering in the Q.93B draft standard at the time this document was produced.

> *Note 2* - The convention of highlighting requirements and options with (R) and (O), respectively, used elsewhere in this document, is not used in §5 or in the Signalling annexes and appendicies. This is done to maintain a higher degree of similarity between the specification of signalling as found in this Implementation Agreement and that found in the emerging Q.93B standard.

5.1.1.1 Reference Configuration

The protocol will be valid for the private and public UNI as defined in Figure 1-3. Moreover, based on the requirement that the protocol be symmetrical, it will also apply in the configuration ATM Endpoint to ATM Endpoint.

The purpose of a reference configuration for the UNI signalling specification is to list all the elements of an ATM network and the links between them, to which this specification will apply.

Network elements in this context are:

- endpoint equipment
- private ATM network
- public ATM network.

For the purpose of this section, a network, public or private, consists of one or more ATM switching platforms under the same administration.

The possible reference configurations that apply to this Implementation Agreement are illustrated in Table 5-1. The table entries 'Public UNI' and 'Private UNI' refer to Phase 1 only.

Table 5-1 Reference Configurations

BETWEEN -> | V	End-point equipment	Private ATM network	Public ATM network
Endpoint equipment	Private UNI	Private UNI	Public UNI
Private ATM network	Private UNI	Note 1	Public UNI
Public ATM network	Public UNI	Public UNI	Note 2

Note 1 - Private ATM networks may be connected using the private UNI signalling. However, features specific to private network interworking are not a requirement for Phase 1 of the protocol. In releases after Phase 1, such internetworking features may be implemented in a private NNI specification.

Note 2 - The table entry for the connection between public networks is outside the domain of the UNI specification. It is addressed by the B-ICI (Broadband Intercarrier Interface) specification of the ATM Forum.

5.1.2 Capabilities Supported by Phase 1 Signalling

The basic capabilities supported by the Phase 1 Signalling specified in this document are listed below:

1. Demand (switched) channel connections.
2. Point-to-point and point-to-multipoint switched channel connections.
3. Connections with symmetric or asymmetric bandwidth requirements.
4. Single-connection (point-to-point or point-to-multipoint) calls.

5. Basic signalling functions via protocol messages, information elements, and procedures.

6. Class X, Class A, and Class C ATM Transport services.

7. Request and Indication of signalling parameters.

8. VPCI/VPI/VCI assignment.

9. A single, statically defined out-of-band channel for all signalling messages.

10. Error recovery.

11. Public UNI and Private UNI addressing formats for unique identification of ATM endpoints.

12. A client registration mechanism for exchange of addressing information across a UNI.

13. End-to-end Compatibility Parameter Identification.

The following sections describe each capability in more detail.

5.1.2.1 Support of Demand (Switched) Channel Connections

The purpose of this specification is to support demand (switched) channel connections. These connections are established in real time using signalling procedures. Demand connections can remain active for an arbitrary amount of time but would not automatically be re-established after a network failure.

In contrast, permanent connections are those that are set up and torn down via provisioning. Permanent connections generally remain established for long periods of time and should automatically be re-established in the event of network failure. The Phase 1 Signalling specified in this document does not support permanent connections.

5.1.2.2 Support of Point-to-Point and Point-to-Multipoint Channel Connections

A Point-to-Point Connection is a collection of associated ATM virtual channel (VC) or virtual path (VP) links that connect two endpoints. The Phase 1 Signalling specified in this document supports point-to-point virtual channel (VC) connections.

5.1.2.2.1 Definition of Point-to-Multipoint Connection

A Point-to-Multipoint Connection is a collection of associated ATM VC or VP links, with associated endpoint nodes, with the following properties:

1. One ATM link, called the Root Link, serves as the root in a simple tree topology. When the Root node sends information, all of the remaining nodes on the connection, called Leaf Nodes, receive copies of the information.

2. For Phase 1, only zero return bandwidth (i.e., from the Leaves to the Root) is supported.

3. The Leaf Nodes can not communicate directly to each other with this connection type.

4. A distributed implementation can be used to connect leaves to the tree.

5.1.2.2.2 Support of Point-to-Multipoint Channel Connections

The Phase 1 Signalling specified in this document supports point-to-multipoint virtual channel (VC) connections as follows:

A point-to-multipoint connection is set up by first establishing a point-to-point connection between the root node and one leaf node. After this set up is complete, additional leaf nodes can be added to the connection by "add party" requests from the root node. The Phase 1 Signalling specified in this document supports the ability of the root to have multiple "add party" requests pending at one time (that is, the root node does not have to wait for a response from one "add party" request before issuing the next). The "add party" response identifies the leaf that was added (or that failed to be added) so that responses can be paired with requests. Note that the root node could choose to add leaf nodes serially (that is, the root could wait for each "add party" to complete before issuing the next), even though the network allows leaf nodes to be added in parallel.

A leaf node may be added or dropped from a point-to-multipoint connection at any time after the establishment of the connection. A new leaf node can be added to an existing connection via the root node issuing an "add party" request, as described above. A leaf node can be dropped from a connection as a result of a request sent by either the root node or by the leaf node to be dropped (but not by another leaf).

> *Note* - Multipoint-to-Multipoint connections are not supported in Phase 1. Instead, techniques such as the following, involving point-to-multipoint connections, can be used:

A. Each node in a group that wishes to communicate can establish a Point-to-Multipoint connection to all of the other nodes in the group. For a group of N nodes, this requires N Point-to-Multipoint connections.

B. Each node in the group that wishes to communicate can establish a Point-to-Point connection to a "Multicast Server." The Multicast Server is the Root Node in a Point-to-Multipoint connection to each node in the group. Any information sent by a node in the group to the Multicast Server is transmitted back from the Multicast Server through the Point-to-Multipoint connection to each of the nodes in the group. For a group of N nodes, this requires N Point-to-Point connections and one Point-to-Multipoint connection.

5.1.2.3 Support of Connections with Symmetric or Asymmetric Bandwidth

Phase 1 Signalling specified in this document supports point-to-point, bi-directional connections that have bandwidth specified independently in the forward and backward directions. The forward direction is from the calling party to the called party, while the backward direction is from the called party to the calling party.

For point-to-multipoint connections, the Phase 1 Signalling specified in this document supports only non-zero, identical bandwidth in the forward direction from the root node to each leaf node, and zero bandwidth in the backward direction from each leaf node to the root node.

5.1.2.4 Support of a Single Connection per Call

The Phase 1 Signalling specified in this document will support one and only one connection per call. The single connection can be either a point-to-point or point-to-multipoint (as described in §5.1.2.2.2) connection.

5.1.2.5 Protocol Support for Basic Signalling Functions

The signalling protocol supports the following basic functions at the UNI interface:

Connection/Call Setup	This is the aspect of the protocol which supports the establishment of a connection/call between different parties. It includes Connection/Call Request and Connection/Call Answer.
Connection/Call Request	This protocol function allows an originating party to request the establishment of a connection/call to a certain destination. In this request the originating party may provide information related to the connection/call.
Connection/Call Answer	This protocol function allows the destination party to respond to an incoming connection/call request. The destination party may include information related to the connection/call. (Rejecting the connection/call request is considered part of the Connection/Call Clearing function).
Connection/Call Clearing	This protocol function allows any party involved in a connection/call to initiate its removal from an already established connection/call. If the connection/call is between two parties only, then the whole connection/call is removed. This function also allows a destination party to reject its inclusion in a connection/call.
Reason for Clearing	This protocol function allows the clearing party to indicate the cause for initiating its removal from a connection/call.
Out of Band Signalling	This function specifies that connection/call control information uses a channel different from the channels used for exchanging data information between the end-parties (i.e., a specific VPCI/VCI value will be used for the connection/call control signalling channel).

5.1.2.6 Support of Class X, Class A, and Class C ATM Transport Services

Class X service is a connection oriented ATM transport service where the AAL, traffic type (VBR or CBR) and timing requirements are user defined (i.e., transparent to the network). The user chooses only the desired bandwidth and QoS with appropriate information elements in a SETUP message to establish a class X connection.

Class A service is a connection oriented, constant bit rate ATM transport service. Class A service has end-to-end timing requirements. Class A service may require stringent cell loss, cell delay and cell delay variation performance. The user chooses the desired bandwidth and the appropriate QoS in the SETUP message to establish a class A connection.

Class C service is a connection oriented, variable bit rate ATM transport service. Class C service has no end-to-end timing requirements. The user chooses the desired bandwidth and QoS with appropriate information elements in a SETUP message to establish a class C connection.

The Phase 1 Signalling specified in this document supports class X, class A and class C service. Class D service is not directly supported by signalling. It can be supported via a class X or class C connection to a connectionless server.

5.1.2.7 Support of Signalling Parameter "Request and Indication"

The Phase 1 Signalling specified in this document does not provide support for the negotiation of signalling parameters (e.g., QoS, cell transfer rate) between the users and the network. Instead, the sender chooses a value for each parameter to be sent in the connection setup request, and the receiver indicates whether or not the chosen values can be accommodated.

5.1.2.8 VPI/VPCI/VCI Support

The Phase 1 Signalling specified in this document supports the VPCI as the way of identifying the virtual path across the UNI, with the restriction that there is a one-to-one mapping between VPCI and VPI, hence values beyond 8 bits are restricted.

The following list describes the Phase 1 Signalling capabilities with respect to VPIs, VPCIs, and VCIs. The Phase 1 Signalling specified in this document:

1. provides for the identification of virtual paths (using VPCIs) and virtual connections within virtual paths (using VCIs);

2. does not (in Phase 1) include negotiations of VPCIs and/or VCIs, but does not preclude negotiation in future releases;

3. does not (in Phase 1) include provisions to negotiate or modify allowed ranges for VPCIs and/or VCIs within virtual paths but does not preclude this in future releases. (Negotiation and/or provisioning of VPCI/VCI ranges is outside the scope of the signalling protocol for Phase 1.)

155

5.1.2.9 Support of a Single Signalling Virtual Channel

The point-to-point signalling virtual channel (i.e., VCI=5, VPCI=0) will be used for all signalling in Phase 1. The association between signalling entities should be permanently established. Metasignalling is not supported in Phase 1. The broadcast signalling virtual channel is not supported.

5.1.2.10 Support of Error Recovery

The error recovery capabilities of the Phase 1 Signalling specified in this document include:

1. Detailed error handling procedures, including means for one signalling entity to inform its peer when it has encountered a non-fatal error (i.e., insufficiently severe to force call clearing); examples of non-fatal errors are message format errors, message content errors and procedural errors (e.g., messages or message contents received in a state in which they are not expected).

2. Procedures for recovery from signalling AAL reset and failure (and, by extension, from Physical layer outages and glitches).

3. Mechanisms for signalling entities to exchange state information for calls and interfaces, and to recover gracefully if there is a disagreement; these procedures must operate both in error conditions as a side-effect of (1) and on request by either signalling entity (i.e., "status enquiry").

4. Capability to force calls, VCCs, and interfaces to an idle state, either due to manual intervention or as a result of severe errors.

5. Cause and diagnostic information for fault resolution provided with call clearing (see §5.1.3), non-fatal errors, and recovery from errors affecting the whole interface.

6. Mechanisms (e.g., timers and associated procedures) to recover from loss of individual messages.

5.1.2.11 Support of Public UNI and Private UNI ATM Addressing

The Phase 1 Signalling specified in this document supports a number of ATM address formats to be used across the Public UNI and/or Private UNI to unambiguously identify the endpoints in an ATM connection. Refer to §5.1.3 and Annex A for a detailed description of the ATM address formats supported, and for guidelines on their use.

5.1.2.12 Support of a Client Registration Mechanism

This implementation agreement (see §5.8) supports a mechanism for the exchange of identifier and address information between an end system and a switch across a UNI. The basic capability allows a network administrator to manually configure ATM network address information into a switch port, without having to also configure that information into any terminal that is later attached to that port. Instead, the terminal will use the client registration mechanism to exchange its identifier information for the ATM address information configured in the switch port. The client registration mechanism allows this exchange to take place whenever, for example, the terminal is initialized, re-initialized, or reset.

At the conclusion of the client registration exchange, the terminal will have automatically acquired the ATM network address as configured by the network provider, without any requirement for the same address to have been manually provisioned into the terminal. The terminal can then use and transfer its network address as needed by higher level protocols and applications.

5.1.2.13 Support of End-to-end Compatibility Parameter Identification

On a per-connection basis the following end-to-end compatibility parameters can be specified:

1. The AAL type (e.g., Type 1, 3/4, or 5).

2. The method of protocol multiplexing (e.g., LLC vs. VC).

3. For VC-based multiplexing, the protocol which is encapsulated (e.g., any of the list of known routed protocols or bridged protocols).

4. Protocols above the network layer.

5.1.2.14 Support of Multicast Service Addresses

The use of Multicast Service Addresses is not described in this implementation agreement, but it intended to be specified when this agreement is next revised.

5.1.3 Addressing

5.1.3.1 Private Networks

For the purposes of switched virtual connections established by the procedures of this specification, an ATM private network address uniquely identifies an ATM endpoint. The format of an ATM Address for endpoints in private ATM networks is modeled after the format of an OSI Network Service Access Point, as specified in ISO 8348 and CCITT X.213; specifically, using the same structure, abstract semantics, abstract syntax, and preferred binary encoding. The structure of the low-order part (ESI and SEL) of the Domain Specific Part (DSP) is as specified in ISO 10589. Three Initial Domain Identifier (IDI) formats are specified in this implementation agreement. The structure of the ATM address with the IDI in each of these formats is illustrated in Figures 5-1a, 5-1b, and 5-1c.

> *Note 1* - In the context of OSI Network Layer addressing, an ATM private network address is a subnetwork point of attachment.

Note 2 - The technical issues surrounding addressing and routing architecture are strongly interrelated. In general, routing has implications on addressing. Further study is needed of the routing architecture.

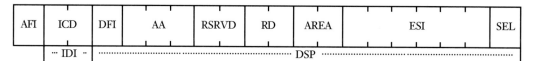

Figure 5-1a DCC ATM Format

Figure 5-1b ICD ATM Format

Figure 5-1c E.164 ATM Format

The ability of an endpoint to originate a call to any other endpoint shall be independent of the structure of the ATM address of the called system. All private networks shall be able to accept initial call setup messages containing ATM addresses with any of the IDI formats which are approved in this document, and progress the corresponding call towards the destination endpoint, if it is reachable. Selection of one of the IDI formats to be used for the addresses of endpoints attached to any particular private ATM network is beyond the scope of this implementation agreement.

In addition to the structure, abstract semantics, abstract syntax, and coding specified in this implementation agreement, endpoints and private networks may, by mutal agreement, support other forms of ATM address. However, the ATM address will always be 20 octets.

Guidelines for ATM addresses are provided in Annex A.

Each of the address fields in the formats above are specified below.

5.1.3.1.1 Authority and Format Identifier (AFI)

The Authority and Format Identifier identifies the authority allocating the Data Country Code, International Code Designator, or E.164 number; the format of the IDI, and the syntax of the remainder of the address. The length of this field is 1 octet.

The following codes are specifiemd:

AFI	Format
39	DCC ATM Format
47	ICD ATM Format
45	E.164 ATM Format

All other code values are reserved.

5.1.3.1.2 Data Country Code (DCC)

The Data Country Code specifies the country in which an address is registered. The codes are given in ISO 3166. The length of this field is two octets. The digits of the Data Country Code are encoded in Binary Code Decimal (BCD) syntax. The codes will be left justified and padded on the right with the hexadecimal value 'F' to fill the two octets.

5.1.3.1.3 International Code Designator (ICD)

The International Code Designator identifies an international organization. The registration authority for the International Code Designator is maintained by the British Standards Institute. The length of this field is two octets. The digits of the International Code Designator are encoded in Binary Coded Decimal (BCD) syntax. The codes will be left justified and padded on the right with the hexadecimal value 'F' to fill the two octets.

5.1.3.1.4 E.164 (E.164)

E.164 specifies Integrated Services Digital Network numbers. These numbers include telephone numbers. The international format of these numbers will be used. These numbers can be up to 15 digits long. The length of this field is eight octets. The digits of the E.164 number are encoded in Binary Coded Decimal (BCD) syntax. The E.164 address is padded with leading semi octet 0000 to obtain the maximum length (15 digits). Semi octet value 1111 is used as a pad after the final semi octet to obtain an integral number of octets.

5.1.3.1.5 Domain Specific Part Format Identifier (DFI)

The Domain Specific Part Format Identifier specifies the structure, semantics, and administrative requirements for the remainder of the address. The length of this field is 1 octet.

5.1.3.1.6 Administrative Authority (AA)

The value of the Administrative Authority[1] (AA) field is assigned to an organizational entity which is the administrative authority for allocation of addresses in the remainder of the DSP. This organizational entity could be, for example, an ATM service provider, the administrator of a private ATM network, or an ATM vendor.

For the ISO DCC IDI Format, the Administrative Authority (AA) is an organization identifier assigned by the ISO national member body. In the United States (IDI = '0x840f'), it is allocated and assigned by the ANSI-administered USA Registration Authority for OSI Organization Names.

For the ISO ICD IDI Format, the Administrative Authority (AA) is an organization identifier assigned by the international organization identified by the ICD.

The length of this field is 3 octets.

5.1.3.1.7 Reserved (RSRVD)

The Reserved field is reserved for future use, e.g., possible extension of the AA, RD, or Area field. The length of this field is 2 octets, and is set to zero when not used.

5.1.3.1.8 Routing Domain (RD)

The Routing Domain identifier specifies a domain that shall be unique within one of the following: E.164, DCC/DFI/AA, or ICD/DFI/AA. The length of this field is 2 octets.

5.1.3.1.9 Area (AREA)

The Area identifies a unique area within a Routing Domain. The length of this field is 2 octets.

5.1.3.1.10 End System Identifier (ESI)

The end system identifier identifies an end system within an Area. This identifier must be unique within an Area. In addition, to ensure the ability of an end system to autoconfigure its address, this end system identifier can be a globally unique identifier specified by an IEEE MAC address. The length of this field is 6 octets.

5.1.3.1.11 Selector

The selector is not used for ATM routing, but may be used by endsystems. The length of this field is 1 octet.

---

[1] Where Administrative Authority is capitalized in this document, it signifies this field in the DCC and ICD NSAP formats. If not capitalized, it is used in a generic sense.

5.1.3.2 Public Networks

The Public UNI shall support one of the following:

1. E.164 address structure:
    > Type of Number field = international
    > Numbering Plan Indication = E.164

2. Private ATM Address Structure (all 3 formats, as defined in 5.1.3.1):
    > Type of Number = Unknown
    > Numbering Plan Indication = ISO NSAP, as discussed in §5.1.3.1

3. Both

Note - E.164 numbers are covered by the following definitions:
1. E.164 numbering is defined by CCITT Recommendation E.164.
2. E.164 numbers are administered by public networks.
3. E.164 numbers uniquely identify interfaces to public networks.
4. Several E.164 numbers can identify the same interface to the public network.
5. Routing internal to public networks bases on E.164 is outside the scope of this Implementation Agreement.

5.2 Overview of Call Control

In this Implementation Agreement, the terms "incoming" and "outgoing" are used to describe the call as viewed by the user side of the interface.

This section defines the basic call control states that individual calls may have. These definitions do not apply to the state of the interface itself, any attached equipment, or the signalling virtual channel. Because several calls may exist simultaneously at a User-Network Interface, and each call may be in a different state, the state of the interface cannot be unambiguously defined.

5.2.1 ATM Call States

This section defines the basic call control states for ATM calls.

5.2.1.1 Call States at the User Side of the Interface

The states which may exist on the user side of the user-network interface are defined in this section.

5.2.1.1.1 Null (U0)

No call exists.

5.2.1.1.2 Call Initiated (U1)

This state exists for an outgoing call when the user requests call establishment from the network.

5.2.1.1.3 Outgoing Call Proceeding (U3)

This state exists for an outgoing call when the user has received acknowledgment that the network has received all call information to effect call establishment.

5.2.1.1.4 Call Delivered (U4)

Not supported in this Implementation Agreement.

5.2.1.1.5 Call Present (U6)

This state exists for an incoming call when the user has received a call establishment request but has not yet responded.

5.2.1.1.6 Call Received (U7)

Not supported in this Implementation Agreement.

5.2.1.1.7 Connect Request (U8)

This state exists for an incoming call when the user has answered the call and is waiting to be awarded the call.

5.2.1.1.8 Incoming Call Proceeding (U9)

This state exists for an incoming call when the user has sent acknowledgment that the user has received all call information necessary to effect call establishment.

5.2.1.1.9 Active (U10)

This state exists for an incoming call when the user has received an acknowledgment from the network that the user has been awarded the call. This state exists for an outgoing call when the user has received an indication that the remote user has answered the call.

5.2.1.1.10 Release Request (U11)

This state exists when the user has requested the network to clear the end-to-end connection (if any) and is waiting for a response.

5.2.1.1.11 Release Indication (U12)

This state exists when the user has received an invitation to disconnect because the network has disconnected the end-to-end connection (if any).

5.2.1.2 Call States at the Network Side of the Interface

The call states that may exist on the network side of the user-network interface are defined in this section.

5.2.1.2.1 Null (N0)

No call exists.

5.2.1.2.2 Call Initiated (N1)

This state exists for an outgoing call when the network has received a call establishment request but has not yet responded.

5.2.1.2.3 Outgoing Call Proceeding (N3)

This state exists for an outgoing call when the network has sent acknowledgment that the network has received all call information to effect call establishment.

5.2.1.2.4 Call Delivered (N4)

Not supported in this Implementation Agreement.

5.2.1.2.5 Call Present (N6)

This state exists for an incoming call when the network has sent a call establishment request but not yet received a satisfactory response.

5.2.1.2.6 Call Received (N7)

Not supported in this Implementation Agreement.

5.2.1.2.7 Connect Request (N8)

This state exists for an incoming call when the network has received an answer but the network has not yet awarded the call.

5.2.1.2.8 Incoming Call Proceeding (N9)

This state exists for an incoming call when the network has received acknowledgment that the user has received all call information necessary to effect call establishment.

5.2.1.2.9 Active (N10)

This state exists for an incoming call when the network has awarded the call to the called user. This state exists for an outgoing call when the network has indicated that the remote user has answered the call.

5.2.1.2.10 Release Request (N11)

This state exists when the network has received a request from the user to clear the end-to-end connection (if any).

5.2.1.2.11 Release Indication (N12)

This state exists when the network has disconnected the end-to-end connection (if any) and has sent an invitation to disconnect the user-network connection.

5.2.1.2.12 Call Abort (N22)

Not supported in this Implementation Agreement.

5.2.2 ATM Call States Relating to Interworking Requirements

Not supported in this Implementation Agreement.

5.2.3 States Associated with the Global Call Reference

This section defines the states that the protocol may adopt using the global call reference. The procedures for use of the global call reference for restart procedures are contained in §5.5.5.

There is only one global call reference per interface.

5.2.3.1 Call States at the User Side of the Interface

The states which may exist on the user side of the user-network interface are defined in this section.

5.2.3.1.1 Null (Rest 0)

No transaction exists.

5.2.3.1.2 Restart Request (Rest 1)

This state exists for a restart transaction when the user has sent a restart request but has not yet received an acknowledgment response from the network.

5.2.3.1.3 Restart (Rest 2)

This state exists when a request for a restart has been received from the network and responses have not yet been received from all locally active call references.

5.2.3.2 Call States at the Network Side of the Interface

The states which may exist on the network side of the user-network interface are defined in this section.

5.2.3.2.1 Null (Rest 0)

No transaction exists.

5.2.3.2.2 Restart Request (Rest 1)

This state exists for a restart transaction when the network has sent a restart request but has not yet received an acknowledgment response from the user.

5.2.3.2.3 Restart (Rest 2)

This state exists when a request for a restart has been received from the user and a response has not yet been received from all locally active call references.

5.3 Message Functional Definitions and Contents

This section provides an overview of the message structure, which highlights the functional definitions and information content (i.e., semantics) of each message. Each definition includes:

1. A brief description of the message direction and use, including whether the message has:

   a) Local significance, i.e., relevant only in the originating or terminating access;

   b) Access significance, i.e., relevant in the originating and terminating access, but not in the network;

   c) Dual significance, i.e., relevant in either the originating or terminating access and in the network; or

   d) Global significance, i.e., relevant in the originating and terminating access and in the network.

   Note - Messages of access significance and dual significance are not supported in this Implementation Agreement

2. A table listing the codeset 0 (ITU-TS [CCITT] standardized) information elements. For each information element the table indicates:

   a) the section of this Implementation Agreement describing the information element;

   b) the direction in which it may be sent; i.e., user to network ('u -> n'), network to user ('n -> u'), or both;

Note - The user-network terminology in this section refers to the interface structures between ATM terminal equipment and ATM public or private network (TE-LCRF/CN) and between ATM customer network and ATM public network (CN-LCRF); the terms TE, CN, and LCRF being used as defined in CCITT Recommendation I.327.

c) whether inclusion is mandatory ('M') or optional ('O'), with a reference to notes explaining the circumstances under which the information element shall be included; and

d) the length of the information element (or permissible range of lengths), in octets.

3. Further explanatory notes, as necessary.

5.3.1 Messages for ATM point-to-point call and connection control

Table 5-2 summarizes the messages for ATM point-to-point call and connection control.

Table 5-2 Messages for ATM Call and Connection Control

Message	Reference
Call establishment messages:	
CALL PROCEEDING	5.3.1.2
CONNECT	5.3.1.3
CONNECT ACKNOWLEDGE	5.3.1.4
SETUP	5.3.1.7
Call clearing messages:	
RELEASE	5.3.1.5
RELEASE COMPLETE	5.3.1.6
Miscellaneous messages:	
STATUS	5.3.1.8
STATUS ENQUIRY	5.3.1.9

5.3.1.1 ALERTING

Not supported in this Implementation Agreement.

5.3.1.2 CALL PROCEEDING

This message is sent by the called user to the network or by the network to the calling user to indicate that the requested call establishment has been initiated and no more call establishment information will be accepted.

The sending of this message is optional; the receiving of this message is required (see §5.5.)

Message Type: CALL PROCEEDING
Significance: local
Direction: both

Information Element	Reference	Direction	Type	Length
Protocol discriminator	5.4.2	both	M	1
Call reference	5.4.3	both	M	4
Message type	5.4.4.1	both	M	2
Message length	5.4.4.2	both	M	2
Connection identifier	5.4.5.16	both	$O^{(1)}$	4-9
Endpoint reference	5.4.8.1	both	$O^{(2)}$	4-7

Note 1 - Mandatory in the network-to-user direction if this message is the first message in response to a SETUP message. It's mandatory in the user-to-network direction if this message is the first response to a SETUP message, unless the user accepts the connection identifier indicated in the SETUP message.

Note 2 - Mandatory if an Endpoint reference was included in the SETUP message.

Figure 5-2 CALL PROCEEDING Message Contents

5.3.1.3 CONNECT

This message is sent by the called user to the network and by the network to the calling user to indicate call acceptance by the called user.

Message Type: CONNECT
Significance: global
Direction: both

Information Element	Reference	Direction	Type	Length
Protocol discriminator	5.4.2	both	M	1
Call reference	5.4.3	both	M	4
Message type	5.4.4.1	both	M	2
Message length	5.4.4.2	both	M	2
AAL parameters	5.4.5.5	both	O(1)	4-11
Broadband low layer information	5.4.5.9	both	O(2)	4-17
Connection identifier	5.4.5.16	both	O(3)	4-9
Endpoint reference	5.4.8.1	both	O(4)	4-7

Note 1 - Included in the user to network direction when the called user wants to pass ATM adaptation layer parameters information to the calling user, and the ATM adaptation layer parameters information element was present in the SETUP message. Included in the network to user direction if the called user included an ATM adaptation layer parameters information element in the CONNECT message. The ATM adaptation layer parameters information element shall not be present when the endpoint reference information element was present in the SETUP message and contained a non-zero value.

Note 2 - Included in the user-to-network direction when the answering user wants to return low layer information to the calling user. Included in the network-to-user direction if the user awarded the call included a Broadband low layer information element in the CONNECT message. Optionally included for Broadband low layer information negotiation, but some networks may not transport this information element to the calling user (see Annex C).

Note 3 - Mandatory in the network-to-user direction if this message is the first message in response to a SETUP message. It's mandatory in the user-to-network direction if this message is the first response to a SETUP message, unless the user accepts the connection identifier indicated in the SETUP message.

Note 4 - Mandatory if the Endpoint reference was included in the SETUP message.

Figure 5-3 CONNECT Message Contents

5.3.1.4 CONNECT ACKNOWLEDGE

This message is sent by the network to the called user to indicate the user has been awarded the call. It is also sent by the calling user to the network to allow symmetrical call control procedures.

Message Type: CONNECT ACKNOWLEDGE
Significance: local
Direction: both

Information Element	Reference	Direction	Type	Length
Protocol discriminator	5.4.2	both	M	1
Call reference	5.4.3	both	M	4
Message type	5.4.4.1	both	M	2
Message length	5.4.4.2	both	M	2

Figure 5-4 CONNECT ACKNOWLEDGE Message Contents

5.3.1.5 RELEASE

This message is sent by the user to request the network to clear the end-to-end connection (if any) or is sent by the network to indicate that the end-to-end connection is cleared and that the receiving equipment should release the virtual channel and prepare to release the call reference after sending a RELEASE COMPLETE.

Message Type: RELEASE
Significance: global
Direction: both

Information Element	Reference	Direction	Type	Length
Protocol discriminator	5.4.2	both	M	1
Call reference	5.4.3	both	M	4
Message type	5.4.4.1	both	M	2
Message length	5.4.4.2	both	M	2
Cause	5.4.5.15	both	M	6-34

Figure 5-5 RELEASE message content

5.3.1.6 RELEASE COMPLETE

This message is sent by the user or the network to indicate that the equipment sending the message has released the virtual channel (if any) and call reference, the virtual channel is available for reuse, and the receiving equipment shall release the call reference.

Message Type: RELEASE COMPLETE
Significance: local [1]
Direction: both

Information Element	Reference	Direction	Type	Length
Protocol discriminator	5.4.2	both	M	1
Call reference	5.4.3	both	M	4
Message type	5.4.4.1	both	M	2
Message length	5.4.4.2	both	M	2
Cause	5.4.5.15	both	O[2]	4-34

Note 1 - This message has local significance; however, it may carry information of global significance when used as the first call clearing message.

Note 2 - Mandatory in the first call clearing message; including when the RELEASE COMPLETE message is sent as a result of an error condition.

Figure 5-6 RELEASE COMPLETE message content

5.3.1.7 SETUP

This message is sent by the calling user to the network and by the network to the called user to initiate call establishment.

Message Type: SETUP
Significance: global
Direction: both

Information Element	Reference	Direction	Type	Length
Protocol discriminator	5.4.2	both	M	1
Call reference	5.4.3	both	M	4
Message type	5.4.4.1	both	M	2
Message length	5.4.4.2	both	M	2
AAL parameters	5.4.5.5	both	O[1]	4-20
ATM user cell rate	5.4.5.6	both	M	12-30
Broadband bearer capability	5.4.5.7	both	M	6-7
Broadband high layer information	5.4.5.8	both	O[2]	4-13
Broadband repeat indicator	5.4.5.19	both	O[3]	4-5
Broadband low layer information	5.4.5.9	both	O[4]	4-17
Called party number	5.4.5.11	both	M	[5]
Called party subaddress	5.4.5.12	both	O[6]	4-25
Calling party number	5.4.5.13	both	O[7]	4-26
Calling party subaddress	5.4.5.14	both	O[8]	4-25
Connection identifier	5.4.5.16	N -> U	M	9
QoS parameter	5.4.5.18	both	M	6
Broadband sending complete	5.4.5.21	both	O[9]	4-5
Transit network selection	5.4.5.22	U -> N	O[10]	4-8
Endpoint reference	5.4.8.1	both	O[11]	4-7

Note 1 - Included in the user-to-network direction when the calling user wants to pass ATM adaptation layer parameters information to the called user. Included in the network-to-user direction if the calling user included an ATM adaptation layer parameters information element in the SETUP message.

Note 2 - Included in the user-to-network direction when the calling user wants to pass broadband high layer information to the called user. Included in the network-to-user direction if the calling user included a Broadband high layer information information element in the SETUP message.

Note 3 - Included when two or more Broadband low layer information information elements are included for Broadband low layer information negotiation.

Note 4 - Included in the user-to-network direction when the calling user wants to pass broadband low layer information to the called user. Included in the network-to-user direction if the calling user included a Broadband low layer information information element in the SETUP message. Two or three information elements may be included in descending order of priority, i.e., highest priority first, if the Broadband low layer information negotiation procedures are used (see Annex C).

Note 5 - Minimum length depends on the numbering plan. Maximum length is 25 octets.

Note 6 - Included in the user-to-network direction when the calling user wants to indicate the called party subaddress. Included in the network-to-user direction if the calling user included a Called party subaddress information element in the SETUP message.

Note 7 - May be included by the calling user or by the network to identify the calling user.

Note 8 - Included in the user-to-network direction when the calling user wants to indicate the calling party subaddress. Included in the network-to-user direction if the calling user included a Calling party subaddress information element in the SETUP message.

Note 9 - It is optional for the user to include the Broadband sending complete information element when enbloc sending procedures (i.e., complete address information is included) are used; its interpretation by the network is optional. It is optional for the network to include the Broadband sending complete information element when enbloc receiving procedures (i.e., complete address information is included) are used.

Note 10 - Included by the calling user to select a particular transit network (see Annex D.)

Note 11 - Not used for point-to-point connection establishment. Must be included in SETUP messages involved in point-to-multipoint connection establishment.

Figure 5-7 SETUP message content

5.3.1.8 STATUS

This message is sent by the user or the network in response to a STATUS ENQUIRY message or at any time to report certain error conditions listed in §5.5.

Message type: STATUS
Significance: local
Direction: both

Information Element	Reference	Direction	Type	Length
Protocol discriminator	5.4.2	both	M	1
Call reference	5.4.3	both	M	4
Message type	5.4.4.1	both	M	2
Message length	5.4.4.2	both	M	2
Call state	5.4.5.10	both	M	5
Cause	5.4.5.15	both	M	6-34
Endpoint reference	5.4.8.1	both	$O^{(1)}$	4-7
Endpoint state	5.4.8.2	both	$O^{(2)}$	4-5

Note 1 - Included when responding to a status enquiry about a party state or at any time to report certain error conditions in the point-to-multipoint procedures.

Note 2 - Included when the Endpoint reference information element is included.

Figure 5-8 STATUS message content

5.3.1.9 STATUS ENQUIRY

The STATUS ENQUIRY message is sent by the user or the network at any time to solicit a STATUS message from the peer layer 3 entity. Sending a STATUS message in response to a STATUS ENQUIRY message is mandatory.

Message type: STATUS ENQUIRY
Significance: local
Direction: both

Information Element	Reference	Direction	Type	Length
Protocol discriminator	5.4.2	both	M	1
Call reference	5.4.3	both	M	4
Message type	5.4.4.1	both	M	2
Message length	5.4.4.2	both	M	2
Endpoint reference	5.4.8.1	both	$O^{(1)}$	4-7

Note 1 - Included when enquiring about a party state in the point-to-multipoint procedures.

Figure 5-9 STATUS ENQUIRY message content

5.3.2 Messages for the Support of 64 kbit/s based ISDN Circuit Mode Services

Not supported in this Implementation Agreement.

5.3.3 Messages Related to Release 1 Supplementary Services

Not supported in this Implementation Agreement.

5.3.4 Messages Used with the Global Call Reference

Table 5-3 Messages Used with the Global Call Reference

Message	Reference
RESTART	5.3.4.1
RESTART ACKNOWLEDGE	5.3.4.2
STATUS	5.3.1.8

5.3.4.1 RESTART

This message is sent by the user or the network to request the recipient to restart (i.e., release all resources associated with) the indicated virtual channel or all virtual channels controlled by the Signalling Virtual Channel.

Message type: RESTART
Significance: local
Direction: both

Information Element	Reference	Direction	Type	Length
Protocol discriminator	5.4.2	both	M	1
Call reference	5.4.3	both	M[1]	4
Message type	5.4.4.1	both	M	2
Message length	5.4.4.2	both	M	2
Connection identifier	5.4.5.16	both	O[2]	4-9
Restart indicator	5.4.5.20	both	M	5

Note 1 - This message is sent with the global call reference defined in §5.4.3.

Note 2 - Included when necessary to indicate the particular virtual channel to be restarted.

Figure 5-10 RESTART message content

5.3.4.2 RESTART ACKNOWLEDGE

This message is sent to acknowledge the receipt of a RESTART message and to indicate that the requested restart is complete.

Message type: RESTART ACKNOWLEDGE
Significance: local
Direction: both

Information Element	Reference	Direction	Type	Length
Protocol discriminator	5.4.2	both	M	1
Call reference	5.4.3	both	M[1]	4
Message type	5.4.4.1	both	M	2
Message length	5.4.4.2	both	M	2
Connection identifier	5.4.5.16	both	O[2]	4-9
Restart indicator	5.4.5.20	both	M	5

Note 1 - This message is sent with the global call reference defined in §5.4.3.

Note 2 - Included when necessary to indicate the particular virtual channel which has been restarted.

Figure 5-11 RESTART ACKNOWLEDGE message content

5.3.5 Messages for Point-to-multipoint call and connection control

Table 5-4 Messages Used with ATM Point-to-multipoint call and connection control

Message	Reference
ADD PARTY	5.3.5.1
ADD PARTY ACKNOWLEDGE	5.3.5.2
ADD PARTY REJECT	5.3.5.3
DROP PARTY	5.3.5.4
DROP PARTY ACKNOWLEDGE	5.3.5.5

5.3.5.1 ADD PARTY

This message is sent to add a party to an existing connection (see §5.6).

Message type: ADD PARTY
Significance: global
Direction: both

Information Element	Reference	Direction	Type	Length
Protocol discriminator	5.4.2	both	M	1
Call reference	5.4.3	both	M	4
Message type	5.4.4.1	both	M	2
Message length	5.4.4.2	both	M	2
AAL parameters	5.4.5.5	both	$O^{(1)}$	4-20
Broadband high layer information	5.4.5.8	both	$O^{(2)}$	4-13
Broadband low layer information	5.4.5.9	both	$O^{(3)}$	4-17
Called party number	5.4.5.11	both	M	(4)
Called party subaddress	5.4.5.12	both	$O^{(5)}$	4-25
Calling party number	5.4.5.13	both	$O^{(6)}$	4-26
Calling party subaddress	5.4.5.14	both	$O^{(7)}$	4-25
Broadband sending complete	5.4.5.21	both	$O^{(8)}$	4-5
Transit network selection	5.4.5.22	U->N	$O^{(9)}$	4-8
Endpoint Reference	5.4.8.1	both	$M^{(10)}$	7

Note 1 - Included in the user-to-network direction when the calling user wants to pass ATM adaptation layer parameters information to the called user. Included in the network-to-user direction if the calling user included an ATM adaptation layer parameters information element in the ADD PARTY message. Must be the same as in the initial SETUP of the call, but is not checked by the network.

Note 2 - Included in the user-to-network direction when the calling user wants to pass broadband high layer information to the called user. Included in the network-to-user direction if the calling user included a Broadband high layer information information element in the ADD PARTY message. Must be the same as in the initial SETUP of the call, but is not checked by the network.

Note 3 - Included in the user-to-network direction when the calling user wants to pass broadband low layer information to the called user. Included in the network-to-user direction if the calling user included a Broadband low layer information information element in the ADD PARTY message. Must be the same as the one negotiated during the initial SETUP of the call, but is not checked by the network. Only one Broadband low layer information information element is permitted in the ADD PARTY message.

Note 4 - Minimum length depends on the numbering plan. Maximum length is 25 octets.

Note 5 - Included in the user-to-network direction when the calling user wants to indicate the called party subaddress. Included in the network-to-user direction if the calling user included a Called Party Subaddress information element in the ADD PARTY message.

Note 6 - May be included by the calling user, or by the network to identify the calling user.

Note 7 - Included in the user-to-network direction when the calling user wants to indicate the calling party subaddress. Included in the network-to-user direction if the calling user included a Calling Party Subaddress information element in the ADD PARTY message.

Note 8 - It is optional for the user to include the Broadband sending complete information element when enbloc sending procedures (i.e., complete address information is included) are used; its interpretation by the network is optional. It is optional for the network to include the Broadband sending complete information element when enblock receiving (i.e., complete address information is included) are used.

Note 9 - Included by the calling user to select a particular transit network (see Annex D.)

Note 10 - The endpoint reference must be unique within a given call reference on a given link.

Figure 5-12 ADD PARTY message content

5.3.5.2 ADD PARTY ACKNOWLEDGE

This message is sent to acknowledge that the ADD PARTY request was successful.

Message type: ADD PARTY ACKNOWLEDGE
Significance: global
Direction: both

Information Element	Reference	Direction	Type	Length
Protocol discriminator	5.4.2	both	M	1
Call reference	5.4.3	both	M	4
Message type	5.4.4.1	both	M	2
Message length	5.4.4.2	both	M	2
Endpoint reference	5.4.8.1	both	M[(1)]	7

Note 1 - The endpoint reference must be the same value as in the ADD PARTY message being responded to.

Figure 5-13 ADD PARTY ACKNOWLEDGE message content

5.3.5.3 ADD PARTY REJECT

This message is sent to acknowledge that the ADD PARTY request was not successful.

Message type: ADD PARTY REJECT
Significance: global
Direction: both

Information Element	Reference	Direction	Type	Length
Protocol discriminator	5.4.2	both	M	1
Call reference	5.4.3	both	M	4
Message type	5.4.4.1	both	M	2
Message length	5.4.4.2	both	M	2
Cause	5.4.5.15	both	M	6-34
Endpoint reference	5.4.8.1	both	M[(1)]	7

Note 1 - The endpoint reference must be the same value as in the ADD PARTY message being responded to.

Figure 5-14 ADD PARTY REJECT message content

5.3.5.4 DROP PARTY

This message is sent to drop (clear) a party from an existing point-to-multipoint connection.

Message type: DROP PARTY
Significance: global
Direction: both

Information Element	Reference	Direction	Type	Length
Protocol discriminator	5.4.2	both	M	1
Call reference	5.4.3	both	M	4
Message type	5.4.4.1	both	M	2
Message length	5.4.4.2	both	M	2
Cause	5.4.5.15	both	M	6-34
Endpoint reference	5.4.8.1	both	M	7

Figure 5-15 DROP PARTY message content

5.3.5.5 DROP PARTY ACKNOWLEDGE

This message is sent in response to a DROP PARTY message to indicate that the party was dropped from the connection.

Message type: DROP PARTY ACKNOWLEDGE
Significance: local
Direction: both

Information Element	Reference	Direction	Type	Length
Protocol discriminator	5.4.2	both	M	1
Call reference	5.4.3	both	M	4
Message type	5.4.4.1	both	M	2
Message length	5.4.4.2	both	M	2
Cause	5.4.5.15	both	O[1]	4-34
Endpoint reference	5.4.8.1	both	M	7

Note 1 - Mandatory when DROP PARTY ACKNOWLEDGE is sent as a result of an error condition.

Figure 5-16 DROP PARTY ACKNOWLEDGE message content

5.4 General Message Format and Information Element Coding

The figures and text in this section describe message contents.

5.4.1 Overview

Within this protocol, every message shall consist of the following parts:

    a) protocol discriminator;

    b) call reference;

    c) message type;

    d) message length;

    e) variable length information elements, as required.

Information elements a), b), c), and d) are common to all the messages and shall always be present, while information element e) is specific to each message type.

This organization is illustrated in the example shown in Figure 5-17.

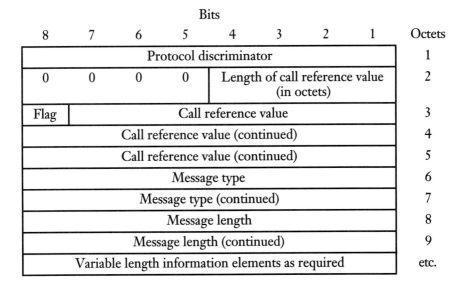

				Bits				
8	7	6	5	4	3	2	1	Octets
Protocol discriminator								1
0	0	0	0	Length of call reference value (in octets)				2
Flag	Call reference value							3
Call reference value (continued)								4
Call reference value (continued)								5
Message type								6
Message type (continued)								7
Message length								8
Message length (continued)								9
Variable length information elements as required								etc.

Figure 5-17 General Message Organization Example

A particular message may contain more information than a particular (user or network) equipment needs or can understand. All equipment shall be able to ignore any extra information, present in a message, which is not required for the proper operation of that equipment. For example, a user may ignore the calling party number if that number is of no interest to the user when a SETUP message is received.

Unless specified otherwise, a particular information element may be present only once in a given message.

The term "default" implies that the value defined should be used in the absence of any assignment, or the negotiation of alternative values.

When a field, such as the message length, extends over more than one octet, the order of bit values progressively decreases as the octet number increases. The least significant bit of the field is represented by the lowest numbered bit of the highest-numbered octet of the field.

5.4.2 Protocol Discriminator

The purpose of the protocol discriminator is to distinguish messages for user-network call control from other messages (to be defined) within this Implementation Agreement. It also distinguishes messages of this Implementation Agreement from those OSI network layer protocol units which are coded to other CCITT and ITU-TS Recommendations and other standards.

The protocol discriminator is the first part of every message. The protocol discriminator is coded according to Figure 5-18.

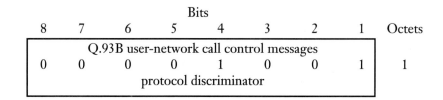

Figure 5-18 Protocol Discriminator

Bits 8 7 6 5 4 3 2 1	Meaning
0 0 0 0 0 0 0 0 through 0 0 0 0 0 1 1 1	) assigned in §4.5.30/Q.931; not available for use in the) message protocol discriminator)
0 0 0 0 1 0 0 0	Q.931/(I.451) user-network call control messages
0 0 0 0 1 0 0 1	Q.93B user-network call control messages
0 0 0 1 0 0 0 0 through 0 0 1 1 1 1 1 1	) reserved for other network layer or layer 3 protocols,) including Recommendation X.25 (Note))
0 1 0 0 0 0 0 0 through 0 1 0 0 1 1 1 1	)) national use)
0 1 0 1 0 0 0 0 through 1 1 1 1 1 1 1 0	) reserved for other network layer or layer) 3 protocols, including Recommendation X.25 (Note))

All other values are reserved

Note - These values are reserved to discriminate these protocol discriminators from the
first octet of a Recommendation X.25 packet including general format identifier.

5.4.3 Call Reference

The purpose of the call reference is to identify the call at the local user-network interface to
which the particular message applies. The call reference does not have end-to-end significance
across ATM networks.

The call reference is the second part of every message. The call reference is coded as shown
in Figure 5-19. The length of the call reference value is indicated in octet 1, bits 1-4. The
length of the call reference information element is four octets long. The actions taken by the
receiver are based on the numerical value of the call reference and are independent of the
length of the call reference information element.

The call reference information element includes the call reference value and the call
reference flag.

Call reference values are assigned by the originating side of the interface for a call. These
values are unique to the originating side only within a particular signalling virtual channel.
The call reference value is assigned at the beginning of a call and remains fixed for the

lifetime of a call. After a call ends, the associated call reference value may be reassigned to a later call. Two identical call reference values on the same signalling virtual channel may be used when each value pertains to a call originated at opposite ends of the signalling virtual channel.

> Note - To avoid race conditions in certain SAAL error scenarios, it is suggested that implementors avoid immediate reuse of the call reference values after they are released.

The call reference flag can take the values "0" or "1". The call reference flag is used to identify which end of the signalling virtual channel originated a call reference. The origination side always sets the call reference flag to "0". The destination side always sets the call reference flag to a "1".

Hence the call reference flag identifies who allocated the call reference value and the only purpose of the call reference flag is to resolve simultaneous attempts to allocate the same call reference value. The call reference flag also applies to functions which use the global call reference (e.g., restart procedures).

> Note - The numerical value of the global call reference is zero. The equipment receiving a message containing the global call reference should interpret the message as pertaining to all call references associated with the appropriate signalling virtual channel. See Figure 5-20.

				Bits				
8	7	6	5	4	3	2	1	Octets
0	0	0	0	Length of call reference value (in octets) 0 0 1 1				1
flag	Call reference value							2
Call reference value (continued)								3
Call reference value (continued)								4

Call reference flag (octet 2)

Bit 8	Meaning
0	the message is sent from the side that originates the call reference.
1	the message is sent to the side that originates the call reference.

Figure 5-19 Call Reference Information Element

Bits								Octets
8	7	6	5	4	3	2	1	

					Length of call reference value			
0	0	0	0	0	0 1		1	1
0/1 flag	0	0	0	0	0	0	0	2
0	0	0	0	0	0	0	0	3
0	0	0	0	0	0	0	0	4

Figure 5-20 Encoding for Global Call Reference

5.4.4 Message Type and Message Length

5.4.4.1 Message Type

The purpose of the message type is to identify the function of the message being sent and to allow the sender of a message to indicate explicitly the way the receiver should handle unrecognized messages.

The message type is the third part of every message. The message type is coded as shown in Figure 5-21.

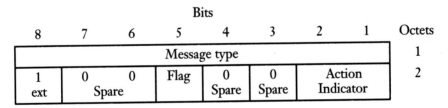

Bits								Octets
8	7	6	5	4	3	2	1	
Message type								1
1 ext	0 Spare	0	Flag	0 Spare	0 Spare	Action Indicator		2

Figure 5-21 Message Type

Message Type (Octet 1)

Bits 8 7 6 5	4 3 2 1	Meaning
0 0 0 -	- - - -	Call establishment messages:
0	0 0 1 0	CALL PROCEEDING
0	0 1 1 1	CONNECT
0	1 1 1 1	CONNECT ACKNOWLEDGE
0	0 1 0 1	SETUP
0 1 0 -	- - - -	Call clearing messages:
0	1 1 0 1	RELEASE
1	1 0 1 0	RELEASE COMPLETE
0	0 1 1 0	RESTART
0	1 1 1 0	RESTART ACKNOWLEDGE
0 1 1 -	- - - -	Miscellaneous messages:
1	1 1 0 1	STATUS
1	0 1 0 1	STATUS ENQUIRY
1 0 0 -	- - - -	Point-to-Multipoint messages:
0	0 0 0 0	ADD PARTY
0	0 0 0 1	ADD PARTY ACKNOWLEDGE
0	0 0 1 0	ADD PARTY REJECT
0	0 0 1 1	DROP PARTY
0	0 1 0 0	DROP PARTY ACKNOWLEDGE

Flag (Octet 2) (Note 1)

Bit 5	Meaning
0	Message instruction field not significant (regular error handling procedures apply)
1	Follow explicit instructions (supersedes regular error handling procedures)

Action Indicator (Octet 2) (Note 1)

Bits 2 1	Meaning
0 0	Clear call
0 1	Discard and ignore
1 0	Discard and report status
1 1	Reserved

Note 1 - For this Implementation Agreement, the Flag field (bit 5) and Action Indicator field (bits 2-1) shall be coded to zero. If any other codings are received, the following procedures apply:

- If the Flag field is set to zero, the receiving entity shall ignore the content of the Action Indicator field.

- If the Flag field is set to one, the receiving entity shall either treat the message as if the Flag field is coded to zero or shall follow the explicit instruction in the Action Indicator field.

5.4.4.2 Message Length

The purpose of the message length is to identify the length of the contents of a message. It is the binary coding of the number of octets of the message contents, excluding the octets used for "protocol discriminator", "call reference", "message type" and for the message length indication itself.

If the message contains no further octets, the message length value is coded to all "0's".

The message length is the fourth information element of every message. The message length is a 16-bit value, coded as shown in Figure 5-22.

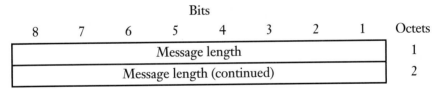

Figure 5-22 Message Length

5.4.5 Variable Length Information Elements

5.4.5.1 Coding Rules

The coding of variable length information elements follows the coding rules described below. These rules are formulated to allow each equipment which processes a message to find information elements important to it, and yet remain ignorant of information elements not important to that equipment.

For the information elements listed below, the coding of the information element identifier bits is summarized in Table 5-5 and Figure 5-23.

The descriptions of the information elements in this section are organized in alphabetical order.

The specific variable length information elements within a message may appear in any order except for the following:

    a.   If information elements are repeated without using the Broadband repeat indicator information element, the following rules applies: The second occurrence of a repeated information element must immediately follow the first occurrence of the repeated information element. The third occurrence of a repeated information element must immediately follow the second occurrence of the repeated information element. Etc.

    b.   When information elements are repeated and the Broadband repeat indicator information element is used, the following rules apply:

        -   The Broadband repeat indicator must immediately precede the first occurrence of the repeated information element.

        -   The first occurrence of the repeated information element (immediately following the Broadband repeat indicator) is interpreted as the highest priority. The second, third, fourth, etc., occurrences of the repeated information element are interpreted in descending order of priority.

        -   The second occurrence of the repeated information element must immediately follow the first occurrence of the repeated information element. The third occurrence of the repeated information element must immediately follow the second occurrence of the repeated information element. Etc.

    c.   Repetition rules with respect to locking shift are not supported in this Implementation Agreement. See §5.4.5.3.

    d.   Repetition rules with respect to non-locking shift are not supported in this Implementation Agreement. See §5.4.5.4.

Where the description of information elements in this Implementation Agreement contains spare bits, these bits are indicated as being set to "0". In order to allow compatibility with future implementation, messages should not be rejected simply because a spare bit is set to "1".

The second octet group of an information element contains the information element compatibility instruction indicator. The coding of the information element compatibility instruction indicator is shown in Table 5-6.

The third octet group of an information element indicates the length of that information element. The length of an information element does not include the length of the information element identifier field, the length of the information element compatibility instruction indicator, or the length of the length field itself. The information element length indication has a fixed length of 2 octets (16 bit value). The coding of the information element length follows the coding rules for integer values described in item g) below.

An optional information element may be present, but empty. For example, a SETUP message may contain a calling party number information element, the content of which is of zero length. This should be interpreted by the receiver as equivalent to that information element being absent. Similarly, an absent information element should be interpreted by the receiver as equivalent to that information element being empty.

An empty information element is an information element that satisfies the following conditions: has a valid information element identifier and has an information element length set to 0.

The following rules apply for the coding of information elements (octets 5, etc.):

a) The first digit in the octet number identifies one octet or a group of octets.

b) Each octet group is a self contained entity. The internal structure of an octet group may be defined in alternative ways.

c) An octet group is formed by using some extension mechanism. The preferred extension mechanism is to extend an octet (N) through the next octet(s) (Na, Nb, etc.) by using bit 8 in each octet as an extension bit. The bit value "0" indicates that the octet group continues through the next octet. The bit value "1" indicates that this octet is the last octet. If one octet (Nb) is present, also the preceding octets (N and Na) must be present.

   In the format descriptions appearing in §5.4.5.5, etc., bit 8 is marked:

   "0 ext"   if another octet of this octet group always follows,
   "1 ext"   if this is the last octet in this group,
   "0/1 ext"   if other octets of this group may or may not follow.

   Additional octets may be defined later ("1 ext" changed to "0/1 ext") and equipment shall be prepared to receive such additional octets although the equipment need not be able to interpret or act upon the content of these octets.

d) In addition to the extension mechanism defined above, an octet (N) may be extended through the next octet(s) (N.1, N.2, etc.) by indications in bits 7-1 (of octet N).

e) The mechanisms in c) and d) may be combined.

f) Optional octets are marked with asterisks (*).

g) Unless specified otherwise, integers are coded such that the Most Significant Bit (MSB) is placed in the highest order bit (excluding the extension bit, if used) in the first octet containing the integer (e.g., bit 8, octet 1 for Message Length), and the Least Significant Bit is placed in the lowest order bit in the last octet containing the integer (e.g., bit 1, octet 2 for Message Length). Where integer values are represented by a variable number of octets (e.g., by using bit 8 as an extension mechanism), the integer value shall be coded with a minimum number of octets (i.e., no leading all-zero octets are present).

Note 1 - It is not possible to use mechanism c) repeatedly, i.e., it is not possible to construct an octet 4aa as this would become octet 4b.

Note 2 - Protocol designers should exercise care in using multiple extension mechanisms to insure that a unique interpretation of the resultant coding is possible.

Note 3 - For all information elements there is a field that defines the coding standard. When the coding standard defines a national standard it is recommended that the national standard be structured similar to the information element defined in ITU-T draft Recommendation Q.93B [29].

Table 5-5 Information Element Identifier Coding (Codeset 0)

Bits 8 7 6 5	4 3 2 1	Information Element	Section Reference	Max Length	Max no. of occurrences
0 0 0 0	1 0 0 0	Cause[1]	5.4.5.15	34	2
0 0 0 1	0 1 0 0	Call state	5.4.5.10	5	1
0 1 0 1	0 1 0 0	Endpoint reference	5.4.8.1	7	1
0 1 0 1	0 1 0 1	Endpoint state	5.4.8.2	5	1
0 1 0 1	1 0 0 0	ATM adaptation layer parameters	5.4.5.5	20	1
0 1 0 1	1 0 0 1	ATM user cell rate	5.4.5.6	30	1
0 1 0 1	1 0 1 0	Connection identifier	5.4.5.16	9	1
0 1 0 1	1 1 0 0	Quality of service parameter	5.4.5.18	6	1
0 1 0 1	1 1 0 1	Broadband high layer information	5.4.5.8	13	1
0 1 0 1	1 1 1 0	Broadband bearer capability	5.4.5.7	7	1
0 1 0 1	1 1 1 1	Broadband low-layer information[2]	5.4.5.9	17	3
0 1 1 0	0 0 0 0	Broadband locking shift	5.4.5.3	5	-
0 1 1 0	0 0 0 1	Broadband non-locking shift	5.4.5.4	5	-
0 1 1 0	0 0 1 0	Broadband sending complete	5.4.5.21	5	1
0 1 1 0	0 0 1 1	Broadband repeat indicator	5.4.5.19	5	1
0 1 1 0	1 1 0 0	Calling party number	5.4.5.13	26	1
0 1 1 0	1 1 0 1	Calling party subaddress	5.4.5.14	25	1
0 1 1 1	0 0 0 0	Called party number	5.4.5.11	25	1
0 1 1 1	0 0 0 1	Called party subaddress	5.4.5.12	25	1
0 1 1 1	1 0 0 0	Transit network selection	5.4.5.22	8[3]	1
0 1 1 1	1 0 0 1	Restart indicator	5.4.5.20	5	1

Note 1 - This information element may be repeated without the Broadband repeat indicator information element.

Note 2 - This information element may be repeated in conjunction with the Broadband repeat indicator information element.

Note 3 - The Transit network selection information element will be expanded to 9 octets to allow for the planned expansion of Carrier Identification Codes (CICs) in the first half of 1995. Carrier Identification Codes (CICs) are currently 3 digits in length. The length of CICs will be expanded to 4 digits in 1995.

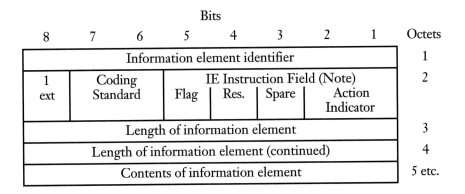

Figure 5-23 General Information Element Format

Note - The IE instruction field (Bits 5-1 of octet 2) is only interpreted in case of unrecognized information element identifier or unrecognized information element contents. For the information elements in this Implementation Agreement, the allocation of values to the IE instruction field is restricted (see Table 5-6).

The ITU-TS standardized escape for extension mechanism for the information element identifier (octet 1) is not supported in this Implementation Agreement.

Table 5-6 General Information Element Format

Coding Standard (octet 2) (Note 1)

Bits 7 6	Meaning
0 0	ITU-TS (CCITT) standardized
1 1	Standard defined for the network (either public or private) present on the network side of the interface. (Note 2)

Flag (octet 2) (Note 3)

Bit 5	Meaning
0	IE instruction field not significant (regular error handling procedures apply)
1	Follow explicit instructions (supersedes regular error handling procedures)

Reserved (octet 2) (Note 4)

Bit 4	Meaning
0	Reserved

Spare (octet 2)

Bit 3	Meaning
0	Spare

Action Indicator (octet 3) (Note 3)

Bits 2 1	Meaning
0 0	Clear call
0 1	Discard and proceed
1 0	Discard, proceed, and report status
1 1	Reserved

Note 1 - For this Implementation Agreement, the coding standard shall be coded as "ITU-TS (CCITT) Standardized" or "Standard defined for the network (either public or private) present on the network side of the interface" as defined by each information element. If an information element is received with an invalid coding standard, the receiving entity shall follow procedures for information element content error as described in §§ 5.5.6.7.2 and 5.5.6.8.2.

Note 2 - This coding standard should be used only when the information element contents cannot be represented with the CCITT standardized coding.

Note 3 - For this Implementation Agreement, the Flag field (bit 5) and Action Indicator field (bits 2-1) shall be coded to zero. If any other codings are received, the following procedures apply:

- If the Flag field is set to zero, the receiving entity shall ignore the content of the Action Indicator field.

- If the Flag field is set to one, the receiving entity shall either treat the message as if the Flag field is coded to zero or shall follow the explicit instruction in the Action Indicator field.

Note 4 - This field is reserved for a possible use of indicating a pass along request.

5.4.5.2 Extension of Codesets

This Implementation Agreement does not support the Broadband locking shift and Broadband non-locking shift information elements since it is not necessary to use information elements in codesets other than codeset 0. For this Implementation Agreement, it is necessary to recognize the Broadband locking shift and Broadband non-locking shift information elements to allow the proper interpretation of the receipt of non-ITU-TS (CCITT) standardized information elements.

For additional details on codesets, see §4.5.2 of ITU-T draft Recommendation Q.93B [29].

5.4.5.3 Broadband Locking Shift Procedures

If a Broadband locking shift information element is received, the Broadband locking shift information element and all information elements in the new active codeset are discarded and the procedures in §5.5.6.8.1 are followed, with the exception that only the Broadband locking shift information element identifier is returned in the diagnostic field of the Cause information element. The information element identifier(s) of the information element(s) in the new codeset are not included.

For additional details of the Broadband locking shift information element, see §4.5.3 of ITU-T draft Recommendation Q.93B [29].

5.4.5.4 Broadband Non-Locking Shift Procedures

If a Broadband non-locking shift information element is received, the Broadband non-locking shift information element and the information element that follows it are discarded and the procedures in §5.5.6.8.1 are followed, with the exception that only the Broadband non-locking shift information element identifier is returned in the diagnostic field of the Cause information element. The information element identifier of the information element in the new codeset is not included.

For additional details of the Broadband non-locking shift information element, see §4.5.4 of ITU-T draft Recommendation Q.93B [29].

5.4.5.5 ATM Adaptation Layer Parameters

The purpose of the ATM adaptation layer parameters information element is to indicate the requested ATM adaptation layer parameter values (end-to-end significance) for the ATM connection. It contains the parameters selectable by the user for all AAL sublayers.

The ATM adaptation layer parameters information element may also be included in the CONNECT message to indicate that the called party to a point-to-point call (or the first leaf of a point-to-multipoint call) wishes to indicate the Forward and Backward Maximum CPCS-SDU size (for AAL 3/4 and AAL5), reduce the value of the MID (for AAL 3/4), or indicate user-defined AAL information.

> *Note* - Other uses of the ATM adaptation layer parameters information element in the connect message (e.g., for interworking) are for further study.

The contents of this information element is transparent for the network, except for the case of interworking.

Bits								Octets
8	7	6	5	4	3	2	1	Octets
ATM adaptation layer parameters								
0	1	0	1	1	0	0	0	1
Information element identifier								
1 ext	Coding Standard		IE Instruction Field					2
Length of AAL parameters contents								3
Length of AAL parameters contents (continued)								4
AAL Type								5
Further content depending upon AAL type								6 etc.

Figure 5-24 ATM Adaptation Layer Parameters Information Element (For all AAL Types)

Bits								Octets
8	7	6	5	4	3	2	1	
Subtype identifier								6
1	0	0	0	0	1	0	1	
Subtype								6.1
CBR Rate Identifier								7
1	0	0	0	0	1	1	0	
CBR Rate								7.1
Multiplier Identifier								8* (Note 1)
1	0	0	0	0	1	1	1	
Multiplier								8.1* (Note 1)
Multiplier (continued)								8.2* (Note 1)
Clock Recovery Type Identifier								9*
1	0	0	0	1	0	0	0	
Clock Recovery Type								9.1*
Error Correction Identifier								10*
1	0	0	0	1	0	0	1	
Error Correction								10.1*
Structured Data Transfer Identifier								11*
1	0	0	0	1	0	1	0	
Structured Data Transfer								11.1*
Partially Filled Cells Identifier								12*
1	0	0	0	1	0	1	1	
Partially Filled Cells								12.1*

Note 1 - These octets are only present if octet 7.1 indicates "n x 64 kbit/s".

**Figure 5-25 ATM Adaptation Layer Parameters Information Element
(Octet Groups 6-12 for AAL Type 1)**

				Bits					
8	7	6	5	4	3	2	1		Octets
Forward Maximum CPCS-SDU Size Identifier									6* (Note 1)
1	0	0	0	1	1	0	0		
Forward Maximum CPCS-SDU Size									6.1*
Forward Maximum CPCS-SDU Size (continued)									6.2*
Backward Maximum CPCS-SDU Size Identifier									7* (Note 1)
1	0	0	0	0	0	0	1		
Backward Maximum CPCS-SDU Size									7.1*
Backward Maximum CPCS-SDU Size (continued)									7.2*
MID Size Identifier									8*
1	0	0	0	0	0	1	0		
MID Size									8.1*
MID Size (continued)									8.2*
Mode Identifier									9*
1	0	0	0	0	0	1	1		
Mode									9.1*
SSCS Type Identifier									10*
1	0	0	0	0	1	0	0		
SSCS Type									10.1*

Note 1 - If the Forward Maximum CPCS-SDU Size is included, the Backward Maximum CPCS-SDU size shall be included. If the Backward Maximum CPCS-SDU Size is included, the Forward Maximum CPCS-SDU Size shall be included.

Figure 5-26 ATM Adaptation Layer Parameters Information Element (Octet Groups 6-10 for AAL Type 3/4)

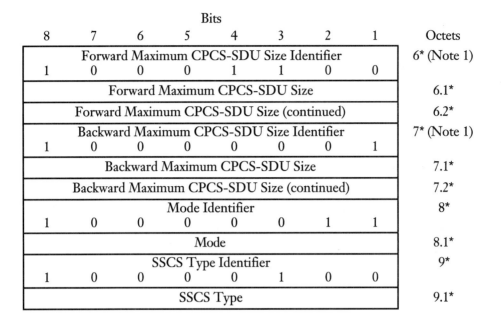

Bits								Octets
8	7	6	5	4	3	2	1	
Forward Maximum CPCS-SDU Size Identifier								6* (Note 1)
1	0	0	0	1	1	0	0	
Forward Maximum CPCS-SDU Size								6.1*
Forward Maximum CPCS-SDU Size (continued)								6.2*
Backward Maximum CPCS-SDU Size Identifier								7* (Note 1)
1	0	0	0	0	0	0	1	
Backward Maximum CPCS-SDU Size								7.1*
Backward Maximum CPCS-SDU Size (continued)								7.2*
Mode Identifier								8*
1	0	0	0	0	0	1	1	
Mode								8.1*
SSCS Type Identifier								9*
1	0	0	0	0	1	0	0	
SSCS Type								9.1*

Note 1 - If the Forward Maximum CPCS-SDU Size is included, the Backward Maximum
CPCS-SDU size shall be included. If the Backward Maximum CPCS-SDU Size is
included, the Forward Maximum CPCS-SDU Size shall be included.

**Figure 5-27 ATM Adaptation Layer Parameters Information Element
(Octet Groups 6-9 for AAL Type 5)**

Bits								Octets
8	7	6	5	4	3	2	1	
User Defined AAL Information								6*
User Defined AAL Information								6.1*
User Defined AAL Information								6.2*
User Defined AAL Information								6.3*

**Figure 5-28 ATM Adaptation Layer Parameters Information Element
(Octet Group 6 for User Defined AAL)**

Coding Standard (octet 2)

Bits 7 6	Meaning
0 0	ITU-TS (CCITT) standardized

IE Instruction Field (octet 2)

Bits 5 4 3 2 1	Meaning
0 0 0 0 0	IE instruction field not significant

AAL type (octet 5)

Bits 8 7 6 5 4 3 2 1	Meaning
0 0 0 0 0 0 0 1	AAL type 1
0 0 0 0 0 0 1 1	AAL type 3/4
0 0 0 0 0 1 0 1	AAL type 5
0 0 0 1 0 0 0 0	User-Defined AAL

Subtype (octet 6.1 for AAL type 1)

Bits 8 7 6 5 4 3 2 1	Meaning
0 0 0 0 0 0 0 0	Null/empty
0 0 0 0 0 0 0 1	Voice-band based on 64 kbit/s
0 0 0 0 0 0 1 0	Circuit emulation (synchronous)
0 0 0 0 0 0 1 1	Circuit emulation (asynchronous)
0 0 0 0 0 1 0 0	High-quality audio
0 0 0 0 0 1 0 1	Video

CBR rate (octet 7.1 for AAL type 1)

Bits 8 7 6 5 4 3 2 1	Meaning
0 0 0 0 0 0 0 1	64 kbit/s
0 0 0 0 0 1 0 0	1544 kbit/s (DS1)
0 0 0 0 0 1 0 1	6312 kbit/s (DS2)
0 0 0 0 0 1 1 0	32064 kbit/s
0 0 0 0 0 1 1 1	44736 kbit/s (DS3)
0 0 0 0 1 0 0 0	97728 kbit/s
0 0 0 1 0 0 0 0	2048 kbit/s (E1)
0 0 0 1 0 0 0 1	8448 kbit/s (E2)
0 0 0 1 0 0 1 0	34368 kbit/s (E3)
0 0 0 1 0 0 1 1	139264 kbit/s
0 1 0 0 0 0 0 0	n x 64 kbit/s

Multiplier (octets 8.1 and 8.2 for AAL type 1 and nx64kbit/s indication in octet 7.1)
  Integer representation of multiplier values between 2 and 2^{16}-1.

Clock recovery type (octet 9.1 for AAL type 1)

Bits 8 7 6 5 4 3 2 1	Meaning
0 0 0 0 0 0 0 0	Null (Timing is derived from physical interface)
0 0 0 0 0 0 0 1	SRTS (Synchronous Residual Time Stamp)
0 0 0 0 0 0 1 0	Adaptive Clock Recovery

Error correction type (octet 10.1 for AAL type 1)

Bits 8 7 6 5 4 3 2 1	Meaning
0 0 0 0 0 0 0 0	Null
0 0 0 0 0 0 0 1	Interleaving FEC (Reed Solomon 128, 124). *Note* - This codepoint precludes the indication of SDT in Octet 11.1.

Structured Data Transfer (octet 11.1 for AAL type 1)

Bits 8 7 6 5 4 3 2 1	Meaning
0 0 0 0 0 0 0 0	Null
0 0 0 0 0 0 0 1	Structured Data Transfer (SDT). *Note* - This codepoint precludes the use of Interleaving FEC in Octet 10.1.

Partially Filled Cells (octet 12.1 for AAL type 1)
  Integer representation of the number of leading octets in use (values between 1 and 47).

Forward Maximum CPCS-SDU Size (octets 6.1 and 6.2 for AAL type 3/4 and type 5)
  16 bit integer representation of the values between 1 and 65,535, i.e., 2^{16}-1. This parameter indicates the Maximum CPCS-SDU size sent in the direction from the calling user to the called user.

Backward Maximum CPCS-SDU Size (octets 7.1 and 7.2 for AAL type 3/4 and type 5)
  16 bit integer representation of the values between 1 and 65,535, i.e., 2^{16}-1. This parameter indicates the Maximum CPCS-SDU size sent in the direction from the called user to the calling user.

MID Size (octets 8.1 and 8.2 for AAL type 3/4)
  Integer representation of the number of MID values, only values between 1 and 1023.

Mode (octet 9.1 for AAL type 3/4; octet 8.1 for AAL type 5)

Bits 8 7 6 5 4 3 2 1	Meaning
0 0 0 0 0 0 0 1	Message mode
0 0 0 0 0 0 1 0	Streaming mode

SSCS Type (octet 10.1 for AAL type 3/4; octet 9.1 for AAL type 5)

Bits 8 7 6 5 4 3 2 1	Meaning
0 0 0 0 0 0 0 0	Null
0 0 0 0 0 0 0 1	Data SSCS based on SSCOP (assured operation)
0 0 0 0 0 0 1 0	Data SSCS based on SSCOP (non-assured operation)
0 0 0 0 0 1 0 0	Frame relay SSCS

User Defined AAL Information (octets 6 to 6.3 for User-Defined AAL)
   The use and coding of octets 6-6.3 is according to user defined requirements.

5.4.5.6 ATM User Cell Rate

The purpose of the ATM user cell rate information element is to specify the set of traffic parameters which, together, specify a traffic control capability.

Bits

8	7	6	5	4	3	2	1	Octets
ATM user cell rate								1
0	1	0	1	1	0	0	1	
Information element identifier								
1 ext	Coding Standard	IE Instruction Field						2
Length of ATM user cell rate contents								3
Length of ATM user cell rate contents (continued)								4
1	0	0	0	0	0	1	0	5*
Forward Peak Cell Rate Identifier (CLP=0)								
Forward Peak Cell Rate								5.1*
Forward Peak Cell Rate (continued)								5.2*
Forward Peak Cell Rate (continued)								5.3*
1	0	0	0	0	0	1	1	6*
Backward Peak Cell Rate Identifier (CLP=0)								
Backward Peak Cell Rate								6.1*
Backward Peak Cell Rate (continued)								6.2*
Backward Peak Cell Rate (continued)								6.3*
1	0	0	0	0	1	0	0	7 (Note 3)
Forward Peak Cell Rate Identifier (CLP=0+1)								
Forward Peak Cell Rate								7.1 (Note 3)
Forward Peak Cell Rate (continued)								7.2 (Note 3)
Forward Peak Cell Rate (continued)								7.3 (Note 3)
1	0	0	0	0	1	0	1	8 (Notes 3,4)
Backward Peak Cell Rate Identifier (CLP=0+1)								
Backward Peak Cell Rate								8.1 (Notes 3,4)
Backward Peak Cell Rate (continued)								8.2 (Notes 3,4)
Backward Peak Cell Rate (continued)								8.3 (Notes 3,4)
1	0	0	0	1	0	0	0	9* (Note 5)
Forward Sustainable Cell Rate Identifier (CLP=0)								
Forward Sustainable Cell Rate								9.1* (Note 5)
Forward Sustainable Cell Rate (continued)								9.2* (Note 5)

Forward Sustainable Cell Rate (continued)								9.3* (Note 5)
1	0	0	0	1	0	0	1	10* (Note 5)
Backward Sustainable Cell Rate Identifier (CLP=0)								
Backward Sustainable Cell Rate								10.1* (Note 5)
Backward Sustainable Cell Rate (continued)								10.2* (Note 5)
Backward Sustainable Cell Rate (continued)								10.3* (Note 5)
1	0	0	1	0	0	0	0	11* (Note 5)
Forward Sustainable Cell Rate Identifier (CLP=0+1)								
Forward Sustainable Cell Rate								11.1* (Note 5)
Forward Sustainable Cell Rate (continued)								11.2* (Note 5)
Forward Sustainable Cell Rate (continued)								11.3* (Note 5)
1	0	0	1	0	0	0	1	12* (Note 5)
Backward Sustainable Cell Rate Identifier (CLP=0+1)								
Backward Sustainable Cell Rate								12.1* (Note 5)
Backward Sustainable Cell Rate (continued)								12.2* (Note 5)
Backward Sustainable Cell Rate (continued)								12.3* (Note 5)
1	0	1	0	0	0	0	0	13* (Note 5)
Forward Maximum Burst Size Identifier (CLP=0)								
Forward Maximum Burst Size								13.1* (Note 5)
Forward Maximum Burst Size (continued)								13.2* (Note 5)
Forward Maximum Burst Size (continued)								13.3* (Note 5)
1	0	1	0	0	0	0	1	14* (Note 5)
Backward Maximum Burst Size Identifier (CLP=0)								
Backward Maximum Burst Size								14.1* (Note 5)
Backward Maximum Burst Size (continued)								14.2* (Note 5)
Backward Maximum Burst Size (continued)								14.3* (Note 5)
1	0	1	1	0	0	0	0	15* (Note 5)
Forward Maximum Burst Size Identifier (CLP=0+1)								
Forward Maximum Burst Size								15.1* (Note 5)
Forward Maximum Burst Size (continued)								15.2* (Note 5)
Forward Maximum Burst Size (continued)								15.3* (Note 5)
1	0	1	1	0	0	0	1	16* (Note 5)
Backward Maximum Burst Size Identifier (CLP=0+1)								
Backward Maximum Burst Size								16.1* (Note 5)
Backward Maximum Burst Size (continued)								16.2* (Note 5)
Backward Maximum Burst Size (continued)								16.3* (Note 5)

1	0	1	1	1	1	1	0	17* (Note 6)
		Best Effort Indicator						
1	0	1	1	1	1	1	1	18* (Note 7)
		Traffic Management Options Identifier						
0	0	0	0	0	0	Tag-ging Back-ward	Tag-ging For-ward	18.1* (Note 7)
			Reserved					

Note 1 - All the parameters are position independent. The term "Forward" indicates the direction from calling user to the called user. The term "Backward" indicates the direction from the called user to the calling user.

Note 2 - The traffic parameters encoded in this information element do not include OAM cells. Traffic descriptors for OAM cells are not supported in this Implementation Agreement.

Note 3 - If only Peak cell rate for CLP = 0+1 is specified, the network resource allocation will assume the entire peak cell rate can be used for CLP=0.

Note 4 - For point-to-multipoint calls (see §5.6), the backward peak cell rate (CLP=0+1) value shall be coded as zero. No other backwards traffic descriptors shall be included.

Note 5 - If either forward sustainable cell rate (CLP=0), forward sustainable cell rate (CLP=0+1), backward sustainable cell rate (CLP=0), or backward sustainable cell rate (CLP=0+1) are included, the corresponding maximum burst size shall be included. Similarly, if forward maximum burst size (CLP=0), forward maximum burst size (CLP=0+1), backward maximum burst size (CLP=0), or backward maximum burst size (CLP=0+1) are included, the corresponding sustainable cell rate shall be included.

Note 6 - QoS class 0 is used with the best effort indication. The interpretation of the Forward Peak Cell Rate (CLP=0+1) parameter and the Backward Peak Cell Rate (CLP=0+1) parameter is modified by the best effort indication (see §3.6.2.4).

Note 7 - When these octets are not present, it is assumed that tagging is not requested.

Figure 5-29 ATM User Cell Rate Information Element

Coding Standard (octet 2)

Bits 7 6	Meaning
0 0	ITU-TS (CCITT) standardized (Note 1)
1 1	Standard defined for the network (either public or private) present on the network side of the interface. (Note 2)

Note 1 - This codepoint is used when the combinations of traffic parameter subfields in Tables 5-7 and 5-8 are used.

Note 2 - This codepoint can be used to specify additional experimental parameters. These parameters may be used to provide a more detailed traffic characterization (e.g., Average cell rate, Average burst size, etc.)

IE Instruction Field (octet 3)

Bits 5 4 3 2 1	Meaning
0 0 0 0 0	IE instruction field not significant

Forward/Backward Peak Cell Rate
(octets i.1 - i.3, where i may have values 5, 6, 7, or 8)
The forward and backward peak cell rate parameters indicate the peak cell rate (see §3.6), expressed in cells per second. It is coded as a 24-bit binary integer, with Bit 8 of the first octet being the most significant bit and Bit 1 of the third octet being the least significant bit.

Forward/Backward Sustainable Cell Rate
(octets i.1 - i.3, where i may have values 9, 10, 11, or 12)
The forward and backward sustainable cell rate parameters indicate the sustainable cell rate (see §3.6), expressed in cells per second. It is coded as a 24-bit binary integer, with Bit 8 of the first octet being the most significant bit and Bit 1 of the third octet being the least significant bit.

Forward/Backward Maximum Burst Size
(octets i.1 - i.3, where i may have values 13, 14, 15, or 16)
The forward and backward maximum burst size parameters indicate the maximum burst size (see §3.6), expressed in cells. It is coded as a 24-bit binary integer with Bit 8 of the first octet being the most significant bit and Bit 1 of the third octet being the least significant bit.

Best Effort Indication (octet 17)
This octet is included when best effort is requested (see §3.6).

Tagging Backward (octet 18.1) (Note)

Bit 2	Meaning
0	Tagging not requested
1	Tagging requested

Note -   The tagging backward parameter is coded as a one (1) when the tagging is requested and is coded as a zero (0) when tagging is not requested. (See §3.6 for more information.)

Tagging Forward (octet 18.1) (Note)

Bit 1	Meaning
0	Tagging not requested
1	Tagging requested

Note -   The tagging forward parameter is coded as a one (1) when the tagging is requested and is coded as a zero (0) when tagging is not requested. (See §3.6 for more information.)

The valid combinations of the traffic descriptor subfields in the ATM user cell rate information element are shown in Tables 5-7 and 5-8. Table 5-7 shows the valid combinations of traffic parameter subfields for a given direction (i.e., the forward direction may use one combination of traffic descriptors, while the backward direction uses a different combination of traffic descriptors). Total information element length will depend upon the combinations of traffic parameter subfields chosen for each direction. Table 5-8 shows the valid combination of traffic parameter subfields for best effort (best effort always applies to both directions of the connection).

Table 5-7 Allowable Combinations of Traffic Parameters in a Given Direction

Allowable Combinations of Traffic Parameter Subfields in the ATM User Cell Rate Information Element for a Given Direction
Peak Cell Rate CLP=0 Peak Cell Rate CLP=0+1
Peak Cell Rate CLP=0 Peak Cell Rate CLP=0+1 Tagging=tagging requested
Peak Cell Rate CLP=0+1 Sustainable Cell Rate CLP=0 Maximum Burst Size CLP=0
Peak Cell Rate CLP=0+1 Sustainable Cell Rate CLP=0 Maximum Burst Size CLP=0 Tagging=tagging requested
Peak Cell Rate CLP=0+1
Peak Cell Rate CLP=0+1 Sustainable Cell Rate CLP=0+1 Maximum Burst Size CLP=0+1

Table 5-8 Combination of Traffic Parameters for Best Effort

Combination of Traffic Parameter Subfields in the ATM User Cell Rate Information Element for Best Effort	Total information element length in octets (including overhead)
Peak Cell Rate Forward CLP=0+1 Peak Cell Rate Backward CLP=0+1 Best Effort Indication	13

5.4.5.7 Broadband Bearer Capability

The purpose of the Broadband bearer capability information element is to indicate a requested broadband connection oriented bearer service (see CCITT Recommendation F.811) to be provided by the network.

				Bits				
8	7	6	5	4	3	2	1	Octets
			Broadband bearer capability					
0	1	0	1	1	1	1	0	1
			Information element identifier					
1 ext	Coding Standard		IE Instruction Field					2
Length of B-BC contents								3
Length of B-BC contents (continued)								4
0/1 ext	0 0 Spare		Bearer Class					5
1 ext	0 0 Spare		Traffic Type			Timing Requirements		5a* (Note 1)
1 ext	Susceptibility to clipping	0 0 0 Spare				User plane connection configuration		6

Note 1 - This octet will only be present if Bearer Class X is indicated in Octet 5.

Figure 5-30 Broadband Bearer Capability Information Element

Coding Standard (octet 2)

Bits 76	Meaning
0 0	ITU-TS (CCITT) standardized

IE Instruction Field (octet 2)

Bits 5 4 3 2 1	Meaning
0 0 0 0 0	IE instruction field not significant

Bearer Class (octet 5)

Bits 5 4 3 2 1	Meaning
0 0 0 0 1	BCOB-A
0 0 0 1 1	BCOB-C
1 0 0 0 0	BCOB-X

Traffic Type (octet 5a)

Bits 5 4 3	Meaning
0 0 0	No indication
0 0 1	Constant bit rate
0 1 0	Variable bit rate

Timing Requirements (octet 5a)

Bits 2 1	Meaning
0 0	No indication
0 1	End-to-end timing required
1 0	End-to-end timing not required
1 1	Reserved

Susceptibility to clipping (octet 6)

Bits 7 6	Meaning
0 0	Not susceptible to clipping
0 1	Susceptible to clipping

User plane connection configuration (octet 6)

Bits 2 1	Meaning
0 0	Point-to-point
0 1	Point-to-multipoint

5.4.5.8 Broadband High Layer Information

The purpose of the Broadband high layer information element is to provide a means which should be used for compatibility checking by an addressed entity (e.g., a remote user or an interworking unit or a high layer function network node addressed by the calling user). The Broadband high layer information element is transferred transparently by an ATM network between the call originating entity (e.g., the calling user) and the addressed entity. For the Public UNI, the availability of this information element must be negotiated with the network provider. At the Public UNI, the network provider has the option of not supporting this element in the SETUP message. At the Private UNI, support for this information element is mandatory.

8	7	6	5	4	3	2	1	Octets
Broadband high layer information								
0	1	0	1	1	1	0	1	1
Information element identifier								
1 ext	Coding Standard		IE Instruction Field					2
Length of B-HLI contents								3
Length of B-HLI contents (continued)								4
1 ext	High Layer Information Type							5
High Layer Information								6-13*

Figure 5-31 Broadband High Layer Information Information Element

Coding Standard (octet 2)

Bits 76	Meaning
0 0	ITU-TS (CCITT) standardized

IE Instruction Field (octet 2)

Bits 5 4 3 2 1	Meaning
0 0 0 0 0	IE instruction field not significant

High Layer Information Type (octet 5)

Bits 765 4321	Meaning
000 0000	ISO (Note 1)
000 0001	User Specific (Note 1)
000 0010	High layer profile (Note 2)
000 0011	Vendor-Specific Application identifier (Note 3)

Note 1 - The exact coding of octets 6-13, when this high layer information type is used is for further study.

Note 2 - High Layer profiles consist of a 4 byte field containing a user to user profile identifier.

Note 3 - Vendor-Specific Application identifier: consists of a 7-byte field; the left-most three octets consist of a globally-administered Organizationally Unique Identifier (OUI) (as per IEEE standard 802-1990), the right-most four octets are an application identifier, which is administered by the vendor identified by the OUI.

High Layer Information (octets 6-13)

The contents of these octets depends on the high layer information type.

5.4.5.9 Broadband Low Layer Information

The purpose of the Broadband low layer information element is to provide a means which should be used for compatibility checking by an addressed entity (e.g., a remote user or an interworking unit or a high layer function network node addressed by the calling user). The Broadband Low layer information information element is transferred transparently by an ATM network between the call originating entity (e.g., the calling user) and the addressed entity. Support of this information element by the network is mandatory.

Bits

8	7	6	5	4	3	2	1	Octets
Broadband low layer information								1
0	1	0	1	1	1	1	1	
Information element identifier								
1 ext	Coding Standard		IE Instruction Field					2
Length of B-LLI contents								3
Length of B-LLI contents (continued)								4
1 ext	0	1	User information layer 1 protocol					5*
	Layer 1 id							
0/1 ext	1	0	User information layer 2 protocol					6*
	Layer 2 id							
0/1 ext	Mode		0	0	0	Q.933 use		6a* (Note 1)
			Spare					
1 ext	Window size (k)							6b* (Note 1)
1 ext	User specified layer 2 protocol information							6a* (Note 2)
0/1 ext	1	1	User information layer 3 protocol					7*
	Layer 3 id							
0/1 ext	Mode		0	0	0	0	0	7a* (Note 3)
			Spare					
0/1 ext	0	0	0	Default Packet Size				7b* (Note 3)
	Spare							
1 ext	Packet window size							7c* (Note 3)
1 ext	User specified layer 3 protocol information							7a* (Note 4)
0 ext	ISO/IEC TR 9577 Initial Protocol Identifier (IPI) (bits 8-2)							7a* (Note 5)
1 ext	IPI (bit1)	0	0	0	0	0	0	7b* (Note 5)
		Spare						
1 ext	0	0	0	0	0	0	0	8* (Note 6)
	SNAP ID		Spare					
OUI Octet 1								8.1*
OUI Octet 2								8.2*
OUI Octet 3								8.3*
PID Octet 1								8.4*
PID Octet 2								8.5*

211

Note 1 - This octet may be present only if octet 6 indicates certain acknowledged mode HDLC elements of procedures as indicated in User information layer 2 protocol (octet 6).

Note 2 - This octet may be present only if octet 6 indicates user specified layer 2 protocol.

Note 3 - This octet may be present only if octet 7 indicates a layer 3 protocol based on Recommendation X.25, ISO/IEC 8208, or X.223/ISO 8878 as indicated in User information layer 3 protocol (octet 7).

Note 4 - This octet may be present only if octet 7 indicates user specified layer 3 protocol.

Note 5 - These octets may be present only if octet 7 indicates ISO/IEC TR 9577.

Note 6 - This octet group shall be present only if octet 7 indicates ISO/IEC TR 9577 and octets 7a and 7b indicate IEEE 802.1 SNAP.

Figure 5-32 Broadband Low Layer Information Information Element

Coding Standard (octet 2)

Bits 7 6	Meaning
0 0	ITU-TS (CCITT) standardized

IE Instruction Field (octet 2)

Bits 5 4 3 2 1	Meaning
0 0 0 0 0	IE instruction field not significant

User information layer 1 protocol (octet 5)
Use of this octet is not supported in this Implementation Agreement.

User information layer 2 protocol (octet 6)

Bits 5 4 3 2 1	Meaning
0 0 0 0 1	Basic mode ISO 1745
0 0 0 1 0	CCITT Recommendation Q.921
0 0 1 1 0	CCITT Recommendation X.25, link layer (Note 1)
0 0 1 1 1	CCITT Recommendation X.25 multilink (Note 1)
0 1 0 0 0	Extended LAPB; for half duplex operation
0 1 0 0 1	HDLC ARM (ISO 4335) (Note 1)
0 1 0 1 0	HDLC ARM (ISO 4335) (Note 1)
0 1 0 1 1	HDLC ARM (ISO 4335) (Note 1)
0 1 1 0 0	LAN logical link control (ISO 8802/2)
0 1 1 0 1	CCITT Recommendation X.75, single link procedure (SLP)
0 1 1 1 0	CCITT Recommendation Q.922 (Note 1)
1 0 0 0 0	User specified (Note 2)
1 0 0 0 1	ISO 7776 DTE-DTE operation (Note 1)

Note 1 - When this coding is included, octets 6a and 6b with CCITT encoding may be included.

Note 2 - When this coding is included, octet 6a will include user coding for the user specified layer 2 protocol.

Octet 6a for CCITT codings
  Mode of operation (octet 6a)

Bits 7 6	Meaning
0 1	normal mode of operation
1 0	extended mode of operation

Q.933 use (octet 6a)

Bits 2 1	Meaning
0 0	for use when the coding defined in Recommendation Q.933 is not used.

Window size (k) (octet 6b)
  Binary coding of k parameter value in the range from 1 to 127.

Octet 6a for user protocol
  User specified layer 2 protocol information (octet 6a)
    The use and coding of octet 6a is according to user defined requirements.

User information layer 3 protocol (octet 7)

Bits 5 4 3 2 1	Meaning
0 0 1 1 0	CCITT Recommendation X.25, packet layer (Note 1)
0 0 1 1 1	ISO/IEC 8208 (X.25 packet level protocol for data terminal equipment) (Note 1)
0 1 0 0 0	X.223/ISO 8878 (use of ISO/ISO 8208 [41] and CCITT X.25 to provide the OSI-CONS) (Note 1)
0 1 0 0 1	ISO/IEC 8473 (OSI connectionless mode protocol)
0 1 0 1 0	CCITT Recommendation T.70 minimum network layer
0 1 0 1 1	ISO/IEC TR 9577 (Protocol Identification in the Network Layer) (Note 2)
1 0 0 0 0	User specified (Note 3)

Note 1 - When this coding is included, octets 7a, 7b, and 7c with CCITT encoding may be included.

Note 2 - If extension octets (7a-7b) are not included, the Layer 3 protocol(s) carried in the user plane are identified by examining each layer 3 protocol data unit, according to ISO/IEC TR 9577. More than one layer 3 protocol may thus be carried on a connection.

If extension octets are present, the ISO/IEC TR 9577 Initial Protocol Identifier (IPI) is not carried in the user plane.

Note 3 - When this coding is included, octet 7a will include user coding for the user specified layer 3 protocol.

Octet 7a for CCITT codings
  Mode of operation (octet 7a)

Bits 7 6	Meaning
0 1	normal packet sequence numbering
1 0	extended packet sequence numbering

Default packet size (octet 7b)

Bits 4 3 2 1	Meaning
0 1 0 0	default packet size 16 octets
0 1 0 1	default packet size 32 octets
0 1 1 0	default packet size 64 octets
0 1 1 1	default packet size 128 octets
1 0 0 0	default packet size 256 octets
1 0 0 1	default packet size 512 octets
1 0 1 0	default packet size 1024 octets
1 0 1 1	default packet size 2048 octets
1 1 0 0	default packet size 4096 octets

Packet window size (octet 7c, bits 7-1)
  Binary coding of packet window size value in the range 1 to 127.

Octet 7a for user protocol
  User specified layer 3 protocol identification (octet 7a)
    The use and coding of octet 7a depends on user defined requirements.

ISO/IEC TR 9577 Network Layer Protocol Identifier (NLPID) and IEEE 802.1 SNAP identifier (octets 7a-7b, 8-8.5)

Octet 7a and bit 8 of octet 7b indicate the ISO/IEC TR 9577 Initial Protocol Identifier (IPI) for the protocol to be carried in the user plane. If octets 7a and 7b are coded as '10000000', indicating an IEEE 802.1 SNAP identifier (see Annex D of ISO/IEC TR 9577), Octets 8.1-8.5 will contain a 40 bit SNAP identifier, consisting of a 24-bit organization unique identifier (OUI) and a 16-bit protocol identifier (PID). The NLPID coding shall only be used if there is no CCITT or ITU-TS standardized coding for the layer 3 protocol being used, and an ISO/IEC TR 9577 or SNAP coding applies for that protocol. The SNAP coding shall be used for a layer 3 protocol only if ISO has not assigned an NLPID for the layer 3 protocol. The SNAP coding can also be used to indicate that bridged LAN frames are to be carried in the user plane.

5.4.5.10 Call State

The purpose of the Call state information element is to describe the current status of a call or a global interface state.

Bits								Octets
8	7	6	5	4	3	2	1	Octets
Call state								1
0	0	0	1	0	1	0	0	1
Information element identifier								
1 ext	Coding Standard		IE Instruction Field					2
Length of call state contents								3
Length of call state contents (continued)								4
0 0 Spare		Call state value/ global interface state value						5

Figure 5-33 Call State Information Element

Coding Standard (octet 2)

Bits 7 6	Meaning
0 0	ITU-TS (CCITT) standardized

IE Instruction Field (octet 2)

Bits 5 4 3 2 1	Meaning
0 0 0 0 0	IE instruction field not significant

Call State Value (octet 5)

Bits 6 5 4 3 2 1	Meaning User state	Network state
0 0 0 0 0 0	U0 - Null	N0 - Null
0 0 0 0 0 1	U1 - Call initiated	N1 - Call initiated
0 0 0 0 1 1	U3 - Outgoing call proceeding	N3 - Outgoing call proceeding
0 0 0 1 1 0	U6 - Call present	N6 - Call present
0 0 1 0 0 0	U8 - Connect request	N8 - Connect request
0 0 1 0 0 1	U9 - Incoming call proceeding	N9 - Incoming call proceeding
0 0 1 0 1 0	U10 - Active	N10 - Active
0 0 1 0 1 1	U11 - Release request	N11 - Release request
0 0 1 1 0 0	U12 - Release indication	N12 - Release indication

Global Interface State Value (octet 5)

Bits 6 5 4 3 2 1	Meaning
0 0 0 0 0 0	REST 0 - Null
1 1 1 1 0 1	REST 1 - Restart request
1 1 1 1 1 0	REST 2 - Restart

5.4.5.11 Called Party Number

The purpose of the Called party number information element is to identify the called party of a call.

			Bits					
8	7	6	5	4	3	2	1	Octets
0	1	1	1	0	0	0	0	1
			Called party number Information element identifier					
1 ext	Coding Standard		IE Instruction Field					2
Length of called party number contents								3
Length of called party number contents (continued)								4
1 ext	Type of number		Addressing/numbering plan identification					5
0	Address/Number Digits (IA5 characters)							6 etc. Note 1
NSAP Address Octets								6 etc. Note 2

Note 1 - If the use of the E.164 numbering plan is indicated in the addressing/numbering plan identification, the number digits appear in multiple octet 6's in the same order in which they would be entered on a numeric keypad; i.e., the number digit which would be entered first is located in first octet 6. Digits are coded in IA5 characters. Bit 8 is set to 0.

Note 2 - If the use of OSI NSAP addressing is indicated in the addressing/numbering plan identification, the address is coded as described in ISO 8348/AD 2, using the preferred binary encoding.

Figure 5-34 Called Party Number Information Element

Coding Standard (octet 2)

Bits 7 6	Meaning
0 0	ITU-TS (CCITT) standardized

IE Instruction Field (octet 2)

Bits 5 4 3 2 1	Meaning
0 0 0 0 0	IE instruction field not significant

Type of Number (octet 5)

Bits 7 6 5	Meaning
0 0 0	Unknown
0 0 1	International number

Addressing/Numbering Plan Identification (octet 5)

Bits 4 3 2 1	Meaning
0 0 0 1	ISDN/telephony numbering plan (Recommendation E.164) (Note 1)
0 0 1 0	ISO NSAP (Note 2)

Note 1 - If the E.164 numbering plan is used, "Type of Number" shall be coded as "International Number"

Note 2 - If the OSI NSAP addressing format is used, "Type of Number" shall be coded as "Unknown"

Address (octet 6, etc.)

If the coding "international number/ISDN/telephony numbering plan (Recommendation E.164)" is used, the address is coded as IA5 characters according to the format specified in the numbering plan. If the coding "unknown/ISO NSAP" is used, the address is coded as described in ISO 8348, Addendum 2, using the preferred binary encoding.

5.4.5.12 Called Party Subaddress

The purpose of the Called party subaddress information element is to identify the subaddress of the called party of a call. It is used in this Implementation Agreement only to convey an ATM address in the OSI NSAP format across a public network which supports only E.164 addresses. Support of this information element by the network is mandatory.

Bits								Octets
8	7	6	5	4	3	2	1	
Called party subaddress								1
0	1	1	1	0	0	0	1	
Information element identifier								
1 ext	Coding standard		IE Instruction Field					2
Length of called party subaddress contents								3
Length of called party subaddress contents (continued)								4
1 ext	Type of subaddress		Odd/even indicator	0	0 Spare		0	5
Subaddress information								6 etc.

Figure 5-35 Called Party Subaddress Information Element

Coding Standard (octet 2)

Bits 7 6	Meaning
0 0	ITU-TS (CCITT) standardized

IE Instruction Field (octet 2)

Bits 5 4 3 2 1	Meaning
0 0 0 0 0	IE instruction field not significant

Type of Subaddress (octet 5)

Bits 7 6 5	Meaning
0 0 0	NSAP (X.213/ISO 8348 AD2)

Odd/even Indicator (octet 5)

    The Odd/even indicator is not used in this Implementation Agreement.

Subaddress information (octet 6)

    The NSAP X.213/ISO8348AD2 address, shall be formatted as specified by octet 6 which contains the Authority and Format Identifier (AFI). The encoding is made according to the "preferred binary encoding" as defined in X.213/ISO 8348 AD2. For the definition of this type of subaddress, see Recommendation I.334.

5.4.5.13 Calling Party Number

The purpose of the calling party number information element is to identify the origin of a call.

			Bits					
8	7	6	5	4	3	2	1	Octets
Calling party number / Information element identifier								
0	1	1	0	1	1	0	0	1
1 ext	Coding Standard	IE Instruction Field						2
Length of calling party number contents								3
Length of calling party number contents (continued)								4
0/1 ext	Type of number		Addressing/numbering plan identification					5
1 ext	Presentation Indicator	0	0	0	Screening Indicator			5a*
0	Address/number digits (IA5 characters)							6* etc. Note 1
NSAP Address Octets								6* etc. Note 2

Note 1 - If the use of the E.164 numbering plan is indicated in the addressing/numbering plan identification, the number digits appear in multiple octet 6's in the same order in which they would be entered on a numeric keypad; i.e., the number digit which would be entered first is located in first octet 6. Digits are coded in IA5 characters. Bit 8 is set to 0.

Note 2 - If the use of OSI NSAP addressing is indicated in the addressing/numbering plan identification, the address is coded as described in ISO 8348/AD 2, using the preferred binary encoding.

Figure 5-36 Calling Party Number Information Element

Coding Standard (octet 2)

Bits 7 6	Meaning
0 0	ITU-TS (CCITT) standardized

IE Instruction Field (octet 2)

Bits 5 4 3 2 1	Meaning
0 0 0 0 0	IE instruction field not significant

Type of Number (octet 5)

Bits 7 6 5	Meaning
0 0 0	Unknown
0 0 1	International number

Addressing/Numbering Plan Identification (octet 5)

Bits 4 3 2 1	Meaning
0 0 0 1	ISDN/telephony numbering plan (Recommendation E.164) (Note 1)
0 0 1 0	ISO NSAP (Note 2)

Note 1 - If the E.164 numbering plan is used, "Type of Number" shall be coded as "International Number"

Note 2 - If the OSI NSAP addressing format is used, "Type of Number" shall be coded as "Unknown"

Presentation indicator (octet 5a)

Bits 7 6	Meaning
0 0	Presentation allowed
0 1	Presentation restricted
1 0	Number not available
1 1	Reserved

Note - At the originating user-network interface, the presentation indicator is used for indicating the intention of the calling user for the presentation of the calling party number to the called user. This may also be requested on a subscription basis. If octet 5a is omitted, and the network does not support subscription information for the calling party number information restrictions, the value "00 - presentation allowed" is assumed.

Screening indicator (octet 5a)

Bits 2 1	Meaning
0 0	User-provided, not screened
0 1	User-provided, verified and passed
1 0	User-provided, verified and failed
1 1	Network provided

Note - If octet 5a is omitted, "00 - User provided, not screened" is assumed.

Address (octet 6, etc.)

If the coding "international number/ISDN/telephony numbering plan (Recommendation E.164)" is used, the address is coded as IA5 characters according to the format specified in the numbering plan. If the coding "unknown/ISO NSAP" is used, the address is coded as described in ISO 8348, Addendum 2, using the preferred binary encoding.

5.4.5.14 Calling Party Subaddress

The purpose of the Calling party subaddress information element is to identify a subaddress associated with the origin of a call. It is used in this Implementation Agreement only to convey an ATM address in the OSI NSAP format across a public network which supports only E.164 addresses. Support of this information element by the network is mandatory.

			Bits					
8	7	6	5	4	3	2	1	Octets
Calling party subaddress								
0	1	1	0	1	1	0	1	1
Information element identifier								
1 ext	Coding standard	IE Instruction Field						2
Length of calling party subaddress contents								3
Length of calling party subaddress contents (continued)								4
1 ext	Type of subaddress	Odd/even indicator	0	0 Spare	0			5
Subaddress information								6 etc.

Figure 5-37 Calling Party Subaddress Information Element

Coding Standard (octet 2)

Bits 7 6	Meaning
0 0	ITU-TS (CCITT) standardized

IE Instruction Field (octet 2)

Bits 5 4 3 2 1	Meaning
0 0 0 0 0	IE instruction field not significant

Type of Subaddress (octet 5)

Bits 7 6 5	Meaning
0 0 0	NSAP (X.213/ISO 8348 AD2)

Odd/even Indicator (octet 5)
    The Odd/even indicator is not used in this Implementation Agreement.

Subaddress information (octet 6)
    The NSAP X.213/ISO8348AD2 address shall be formatted as specified by octet 6 which contains the Authority and Format Identifier (AFI). The encoding is made according to the "preferred binary encoding" as defined in X.213/ISO 8348 AD2. For the definition of this type of subaddress, see Recommendation I.334.

5.4.5.15 Cause

The Cause information element describes the reason for generating certain messages, provides diagnostic information in the event of procedural errors, and indicates the location of the cause originator. The Cause information element and diagnostic may be repeated in a message.

8	7	6	5	Bits 4	3	2	1	Octets
0	0	0	0	Cause 1	0	0	0	1
				Information element identifier				
1 ext	Coding Standard		IE Instruction Field					2
Length of cause information contents								3
Length of cause information contents (continued)								4
1 ext	0	0 Spare	0	Location				5
1 ext	Cause value							6
Diagnostic(s) (if any)								7*

Figure 5-38 Cause Information Element

223

Coding Standard (octet 2)

Bits 7 6	Meaning
0 0 1 1	ITU-TS (CCITT) standardized Standard defined for the network (either public or private) present on the network side of the interface.

IE Instruction Field (octet 2)

Bits 5 4 3 2 1	Meaning
0 0 0 0 0	IE instruction field not significant

Location (octet 5)

Bits 4 3 2 1	Meaning
0 0 0 0	user
0 0 0 1	private network serving the local user
0 0 1 0	public network serving the local user
0 0 1 1	transit network
0 1 0 0	public network serving the remote user
0 1 0 1	private network serving the remote user
0 1 1 1	international network
1 0 1 0	network beyond interworking point

Cause value (octet 6) (Note 1)

Bits 7 6 5 4 3 2 1	Number	Meaning	Diagnostics
0 0 0 0 0 0 1	1	unallocated (unassigned) number	Note 2
0 0 0 0 0 1 0	2	no route to specified transit network	-
0 0 0 0 0 1 1	3	no route to destination	Note 2
0 0 0 1 0 1 0	10	VPCI/VCI unacceptable	-
0 0 1 0 0 0 1	17	user busy	-
0 0 1 0 0 1 0	18	no user responding	-
0 0 1 0 1 0 1	21	call rejected	Note 3
0 0 1 0 1 1 0	22	number changed	New destination (Note 4)
0 0 1 0 1 1 1	23	user rejects all calls with calling line identification restriction (CLIR) (Note 5)	-
0 0 1 1 0 1 1	27	destination out of order	-
0 0 1 1 1 0 0	28	invalid number format (address incomplete)	-
0 0 1 1 1 1 0	30	response to STATUS ENQUIRY	-
0 0 1 1 1 1 1	31	normal, unspecified	-
0 1 0 0 0 1 1	35	requested VPCI/VCI not available	-
0 1 0 0 1 1 0	38	network out of order (*)	-
0 1 0 1 0 0 1	41	temporary failure	-
0 1 0 1 0 1 1	43	access information discarded	Note 6, Note 7
0 1 0 1 1 0 1	45	no VPCI/VCI available	-
0 1 0 1 1 1 1	47	resource unavailable, unspecified	-
0 1 1 0 0 0 1	49	Quality of Service unavailable	Note 2
0 1 1 0 0 1 1	51	user cell rate not available	Note 8
0 1 1 1 0 0 1	57	bearer capability not authorized	-
0 1 1 1 0 1 0	58	bearer capability not presently available	-
0 1 1 1 1 1 1	63	Service or option not available, unspecified	-
1 0 0 0 0 0 1	65	bearer capability not implemented	-
1 0 0 1 0 0 1	73	unsupported combination of traffic parameters	-
1 0 1 0 0 0 1	81	invalid call reference value	-
1 0 1 0 0 1 0	82	identified channel does not exist	Note 9
1 0 1 1 0 0 0	88	incompatible destination	Note 6
1 0 1 1 0 0 1	89	invalid endpoint reference	-
1 0 1 1 0 1 1	91	invalid transit network selection	-
1 0 1 1 1 0 0	92	too many pending add party requests	-
1 0 1 1 1 0 1	93	AAL parameters cannot be supported	-
1 1 0 0 0 0 0	96	mandatory information element is missing	Note 6, Note 7
1 1 0 0 0 0 1	97	message type non-existent or not implemented	Note 10
1 1 0 0 0 1 1	99	information element non-existent or not implemented	Note 6, Note 7
1 1 0 0 1 0 0	100	invalid information element contents	Note 6, Note 7
1 1 0 0 1 0 1	101	message not compatible with call state	Note 10
1 1 0 0 1 1 0	102	recovery on timer expiry	Timer Number (Note 11)
1 1 0 1 0 0 0	104	incorrect message length	-
1 1 0 1 1 1 1	111	protocol error, unspecified	-

(*) Not used in this Implementation Agreement

The use of diagnostics and the coding format of diagnostics varies among the different cause values. The diagnostics column of the table above indicates whether diagnostics are applicable and the coding format of the diagnostics field.

Note 1 - The cause value can be viewed as being comprised of two fields, a class (bits 5 through 7) indicating the general nature of the event, and a value within the class (bits 1 through 4). Classes are:

Bits 7 6 5	Meaning
0 0 0	normal event
0 0 1	normal event
0 1 0	resource unavailable
0 1 1	service or option not available
1 0 0	service or option not implemented
1 0 1	invalid message
1 1 0	protocol error
1 1 1	interworking event/error

Note 2 - The following coding is used:

Bits

8	7	6	5	4	3	2	1	Octet
1 ext	0	Spare 0	0	P-U	N-A	Condition		7

P-U (octet 7)

Bit 4	Meaning
0	Network service - Provider
1	Network service - User

N-A (octet 7)

Bit 3	Meaning
0	Normal
1	Abnormal

Condition (octet 7)

Bits 2 1	Meaning
0 0	Unknown
0 1	Permanent
1 0	Transient

Note 3 - The following coding is used:

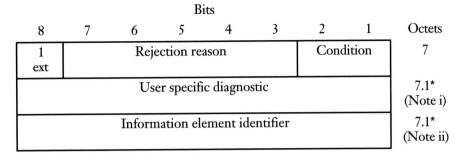

Bits

8	7	6	5	4	3	2	1	Octets
1 ext	Rejection reason					Condition		7
User specific diagnostic								7.1* (Note i)
Information element identifier								7.1* (Note ii)

Note i - This octet may be present only if octet 7 indicates user specific diagnostic.

Note ii - This octet may be present only if octet 7 indicates information element missing or information element contents are not sufficient.

Rejection reason (octet 7)

Bits 7 6 5 4 3	Meaning
0 0 0 0 0	User specific
0 0 0 0 1	Information element missing
0 0 0 1 0	Information element contents are not sufficient

Condition (octet 7)

Bits 2 1	Meaning
0 0	Unknown
0 1	Permanent
1 0	Transient

User specific diagnostic (octet 7.1)
> Coded according to the user specification, subject to the maximum length of the Cause information element.

Information element identifier (octet 7.1)
> Bits 8-1 encoded with the information element identifier of the missing or insufficient information element.

Note 4 - New destination is formatted as the called party number information element, including information element identifier. Transit network selection may also be included.

Note 5 - This cause value is used with coding standard "1 1", Standard defined for the network (either public or private) present on the network side of the interface.

Note 6 - The following coding is used:

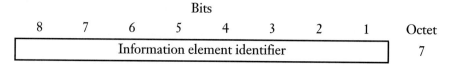

Note 7 - Multiple information identifiers may be included.

Note 8 - The following coding is used:

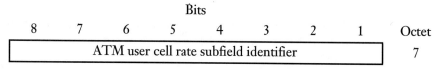

Octet 7 may be repeated to identify multpile ATM user cell rate subfield identifiers.

Note 9 - The following coding is used:

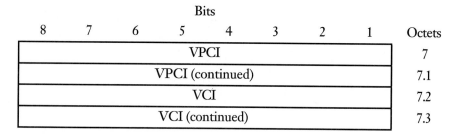

Note 10 - The following coding is used:

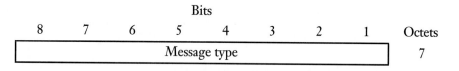

Note 11 - The timer number is coded in IA5 characters, e.g., T308 is coded as "3" "0" "8". The following is used in each octet:

        Bit 8:   Spare "0"
        Bit 7 - 1: IA5 character

The following coding is used:

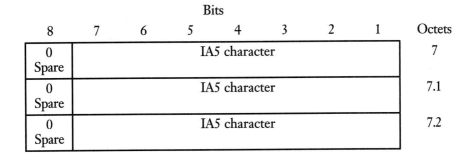

			Bits					
8	7	6	5	4	3	2	1	Octets
0 Spare	IA5 character							7
0 Spare	IA5 character							7.1
0 Spare	IA5 character							7.2

5.4.5.16 Connection Identifier

The Connection identifier information element identifies the local ATM connection resources on the interface.

			Bits					
8	7	6	5	4	3	2	1	Octets
Connection identifier								
0	1	0	1	1	0	1	0	1
Information element identifier								
1 ext	Coding standard		IE Instruction Field					2
Length of connection identifier contents								3
Length of connection identifier contents (continued)								4
1 ext	0 0 Spare		VP Associated Signalling		Preferred/Exclusive			5
Virtual Path Connection Identifier								6
Virtual Path Connection Identifier (continued)								7
Virtual Channel Identifier								8
Virtual Channel Identifier (continued)								9

Figure 5-39 Connection Identifier Information Element

Coding Standard (octet 2)

Bits 7 6	Meaning
0 0	ITU-TS (CCITT) standardized

229

IE Instruction Field (octet 2)

Bits 5 4 3 2 1	Meaning
0 0 0 0 0	IE instruction field not significant

VP Associated Signalling (octet 5)

Bits 5 4	Meaning
0 1	Explicit indication of VPCI

Preferred/Exclusive (octet 5) (Note)

Bits 3 2 1	Meaning
0 0 0	Exclusive VPCI; Exclusive VCI

Note - The network always assigns the VPCI and VCI in this Implementation Agreement.

Virtual Path Connection Identifier (octets 6 and 7)

A two octet binary number assigned to the ATM connection representing the identifier of the Virtual Path Connection.

For this Implementation Agreement, the VPCI value is numerically equivalent to the VPI value assigned for the call. The VPI value is coded in bits 8-1 of Octet 7. Bits 8-1 of Octet 6 are coded to all "0's".

Virtual Channel Identifier (octets 8 and 9)

A two octet binary number assigned to the ATM connection representing the identifier of the Virtual Channel Connection.

VCI Value	
0-15	Reserved by CCITT
16-31	Reserved by ATM Forum
32-65535	Available for assignment by these procedures. Some values in this range may not be available for use (e.g., permanent connections)

5.4.5.17 End-to-End Transit Delay

Not supported in this Implementation Agreement.

5.4.5.18 Quality of Service Parameter

The purpose of the Quality of Service parameter information element is to request and indicate the Quality of Service Class for a connection.

			Bits					
8	7	6	5	4	3	2	1	Octets
Quality of Service parameter								

Bits

8	7	6	5	4	3	2	1	Octets
0	1	0	1	1	1	0	0	1
Quality of Service parameter Information element identifier								
1 ext	Coding standard		IE Instruction Field					2
Length of quality of service parameter contents								3
Length of quality of service parameter contents (continued)								4
QoS Class Forward								5
QoS Class Backward								6

Figure 5-40 Quality of Service parameter Information Element

Coding Standard (octet 2)

Bits 7 6	Meaning
1 1	Standard defined for the network (either public or private) present on the network side of the interface.

IE Instruction Field (octet 2)

Bits 5 4 3 2 1	Meaning
0 0 0 0 0	IE instruction field not significant

QoS Class Forward (octet 5) (Note 1)

Bits 8 7 6 5 4 3 2 1	Meaning
0 0 0 0 0 0 0 0	QoS class 0 - Unspecified QoS class
0 0 0 0 0 0 0 1	QoS class 1
0 0 0 0 0 0 1 0	QoS class 2
0 0 0 0 0 0 1 1	QoS class 3
0 0 0 0 0 1 0 0	QoS class 4

QoS Class Backward (octet 6) (Note 1)

Bits 8 7 6 5 4 3 2 1	Meaning
0 0 0 0 0 0 0 0	QoS class 0 - Unspecified QoS class
0 0 0 0 0 0 0 1	QoS class 1
0 0 0 0 0 0 1 0	QoS class 2
0 0 0 0 0 0 1 1	QoS class 3
0 0 0 0 0 1 0 0	QoS class 4

Note 1 - These codepoints are taken from the Coding Standard value 11. The ATM Forum reserved the right to assign all values. However, these values will be assigned in ascending sequence.

5.4.5.19 Broadband Repeat Indicator

The purpose of the Broadband repeat indicator information element is to indicate how repeated information elements shall be interpreted, when included in a message. The Broadband repeat indicator information element is included before the first occurrence of the information element which will be repeated in a message.

Note - Use of the Broadband repeat indicator information element in conjunction with an information element that occurs only once in a message shall not of itself constitute an error.

Bits								Octets
8	7	6	5	4	3	2	1	Octets
Broadband repeat indicator								1
0	1	1	0	0	0	1	1	1
Information element identifier								
1 ext	Coding Standard		IE Instruction Field					2
Length of broadband repeat indicator contents								3
Length of broadband repeat indicator contents (continued)								4
1 ext	0	0	0	Broadband repeat indication				5
	Spare							

Figure 5-41 Broadband Repeat Indicator Information Element

Coding Standard (octet 2)

Bits 7 6	Meaning
0 0	ITU-TS (CCITT) standardized

IE Instruction Field (octet 2)

Bits 5 4 3 2 1	Meaning
0 0 0 0 0	IE instruction field not significant

Broadband repeat indication (octet 5)

Bits 4 3 2 1	Meaning
0 0 1 0	Prioritized list for selecting one possibility

5.4.5.20 Restart Indicator

The purpose of the Restart indicator information element is to identify the class of the facility to be restarted.

			Bits					
8	7	6	5	4	3	2	1	Octets
Restart indicator								
0	1	1	1	1	0	0	1	1
Information element identifier								
1 ext	Coding Standard		IE Instruction Field					2
Length of restart indicator contents								3
Length of restart indicator contents (continued)								4
1 ext	0	0	0	0	Class			5
	Spare							

Figure 5-42 Restart Indicator Information Element

Coding Standard (octet 2)

Bits 7 6	Meaning
0 0	ITU-TS (CCITT) standardized

IE Instruction Field (octet 2)

Bits 5 4 3 2 1	Meaning
0 0 0 0 0	IE instruction field not significant

Class (octet 5)

Bits 3 2 1	Meaning
0 0 0	Indicated virtual channel (Note 1)
0 1 0	All virtual channels controlled by the Layer 3 entity which sends the RESTART message (Note 2)

Note 1 - The Connection identifier information element must be included and indicates the virtual channel to be restarted.

Note 2 - The Connection identifier information element is not included. All virtual channels controlled by the point-to-point signalling channel are to be restarted.

5.4.5.21 Broadband Sending Complete

The purpose of the Broadband sending complete information element is to optionally indicate completion of the called party number. It is provided in this Implementation Agreement to provide for compatibility with certain public networks. It is optional for user equipment to send, and shall be ignored by network equipment when received. It is optional for the network to send the Broadband sending complete information element in the SETUP message.

				Bits					
8	7	6	5	4	3	2	1		Octets
		Broadband Sending Complete							
0	1	1	0	0	0	1	0		1
		Information element identifier							
1 ext	Coding Standard		IE Instruction Field						2
Length of broadband sending complete contents									3
Length of broadband sending complete contents (continued)									4
1 ext	Broadband sending complete indication								5
	0	1	0	0	0	0	1		

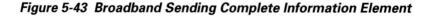

Figure 5-43 Broadband Sending Complete Information Element

Coding Standard (octet 2)

Bits 7 6	Meaning
0 0	ITU-TS (CCITT) standardized

IE Instruction Field (octet 2)

Bits 5 4 3 2 1	Meaning
0 0 0 0 0	IE instruction field not significant

Broadband Sending Complete Indication (octet 5)

Bits 7 6 5 4 3 2 1	Meaning
0 1 0 0 0 0 1	Sending complete

5.4.5.22 Transit Network Selection

The purpose of the Transit network selection information element is to identify one requested transit network.

			Bits					
8	7	6	5	4	3	2	1	Octets
Transit network selection Information element identifier								1
0	1	1	1	1	0	0	0	
1 ext	Coding Standard		IE Instruction Field					2
Length of transit network selection contents								3
Length of transit network selection contents (continued)								4
1 ext	Type of network identification		Network identification plan					5
0	Network identification (IA5 characters)							6 etc.

Figure 5-44 Transit Network Selection Information Element

Coding Standard (octet 2)

Bits 7 6	Meaning
0 0	ITU-TS (CCITT) standardized

235

IE Instruction Field (octet 2)

Bits 5 4 3 2 1	Meaning
0 0 0 0 0	IE instruction field not significant

Type of Network Identification (octet 5)

Bits 7 6 5	Meaning
0 1 0	National network identification

Network Identification Plan (octet 5)

Bits 4 3 2 1	Meaning
0 0 0 1	Carrier Identification Code (Note)

Note - For use in the US, Carrier Identification Codes are assigned by the North American Numbering Plan Administrator to Interexchange Carriers and International Carriers. CICs are coded in IA5 characters corresponding to the digits "0" - "9". See Annex D. This text addresses only the needs of the US telecommunications environment.

Network identification (octet 6)

These IA5 characters are organized according to the network identification plan specified in octet 5.

5.4.6 Information Elements for Interworking with 64 kbit/s Based ISDN

Not supported in this Implementation Agreement.

5.4.7 Information Elements for Supplementary Services

Not supported in this Implementation Agreement.

5.4.8 ATM Forum Specified Information Elements

5.4.8.1 Endpoint Reference

The purpose of the Endpoint reference information element is to identify the individual endpoints of a point-to-multipoint connection. The Endpoint Reference Identifier Value 0 is always used to identify the first party of a point-to-multipoint call. A non-zero value is always used to identify subsequent parties of a point-to-multipoint call.

Bits								Octets
8	7	6	5	4	3	2	1	Octets
Endpoint reference								1
0	1	0	1	0	1	0	0	
Information element identifier								
1 ext	Coding Standard		IE Instruction Field					2
Length of endpoint reference contents								3
Length of endpoint reference contents (continued)								4
Endpoint Reference Type								5
0 Endpoint Reference Flag	Endpoint Reference Identifier Value							6
Endpoint Reference Identifier Value (continued)								6.1

Figure 5-45 Endpoint Reference Information Element

Coding Standard (octet 2)

Bits 76	Meaning
0 0	ITU-TS (CCITT) standardized

IE Instruction Field (octet 2)

Bits 5 4 3 2 1	Meaning
0 0 0 0 0	IE instruction field not significant

Endpoint Reference Type (octet 5)

Bits 8 7 6 5 4 3 2 1	Meaning
0 0 0 0 0 0 0 0	Locally defined integer

Endpoint Reference Flag (octet 6)

Bit 8	Meaning
0	Root Initiated

237

Endpoint Reference Identifier Value (octet 6, 6.1)

The endpoint Reference Identifier is a 15-bit integer (coded in binary) assigned by the root to uniquely identify an endpoint.

5.4.8.2 Endpoint State

The purpose of the Endpoint state information element is to indicate the state of an endpoint of a point-to-multipoint connection.

8	7	6	5	4	3	2	1	Octets
			Bits					

8	7	6	5	4	3	2	1	Octets
			Endpoint state					
0	1	0	1	0	1	0	1	1
			Information element identifier					
1 ext	Coding Standard		IE Instruction Field					2
Length of endpoint state contents								3
Length of endpoint state contents (continued)								4
0 0 Spare		Endpoint Reference Party-state						5

Figure 5-46 Endpoint State Information Element

Coding Standard (octet 2)

Bits 7 6	Meaning
0 0	ITU-TS (CCITT) standardized

IE Instruction Field (octet 2)

Bits 5 4 3 2 1	Meaning
0 0 0 0 0	IE instruction field not significant

Endpoint Reference Party-state (octet 5)

Bits 6 5 4 3 2 1	Meaning
0 0 0 0 0 0	Null
0 0 0 0 0 1	Add Party Initiated
0 0 0 1 1 0	Add Party Received
0 0 1 0 1 1	Drop Party Initiated
0 0 1 1 0 0	Drop Party Received
0 0 1 0 1 0	Active

5.5 Call/Connection Control Procedures For ATM Point-to-Point Calls

This section describes procedures for point-to-point calls only. Section 5.6 contains additional procedures for point-to-multipoint calls as well as changes to the point-to-point procedures needed to support point-to-multipoint calls.

ITU - T draft Recommendation Q.93B [29] procedures are used to establish ATM connections over a permanent signalling virtual channel connection (VCC). The Signalling virtual channel uses VPI=0, VCI=5.

For a call/connection to be established it must satisfy the following general criteria determined by the network and end systems:

Basic service support;

VC availability;

Physical and virtual network resource availability to provide quality of service requested;

End system resource availability to provide quality of service requested;

End to end compatibility.

The call states referred to in this section cover the states perceived by the network, states perceived by the user and states which are common to both user and network.

On any given interface, one entity always assumes the role of user and the other entity always assumes the role of network.

5.5.1 Call/Connection establishment at the originating interface

Before these procedures are invoked, an assured mode signalling AAL connection must be established between the user and the network. All layer 3 messages shall be sent to the Signalling AAL (SAAL) using an AAL-DATA-REQUEST primitive. For more information on the Signalling AAL, see §5.9.

5.5.1.1 Call/Connection request

The calling party initiates call establishment by transferring a SETUP message on the signalling virtual channel across the interface and starting timer T303. Following the transmission of the SETUP message, the call is considered by the calling party to be in the Call Initiated state. The message shall always contain a call reference, selected according to the procedures given in §5.4.3.

The SETUP message shall contain all the information required by the network to process the call. In particular, the called party address information is contained in the Called party number information element possibly supplemented by the Called party subaddress information element. The ATM user cell rate, Broadband bearer capability, and Quality of service parameter information elements are mandatory in the SETUP message. The Broadband sending complete information element may optionally be included by the user for compatibility with ITU - T draft Recommendation Q.93B [29]; however, if it is received by the network, it shall be ignored.

If no response to the SETUP message is received by the user before the first expiry of timer T303, the SETUP message may be retransmitted and timer T303 restarted. If the user does not receive any response to the SETUP message after the final expiry of timer T303, the user shall internally clear the call.

5.5.1.2 Connection Identifier (VPCI/VCI) Allocation/Selection

5.5.1.2.1 Connection Identifier Allocation/Selection - Origination

In the SETUP message, the user shall not include the Connection identifier information element. If the Connection identifier information element is included by the user in the SETUP message, the network shall treat it as an unexpected recognized information element (see §5.5.6.8.3)

The network selects any available VPCI and VCI.

The selected VPCI/VCI value is indicated in the Connection identifier information element in the first message returned by the network in response to the SETUP message (i.e., CALL PROCEEDING message).

If the network is not able to allocate a VCI in any VPCI, a RELEASE COMPLETE message with cause #45, "*No VPCI/VCI available* ," is sent by the network.

5.5.1.2.2 Use of VPCIs

The Connection identifier information element is used in signalling messages to identify the corresponding user information flow. The Connection identifier information element contains the Virtual Path Connection Identifier (VPCI) and the Virtual Channel Identifier (VCI). The VPCI is used instead of the Virtual Path Identifier (VPI) since Virtual Path Cross Connects may be used in the access and multiple interfaces could be controlled by the signalling virtual channel.

Both the user and the network must understand the relationship between the VPCI used in the signalling protocol and the actual VPI used for the user information flow. VPCIs only have significance with regard to a given signalling virtual channel.

For this Implementation Agreement, the signalling virtual channel controls only a single interface, and the VPI and VPCI have the same numerical value.

5.5.1.2.3 VPCI and VCI Ranges

The range of valid VCI values is indicated below:

VCI Value	
0-15	Reserved by CCITT
16-31	Reserved by ATM Forum
32-65535	Identifier of the Virtual Channel (Note)

Note - Some values in the range may not be available for use (e.g., some values may be used for permanent connections). The upper bound on the VCI range (i.e., 65535) may be further restricted by the number of active VCI bits. In addition, a need might arise to reserve more than 32 VCI values.

The range of valid VPCI values is as indicated below:

VPCI Value	
0-255	Identifier of the Virtual Path (Note)

Note - Some values in the range may not be available for use (e.g., some values may be used for permanent virtual path connections). The upper bound on the VPCI range (i.e., 255) may be further restricted by the number of active VPI bits.

5.5.1.3 QoS and Traffic parameters selection procedures

The user shall indicate the requested QoS class in the Quality of Service information element. The user shall indicate the requested ATM user cell rate in the ATM user cell rate information element.

If the network is able to provide the requested ATM user cell rate and QoS class, the network shall progress the call.

If the network is not able to provide the requested QoS class, the network shall reject the call, returning a RELEASE COMPLETE message with cause #49, *"Quality of Service unavailable"*.

If the network is not able to provide the requested ATM user cell rate, the network shall reject the call, returning a RELEASE COMPLETE message with cause #51, *"User cell rate unavailable"*.

If the network detects that the ATM user cell rate information element contains a non-supported set of traffic parameters (see §3.6 for more information), the network shall return a RELEASE COMPLETE message with cause #73, *"Unsupported combination of traffic parameters."*

5.5.1.4 Invalid Call/Connection control information

Upon receiving the SETUP message, the network determines that the call information received from the user is invalid (e.g., invalid number), then the network shall initiate call clearing in accordance with §5.5.4 with a cause such as the following:

#1 *"unassigned (unallocated) number"*;

#3 *"no route to destination"*;

#22 *"number changed"*;

#28 *"invalid number format (address incomplete)"*.

5.5.1.5 Call/Connection proceeding

If the network can determine that access to the requested service is authorized and available, the network may send a CALL PROCEEDING message to the user to acknowledge the SETUP message and to indicate that the call is being processed, and enter the Outgoing Call Proceeding state. When the user receives the CALL PROCEEDING message, the user shall stop timer T303, start timer T310, and enter the Outgoing Call Proceeding state. If the network chooses not to send the CALL PROCEEDING message, the network shall remain in the Call Initiated state.

If the network determines that a requested service is not authorized or is not available, the network shall initiate call clearing in accordance with §5.5.4 with one of the following causes:

#38 *"network out of order"*;

#57 *"bearer capability not authorized"*;

#58 *"bearer capability not presently available"*;

#63 *"service or option not available, unspecified"*; or

#65 *"bearer service not implemented"*.

If the user has received a CALL PROCEEDING message, but does not receive a CONNECT or RELEASE message prior to the expiration of timer T310, then the user shall initiate clearing procedures towards the network with cause #102, *"Recovery on timer expiry"*.

5.5.1.6 Call/Connection confirmation indication

Not supported in this Implementation Agreement.

5.5.1.7 Call/Connection acceptance

Upon receiving an indication that the call has been accepted, the network shall: send a CONNECT message across the user-network interface to the calling user and enter the Active state.

This message indicates to the calling user that a connection has been established through the network.

On receipt of the CONNECT message, the calling user shall: stop timer T303 or T310; send a CONNECT ACKNOWLEDGE message; and enter the Active state. The network shall not take any action on receipt of a CONNECT ACKNOWLEDGE message when it perceives the call to be in the Active state.

At this point an end-to-end connection is established.

5.5.1.8 Call/Connection rejection

Upon receiving an indication that the network or the called user is unable to accept the call, the network shall initiate clearing at the originating user-network interface as described in §5.5.4, using the cause provided by the terminating network or the called user.

5.5.1.9 Transit network selection

When the Transit network selection information element is present, the call shall be processed according to Annex D. Some networks may not support transit network selection.

5.5.1.10 Extensions for symmetric call operation

An extension to allow the optional sending of a CALL PROCEEDING message is supported in §5.5.1.5.

5.5.2 Call/Connection establishment at the destination interface - Point-to-Point Access Configuration Call Offering

Before these procedures are invoked, an assured mode signalling AAL connection must be established between the user and the network. All layer 3 messages shall be sent to the Signalling AAL using an AAL-DATA-REQUEST primitive. The Signalling AAL is described in §5.9.

5.5.2.1 Incoming Call/Connection request

The network will indicate the arrival of a call at the user-network interface by transferring a SETUP message across the interface. The network shall start timer T303 and enter the Call Present state. The message shall always contain a call reference, selected according to the procedures given in §5.4.3. This message is sent by the network only if resources for the call are available; otherwise, the call is cleared toward the calling user.

The SETUP message shall contain all the information required by the called user to process the call.

Upon receipt of a SETUP message, the user shall enter the Call Present state.

If no response to the SETUP message is received by the network before the first expiry of timer T303, the SETUP message may be retransmitted and timer T303 restarted.

5.5.2.2 Address and Compatibility Check

The procedures to perform compatibility checking are implementation dependent. See §5.5.2 of ITU-T draft Recommendation Q.93B [29] for more information.

5.5.2.3 Connection identifier (VPCI/VCI) allocation/selection — destination

The network shall allocate a VPCI/VCI value and include this value in the SETUP message.

The user receiving the SETUP message accepts the indicated VPCI/VCI for the call.

If the indicated VCI is not available within the indicated VPCI, a RELEASE COMPLETE message with cause #35, *"Requested VPCI/VCI not available"*, is sent by the user.

If the VPCI and VCI values in the first response message are not the VPCI and VCI values offered by the network, a RELEASE message with cause #10, *"VPCI/VCI unacceptable"*, is sent to the called user by the network.

If connection identifier selection fails, the network shall initiate clearing towards the calling party using cause #41, *"temporary failure"*.

5.5.2.4 QoS and Traffic parameter selection procedures

The network shall indicate the QoS class in the Quality of service information element.

If the user is not able to provide the requested QoS class, the user shall reject the call, returning a RELEASE COMPLETE message with cause #49, *"Quality of Service unavailable"*.

The network shall indicate the ATM user cell rate in the ATM user cell rate information element.

If the user is not able to support the indicated ATM user cell rate, the user shall reject the call, returning a RELEASE COMPLETE message with cause #47, *"Resource unavailable, unspecified"*.

5.5.2.5 Call/Connection confirmation

5.5.2.5.1 Response to SETUP

5.5.2.5.1.1 Procedures when the User is an ATM endpoint

When the user receives a SETUP message and wishes to accept the incoming call/connection, the user responds with either a CALL PROCEEDING or CONNECT message (see Note), and enters the Incoming Call Proceeding or Connect Request state, respectively.

> *Note* - The CALL PROCEEDING message may be sent by the user which cannot respond to a SETUP message with a CONNECT or RELEASE COMPLETE message before expiration of timer T303.

An incompatible user shall respond by sending a RELEASE COMPLETE message with cause #88, *"incompatible destination"*, and enter the Null state. The network processes this RELEASE COMPLETE message in accordance with §5.5.2.5.3.

A busy user which satisfies the compatibility requirements indicated in the SETUP message shall normally respond with a RELEASE COMPLETE message with cause #17, *"user busy"*. The network processes this RELEASE COMPLETE message in accordance with §5.5.2.5.3.

If the user wishes to refuse the call, a RELEASE COMPLETE message shall be sent with the cause #21, *"call rejected"*, and the user returns to the Null state. The network processes this RELEASE COMPLETE message in accordance with §5.5.2.5.3.

If the user rejects all incoming calls that don't provide the calling number, the user shall return a RELEASE COMPLETE message with network-specific cause #23, *"User rejects all calls with calling line identification restriction (CLIR)"*, and enter the Null state. The network processes this RELEASE COMPLETE message in accordance with §5.5.2.5.3.

5.5.2.5.1.2 Procedures when the User is not an ATM endpoint

If the user is able to provide the requested ATM user cell rate and the QoS, the user shall progress the call.

5.5.2.5.2 Receipt of CALL PROCEEDING

Upon receipt of the CALL PROCEEDING message from a user, the network shall: stop timer T303; start timer T310; and enter the Incoming Call Proceeding state.

5.5.2.5.3 Called user clearing during incoming call establishment

If a RELEASE COMPLETE or RELEASE message is received before a CONNECT message has been received, the network shall: stop timer T303 or T310; continue to clear the call to the called user as described in §5.5.4.3; and clear the call to the calling user with the cause received in the RELEASE COMPLETE or RELEASE message.

5.5.2.5.4 Call failure

If the network does not receive any response to the SETUP after the final expiry of timer T303, the network shall enter the Null state and initiate clearing procedures towards the calling user with cause #18, *"no user responding"*.

If the network has received a CALL PROCEEDING message, but does not receive a CONNECT or RELEASE message prior to the expiration of timer T310, then the network shall: initiate clearing procedures toward the calling user with cause #18, *"no user responding"*, and initiate clearing procedures towards the called user.

5.5.2.6 Call/Connection acceptance

An ATM endpoint indicates acceptance of an incoming call by sending a CONNECT message to the network. Upon sending the CONNECT message, the user (ATM endpoint) shall: start timer T313 and enter the Connect Request state.

A user that is not an ATM endpoint shall accept an incoming call by sending a CONNECT message to the network after receiving an indication that the call has been accepted from the ATM endpoint. After sending the CONNECT message the user shall: start timer T313 and enter the Connect Request state.

5.5.2.7 Active indication

On receipt of the CONNECT message, the network shall: stop timers T303 or T310; send a CONNECT ACKNOWLEDGE message to the user; initiate procedures to send a CONNECT message towards the calling user; and enter the Active state.

The CONNECT ACKNOWLEDGE message indicates completion of the ATM connection for that interface. There is no guarantee of an end-to-end connection until a CONNECT message is received at the calling user. Upon receipt of the CONNECT ACKNOWLEDGE message the called user shall: stop timer T313 and enter the Active state.

When timer T313 expires prior to receipt of a CONNECT ACKNOWLEDGE message, the called user shall initiate clearing in accordance with §5.5.4.3.

5.5.3 Call/Connection establishment at the destination — Point-to-multipoint access arrangement call offering

Not supported in this Implementation Agreement.

5.5.4 Call/Connection clearing

5.5.4.1 Terminology

The following terms are used in this Implementation Agreement in the description of clearing procedures:

- A virtual channel is *connected* when the virtual channel is part of an ATM virtual channel connection established according to this Implementation Agreement.
- A virtual channel is *disconnected* when the virtual channel is no longer part of an ATM virtual channel connection, but is not yet available for use in a new virtual channel connection.
- A virtual channel is *released* when the virtual channel is not part of an ATM virtual channel connection and is available for use in a new virtual channel connection. Similarly, a call reference that is *released* is available for reuse.

5.5.4.2 Exception conditions

Under normal conditions, call clearing is usually initiated when the user or the network sends a RELEASE message and follows the procedures defined in §§5.5.4.3 and 5.5.4.4 respectively. The only exception to the above rule is in response to a SETUP message, the user or network can reject a call/connection (e.g., because of the unavailability of a suitable virtual channel) by: responding with a RELEASE COMPLETE message provided no other response has previously been sent; releasing the call reference; and entering the Null state.

5.5.4.3 Clearing initiated by the user

Apart from the exceptions identified in §§5.5.4.2 and 5.5.6, the user shall initiate clearing by: sending a RELEASE message; starting timer T308; disconnecting the virtual channel; and entering the Release Request state.

The network shall enter the Release Request state upon receipt of a RELEASE message. This message then prompts the network to disconnect the virtual channel, and to initiate procedures for clearing the network connection to the remote user. Once the virtual channel used for the call has been disconnected, the network shall: send a RELEASE COMPLETE message to the user; release both the call reference and virtual channel (i.e., connection identifier); and enter the Null state.

> *Note* - The RELEASE COMPLETE message has only local significance and does not imply an acknowledgment of clearing from the remote user.

On receipt of the RELEASE COMPLETE message the user shall: stop timer T308; release the virtual channel; release the call reference; and return to the Null state.

If timer T308 expires for the first time, the user shall: retransmit a RELEASE message to the network with the cause number originally contained in the first RELEASE message; restart timer T308 and remain in the Release Request state. In addition, the user may indicate a second Cause information element with cause #102, *"recovery on timer expiry"*. If no RELEASE COMPLETE message is received from the network before timer T308 expires a second time, the user shall: release the call reference; and return to the Null state. Equipment shall perform implementation dependent recovery, such as initiating restart procedures.

5.5.4.4 Clearing initiated by the network

Apart from the exception conditions identified in §§5.5.4.2 and 5.5.6, the network shall initiate clearing by: sending a RELEASE message; starting timer T308; disconnecting the virtual channel; and entering the Release Indication state.

The user shall enter the Release Indication state upon receipt of a RELEASE message. Once the virtual channel used for the call has been disconnected, the user shall: send a RELEASE COMPLETE message to the network; release both its call reference and the virtual channel; and return to the Null state.

On receipt of the RELEASE COMPLETE message, the network shall: stop timer T308; release both the virtual channel and call reference; and return to the Null state.

If timer T308 expires for the first time, the network shall retransmit the RELEASE message to the user with the cause number originally contained in the first RELEASE message; start timer T308 and remain in the Release Indication state. In addition, the network may indicate a second Cause information element with cause #102, *"recovery on timer expiry"*. If no RELEASE COMPLETE message is received from the user before timer T308 expires a second time, the network shall: release the call reference and return to the Null state. Equipment shall perform implementation dependent recovery, such as initiating restart procedures.

5.5.4.5 Clear collision

Clear collision can occur when both sides simultaneously transfer RELEASE messages related to the same call reference value. If the user receives a RELEASE message while in the Release Request state, the user shall: stop timer T308; release the call reference and virtual channel; and enter the Null state (without sending or receiving a RELEASE COMPLETE message). If the network receives a RELEASE message while in the Release Indication state, the network shall: stop timer T308; release the call reference and virtual channel; and enter the Null state (without sending or receiving a RELEASE COMPLETE message).

5.5.5 Restart procedure

The user and the network shall implement these procedures.

The restart procedure is used to return a virtual channel or all virtual channels controlled by the signalling virtual channel to the Null state. The procedure is usually invoked when the other side of the interface does not respond to other call control messages or a failure has occurred (e.g., following the expiry of timer T308 due to the absence of response to a clearing message). It may also be initiated as a result of local failure, maintenance action or mis-operation.

> *Note* - The call reference flag of the global call reference applies to restart procedures. In the case when both sides of the interface initiate simultaneous restart requests, they shall be handled independently. In the case when the same virtual channel(s) are specified, they shall not be considered free for reuse until all the relevant restart procedures are completed.

5.5.5.1 Sending RESTART

A RESTART message is sent by the network or user equipment in order to return virtual channels to the idle condition. The Restart indicator information element shall be present in the RESTART message to indicate whether an *indicated virtual channel* or *all virtual channels controlled by the layer 3 entity* are to be restarted. If the Restart indicator information element is coded as "indicated virtual channel", then the Connection identifier information element shall be present to indicate which virtual channel is to be returned to the idle condition. If the Restart indicator information element is coded as "all virtual channels controlled by the layer

3 entity which sends the RESTART message", then the Connection identifier information element shall not be included.

Upon transmitting the RESTART message the sender enters the Restart Request state, starts timer T316, and waits for a RESTART ACKNOWLEDGE message. Also, no further RESTART messages shall be sent until a RESTART ACKNOWLEDGE is received or timer T316 expires. Receipt of a RESTART ACKNOWLEDGE message stops timer T316 and indicates that the virtual channel(s) and associated resources (e.g., call reference value(s)) can be freed for reuse. The Null state shall be entered after the virtual channel and call reference value are released .

If a RESTART ACKNOWLEDGE message is not received prior to the expiry of timer T316 one or more subsequent RESTART messages may be sent until a RESTART ACKNOWLEDGE message is returned. While timer T316 is running, no calls shall be placed or accepted over the virtual channel(s) by the originator of the RESTART message. The number of consecutive unsuccessful restart attempts has a default limit of two. When this limit is reached, the originator of the RESTART message shall make no further restart attempts and shall enter the Null state (REST 0). An indication will be provided to the appropriate maintenance entity. The virtual channel(s) is considered to be in an out-of-service condition until maintenance action has been taken.

If a RESTART ACKNOWLEDGE message is received indicating a different set of virtual channels from the set indicated in the RESTART message, an indication shall be given to the maintenance entity. It is the responsibility of the maintenance entity to determine what actions shall be taken on the channels which have not been returned to the idle condition. Those virtual channels that are acknowledged shall be considered free for reuse.

The RESTART and RESTART ACKNOWLEDGE message shall contain the global call reference value (all zeros) to which the Restart Request state is associated. These messages are transferred using the AAL-DATA-REQUEST primitive.

The remote parties are cleared using cause #41, *"temporary failure"*.

5.5.5.2 Receipt of RESTART

Upon receiving a RESTART message the recipient shall enter the Restart state associated to the global call reference and start timer T317; it shall then initiate the appropriate internal actions to return the specified virtual channels to the idle condition and release all call references associated with the specified virtual channels. Upon completion of internal clearing, timer T317 shall be stopped and a RESTART ACKNOWLEDGE message transmitted to the originator, and the Null state (REST 0) entered.

If timer T317 expires prior to completion of internal clearing, an indication shall be sent to the maintenance entity (i.e., a primitive should be transmitted to the system management entity) and the Null state (REST 0) shall be entered.

The remote parties are cleared using cause #41, *"temporary failure"*.

Even if all the specified virtual channels are in the idle condition, the receiving entity shall transmit a RESTART ACKNOWLEDGE message to the originator upon receiving a RESTART message.

If the Restart indicator information element is coded as "all virtual channels controlled by the layer 3 entity which sends the RESTART message", then all calls on all interfaces associated with the signalling virtual channel shall be cleared.

If the Restart indicator information element is coded as "all virtual channels controlled by the layer 3 entity which sends the RESTART message" and a Connection identifier information element is included, the Connection identifier information element is treated as described in §5.5.6.8.3.

If the Restart indicator information element is coded as "indicated virtual channel" and the Connection identifier information element is not included, then the procedures in §5.5.6.7.1 shall be followed.

If the Restart indicator information element is coded as "indicated virtual channel" and the Connection identifier information element contains an unrecognized VPCI, then the procedures in §5.5.6.7.2 shall be followed.

If permanent virtual connections established by management procedures are implicitly specified (by specifying "all virtual channels controlled by the layer 3 entity which sends the RESTART message") no action shall be taken on these virtual channels, but a RESTART ACKNOWLEDGE message shall be returned containing the appropriate indications (i.e., "all virtual channels controlled by the layer 3 entity which sends the RESTART message").

If a permanent virtual connection established by management procedures or a reserved VPCI/VCI (e.g., the point-to-point signalling virtual channel) is explicitly specified (by including a Connection identifier information element in the RESTART message), no action shall be taken on the virtual channel and a STATUS message should be returned with cause #82, *"identified channel does not exist"*, indicating in the diagnostics field the virtual channel that could not be handled.

The following entities are released as a result of the Restart Procedures:
- virtual channels established by Q.93B procedures,
- all resources associated with the released virtual channel (e.g., call reference value)

The following entities are not released as a result of the Restart Procedures:
- permanent connections established by a network management system
- reserved virtual channels (e.g., point-to-point signalling virtual channel)

5.5.6 Handling of error conditions

All messages which use the protocol discriminator *Q.93B user-network call control message* must pass the checks described in §§5.5.6.1 through 5.5.6.8.

Detailed error handling procedures are implementation dependent and may vary from network to network. However, capabilities facilitating the orderly treatment of error conditions are provided for in this section and shall be provided in each implementation.

Sections 5.5.6.1 through 5.5.6.8 are listed in order of precedence.

5.5.6.1 Protocol discrimination error

When a message is received with a protocol discriminator coded other than *Q.93B user-network call control message*, that message shall be ignored. "Ignore" means to do nothing, as if the message had never been received.

5.5.6.2 Message too short

When a message is received that is too short to contain a complete Message type information element, that message shall be ignored.

5.5.6.3 Call reference error

5.5.6.3.1 Invalid call reference format

If the call reference information element octet 1, bits 5 through 8 do not equal 0000, then the message shall be ignored.

If the call reference information element octet 1, bits 1 through 4 indicate a length other than 3 octets (see §5.4.3), then the message shall be ignored.

5.5.6.3.2 Call reference procedural errors

a) Whenever any message except SETUP, RELEASE COMPLETE, STATUS EN-QUIRY, or STATUS is received specifying a call reference which is not recognized as relating to an active call or to a call in progress, the receiver shall initiate clearing by sending a RELEASE COMPLETE message with cause #81, "*invalid call reference value*", specifying the call reference in the received message and shall remain in the Null state.

b) When a RELEASE COMPLETE message is received specifying a call reference which is not recognized as relating to an active call or to a call in progress, no action should be taken.

c) When a SETUP message is received specifying a call reference which is not recognized as relating to an active call or to a call in progress, and with a call reference flag incorrectly set to "1", this message shall be ignored.

251

d) When a SETUP message is received specifying a call reference which is recognized as relating to an active call or to a call in progress, this SETUP message shall be ignored.

e) When any message except RESTART, RESTART ACKNOWLEDGE, or STATUS is received using the global call reference, no action should be taken on this message and a STATUS message using the global call reference with a call state indicating the current state associated with the global call reference and cause #81, "*invalid call reference*", shall be returned.

f) When a STATUS message is received specifying a call reference which is not recognized as relating to an active call or to a call in progress, the procedures of §5.5.6.12 shall apply.

g) When a STATUS ENQUIRY message is received which is not recognized as relating to an active call or a call in progress, the procedures of §5.5.6.11 shall apply.

5.5.6.4 Message type or message sequence errors

Whenever an unexpected message (including messages that are standardized by the ITU-TS but which are not included in this specification), except RELEASE, RELEASE COMPLETE, or an unrecognized message is received in any state other than the Null state, a STATUS message shall be returned with one of the following causes:

#97   "*message type non-existent or not implemented*"; or,

#101 "*message not compatible with call state*".

However, two exceptions to this procedure exist. The first exception is when the network or the user receives an unexpected RELEASE message in response to a SETUP message. In this case no STATUS or STATUS ENQUIRY message is sent. Whenever the network receives an unexpected RELEASE message, the network shall: release the virtual channel; clear the network connection and the call to the remote user with the cause in the RELEASE message sent by the user or, if not included, cause #31, "*normal, unspecified*"; return a RELEASE COMPLETE message to the user; release the call reference; stop all timers; and enter the Null state. Whenever the user receives an unexpected RELEASE message, the user shall: release the virtual channel; return a RELEASE COMPLETE message to the network; release the call reference; stop all timers; and enter the Null state.

The second exception is when the network or user receives an unexpected RELEASE COMPLETE message. Whenever the network receives an unexpected RELEASE COM-PLETE message, the network shall: disconnect and release the virtual channel; clear the network connection and the call to the remote user with the cause indicated by the user or, if not included, cause #111, "*protocol error, unspecified*"; release the call reference; stop all timers; and enter the Null state. Whenever the user receives an unexpected RELEASE COMPLETE message, the user shall: disconnect and release the virtual channel; release the call reference; stop all timers; and enter the Null state.

5.5.6.5 Message length error

If the message length indicated in the Message length information element is inconsistent with the length of the message received, the message shall be discarded and a STATUS message with cause #104, "*incorrect message length*," is returned.

5.5.6.6 General information element errors

5.5.6.6.1 Information element sequence

The first four information elements (Protocol discriminator, Call reference, Message type, and Message length) shall appear in the order specified in §5.4.1. Variable length information elements may appear in any order within a message except for the cases described in §5.4.5.1.

5.5.6.6.2 Duplicated information elements

If an information element is repeated in a message in which repetition of the information element is not permitted, only the contents of information element appearing first shall be handled and all subsequent repetitions of the information element shall be ignored. When repetition of information elements is permitted, only the contents of permitted information elements shall be handled. If the limit on repetition of information elements is exceeded, the contents of information elements appearing first up to the limit of repetitions shall be handled and all subsequent repetitions of the information element shall be ignored.

5.5.6.7 Mandatory information element error

5.5.6.7.1 Mandatory information element missing

When a message other than SETUP, RELEASE, or RELEASE COMPLETE is received which has one or more mandatory information elements missing, no action should be taken on the message and no state change should occur. A STATUS message is then returned with cause #96, "*mandatory information element is missing*".

When a SETUP message is received which has one or more mandatory information elements missing, a RELEASE COMPLETE message with cause #96, "*mandatory information element is missing*" shall be returned.

When a RELEASE message is received with the Cause information element missing, the actions taken shall be the same as if a RELEASE message with cause #31, "*normal, unspecified*", was received (see §5.5.4), with the exception that the RELEASE COMPLETE message sent on the local interface contains cause #96, "*mandatory information element is missing*".

When a RELEASE COMPLETE message is received with a Cause information element missing, it will be assumed that a RELEASE COMPLETE message was received with cause #31, "*normal, unspecified*".

5.5.6.7.2 Mandatory information element content error

When a message other than SETUP, RELEASE, or RELEASE COMPLETE is received which has one or more mandatory information elements with invalid content, no action should be taken on the message and no state change should occur. A STATUS message is then returned with cause #100, "*invalid information element contents*".

When a SETUP message is received which has one or more mandatory information elements with invalid content, a RELEASE COMPLETE message with cause #100, "*invalid information element contents*", shall be returned.

When a RELEASE message is received with invalid content of the Cause information element, the actions taken shall be the same as if a RELEASE message with cause #31, "*normal, unspecified*" was received (see §5.5.4), with the exception that the RELEASE COMPLETE message sent on the local interface contains cause #100, "*invalid information element contents*".

When a RELEASE COMPLETE message is received with invalid content of the Cause information element, it will be assumed that a RELEASE COMPLETE message was received with cause #31, "*normal, unspecified*".

Information elements with a length exceeding the maximum length (given in §5.3) will be treated as information elements with content error.

> Note - As an option of user equipment, cause values, location codes, and diagnostics which are not understood by the user equipment may be passed on to another entity (e.g., user) instead of treating the cause value as if it were cause #31, "*normal, unspecified*", and sending cause #100, "*invalid information element contents*", with the RELEASE COMPLETE message. This option is intended to aid user equipment to be compatible to future additions of cause values, location codes and diagnostics to the Implementation Agreement.

5.5.6.8 Non-mandatory information element errors

The following sections identify actions on information elements not recognized as mandatory.

5.5.6.8.1 Unrecognized information element

When a message is received that has one or more unrecognized information elements, then the receiving entity shall proceed as follows:

Action shall be taken on the message and those information elements which are recognized and have valid content. When the received message is other than RELEASE or RELEASE COMPLETE, a STATUS message may be returned containing one Cause information element. The STATUS message indicates the call state of the receiver after taking action on the message. The Cause information element shall contain cause #99, "*information element non-existent or not implemented*", and the diagnostic field, if present, shall contain the information element identifier for each information element which was unrecognized. Subsequent actions are determined by the sender of the unrecognized information elements.

If a clearing message contains one or more unrecognized information elements, the error is reported to the local user in the following manner:

a) When a RELEASE message is received which has one or more unrecognized information elements, a RELEASE COMPLETE message with cause #99, "*information element non-existent or not implemented*", shall be returned. The Cause information element diagnostic field, if present, shall contain the information element identifier for each information element which was unrecognized.

b) When a RELEASE COMPLETE message is received which has one or more unrecognized information elements, no action shall be taken on the unrecognized information.

Note - The diagnostic(s) of cause #99, "*information element non-existent or not implemented*", facilitates the decision in selecting an appropriate recovery procedure at the reception of a STATUS message. Therefore, it is recommended to provide cause #99, "*information element non-existent or not implemented*", with diagnostic(s) if a layer 3 entity expects the peer to take an appropriate action at the receipt of a STATUS message, although inclusion of diagnostic(s) is optional.

5.5.6.8.2 Non-mandatory information element content error

When a message is received which has one or more non-mandatory information elements with invalid content, action shall be taken on the message and those information elements which are recognized and have valid content. A STATUS message may be returned containing one Cause information element. The STATUS message indicates the call state of the receiver after taking action on the message. The Cause information element shall contain cause #100, "*invalid information element contents*", and the diagnostic field, if present, shall contain the information element identifier for each information element which has invalid contents.

Information elements with a length exceeding the maximum length (given in §5.3) will be treated as an information element with content error. But for access information elements (i.e., Calling party subaddress, Called party subaddress, Broadband low layer information, AAL parameters, and Broadband high layer information information elements), cause #43, "*access information discarded*", is used instead of cause #100, "*invalid information element contents*".

Note - As an option of user equipment, cause values, location codes, and diagnostics which are not understood by the user equipment may be accepted and passed on to another entity (e.g., user) instead of ignoring the Cause information element contents and optionally sending a STATUS message with cause #100, "*invalid information element contents*". This option is intended to aid user equipment to be compatible to future additions of cause values, location codes and diagnostics to the Implementation Agreement.

5.5.6.8.3 Unexpected recognized information element

When a message is received with a recognized information element that is not defined to be contained in that message, the receiving entity shall (except as noted below) treat the information element as an unrecognized information element and follow the procedures defined in §5.5.6.8.1.

> *Note* - Some implementations may choose to process unexpected recognized information elements when the procedure for processing the information element is independent of the message in which it is received.

5.5.6.9 Signalling AAL reset

Whenever indication of a Signalling AAL reset is received from the Q.SAAL layer (see §5.9) by means of the AAL-ESTABLISH-INDICATION primitive, the following procedures apply:

a) For calls in the clearing phase (states N11, N12, U11, and U12), no action shall be taken.

b) For calls in the establishment phase (states N1, N3, N6, N8, N9, U1, U3, U6, U8, and U9), the entity shall initiate clearing with cause #41, "*temporary failure*".

c) Calls in the active state shall be maintained according to the procedures in other parts of §5.5.

5.5.6.10 Signalling AAL failure

Whenever the network layer entity is notified by its Signalling AAL entity via the AAL-RELEASE-INDICATION primitive that there is a Signalling AAL malfunction, the following procedure shall apply:

a) Any calls not in the Active state shall be cleared internally.

b) For any call in the Active state a timer T309 shall be started (if implemented). If timer T309 is already running, it shall not be restarted.

Signalling AAL re-establishment shall be requested by sending an AAL-ESTABLISH-REQUEST primitive.

When informed of Signalling AAL re-establishment by means of the AAL-ESTABLISH-CONFIRM primitive, the following procedure shall apply:

- Stop timer T309; and

- Perform the Status Enquiry procedure according to §5.5.6.11.

If timer T309 expires prior to Signalling AAL re-establishment, the network shall: clear the network connection and call to the remote user with cause #27, "*destination out of order*"; disconnect and release the virtual channel; release the call reference; and enter the Null state.

If timer T309 expires prior to Signalling AAL re-establishment, the user shall: clear the attached connection (if any) with cause #27, "*destination out of order*"; disconnect and release the virtual channel; release the call reference; and enter the Null state.

The implementation of timer T309 is optional in the user side and mandatory in the network side.

When timer T309 is not implemented, the user shall: clear the attached connection (if any) with cause #27, "*destination out of order*"; disconnect and release the virtual channel; release the call reference; and enter the Null state.

5.5.6.11 Status enquiry procedure

To check the correctness of a call state at a peer entity, a STATUS ENQUIRY message may be sent requesting the call state. This may, in particular, apply to procedural error conditions described in 5.5.6.9 and 5.5.6.10.

In addition whenever indication is received from the Signalling AAL that a disruption has occurred at the data link layer, a STATUS ENQUIRY message shall be sent to check the correctness of the call state at the peer entity.

Upon sending the STATUS ENQUIRY message, timer T322 shall be started in anticipation of receiving a STATUS message. While timer T322 is running, only one outstanding request for call state information shall exist. Therefore, if timer T322 is already running, it shall not be restarted. If a clearing message is received before timer T322 expires, timer T322 shall be stopped and call clearing shall continue.

Upon receipt of a STATUS ENQUIRY message, the receiver shall respond with a STATUS message, reporting the current call state (the current state of an active call or a call in progress, or the Null state if the call reference does not relate to an active call or a call in progress) and cause #30, "*response to status enquiry*". Receipt of the STATUS ENQUIRY message does not result in a state change.

The sending or receipt of the STATUS message in such a situation will not directly affect the call state of either the sender or receiver. The side having received the STATUS message shall inspect the Cause information element. If a STATUS message is received that contains cause #30, "*response to STATUS ENQUIRY*", timer T322 shall be stopped and the appropriate action taken, based on the information in that STATUS message, relative to the current state of the receiver.

If timer T322 expires, and no STATUS message was received, the STATUS ENQUIRY message may be retransmitted one or more times until a response is received. The number of times the STATUS ENQUIRY message is retransmitted is an implementation dependent value. The call shall be cleared to the local interface with cause #41, "*temporary failure*", if the STATUS ENQUIRY is retransmitted the maximum number of times. If appropriate, the network shall also clear the network connection, using cause #41, "*temporary failure*".

5.5.6.12 Receiving a STATUS message

On receipt of a STATUS message reporting an incompatible state, the receiving entity shall:

a) clear the call by sending the appropriate clearing message with cause #101, *"message not compatible with call state"*; or,

b) take other actions which attempt to recover from a mismatch and which are an implementation option.

Except for the following rules, the determination of which states are incompatible is left as an implementation decision:

a) If a STATUS message indicating any call state except the Null state is received in the Null state, then the receiving entity shall send a RELEASE COMPLETE message with cause #101, *"message not compatible with call state"*; and remain in the Null state.

b) If a STATUS message indicating any call state except the Null state is received in the Release Request or Release Indication state, no action shall be taken.

c) If a STATUS message, indicating the Null state, is received in any state except the Null state, the receiver shall release all resources and move into the Null state.

When in the Null state, the receiver of a STATUS message indicating the Null state shall take no action other than to discard the message and shall remain in the Null state.

A STATUS message may be received indicating a compatible call state but containing one of the following causes:

#96 *"mandatory information element is missing"*;

#97 *"message type non-existent or not implemented"*;

#99 *"information element non-existent or not implemented"*; or

#100 *"invalid information element contents"*.

In this case, the actions to be taken are an implementation option. If other procedures are not defined, the receiver shall clear the call with the appropriate procedure defined in §5.5.4, using the cause specified in the received STATUS message.

On receipt of a STATUS message specifying the global call reference and reporting an incompatible state in the Restart Request or Restart state, layer management shall be informed and take no further action on this message.

When in the null state, then on receipt of a STATUS message with the global call reference, no action shall be taken.

Note - Further actions as a result of higher layer activity (e.g., system or layer management) are implementation dependent (including the retransmission of RESTART).

Except for the above case, the error handling procedures when receiving a STATUS message specifying the global call reference are an implementation option.

5.5.7 Forward Compatibility Procedures

Not supported in this Implementation Agreement

5.6 Call/Connection Control Procedures for Point-to-Multipoint Calls

This section describes procedures for point-to-multipoint calls. The signalling channel used is the same as the one assigned for point-to-point connections. This signalling specification supports point-to-multipoint calls where information is multicasted unidirectionally from one calling user to a set of called users. The calling user is also referred to as the Root; the called users are also referred to as Leaves. In this document the Root initiates the joining of all parties to the call. Point-to-multipoint calls are initiated with a SETUP message which contains an Endpoint reference information element and a Broadband bearer capability information element indicating point-to-multipoint in the user plane connection configuration field.

At an interface involved in a point-to-multipoint call there will be two types of states associated with this call:

1) States on both sides of the interface which coincide with the subset of Q.93B states defined in §5.2, i.e., the states of the Q.93B protocol handlers on both sides of the UNI and identified by their respective Call reference.

   These states will henceforward be called the *link-states* of the point-to-multipoint call at that interface.

2) States for each party in the call which are known at the interface; These parties are identified by their Endpoint reference.

   These states will henceforward be called the *party-states* of the party associated with the call.

Note: In each network there will be:

For each point-to-multipoint call, one incoming link-state (on the link from the root) and one outgoing link-state for each branch leading to one or more leaves (i.e., parties) participating in the call. The network may remap the call reference such that different call reference values may be associated with the incoming and outgoing links, where all pertain to different links of the same point-to-multipoint call.

For each party associated with the point-to-multipoint call, one incoming party-state and one outgoing party-state is maintained for each leaf reached through the network. Additionally, an endpoint reference value is associated with each reachable party, where this value may be remapped by the network such that a different value is used on the incoming link from that used on the outgoing link heading towards the associated party.

The party-states which may exist on the user side or the network side of the user network interface are:

Null:

The party does not exist, no Endpoint Reference value has been allocated.

Add Party Initiated :

A SETUP or an ADD PARTY message has been sent to the other side of the interface for this party for the call.

Add Party Received:

A SETUP or an ADD PARTY message has been received from the other side of the interface for this party for the call.

Drop Party Initiated:

A DROP PARTY message has been sent for this party of the call.

Drop Party Received:

A DROP PARTY message has been received for this party of the call.

Active:

On the user side of the UNI, when the user has received a CONNECT, CONNECT ACKNOWLEDGE or ADD PARTY ACKNOWLEDGE message identifying this party, or sent an ADD PARTY ACKNOWELDGE.

On the network side of the UNI, when the network has sent a CONNECT, CONNECT ACKNOWLEDGE or ADD PARTY ACKNOWLEDGE message identifying this party, or when the network has received an ADD PARTY ACKNOWLEDGE message identifying this party.

These states apply to both sides of the interface.

In the Root, party-states of each party are maintained along with the link-state for the outgoing link. A Leaf terminal which expects to never terminate more than one party of a point-to-multipoint call need only maintain the link-states.

Note - For a more detailed description of the underlying architecture see Appendix C of this specification.

5.6.1 Adding a party at the originating interface

5.6.1.1 Set up of the first party

The set up of the first party of a point-to-multipoint call is always initiated by the Root (terminal) and follows the procedures of Q.93B for call set-up as described in §5.5 for point-to-point calls; in particular only messages of the basic Q.93B and no messages specific to point-to-multipoint control, such as ADD PARTY will be used. The link-states for the call change according to the call state changes as described in §5.5.

The following additions apply:

The SETUP message sent by the Root (terminal) must contain the Endpoint Reference value set to zero for the first party and with the Broadband bearer capability information element indicating point-to-multipoint in the user plane connection configuration field.

The party-state changes from Null to Add Party Initiated at the Root (terminal) after the SETUP message has been sent to the network. Upon reception of the SETUP message, the party-state at the network side of the interface changes from Null to Add Party Received. The party-state changes to Active when:

- at the network side of the Root UNI after CONNECT has been sent to the user side of the Root UNI

- at the user side of the root UNI after CONNECT has been received from the network side of the Root UNI

No party-state change occurs when:

- the user sends or receives a CALL PROCEEDING message.

- the network sends a CALL PROCEEDING message.

- the network receives a CALL PROCEEDING or CONNECT ACKNOWLEDGE message.

- the user sends a CONNECT message.

If the SETUP contains a non-zero backward user cell rate parameter the network shall reject the SETUP request with cause #73, *"Unsupported combination of traffic parameters"*.

If the SETUP contains an Endpoint reference information element and the Broadband bearer capability information element does not indicate point-to-multipoint in the user plane connection configuration field, the network shall reject the SETUP request with cause #100, *"invalid information element contents"*, and include both the Endpoint reference information element and the Broadband bearer capability information element identifiers in the diagnostic field.

If the SETUP contains a Broadband bearer capability information element indicating point-to-multipoint in the user plane connection configuration field and does not contain an Endpoint reference information element, the network shall reject the SETUP request with cause #96, *"mandatory information element is missing"*, and include the Endpoint reference information element identifier in the diagnostic field.

5.6.1.2 Adding a Party

The calling party (Root) initiates the addition of a party by transferring an ADD PARTY message on the assigned signalling VCC across the interface. The user shall send an ADD PARTY message only if the link is in the Active link-state.

After sending the ADD PARTY message, the user starts timer T399. The ADD PARTY message must have the same call reference value as specified in the initial setup of the call to which the party is to be added. The message shall always contain an endpoint reference value as described in §5.4.8.1. Following the transmission of the ADD PARTY message, the party-state is considered by the calling party to be in the Add Party Initiated party-state.

The connection identifier (VPCI/VCI) used for the new party is the same as for the original call and is not indicated in the ADD PARTY message.

The QoS, Bearer capability and ATM user cell rate for the new party shall be the same as for the original call and are not indicated in the ADD PARTY message.

If the Connection identifier, QoS parameter, Broadband bearer capability, or ATM user cell rate information elements are included in the ADD PARTY message, these information elements shall be ignored and a status message sent as described in §5.6.5.

If the network rejects an Add Party request an ADD PARTY REJECT message shall be sent to the user. After sending the ADD PARTY REJECT message, if there are no remaining parties in the Active or Add Party Received party-state, then the network shall send a RELEASE message to the user. The cause used in the RELEASE message is #31, *"Normal, unspecified"*. The cause used in the ADD PARTY REJECT message is specified below:

If the network is not able to provide the requested QoS class, the network shall reject the add request with cause #49, *"Quality of Service unavailable"*.

If the network is not able to provide the user cell rate of the original connection, the network shall reject the add party request with cause #51, *"User cell rate not available"*. The diagnostics field of the cause information element should indicate those parameters that exceed the capacity of the network.

If a user receives a RELEASE message for a call which has one or more parties which have not progressed past the Add Party Initiated party-state, as an option the User may transmit one of the ADD PARTY messages as a SETUP message with a new call reference value and the same information element values as the previous call. After the user receives the CONNECT message for this SETUP message, the remaining ADD PARTY messages will be retransmitted by the user using the new call reference value.

If the user does not use this option, the user shall clear all the parties associated with this call on this link.

5.6.1.3 Invalid Call/Connection Control Information or Service Request in the ADD PARTY message

Upon receiving the ADD PARTY message the network enters the Add Party Received party-state. If the network determines that the call information received from the user is invalid (e.g., invalid number), then the network will send an ADD PARTY REJECT message. The cause used in rejection is specified below.

#1   *"unassigned (unallocated) number"*;

#3   *"no route to destination"*;

#22 *"number changed"*;

#28 *"invalid number format (incomplete number)"*.

Similarly, if the network determines that a requested service is not authorized, not implemented or is not available, the network will send an ADD PARTY REJECT message with one of the following causes:

#47 *"resource unavailable, unspecified"*;

#58 *"bearer capability not presently available"*.

After sending the ADD PARTY REJECT message, if there are no remaining parties in the Active or Add Party Received party-state then the network shall send a RELEASE message to the user. The cause used in the RELEASE message is #31, *"normal unspecified"*.

5.6.1.4 Add Party Received

If the network can determine that access to the requested service is authorized and available, the network shall progress the call.

5.6.1.5 Add Party Connected

Upon receiving an indication that the add has been accepted, the network shall: send an ADD PARTY ACKNOWLEDGE message across the user-network interface to the calling (Root) user and enter the Active party-state for that party.

This message indicates to the calling user (Root) that an additional party has been added to the original connection.

On receipt of the ADD PARTY ACKNOWLEDGE message, the calling user shall enter the Active party-state, and stop timer T399.

If timer T399 expires, the user shall internally clear the party.

5.6.1.6 Add Party Rejection

Upon receiving an indication that the network or the called user is unable to accept the call, the network shall send an ADD PARTY REJECT at the originating user-network interface, using the cause provided by the terminating network or the called user, and enter the Null party-state for that party. After sending the ADD PARTY REJECT message, if there are no remaining parties in the Active or Add Party Received party-state then the network shall send a RELEASE message to the user. The cause used in the release message is #31, *"Normal unspecified."*

5.6.2 Add party establishment at the destination interface

For a party in a call, the call reference and endpoint reference information elements, in those messages that contain these information elements and are exchanged across the user-network interface, shall contain the same call reference and endpoint reference values specified in the SETUP or ADD PARTY messages delivered by the network.

5.6.2.1 Incoming add party request

The network will indicate the arrival of an add party request at the user-network interface by transferring a SETUP or ADD PARTY message across the interface.

The network shall transfer a SETUP message with a new Call Reference value across the UNI if the link-state is either Null or in a clearing state. For the first party of a point-to-multipoint connection, the endpoint reference value used must remain equal to zero.

When a SETUP message is used the point-to-point procedure of §5.2 shall be used except that the Endpoint reference information element must be included in the message and the party-states are tracked.

The network shall transfer an ADD PARTY message across the UNI, start timer T399, and enter the Add Party Initiated party-state only if the link is in the Active link-state. Information such as bandwidth, bearer capability and QoS shall be the same as those contained in the original SETUP message, although these are not contained within the ADD PARTY message. The ADD PARTY message shall contain all the additional information required by the called user to process the call. This message is sent by the network only if resources are available; otherwise the add request is cleared toward the calling user.

Upon receipt of an ADD PARTY message, the user shall enter the Add Party Received party-state.

If there is one and only one party in the Add Party Initiated party-state and the link is not yet in the Active link-state, additional ADD PARTY messages shall be queued by the network until the link either becomes active or is cleared. At this point the queued ADD PARTY messages are treated as if they had just arrived. If the network is unable to queue any additional ADD PARTY messages, the network shall return an ADD PARTY REJECT message to the calling user with cause #92, "*Too many pending add party requests*", and enter the Null party-state.

If the Network receives a RELEASE message for a call which has one or more parties which have not progressed past the Add Party Initiated party-state, the Network shall transmit one of the ADD PARTY messages as a SETUP message with a new call reference value and the same information element values as the previous call. The network node will clear the call reference and initiate party dropping procedures towards the calling user for the party previously in the Active party-state. After the network receives the CONNECT message for this SETUP message, the remaining ADD PARTY messages will be retransmitted by the network using the new call reference value.

5.6.2.2 Address and compatibility check

Not supported in this Implementation Agreement.

The procedures to perform the compaiibility checking are implementation dependent. (See §5.2.2, Q.93B [29] for more information.)

5.6.2.3 Connection identifier (VPCI/VCI) allocation/selection — destination

The VPCI/VCI is the same as the connection that already exists on the interface. The VPCI/VCI is not included in the ADD PARTY message.

5.6.2.4 QoS and Traffic parameter selection procedures

With an ADD PARTY message, the QoS and bandwidth must be the same as the existing connection and are not explicitly indicated in the ADD PARTY message.

If the user is not able to support the requested ATM user cell rate or QoS class, the user shall reject the Add Party request, returning an ADD PARTY REJECT message with cause #47, "*Resources unavailable, unspecified*" or cause #49, "*Quality of Service unavailable*", respectively.

If the user is able to support the indicated ATM user cell rate and QoS, the procedures in §5.6.2.5 shall be followed.

5.6.2.5 Call/Connection confirmation

5.6.2.5.1 Response to ADD PARTY

5.6.2.5.1.1 Procedures when the user is an ATM endpoint

When the user receives an ADD PARTY message and wishes to accept the call/connection, the user responds with an ADD PARTY ACKNOWLEDGE message, and enters the Active party-state.

If a user rejects an Add Party request it will use an ADD PARTY REJECT message and enter the Null party-state. After sending the ADD PARTY REJECT message, if there are no remaining parties in the Active or Add Party Received party-state then the network shall send a RELEASE message to the user. The cause used in the RELEASE message is #31, *"Normal unspecified."* The cause used in the ADD PARTY REJECT message is specified below.

An incompatible user shall respond with cause #88, *"incompatible destination."* The diagnostics field of the cause information element should indicate the incompatible parameter.

A busy user which satisfies the compatibility requirements indicated in the ADD PARTY message shall normally respond with cause #17, *"user busy"*.

If the user wishes to refuse the call, cause #21, *"call rejected,"* shall be used.

If the user rejects all incoming calls that do not provide the calling party number, the user shall use cause #23, *"User rejects all calls with Calling Line Identification Restriction (CLIR)"*.

5.6.2.5.1.2 Procedures when the user is not an ATM endpoint

Upon receiving an indication that the add has been accepted by the ATM endpoint, the user (e.g., private ATM switch) shall: send an ADD PARTY ACKNOWLEDGE message across the user-network interface toward the calling user (Root) and enter the Active party-state.

5.6.2.5.2 Called user rejection of incoming call establishment

If an ADD PARTY REJECT is received before an ADD PARTY ACKNOWLEDGE message has been received, and there are other parties of the call on the interface in the Add Party Initiated or Active party-states, the network shall: stop timer T399, and clear the party toward the calling user with the cause received in the ADD PARTY REJECT message.

If an ADD PARTY REJECT is received before an ADD PARTY ACKNOWLEDGE message has been received, and there are no other parties of the call on the interface in the Add Party Initiated or Active party-states, the network shall: stop timer T399, and clear the party toward the calling user with the cause received in the ADD PARTY REJECT message, and initiate link clearing procedures toward the called user as described in §5.6.3.5.

5.6.2.5.3 Call failure

If the network does not receive any response to the transmitted ADD PARTY message prior to the expiration of timer T399, then the network shall initiate procedures to send an ADD PARTY REJECT message towards the calling user with cause #18, *"no user responding"*. After sending the ADD PARTY REJECT message, if there are no remaining parties in the Active or Add Party Received party-state then the network shall send a RELEASE message to the user. The cause used in the RELEASE message is #31, *"Normal unspecified."*

5.6.2.6 Call/Connection accept

A user indicates acceptance of an incoming add party request by sending an ADD PARTY ACKNOWLEDGE message to the network.

Upon sending the ADD PARTY ACKNOWLEDGE message, the user enters the Active party-state.

5.6.2.7 Active indication

On receipt of the ADD PARTY ACKNOWLEDGE message, the network shall: stop timer T399; enter the Active party-state; and initiate procedures to send an ADD PARTY ACKNOWLEDGE message towards the calling user.

5.6.3 Party clearing

5.6.3.1 Terminology

Terminology is defined in §5.5.4.1.

5.6.3.2 Exception conditions

Under normal conditions, dropping a party is usually initiated when the user or the network sends a RELEASE or DROP PARTY message and follows the procedures defined in §§5.5.4.3, 5.5.4.4, 5.6.3.3 and 5.6.3.4. The only exceptions to the above rule are as follows:

a) In response to a SETUP message (when the call is still in a point-to-point configuration), the call clearing procedures of §5.5.4.2 apply.

b) In response to an ADD PARTY message, the user or network can reject an Add Party request by: responding with an ADD PARTY REJECT provided no other response has previously been sent. In addition, after sending the ADD PARTY REJECT message, if there are no remaining parties in the Active or Add Party Received party-state then the network shall send a RELEASE message to the user. The cause used in the RELEASE message is #31, *"Normal unspecified."*

5.6.3.3 Dropping a party initiated by the user

Apart from the exceptions identified in §§5.6.3.2 and 5.6.5, the user shall initiate dropping a party by sending a RELEASE or DROP PARTY message.

The RELEASE message is sent if all other parties belonging to the same call on the interface are in the Null party-state, a Drop Party Initiated party-state, or a Drop Party Received party-state. When a RELEASE message is sent, the normal clearing procedures of §5.5.4 shall be used and all parties on this interface are cleared (i.e., enter the Null party-state and stop all party-state timers.)

When the network receives a RELEASE message:

- Parties in the Drop Party Initiated and Drop Party Received party-state shall enter the Null party-state

- Parties in the Add Party Received party-state and the Active party-state shall be cleared towards the remote user with the cause contained in the RELEASE message or cause #31, *"Normal unspecified"* if no cause was included in the RELEASE message.

- Parties in the Add Party Initiated party-state shall be reoffered on a new call reference (see §5.6.2.1).

  Note - After sending a RELEASE message, and while in the Release Request link-state, the user shall ignore any ADD PARTY messages pertaining to that call reference until the call reference is available for reuse.

A DROP PARTY message is used to initiate party clearing when:

- The party is in the Active or Add Party Initiated party-states, and

- There are other parties to the call on this interface in the Add Party Initiated, Add Party Received, or Active party-state.

After sending a DROP PARTY message the user shall start timer T398 (the value of timer T398 is specified in §5.7), and enter the Drop Party Initiated party-state.

If one or more parties associated with the call are in the Active party-state, an Add Party Initiated or Add Party Received party-state, this message then prompts the network to release the endpoint reference and to initiate procedures for dropping the party along the path to the remote user. Once the endpoint reference used for the party has been released, the network shall: send a DROP PARTY ACKNOWLEDGE message to the user; and enter the Null party-state.

If all other parties associated with the call are in the Null party-state, a Drop Party Initiated party-state, or a Drop Party Received party-state, this message then prompts the network to release the endpoint reference and to initiate procedures for dropping the party along the path to the remote user. Once the endpoint reference used for the party has been released, the network shall send a RELEASE message to the user.

Note - The DROP PARTY ACKNOWLEDGE message has only local significance and does not imply an acknowledgment of clearing from the remote user.

On receipt of the DROP PARTY ACKNOWLEDGE message the user shall: cancel timer T398; release the endpoint reference; and return to the Null party-state. If all parties on the call at the interface are in the Null party-state, the user shall release the call by sending a RELEASE message.

If timer T398 expires:

If one or more parties associated with the call are in the Active, Add Party Initiated or Add Party Received party-state, the user shall: send a DROP PARTY ACKNOWLEDGE message to the network with the cause number originally contained in the DROP PARTY message; and enter the Null party-state. In addition, the user may indicate a second cause information element with cause #102, *"recovery on timer expiry"*. Equipment may use implementation-dependent recovery procedures, such as initiating status enquiry procedures, to verify that the party has been dropped.

If all parties associated with the call are in the Null, Drop Party Received, or Drop Party Initiated party-state, the user shall: send a RELEASE message to the network with the cause number originally contained in the DROP PARTY message. In addition, the user may indicate a second cause information element with cause #102, *"recovery on timer expiry"*.

5.6.3.4 Dropping a party initiated by the network

Apart from the exception conditions identified in §§5.6.3.2 and 5.6.5, the network shall initiate dropping a party by: sending a RELEASE or DROP PARTY message.

The RELEASE message is used if all other parties belonging to the same call on the interface are in the Null party-state, Drop Party Received party-state, or Drop Party Initiated party-state. When a RELEASE message is used, the normal clearing procedures of §5.5.4 shall be used and all parties are cleared (i.e., enter the Null party-state and stop all party-state timers.)

When the user receives a RELEASE message:

- Parties in the Drop Party Initiated and Drop Party Received party-state shall enter the Null party-state

- Parties in the Add Party Received party-state and the Active party-state shall be cleared towards the remote user with the cause contained in the RELEASE message or cause #31, *"Normal unspecified"* if no cause was included in the RELEASE message.

- Parties in the Add Party Initiated party-state shall be reoffered on a new call reference (see §5.6.2.1).

Note -   After sending a RELEASE message, and while in the Release Indication link-state, the network shall ignore any ADD PARTY messages pertaining to that call reference.

A DROP PARTY message is used to initiate party clearing when:

- The party is in the Active or Add Party Initiated party-states, and

- There are other parties to the call on this interface in the Add Party Initiated, Add Party Received, or Active party-state.

5.6.3.4.1 Clearing with a DROP PARTY message

After sending a DROP PARTY message, the network shall start timer T398 and enter the Drop Party Initiated party-state.

If all other parties associated with the call are in the Null party-state, Drop Party Initiated party-state or Drop Party Received party-state, the user shall respond to a DROP PARTY message by sending a RELEASE message.

If any other parties associated with the call are in the Active party-state, Add Party Initiated party-state, or Add Party Received party-state the user shall respond to a DROP PARTY message by releasing the endpoint reference, sending a DROP PARTY ACKNOWLEDGE message and entering the Null party-state.

On receipt of the DROP PARTY ACKNOWLEDGE message, the network shall: stop timer T398; release the endpoint reference; and return to the Null party-state. If all parties associated with the call are in the Null party-state, a Drop Party Initiated party-state or a Drop Party Received party-state, the network shall: send a RELEASE message to the user.

If timer T398 expires:

If one or more parties associated with the call are in the Active, Add Party Initiated or Add Party Received party-state, the network shall: send a DROP PARTY ACKNOWLEDGE message to the user with the cause number originally contained in the DROP PARTY message; and enter the Null party-state. In addition, the network may indicate a second cause information element with cause #102, *"recovery on timer expiry"*. Equipment may use implementation-dependent recovery procedures, such as initiating status enquiry procedures, to verify that the party has been dropped.

If all parties associated with the call are in the Null party-state, a Drop Party Initiated party-state or a Drop Party Received party-state, the network shall: send a RELEASE message to the user with the cause number originally contained in the DROP PARTY message. In addition, the network may indicate a second cause information element with cause #102, *"recovery on timer expiry"*.

5.6.3.5 Clear collision

Clear collision occurs when both the user and the network transfer simultaneously DROP PARTY messages specifying the same call reference value and endpoint reference value.

Upon receiving a DROP PARTY message whilst in the Drop Party Initiated party-state, and while there are one or more parties associated with the call in the Active, Add Party Initiated or Add Party Received party-state, the recipient shall: stop timer T398; release the endpoint reference; send a DROP PARTY ACKNOWLEDGE message; and enter the Null party-state.

Similarly, upon receiving a DROP PARTY message whilst in the Drop Party Initiated party-state, and while all parties associated with the call are in the Null party-state, Drop Party Initiated party-state, or a Drop Party Received party-state, the recipient shall: stop timer T398; release the endpoint reference; disconnect the bearer virtual channel; and send a RELEASE message.

With point-to-multipoint connections another type of clear collision is when clearing messages (i.e., DROP PARTY, DROP PARTY ACKNOWLEDGE or ADD PARTY REJECT) pertaining to the last two parties on an interface cross. In this case, each entity receiving such a message shall initiate link clearing procedures by returning a RELEASE message and following the clearing procedures in § 5.5.4

5.6.4 Restart Procedure

In addition to the procedures of §5.5.5, when the virtual channel (connection) is restarted, all parties associated with the virtual channel should be cleared. The network will initiate normal drop party procedures toward the remote user(s) for all parties associated with the call. On the interface the party-state of all parties associated with the virtual channel is set to Null.

5.6.5 Handling of error conditions

The point-to-point procedures for handling error conditions should be applied first.

This section discusses error handling that specifically applies to adding or dropping parties in a point-to-multipoint call. The normal error procedures of §5.5.6 also apply.

Sections 5.6.5.1 through 5.6.5.8 are listed in order of precedence.

5.6.5.1 Protocol Discriminator Error

Refer to §5.5.6.1.

5.6.5.2 Message too short

Refer to §5.5.6.2.

5.6.5.3 Call reference and Endpoint Reference errors

5.6.5.3.1 Call reference procedural errors

Whenever an ADD PARTY, ADD PARTY ACKNOWLEDGE, ADD PARTY REJECT, DROP PARTY or DROP PARTY ACKNOWLEDGE message is received while in the Null link-state, a RELEASE COMPLETE message is sent with cause #81, *"invalid call reference value"* and following the procedures in §5.5.4, specifying the call reference in the received message.

5.6.5.3.2 Endpoint reference error

The following section assumes that there are no call reference errors and only the endpoint reference is in error.

5.6.5.3.2.1 Invalid endpoint reference format

If the endpoint reference information element is not properly formatted (i.e., incorrect length, type or flag), then a STATUS message is returned with cause #100, *"invalid information element contents"*, and procedures of 5.5.7.7.2 followed. In this case, no Endpoint reference information element is contained in the STATUS message. No other action is taken on this message.

5.6.5.3.2.2 Endpoint reference procedural errors

a) Whenever any message except SETUP, ADD PARTY, or DROP PARTY ACKNOWLEDGE is received for a party in the NULL party-state, dropping is initiated by sending a DROP PARTY ACKNOWLEDGE message with cause #89 *"invalid endpoint reference value"* and remain in the Null party-state.

b) When a DROP PARTY ACKNOWLEDGE message is received for a party in the NULL party-state, no action should be taken.

c) When an ADD PARTY message is received while not in the NULL or Add Party Received party-state, a STATUS message, containing the Active link-state value, the associated endpoint reference and endpoint state information elements and values, and cause value 101, *"message not compatible with call state"*, is responded.

d) When an Add Party message is received while in the Add Party Received party-state, the Add Party is ignored.

5.6.5.4 Message type or message sequence errors

Procedures specified in § 5.5.6.4 also apply in this section.

When the network or user receives an unexpected RELEASE COMPLETE message, the procedures for handling the party-states will be the same as specified in §5.6.3.3 and §5.6.3.4 on receipt of a RELEASE message with the exception that cause #111, *"protocol error, unspecified"* is used if no cause is specified in the RELEASE COMPLETE message.

Whenever the network receives an unexpected DROP PARTY ACKNOWLEDGE message, the network shall: initiate normal party clearing procedures toward the remote user with the cause indicated by the user or, if not included, cause #111, *"protocol error, unspecified"*; release the endpoint reference; stop all timers; and enter the Null party-state. Whenever the user receives an unexpected DROP PARTY ACKNOWLEDGE message, the user shall: release the endpoint reference; stop all timers; and enter the Null party-state. If no parties remain in the Active, Add Party Initiated or Add Party Received party-state on the call at the interface when either side receives the DROP PARTY ACKNOWLEDGE message, the side receiving the DROP PARTY ACKNOWLEDGE shall disconnect the bearer virtual channel and send a RELEASE message.

The receipt of an ADD PARTY, ADD PARTY ACKNOWLEDGE, or DROP PARTY ACKNOWLEDGE message in any link-state other than the Active link-state is an unexpected message and the procedures of §5.5.6.4 shall apply.

5.6.5.5 Message length errors

Refer to §5.5.6.5.

5.6.5.6 General Information Element errors

Refer to §5.5.6.6.

5.6.5.7 Mandatory information element error

5.6.5.7.1 Mandatory information element missing

When an ADD PARTY message is received which has one or more mandatory information elements missing, an ADD PARTY REJECT message with cause #96, *"mandatory information element is missing"* shall be returned. After sending the ADD PARTY REJECT message, if there are no remaining parties in the Active or Add Party Received party-state then the network shall send a RELEASE message to the user. The cause used in the RELEASE message is #31, *"Normal unspecified."*

When a DROP PARTY message is received with the Cause information element missing, the actions taken shall be the same as if a DROP PARTY message with cause #31, *"normal, unspecified"* was received (see §5.6.3), with the exception that the DROP PARTY ACKNOWLEDGE or RELEASE message, as appropriate, sent on the local interface contains cause #96, *"mandatory information element is missing"*.

When a DROP PARTY ACKNOWLEDGE or ADD PARTY REJECT message is received with a Cause information element missing, it will be assumed that the message was received with cause #31, *"normal, unspecified"*.

5.6.5.7.2 Mandatory information element content error

When an ADD PARTY message is received which has one or more mandatory information elements with invalid content, an ADD PARTY REJECT or RELEASE message, as appropriate, with cause #100, *"invalid information element contents"* shall be returned. After sending the ADD PARTY REJECT message, if there are no remaining parties in the Active or Add Party Received party-state then the network shall send a RELEASE message to the user. The cause used in the RELEASE message is #31, *"Normal unspecified."*

When a DROP PARTY message is received with invalid content of the Cause information element, the actions taken shall be the same as if a DROP PARTY message with cause #31, *"normal, unspecified,"* was received (see §5.5.4), with the exception that the DROP PARTY ACKNOWLEDGE or RELEASE message, as appropriate, sent on the local interface contains cause #100, *"invalid information element contents"*.

When a DROP PARTY ACKNOWLEDGE message is received with invalid content of the Cause information element, it will be assumed that a DROP PARTY ACKNOWLEDGE message was received with cause #31, *"normal, unspecified"*.

Information elements with a length exceeding the maximum length (given in §5.4) will be treated as information elements with content error.

5.6.5.8 Non-mandatory information element errors

The following sections identify actions on information elements not recognized as mandatory.

5.6.5.8.1 Unrecognized information element

When a message is received that has one or more unrecognized information elements, then the receiving entity shall proceed as follows:

Action shall be taken on the message and those information elements which are recognized and have valid content. When the received message is an ADD PARTY, ADD PARTY ACKNOWLEDGE or ADD PARTY REJECT, a STATUS message may be returned containing one cause information element. The STATUS message indicates the link-state and endpoint reference state of the receiver after taking action on the message. The cause information element shall contain cause #99, *"information element non-existent or not implemented"*, and the diagnostic field, if present, shall contain the information element identifier for each information element which was unrecognized, subject to the length constraint of the Cause Information Element size.

Subsequent actions are determined by the sender of the unrecognized information elements. If a clearing message contains one or more unrecognized information elements, the error is reported to the local user in the following manner:

a) When a DROP PARTY message is received which has one or more unrecognized information elements, a DROP PARTY ACKNOWLEDGE or RELEASE message with cause #99, *"information element non-existent or not implemented"*, shall be returned. The cause information element diagnostic field, if present, shall contain the information element identifier for each information element which was unrecognized.

b) When a DROP PARTY ACKNOWLEDGE message is received which has one or more unrecognized information elements, no action shall be taken on the unrecognized information.

Note - The diagnostic(s) of cause #99 facilitates the decision in selecting an appropriate recovery procedure at the reception of a STATUS message. Therefore, it is recommended to provide cause #99 with diagnostic(s) if a layer 3 entity expects the peer to take an appropriate action at the receipt of a STATUS message, although inclusion of diagnostic(s) is optional.

5.6.5.9 Signalling AAL reset

Whenever indication of a Signalling AAL reset is received from the Q.SAAL layer (see §5.9) by means of the AAL-ESTABLISH-INDICATION primitive, the following procedures apply:

a) For parties in the clearing phase (party-states Drop Party Initiated and Drop Party Received), no action shall be taken.
b) For parties in the establishment phase (party-states Add Party Initiated and Add Party Received), the entity shall initiate party clearing with cause #41, *"temporary failure"*.
c) Parties in the active party-state shall be maintained according to the procedures in other parts of §5.6.

5.6.5.10 Signalling AAL failure

Whenever the network layer entity is notified by its Signalling AAL entity via the AAL-RELEASE-INDICATION primitive that there is a Signalling AAL malfunction, the following procedure shall apply:

a) Any Parties not in the Active party-state shall be cleared internally.

5.6.5.11 Status enquiry procedure

To check the correctness of a party-state at a peer entity, a STATUS ENQUIRY message may be sent requesting the party-state, by including the endpoint reference of the party-state to be checked. This may, in particular, apply to procedural error conditions described in 5.6.5.9 and 5.6.5.10.

In addition whenever indication is received from the Signalling AAL that a disruption has occurred at the data link layer, a STATUS ENQUIRY message shall be sent to check the correctness of the party-state at the peer entity.

Upon sending the STATUS ENQUIRY message, timer T322 shall be started in anticipation of receiving a STATUS message. While timer T322 is running, only one outstanding request for party-state information shall exist. Therefore, if timer T322 is already running, it shall not be restarted. If a party clearing message is received before timer T322 expires, timer T322 shall be stopped and party clearing shall continue.

Upon receipt of a STATUS ENQUIRY message, the receiver shall respond with a STATUS message, reporting the current party-state (the current party-state of an active party or a party in progress, or the Null party-state if the endpoint reference does not relate to an active party or a party in progress) and cause #30, *"response to status enquiry"* . Receipt of the STATUS ENQUIRY message does not result in a party-state change.

The sending or receipt of the STATUS message in such a situation will not directly affect the party-state of either the sender or receiver. The side having received the STATUS message shall inspect the Cause information element. If a STATUS message is received that contains cause #30, *"Response to STATUS ENQUIRY"*, timer T322 shall be stopped and the appropriate action taken, based on the information in that STATUS message, relative to the current state of the receiver.

If timer T322 expires, and no STATUS message was received, the STATUS ENQUIRY message may be retransmitted one or more times until a response is received. The number of times the STATUS ENQUIRY message is retransmitted is an implementation dependent value. The party shall be cleared to the local interface with cause #41, *"temporary failure"*, if the STATUS ENQUIRY is retransmitted the maximum number of times. If appropriate, the network shall also clear the network connection, using cause #41, *"temporary failure"*.

5.6.5.12 Receiving a STATUS message

On receipt of a STATUS message reporting an incompatible party-state, the receiving entity shall:

a) clear the party by sending the appropriate clearing message with cause #101, *"message not compatible with call state"*; or,

b) take other actions which attempt to recover from a mismatch and which are an implementation option.

Except for the following rules, the determination of which party-states are incompatible is left as an implementation decision:

a) If a STATUS message indicating any party-state except the Null party-state is received in the Null party-state, then the receiving entity shall send a DROP PARTY ACKNOWLEDGE message with cause #101, *"message not compatible with call state"*; and remain in the Null party-state.

b) If a STATUS message indicating any party-state except the Null party-state is received in the Drop Party Initiated party-state, no action shall be taken.

c) If a STATUS message, indicating the Null party-state, is received in any party-state except the Null party-state, the receiver shall internally clear the party and enter the Null party-state. If no other party of the call is in the Active, Add Party Initiated or Add Party Received party-states call clearing will be initiated with a RELEASE message.

When in the Null party-state, the receiver of a STATUS message indicating the Null party-state shall take no action other than to discard the message and shall remain in the Null party-state.

A STATUS message may be received indicating a compatible party-state but containing one of the following causes:

#96   *"mandatory information element is missing"*;

#97   *"message type non-existent or not implemented"*;

#99   *"information element non-existent or not implemented"*; or

#100 *"invalid information element contents"*.

In this case, the actions to be taken are an implementation option. If other procedures are not defined, the receiver shall clear the party with the appropriate procedure defined in §5.6.3, using the cause specified in the received STATUS message.

5.7 List of Timers

The description of timers in the following tables should be considered a brief summary. The precise details are found in §§5.5 and 5.6, which should be considered the definitive description.

5.7.1 Timers in the Network Side

The timers specified in Table 5-9 are maintained in the network side of the UNI.

Table 5-9 Timers in the network side (page 1 of 2)

TIMER NUM-BER	DEFAULT TIME OUT VALUE	STATE OF CALL	CAUSE FOR START	NORMAL STOP	AT THE FIRST EXPIRY	AT THE SECOND EXPIRY	IMPLEMEN-TATION
T301	Not supported in this Implementation Agreement						
T303	4 s	Call Present	SETUP sent.	CONNECT, CALL PROCEED-ING, or RELEASE COMPLETE received.	Retransmit SETUP; restart T303. If retransmission of SETUP is not supported, clear network connection and enter Null state.	Clear network connection. Enter Null state.	Mandatory
T308	30 s	Release Indication	RELEASE sent.	RELEASE COMPLETE or RELEASE received.	Retransmit RELEASE and restart T308.	Release call reference and enter Null state. (Note 1)	Mandatory
T309	90 s	Any stable state	SAAL disconnec-tion. Calls in the active state are not lost.	SAAL reconnected	Clear network connection. Release virtual channel and call reference	Not applicable.	Mandatory

Table 5-9 Timers in the network side (page 2 of 2)

TIMER NUM-BER	DEFAULT TIME OUT VALUE	STATE OF CALL	CAUSE FOR START	NORMAL STOP	AT THE FIRST EXPIRY	AT THE SECOND EXPIRY	IMPLEMEN-TATION
T310	10 s	Incoming Call Proceeding	CALL PROCEED-ING received.	CONNECT or RELEASE received.	Clear call in accordance with §5.5.4	Not applicable.	Mandatory
T316	2 min	Restart Request	RESTART sent.	RESTART ACKNOWL-EDGE received.	RESTART may be retransmitted several times.	RESTART may be retransmitted several times	Mandatory
T317	(Note 2)	Restart	RESTART received	Internal clearing of call references.	Maintenance notification	Not applicable.	Mandatory
T322	4 s	Any call state	STATUS ENQUIRY sent.	STATUS, RELEASE, or RELEASE COMPLETE received.	STATUS ENQUIRY may be retransmitted several times.	STATUS ENQUIRY may be retransmitted several times	Mandatory
T398	4 s	Drop Party Initiated party-state	DROP PARTY sent	DROP PARTY ACKNOWL-EDGE or RELEASE received.	Send DROP PARTY ACKNOWL-EDGE or RELEASE (see §5.6.3.4.1)	Timer is not restarted.	Mandatory
T399	14 s	Add Party Initiated party-state	ADD PARTY sent	ADD PARTY ACKNOWL-EDGE, ADD PARTY REJECT, or RELEASE received.	Clear the party and enter the Null party-state (see §5.6.2.5.3)	Timer is not restarted.	Mandatory

Note 1 - The restart procedures in §5.5.5 may be used.

Note 2 - The value of this timer is implementation dependent but should be less than the value of T316.

5.7.2 Timers in the User Side

The timers specified in Table 5-10 are maintained in the user side of the UNI.

Table 5-10 Timers in the user side (page 1 of 2)

TIMER NUM-BER	DEFAULT TIME OUT VALUE	STATE OF CALL	CAUSE FOR START	NORMAL STOP	AT THE FIRST EXPIRY	AT THE SECOND EXPIRY	IMPLEMEN-TATION
T303	4 s	Call Initiated	SETUP sent.	CONNECT, CALL PROCEEDING or RELEASE COMPLETE received.	Retransmit SETUP; restart T303. If retransmission of SETUP is not supported, clear internal connection and enter Null state.	Clear internal connection. Enter Null state.	Mandatory
T308	30 s	Release Request	RELEASE sent.	RELEASE COMPLETE or RELEASE received.	Retransmit RELEASE and restart T308.	Release call reference and enter Null state. (Note 1)	Mandatory
T309	90 s	Any stable state	SAAL disconnec-tion. Calls in the active state are not lost.	SAAL reconnected.	Clear network connection. Release virtual channel and call reference.	Not applicable.	Optional
T310	10 s	Outgoing Call Proceeding	CALL PROCEED-ING received.	CONNECT or RELEASE received.	Send RELEASE.	Not applicable.	Mandatory
T313	4 s	Connect Request	CONNECT sent.	CONNECT ACKNOWL-EDGE received.	Send RELEASE.	Not applicable.	Mandatory

Table 5-10 Timers in the user side (page 2 of 2)

TIMER NUMBER	DEFAULT TIME OUT VALUE	STATE OF CALL	CAUSE FOR START	NORMAL STOP	AT THE FIRST EXPIRY	AT THE SECOND EXPIRY	IMPLEMENTATION
T316	2 min	Restart Request	RESTART sent	RESTART ACKNOWL-EDGE received	RESTART may be retransmitted several times	RESTART may be retransmitted several times	Mandatory
T317	(Note 2)	Restart	RESTART received.	Internal clearing of call references.	Maintenance notification.	Not applicable.	Mandatory
T322	4 s	Any call state	STATUS ENQUIRY sent.	STATUS, RELEASE, or RELEASE COMPLETE received.	STATUS ENQUIRY may be retransmitted several times.	STATUS ENQUIRY may be retransmitted several times.	Mandatory
T398	4 s	Drop Party Initiated party-state	DROP PARTY sent.	DROP PARTY ACKNOWL-EDGE or RELEASE received.	Send DROP PARTY ACKNOWL-EDGE or RELEASE (see §5.6.3.3)	Timer is not restarted.	Mandatory
T399	14 s	Add Party Initiated party-state	ADD PARTY sent.	ADD PARTY ACKNOWL-EDGE, ADD PARTY REJECT, or RELEASE received.	Clear the party and enter the Null party-state (see §5.6.2.5.3)	Timer is not restarted.	Mandatory

Note 1 - The restart procedures in §5.5.5 may be used.

Note 2 - The value of timer T317 is implementation dependent but should be less than the value of T316.

5.8 Address Registration

This section specifies the procedures for address registration at the UNI. These procedures are specified as an extension to the Interim Local Management Interface (ILMI) specified in §4.

Equipment at the Private UNI must support the Address Registration procedures described in this section.

Equipment at the Public UNI may support the Address Registration procedures described in this section.

5.8.1 Overview

In order establish an ATM connection at the UNI, both the user and the network must know the ATM address(es) which are in effect at that UNI. These ATM addresses can then be used in Calling Party Number information elements of signalling messages sent by the user, and in Called Party Number information elements of signalling messages sent to the user. The address registration procedures in this section provide the means for the dynamic exchange of addressing information between the user and the network at the UNI, at initialization and at other times as required. Through this dynamic exchange the user and network can agree on the ATM address(es) in effect.

As specified in §5.1.3.1, the Private ATM Address Structure consists of multiple fields. Two of these fields, the End System Identifier (ESI) and the Selector (SEL) fields form the "user part" and are supplied by the user-side of the UNI. All other fields form a "network prefix" for ATM addresses in that they typically have the same value for all ATM addresses on the same ATM UNI; the value of the network prefix is supplied by the network side of the UNI. The network-side is allowed to supply multiple network prefixes for use at a single UNI; however, it is expected that just one will normally be supplied. An ATM address for a terminal on the user-side of a Private UNI is obtained by appending values for the ESI and SEL fields to (one of) the network prefix(es) for that UNI.

For the purposes of address registration, the value of the SEL field is irrelevant, i.e., one user part is a duplicate of another if they have the same ESI value even if they have different SEL values.

ATM addresses in Public networks either have the same Private ATM Address Structure as Private networks, or else they are E.164 addresses (see §5.1.3.2). For Public network E.164 addresses, the network-side supplies the whole ATM address. In effect, the network prefix is the E.164 address and can only be validly combined with a null user part. In this situation, the use of multiple network prefixes at a single UNI occurs whenever multiple E.164 addresses are used at that UNI.

5.8.2 Capabilities

The address registration procedures in this section provide the following capabilities:

- initialization-time exchange of addressing information,
- restrictions on network-prefix/user-part combinations,
- rejection of unacceptable values, either rejection of a specific network prefix by the user, or of a specific user part by the network,
- dynamic addition/deletion of additional network prefixes and user parts,
- de-registration of addresses on a UNI "link down" condition.

The following sections describe each capability in more detail.

5.8.2.1 Initialization-time Exchange of Addressing Information

These procedures allow the user and the network to exchange addressing information to allow ATM addresses to be registered at the UNI and used in signalling messages. This includes the capability for the network to support more than one network prefix (e.g., in a transitional period to allow both an old and a new network prefix value), and for the user to support more than one user part.

5.8.2.2 Restrictions on Network-Prefix/User-Part Combinations

Not all combinations of network prefix and user part may be valid. For example, if the network prefix is an E.164 address (using the E.164 numbering plan), then no user part is necessary or allowed. Alternatively, at a Public UNI which supports Address Registration and connects a Private ATM network and a Public ATM network, the user (the Private ATM network) may wish to restrict combinations of network prefixes offered by the Public network and user parts that it registers (e.g., to simplify its routing task).

5.8.2.3 Rejection of Unacceptable Values

Certain user part values, as specified by the user, may be unacceptable to the network. An example would be if the user attempted to register a user part which is already registered on a different UNI. In this case, the network may wish to block registration of the duplicate. Similarly, a user may wish to block registration of a network prefix supplied by the network. For example, at a Public UNI which supports Address Registration and supports E.164 addresses, both using the E.164 numbering plan and using NSAP encoding, the user might wish to block registration one of the address formats.

5.8.2.4 Dynamic Addition/Deletion

The list of network prefixes and user parts, and their valid combinations may change over time during the operation of the UNI. For example, on the user-side of a private UNI, new user parts may appear or disappear when (individually addressable) components are connected to or disconnected from the access device. On the network-side, the list of valid network prefixes may change due to topology changes.

5.8.2.5 De-registration on UNI "link down" Condition.

The addresses registered at the UNI are de-registered when the UNI is declared to be down. For example, in order for a user device using the Private ATM Address structure to be unplugged from one UNI and plugged in to another UNI on the same network, the user-part(s) registered by the device must be de-registered from the first UNI and re-registered on the second.

5.8.3 General Description of Procedures

For the exchange of addressing information, two MIB tables are defined, one to contain network prefixes, and the other to contain registered ATM addresses. The Network Prefix table contains one entry for each network prefix. The Address table contains one entry for each registered ATM address. The MIB definitions of these tables is given in §5.8.6. The basic approach of the procedures are as follows.

For network prefixes, it is the network-side which supplies the values for the user-side to accept or reject. Thus, it is the user-side which implements the Network Prefix table, and the network-side which issues ILMI SetRequest messages to create/delete entries in the table in order to register/de-register network prefixes.

For registered addresses, it is the user-side which supplies the values for the network-side to accept or reject. Thus, it is the network-side which implements the Address table, and the user-side which issues ILMI SetRequest messages to create/delete entries in the table in order to register/de-register ATM addresses.

At initialization, the registration of network prefixes occurs first. Next, the user-side combines each of the user parts it wishes to use with one or more of the registered network prefixes to form a set of ATM addresses. The user-side then registers these addresses.

After initialization, the network-side issues ILMI SetRequest messages to create/delete entries in the Network Prefix table as and when new network prefixes need to be added or existing network prefixes deleted. Similarly, the user-side issues ILMI SetRequest messages to create/delete entries in the Address table as and when new ATM addresses need to be registered or existing ATM addresses de-registered. If and when the UNI link goes down, all addresses are de-registered.

5.8.4 Management Information Base for Address Registration

Address registration is defined as an extension to the ILMI through the definition of two additional MIB groups: the Prefix group, and the Address group.

5.8.4.1 Prefix Group (CR)

The Prefix group is required to be implemented by the UME on the user-side of the UNI. This group consists of one MIB table, the Network Prefix Table, indexed by the UNI port number and by the value of a network prefix. The information in this group is:

- Interface Index
- Network Prefix
- Network Prefix Status

5.8.4.1.1 Network Prefix

The Network Prefix object has the value of a network prefix.

5.8.4.1.2 Network Prefix Status

The Network Prefix Status object provides an indication of the validity of a network prefix at this UNI. To configure a new network prefix, the network-side uses an ILMI SetRequest to set the Network Prefix Status object for that prefix to be valid. To delete an existing network prefix, the network-side uses an ILMI SetRequest to set the Network Prefix Status object for that prefix to be invalid.

5.8.4.2 Address Group (CR)

The Address group is required to be implemented by the UME on the network-side of the UNI. This group consists of one MIB table, the Address Table, which is indexed by the UNI port number and by the value of an ATM address. The information in this group is:

- Interface Index
- ATM Address
- ATM Address Status

5.8.4.2.1 ATM Address

The ATM Address object has the value of an ATM address.

5.8.4.2.2 ATM Address Status

The ATM Address Status object provides an indication of the validity of an ATM address at this UNI. To configure a new ATM address, the user-side uses an ILMI SetRequest to set the ATM Address Status object for that address to be valid. To delete an existing ATM address, the user-side uses an ILMI SetRequest to set the ATM Address Status object for that address to be invalid.

5.8.5 Address Registration Procedures

5.8.5.1 Network-Side UME

Upon its own restart and before sending the standard ColdStart trap, the network-side UME initializes the Address Table to be empty. It then sends the ColdStart trap and issues an ILMI message (i.e., a GetNext request) to read the first instance of the Network Prefix Status object from the user-side. If the response does not indicate that the Network Prefix table is empty, then this procedure is restarted by retransmitting the ColdStart trap.

The network-side UME also initializes the Address Table to be empty upon receipt of a ColdStart trap from the user-side UME.

In either case, the Network Prefix table will now be empty. Thus, the network-side now issues one (or more) SetRequests to register its network prefix(es), e.g.,

SetRequest { atmfNetPrefixStatus.port.prefix=valid(1) }

Upon receipt of a SetRequest setting an instance of the Address Status object to be valid, the network-side validates the referenced address. If the validation fails, it responds with a Response containing a badValue error. If the validation succeeds, if responds with a Response indicating noError, and if the address is not currently registered, it is registered and the Address table is updated.

Upon receipt of a SetRequest setting an instance of the Address Status object to be invalid, the network-side checks if the referenced address is currently registered. If not, it responds with a Response containing a noSuchName error. If the address is currently registered, then it responds with a Response indicating noError, the address is de-registered and the Address table is updated.

If at any time, the network-side wishes to register an additional network prefix, it issues an appropriate SetRequest, e.g.,

SetRequest { atmfNetPrefixStatus.port.prefix=valid(1) }

If at any time, the network-side wishes to de-register a network prefix, it issues an appropriate SetRequest, e.g.,

SetRequest { atmfNetPrefixStatus.port.prefix=invalid(2) }

If at any time, the network-side wishes to check the consistency of the set of network prefixes currently registered, it issues ILMI messages (e.g., GetNext requests) to read all instances of the Network Prefix Status object from the user-side and checks that the set of those which have a valid status is the correct set.

During operation, if the network-side receives an indication of link down, it de-registers all addresses. Procedures for declaring a link down are specified in §4.7.7.

5.8.5.2 User-Side UME

Upon its own restart and before sending the standard ColdStart trap, the user-side UME initializes the Network Prefix Table to be empty, and then sends the ColdStart trap. The user-side then issues an ILMI message (i.e., a GetNext request) to read the first instance of the ATM Address Status object from the network-side. If the response does not indicate that the ATM Address table is empty, then this procedure is restarted by retransmitting the ColdStart trap.

After ascertaining that the ATM Address table is empty, the user-side awaits one or more ILMI messages (i.e., SetRequests) from the network-side UME which set the Network Prefix Status object to valid for a particular network prefix. In the unlikely event that no such ILMI messages are received for a prolonged period (e.g., 5 seconds) after sending a ColdStart trap, the user-side should retransmit the ColdStart trap.

The user-side UME also initializes the Network Prefix Table to be empty upon receipt of a ColdStart trap from the network-side UME.

Upon receipt of a SetRequest setting an instance of the Network Prefix Status object to be valid, the user-side validates the request. If the validation fails, it responds with a Response containing the appropriate error. If the validation succeeds, it responds with a Response indicating noError, and if the network prefix is one not currently registered, the prefix is registered and the Network Prefix table is updated. For any address which the user-side wishes to register using the new prefix, it forms the address in one of two ways: by appending the ESI and SEL values to the prefix or, for non-NSAP-encoded E.164 addresses, by appending a null user part. It then issues an appropriate SetRequest, e.g.,

    SetRequest { atmfAddressStatus.port.address=valid(1) }

Upon receipt of a SetRequest setting an instance of the Network Prefix Status object to be invalid, the user-side checks if the prefix is currently registered. If not, it responds with a Response containing a noSuchName error. If the prefix is currently registered, then it responds with a Response indicating noError, the prefix is de-registered and the Network Prefix table is updated.

If at any time, the user-side wishes to register an additional address having the Private ATM Address structure, it forms the address by appending the ESI and SEL values to one of the registered prefixes and issues an appropriate SetRequest, e.g.,

    SetRequest { atmfAddressStatus.port.address=valid(1) }

If at any time, the user-side wishes to de-register an address, it issues an appropriate SetRequest, e.g.,

SetRequest { atmfAddressStatus.port.address=invalid(2) }

If the user-side wishes to check periodically that (at least one of) its address(es) is still registered (e.g., that it has not been unplugged from one UNI and plugged into another), then it may wish to poll the first instance of the Address Status object from the network-side and check that the retrieved instance is the one expected.

If at any time, the user-side wishes to check for consistency of all ATM addresses currently registered, it uses ILMI messages (e.g., GetNext requests) to read all instances of the Address Status object from the network-side and checks that the set of those with valid status is the correct set. (Note that when a single address is registered, this consistency check is equivalent to checking just the first address; when multiple addresses are registered, this full consistency check is expected to be needed much less frequently than checking just the first address.)

5.8.5.3 Retransmission of SetRequest Messages

For the above procedures, a UME should retransmit a SetRequest message if it does not receive a Response message within a time-out period. There are two possibilities when a Response is not received, e.g., due to a transmission error/loss, either: A) the SetRequest was processed and the generated Response was lost, or B) the SetRequest was lost before it was processed. When registering a network prefix/address, the retransmission of the appropriate SetRequest message produces the same result no matter which of A or B occurred. When de-registering a network prefix/address, the Response to a retransmission of the appropriate SetRequest message will have an error-status of either noError, noSuchName, or some other error. The noError status indicates that situation B existed, but the de-registration is now complete. The noSuchName status indicates that situation A existed, i.e., the prefix/address was already de-registered. Some other error indicates that the de-registration cannot be completed for some other reason.

5.8.6 MIB Definition

ATM-FORUM-ADDR-REG DEFINITIONS ::= BEGIN

IMPORTS
        atmForumUni   FROM ATM-FORUM-MIB
        OBJECT-TYPE   FROM RFC-1212;

-- Textual Convention

-- Representations in this MIB Module of an ATM address
-- use the data type:

AtmAddress ::= OCTET STRING (SIZE (8 | 20))

-- Representations in this MIB Module of a network-prefix
-- for an ATM address use the data type:

NetPrefix ::= OCTET STRING (SIZE (8 | 13))

-- in both the AtmAddress and NetPrefix conventions, non-NSAP-encoded E.164
-- addresses are represented as 8 octets using the format specified in section 5.1.3.1.4.
-- In contrast, an NSAP-encoded address is 20 octets, and an NSAP-encoded network
-- prefix is 13 octets long.

--   New MIB Groups

atmfAddressGroup   OBJECT IDENTIFIER ::= { atmForumUni 6 }
atmfNetPrefixGroup   OBJECT IDENTIFIER ::= { atmForumUni 7 }

--   The Network Prefix Table
--
-- The Network Prefix Table is implemented by the UNI Management
-- Entity on the user-side of the UNI

atmfNetPrefixTable OBJECT-TYPE
            SYNTAX   SEQUENCE OF AtmfNetPrefixEntry
            ACCESS   not-accessible
            STATUS   mandatory
            DESCRIPTION
                    "A table implemented by the UNI Management Entity on the user-side of an
                    ATM UNI port, containing the network-prefix(es) for ATM-layer addresses
                    in effect on the user-side of the UNI."
            ::= { atmfNetPrefixGroup 1 }

atmfNetPrefixEntry OBJECT-TYPE
            SYNTAX   AtmfNetPrefixEntry
            ACCESS   not-accessible
            STATUS   mandatory
            DESCRIPTION
                    "Information about a single network-prefix for ATM-layer addresses in effect
                    on the user-side of a UNI port. Note that the index variable atmfNetPrefixPrefix
                    is a variable-length string, and as such the rule for variable-length strings in
                    section 4.1.6 of RFC 1212 applies."
            INDEX   { atmfNetPrefixPort, atmfNetPrefixPrefix }
            ::= { atmfNetPrefixTable 1 }

```
AtmfNetPrefixEntry ::=
        SEQUENCE {
                atmfNetPrefixPort        INTEGER,
                atmfNetPrefixPrefix      NetPrefix,
                atmfNetPrefixStatus      INTEGER
        }
```

atmfNetPrefixPort OBJECT-TYPE
        SYNTAX   INTEGER (0..2147483647)
        ACCESS   not-accessible
        STATUS   mandatory
        DESCRIPTION
                "A unique value which identifies the UNI port for which the network prefix
                for ATM addresses is in effect. The value of 0 has the special meaning of iden-
                tifying the local UNI."
        ::= { atmfNetPrefixEntry 1 }

atmfNetPrefixPrefix OBJECT-TYPE
        SYNTAX   NetPrefix
        ACCESS   not-accessible
        STATUS   mandatory
        DESCRIPTION
                "The network prefix for ATM addresses which is in effect on the user-side of
                the ATM UNI port."
        ::= { atmfNetPrefixEntry 2 }

atmfNetPrefixStatus OBJECT-TYPE
        SYNTAX   INTEGER { valid(1), invalid(2) }
        ACCESS   read-write
        STATUS   mandatory
        DESCRIPTION
                "An indication of the validity of the network prefix for ATM addresses on the
                user-side of the UNI port. To configure a new network prefix in this table, the
                network-side must set the appropriate instance of this object to the value
                valid(1). To delete an existing network prefix in this table, the network-side
                must set the appropriate instance of this object to the value invalid(2).

                If circumstances occur on the user-side which cause a prefix to become invalid,
                the user-side modifies the value of the appropriate instance of this object to
                invalid(2).

                Whenever the value of this object for a particular prefix becomes invalid(2),
                the conceptual row for that prefix may be removed from the table at any time,
                either immediately or subsequently."

```
        ::= { atmfNetPrefixEntry 3 }

--          The Address Table
--
-- The Address Table is implemented by the UNI Management Entity
-- on the network-side of the UNI

atmfAddressTable OBJECT-TYPE
        SYNTAX          SEQUENCE OF AtmfAddressEntry
        ACCESS          not-accessible
        STATUS          mandatory
        DESCRIPTION
                "A table implemented by the network-side of an ATM UNI port, containing
                the ATM-layer addresses in effect on the user-side of the UNI."
        ::= { atmfAddressGroup 1 }

atmfAddressEntry OBJECT-TYPE
        SYNTAX          AtmfAddressEntry
        ACCESS          not-accessible
        STATUS          mandatory
        DESCRIPTION
                "Information about a single ATM-layer address in effect on the user-side of a
                UNI port. Note that the index variable atmfAddressAtmAddress is a variable-
                length string, and as such the rule for variable-length strings in section 4.1.6 of
                RFC 1212 applies."
        INDEX   { atmfAddressPort, atmfAddressAtmAddress }
        ::= { atmfAddressTable 1 }

AtmfAddressEntry ::=
        SEQUENCE {
                atmfAddressPort         INTEGER,
                atmfAddressAtmAddress AtmAddress,
                atmfAddressStatus       INTEGER
        }

atmfAddressPort OBJECT-TYPE
        SYNTAX          INTEGER (0..2147483647)
        ACCESS          not-accessible
        STATUS          mandatory
        DESCRIPTION
                "A unique value which identifies the UNI port for which the ATM address is
                in effect. The value of 0 has the special meaning of identifying the local UNI."
        ::= { atmfAddressEntry 1 }
```

atmfAddressAtmAddress OBJECT-TYPE
        SYNTAX   AtmAddress
        ACCESS   not-accessible
        STATUS   mandatory
        DESCRIPTION
            "The ATM address which is in effect on the user-side of the ATM UNI port."
        ::= { atmfAddressEntry 2 }

atmfAddressStatus OBJECT-TYPE
        SYNTAX   INTEGER { valid(1), invalid(2) }
        ACCESS   read-write
        STATUS   mandatory
        DESCRIPTION
            "An indication of the validity of the ATM address at the user-side of the UNI port. To configure a new address in this table, the user-side must set the appropriate instance of this object to the value valid(1). To delete an existing address in this able, the user-side must set the appropriate instance of this object to the value invalid(2).

            If circumstances occur on the network-side which cause an address to become invalid, the network-side modifies the value of the appropriate instance of this object to invalid(2).

            Whenever the value of this object for a particular address becomes invalid(2), the conceptual row for that address may be removed from the table at any time, either immediately or subsequently."
        ::= { atmfAddressEntry 3 }

END

5.9 Signalling ATM Adaptation Layer (SAAL)

This section specifies the Signalling ATM Adaptation Layer (SAAL) for use at the UNI. The SAAL resides between the ATM layer and Q.93B. The purpose of the SAAL is to provide reliable transport of Q.93B messages between peer Q.93B entities (e.g., ATM Switch and host) over the ATM layer. The SAAL is composed of two sublayers, a common part and a service specific part. The service specific part is further subdivided into a Service Specific Coordination Function (SSCF), and a Service Specific Connection Oriented Protocol (SSCOP). Figure 5-47 illustrates the structure of the SAAL.

The SAAL for supporting signalling shall use the protocol structure as illustrated in Figure 5-47.

The Common Part AAL protocol provides unassured information transfer and a mechanism for detecting corruption of SDUs. AAL Type 5 Common Part protocol shall be used to support signalling. The AAL Type 5 Common Part Protocol is specified in Draft Recommendation I.363 [30].

The SAAL for supporting signalling at the UNI shall use AAL Type 5 Common Part protocol as specified in [30] with the following ammendments:

- The "Reserved" fields of all SSCOP PDUs should be encoded as all zeros.

- Upon reception of a BGN PDU while in state 2 (Outgoing Connection Pending), Timer_CC should be stopped, and VT(MS) should only be set BGN.N(MR) and not set to BGAK.N(MR) as illustrated in [31].

- Upon reception of an AA-EST.res while in state 3 (Incoming Connection Pending) VT(MS) should retain its current value and not be set to zero as illustrated in [31].

- Upon reception of a STAT PDU while in state 4 (Data Transfer Ready), VT(PA) is assigned the value N(PS) and not the value of N(PS) + 1 as illustrated in [31].

The Service Specific Connection Oriented Protocol (SSCOP) resides in the Service Specific Convergence Sublayer (SSCS) of the SAAL. SSCOP is used to transfer variable length Service Data Units (SDUs) between users of SSCOP. SSCOP provides for the recovery of lost or corrupted SDUs. SSCOP is specified in Draft Recommendation Q.SAAL1 [31].

The SAAL for supporting signalling shall utilize SSCOP as specified in Q.SAAL1 [31].

An SSCF maps the service of SSCOP to the needs of the SSCF user. Different SSCFs may be defined to support the needs of different AAL users. The SSCF used to support Q.93B at the UNI is specified in Draft Recommendation Q.SAAL2 [32].

The external behavior of theSAAL at the UNI shall appear as if the UNI SSCF as specified in Q.SAAL2 [32] were implemented.

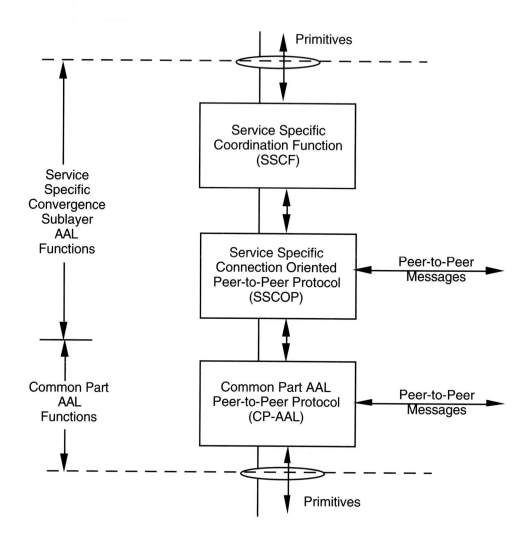

Note: the Figure represents the allocation of functions and is not intended to illustrate sub-layers as defined by OSI modeling principles.

Figure 5-47 SAAL Structure

References

[1] TA-NWT-001113 "Asynchronous Transfer Mode (ATM) and ATM Adaptation Layer (AAL) Protocols Genereic Requirements", Bellcore, Issue 1, August 1992.

[2] FA-NWT-001109 "Broadband ISDN Transport Network Elements Framework Generic Criteria", Bellcore, Dec. 1990.

[3] TA-NWT-001110 "Broadband ISDN Switching System Generic Requirements", Bellcore, Issue 1, August 1992.

[4] TR-NWT-000253 "Synchronous Optical Network (SONET) Transport Systems: Common Generic Criteria", Bellcore, Issue 2, December 1991.

[5] T1S1 LB/91-05 "dpANS - Broadband ISDN User-Network Interfaces: Rates and Formats Specifications".

[6] T1E1.2/92-020 "Broadband ISDN Customer Installation Interfaces, Physical Media Dependent Specification", ANSI Draft Standard, Feb. 1992.

[7] T1 LB 310 "Broadband ISDN ATM Layer Functionality and Specification", January 1993.

[8] T1S1.5/92-029R3 "Broadband ISDN Operations and Maintenance Principles: Technical Report", T1S1.5 August 1992.

[9] ANSI T1.105-1991 "Digital Hiearchy — Optical Interfaces Rates and Formats Specifications (SONET)".

[10] CCITT Recommendation I.413 "B-ISDN User-Network Interface", Matsuyama, December 1990.

[11] Reference Deleted.

[12] CCITT Recommendation I.432, "B-ISDN User-Network Interface - Physical Layer Secification", CCITT SGXVIII, June 1992.

[13] Reference Deleted.

[14] CCITT Recommendation I.610 "OAM principles of B-ISDN access", Geneva, June 1992.

[15] Reference Deleted.

[16] Reference Deleted

[17] Reference Deleted

[18] Reference Deleted

[19] FC-P/91-001R2.1 "Fiber Channel Physical Layer (FC-PH)", Revision 2.1, Working Draft, May 25, 1991.

[20] M.T. Rose and K. McCloghrie, "Structure and Identification of Management Information for TCP/IP-based Internets, Request for Comments 1155. DDN Network Information Center, (May, 1990).

[21] J.D. Case, M.S. Fedor, M.L. Schoffstall, and J.R. Davin, Simple Network Management Protocol, Request for Comments 1157. DDN Network Information Center, (May, 1990).

[22] K. McCloghrie and M.T. Rose (editors), Management Information Base for Network Management of TCP/IP-based internets: MIB-II, Request for Comments 1213. DDN Network Information Center, (March, 1991).

[23] Information processing systems - Open Systems Interconnection - Specification of Abstract Syntax Notation One (ASN.1), International Organization for Standardization. International Standard 8824, (December, 1987).

[24] Information processing systems - Open Systems Interconnection - Specification of Basic Encoding Rules for Abstract Notation One (ASN.1), International Organization for Standardization. International Standard 8825, (December, 1987).

[25] M.T. Rose, K. McCloghrie (editors), Concise MIB Definitions, Request for Comments 1212. DDN Network Information Center, (March, 1991).

[26] M.T. Rose (editor), A Convention for Defining Traps for use with the SNMP, Request for Comments 1215. DDN Network Information Center, (March, 1991).

[27] CCITT Document TD-XVIII/10 "AAL Type 5, Draft Recommendation text for section 6 of I.363", 29 January 1993, Geneva.

[28] T1S1/92-285 "Proposed Procedures, Detailed Service Interface, and Layer Management Interface Description for AAL-5 Common Part", 14 May 1992.

[29] ITU-TS draft Recommendation Q.93B "B-ISDN User-Network Interface Layer 3 Specification for Basic Call/Bearer Control", May 1993.

[30] CCITT Document TD-XVIII/10 (AAL5) "AAL Type 5, Draft Recommendation text for section 6 of I.363", 29 January 1993, Geneva. (Note)

[31] ITU Document DT/11/3-28 (Q.SAAL1) "Service Specific Connection Oriented Protocol (SSCOP) Specification", May 17 1993, Geneva. (Note)

[32] ITU Document DT/11/3-XX (Q.SAAL2) "Service Specific Connection Oriented Protocol (SSCOP) Specification", May 17 1993, Geneva. (Note)

[33] ITU-T I.350, "General Aspects of Quality of Service and Network Performance in Digital Networks, Including ISDN", 6/91.

[34] ITU-T I.35E, "Reference Events for Defining ISDN Performance Parameters", 7/91.

[35] ITU-T I.311, "B-ISDN General Aspects", 6/92.

[36] Richard Colella, Ella Gardner and Ross Callon, Guidelines for OSI NSAP Allocation in the Internet, Request For Comments 1237. DDN Network Information Center, (July, 1991).

[37] Meeting report of Study Group 13 13/2-3, Temporary Document 27 (13/2), July 5-16, 1993 (Expected to be published as part of I.610 in 1994).

[38] ANSI T1.107-1988, "Digital Hierarchy - Format Specification", August 1988.

[39] ANSI T1.107a-1990, "Digital Hierarchy - Suppliment to Format Specification", (DS3 Format Application), 1990.

[40] CCITT, Recommendation I.150, "B-ISDN Asynchronous Transfer Mode Functional Characteristics", SWP-XVII/1, June 1992.

[41] CCITT, Recommendation I.371, "Traffic Control and Congestion Control in B-ISDN", Geneva, 1992.

[42] CCITT, Draft Recommendation I.35B, "Broadband ISDN Performance". WP XVIII/6 (part 2, draft recommendations), TD 15 (XVIII)]

[43] CCITT, Recommendation I.350, "General Aspects of Quality of Service and Network Performance in Digital Networks, Including ISDN," COM XVIII-R 114-E]

[44] "Generic System Requirements in Support of Switched Multi-Megabit Data Service," Bellcore, TR-TSV-000772, Issue 1, May 1991.

[45] "Addendum 1 to T1.606 - Frame Relaying Bearer Service - Architectural Framework and Service Description," Document Number T1S1/91-659, ANSI Approved November 8,1991.

Note - Postscript versions of [30], [31] and [32] are available for anonymous ftp at thumper.bellcore.com : pub/smq. [30] is in AAL5.ps, [31] is available in QSAAL1.ps and [32] is available in QSAAL2.ps. Compressed versions of these files are also available and are identified by the suffix ".Z" on the file name.

Annex A

Guidelines for Use of ATM Address Formats

The goals of the address formats given in this Implementation Agreement are:

 a. to ensure that the addressing scheme is easy to administer,
 b. to construct a scalable address structure,
 c. to provide the ability to uniquely identify an ATM endpoint,
 d. to accommodate public/private interworking using existing technology where appropriate.

The following guidelines are given to clarify the use of addressing in ATM networks from the perspective of users, service providers, and equipment providers:

 1. The ATM address contains an Authority and Format Identifier (AFI), and an Initial Domain Identifier (IDI). In ISO 8348, the purpose of the AFI is to specify: the format of the IDI; the network addressing authority responsible for allocating values of the IDI; whether or not leading zero digits in the IDI are significant; and the abstract syntax of the DSP. The IDI specifies: the network addressing domain from which the values of the DSP are allocated; and the network addressing authority responsible for allocating values of the DSP from that domain. Thus, the combination of the AFI and IDI, which form the Initial Domain Part (IDP) of the ATM address, uniquely specify an administrative authority which has responsibility for allocating and assigning values of the DSP.

 2. For the ISO ICD IDI format, the International Code Designator (ICD) is allocated and assigned by the ISO 6523 registration authority (i.e., the British Standards Institute). The Administrative Authority (AA) is allocated and assigned by the entity specified by the ICD.

 3. For the ISO DCC IDI format, the DCC is allocated and assigned to countries. The ISO National Member Body for that country (or, where no Member Body exists, another appropriate organization) allocates and assigns the Administrative Authority.

 4. The ICD and DCC format are useful for organizations that wish to maintain a private numbering plan that is organizationally based.

 5. The E.164 format is useful for organizations that may wish to use the existing largely geographically based public ISDN/telephony numbering format. The full ISDN number identifies an authority responsible for allocating and assigning values of the DSP. The authority is some entity within the organization which subscribes to the B-ISDN interface.

Note 1 - For private ATM networks which are attached to one or more public ATM networks, this format must be used topologically (i.e. this format must be used with an E.164 address(es) which identify one or more attachment points of the private network to the public network).

For individual private networks that are connected to multiple public networks, there are several alternative methods which may be used for addressing and routing. The best manner to handle this situation is for further study. NSAP Guidelines (RFC 1237 [36]) discusses several alternatives in this case and describes their relative advantages and disadvantages.

6. At the private UNI, the private ATM address will be carried in the Called Party Number information element. The Called Party Subaddress information element is not used.

7. At the public UNI, when the public network supports only the native (non-NSAP) E.164 address format, the gateway of the private network will signal the appropriate native E.164 number in the Called Party information element and the private ATM address in the Called Party Subaddress information element.

8. At the public UNI, when the public network supports the private ATM address format, the private ATM address will be carried in the Called Party Number information element. The Called Party subaddress information element is not used.

9. A call originated on a Private UNI destined for an endsystem which only has a native (non-NSAP) E.164 address (i.e. a system directly attached to a public network supporting the native E.164 format) will code the Called Party Number information element in the (NSAP) E.164 Private ATM address format, with the RD, AREA, and ESI fields set to zero. The Called Party Subaddress information element is not used.

10. The purpose of the RD and Area fields of the private ATM address format is to allow hierarchical routing and efficient use of resources.

Note: These fields shall be assigned with topological significance.

Useful tutorial material and supporting technical information on use of OSI NSAP addresses can be found in RFC 1237 [36].

Annex B

Compatibility Checking

The procedures to perform compatibility checking are implementation dependent.
See Annex B of ITU-T draft Recommendation Q.93B [29] for more information.

Annex C

B-LLI Negotiation

This Annex describes procedures for the use of the Broadband Low Layer Information (B-LLI) information element by endpoint equiment.

C.1 General

The purpose of the B-LLI information element is to provide a means which should be used for conveying information related to lower layer protocols between endpoints. The B-LLI information element is transferred transparently by an ATM network between endpoints.

The user information protocol fields of the B-LLI information element indicate the low layer protocols (i.e., layer 3 and layer 2 protocols above the AAL) used between endpoints. This information is not interpreted by the ATM network and therefore the bearer capability provided by the B-ISDN is not affected by this information.

The B-LLI information element is coded according to §5.4.5.9.

The procedures of this Annex are required in support of some applications (e.g., multiprotocol interconnection). Endpoints should assume that the B-LLI negotiation procedures will be offered by most networks. Therefore it is strongly recommended that networks support all of the procedures of this Annex. At a minimum, all networks shall carry the B-LLI Information Element in the SETUP message.

C.2 B-LLI notification to the called user.

When the calling endpoint wishes to notify the called endpoint of the low layer protocols above the ATM Adaptation Layer (i.e., as identified in octets 6 to 7 of the B-LLI Information element) to be used during the call, then the calling user shall include a B-LLI information element in the SETUP message; this information element is conveyed by the network and delivered to the called user.

C.3 B-LLI negotiation between users

The B-LLI information element supports the indication of certain parameters of acknolwedged mode HDLC elements of procedures. If they are included, parameters(s) may be negotiated for point-to-point calls. In this case, the called endpoint accepting the call may include a B-LLI information element in the CONNECT message if either the endpoint reference information element was not present in the SETUP message or the endpoint reference identifier value was set to 0. This element will be conveyed transparently by the network and delivered to the calling user in the CONNECT message.

> *Note* - The lower layer protocol parameters which may be negotiated by this capability are layer 2 mode (octet 6a), window size (octet 6b), User Specified Layer 2 information (octet 6a), layer 3 mode (octet 7a), default packet size (octet 7b), and packet window size (octet 7c).

If, for any reason, the network is unable to convey this information element, it shall act as described in §5.5.6.8.3 (unexpected recognized information element) except that the cause value #43, *"access information discarded"*, shall be used in the STATUS message. If the called endpoint includes a B-LLI information element in a CONNECT message and it is a leaf (other than the initial leaf) of a point-to-multipoint call, the network shall follow the procedures of §5.5.6.8.3.

If the calling user rejects the B-LLI information element contents in the CONNECT message, the calling user shall initiate clearing with cause #100, *"invalid information element contents"*.

C.4 Alternate requested values

If the calling endpoint wishes to indicate alternative values of B-LLI parameters (i.e., alternative protocols or protocol parameters), the B-LLI information element is repeated in the SETUP message. This procedure applies only for point-to-point calls (and for the initial leaf of a point-to-multipoint call.) Up to three B-LLI information elements may be included in a SETUP message. The first B-LLI information element in the message is preceded by the Broadband Repeat indicator information element specifying "priority list for selection". The order of appearance of the B-LLI information elements indicates the order of preference of end-to-end low layer parameters.

If the network or called endpoint does not support repeating of the B-LLI information element, and therefore discards the Broadband repeat indicator information element and the subsequent B-LLI information elements, only the first B-LLI information element is used in the negotiation. In addition, if the network discards the B-LLI information element, it shall send a STATUS message with cause value #43, *"access information discarded"*.

If the calling endpoint repeats the B-LLI information element in a SETUP message to a leaf (other than the initial leaf) of a point-to-multipoint call, the network shall follow the procedures of §5.5.6.8.3.

The called endpoint indicates a single choice from among the options offered in the SETUP message by including the B-LLI information element in the CONNECT message. Absence of a B-LLI information element in the CONNECT message indicates acceptance of the first B-LLI information element in the SETUP message. If the called endpoint supports none of the choices offered by the calling endpoint (or if acceptable choices have been discarded by the network), it shall clear the call with cause #88, *"incompatible destination"*.

If the calling user rejects the B-LLI information element contents in the CONNECT message, the calling user shall initiate clearing with cause #100, *"invalid information element contents"*.

Annex D

Transit Network Selection

This Annex describes the optional processing of the Transit network selection information element.

Transit network selection procedures are needed in this Implementation Agreement to meet certain regulatory requirements. They may also be used for other reasons.

D.1 Selection not supported

Some networks may not support transit network selection. In this case, when a Transit network selection information element is received, that information element is processed according to the rules for unimplemented non-mandatory information elements (see §5.5.6.8.1).

D.2 Selection supported

When transit network selection is supported, the user identifies the selected transit network in the SETUP message. One Transit network selection information element is used to convey a single network identification.

The Transit network selection information element is not delivered to the destination user.

When a network cannot route the call due to insufficient bandwidth, the network shall initiate call clearing in accordance with §5.5.4 with cause #51, *"user cell rate not available"*.

If a network does not recognize the specified transit network, the network shall initiate call clearing in accordance with §5.5.4, with cause #2, *"no route to specified transit network"*. The diagnostic field shall contain a copy of the contents of the Transit network selection information element identifying the unreachable network.

If the transit network selection is of an incorrect format, the network shall initiate call clearing in accordance with §5.5.4 with cause #91, *"invalid transit network selection"*.

In addition, some networks may, by bilateral agreement, provide screening to the transit network (e.g., to ensure that a business relationship exists between the transit network and the user). Should such screening fail, the network shall initiate call clearing in accordance with §5.5.4, with cause #91, *"invalid transit network selection"*.

When a user includes the Transit network selection information element, pre-subscribed default Transit network selection information (if any) is overridden.

Annex E

Cause Definitions

Normal class definitions

Cause Number 1: unallocated (unassigned) number

> This cause indicates that the called party cannot be reached because, although the number is in a valid format, it is not currently assigned (allocated).

Cause Number 2: no route to specified transit network

> This cause indicates that the equipment sending this cause has received a request to route the call through a particular network which it does not recognize. The equipment sending this cause does not recognize the transit network either because the transit network does not exist or because that particular transit network, while it does exist, does not serve the equipment which is sending this cause.

> This cause is supported on a network-dependent basis.

Cause Number 3: no route to destination

> This cause indicates that the called party cannot be reached because the network through which the call has been routed does not serve the destination desired.

> This cause is supported on a network-dependent basis.

Cause Number 10: VPCI/VCI unacceptable

> This cause indicates that the virtual channel most recently identified is not acceptable to the sending entity for use in this call.

Cause Number 17: user busy

> This cause is used to indicate that the called party is unable to accept another call because the user busy condition has been encountered. This cause value may be generated by the called user or by the network.

Cause Number 18: no user responding

> This cause is used when a called party does not respond to a call establishment message with a connect indication within the prescribed period of time allocated.

Cause Number 21: call rejected

> This cause indicates that the equipment sending this cause does not wish to accept this call, although it could have accepted the call because the equipment sending this cause is neither busy nor incompatible.

Cause Number 22: number changed

This cause is returned to a calling party when the called party number indicated by the calling user is no longer assigned. The new called party number may optionally be included in the diagnostic field. If a network does not support this capability, cause number #1, *"unassigned (unallocated) number"*, shall be used.

Cause Number 23: user rejects all calls with calling line identification restriction (CLIR)

This cause is returned by the called party when the call is offered without calling party number information and the called party requires this information.

Cause Number 27: destination out of order

This cause indicates that the destination indicated by the user cannot be reached because the interface to the destination is not functioning correctly. The term "not functioning correctly" indicates that a signalling message was unable to be delivered to the remote user; e.g., a physical layer or SAAL failure at the remote user, user equipment off-line.

Cause Number 28: invalid number format (address incomplete)

This cause indicates that the called user cannot be reached because the called party number is not in a valid format or is not complete.

Cause Number 30: response to STATUS ENQUIRY

This cause is included in the STATUS message when the reason for generating the STATUS message was the prior receipt of a STATUS ENQUIRY message.

Cause Number 31: normal, unspecified

This cause is used to report a normal event only when no other cause in the normal class applies.

Resource unavailable class definitions

Cause Number 35: requested VPCI/VCI not available

This cause indicates that the requested VPCI/VCI is not available.

Cause Number 38: network out of order

This cause indicates that the network is not functioning correctly and that the condition is likely to last a relatively long period of time; e.g., immediately re-attempting the call is not likely to be successful.

Cause Number 41: temporary failure

This cause indicates that the network is not functioning correctly and that the condition is not likely to last a long period of time; e.g., the user may wish to try another call attempt immediately.

Cause Number 43: access information discarded

This cause indicates that the network could not deliver access information to the remote user as requested: i.e., ATM adaptation layer parameters, Broadband low layer information, Broadband high layer information, or sub-address as indicated in the diagnostic.

Cause Number 45: no VPCI/VCI available

This cause indicates that there is no appropriate VPCI/VCI presently available to handle the call.

Cause Number 47: resource unavailable, unspecified

This cause is used to report a resource unavailable event only when no other cause in the resource unavailable class applies.

Service or option not available class definitions

Cause Number 49: Quality of Service unavailable

This cause is used to report that the requested Quality of Service cannot be provided.

Cause Number 51: User cell rate not available

This cause is used to report that the requested ATM User Cell Rate is unobtainable.

Cause Number 57: bearer capability not authorized

This cause indicates that the user has requested a bearer capability which is implemented by the equipment which generated this cause but the user is not authorized to use.

Cause Number 58: bearer capability not presently available

This cause indicates that the user requested a bearer capability which is implemented by the equipment which generated the cause but which is not available at this time.

Cause Number 63: Service or option not available, unspecified

This cause is used to report a service or option not available event only when no other cause in the service or option not available class applies.

Service or option not implemented class definitions

Cause Number 65: bearer capability not implemented

This cause indicates that the equipment sending this cause does not support the bearer capability requested.

Cause Number 73: unsupported combination of traffic parameters

This cause indicates that the combination of traffic parameters contained in the ATM user cell rate information element is not supported.

Invalid message (e.g., parameter out of range) class definitions

Cause Number 81: invalid call reference value

This cause indicates that the equipment sending this cause has received a message with a call reference which is not currently in use on the user-network interface.

Cause Number 82: identified channel does not exist

This cause indicates that the equipment sending this cause has received a request to use a channel not activated on the interface for a call.

Cause Number 88: incompatible destination

This cause indicates that the equipment sending this cause has received a request to establish a call which has Broadband low layer information, Broadband high layer information, or other compatibility attributes which cannot be accommodated.

Cause Number 89: invalid endpoint reference value

This cause indicates that the equipment sending this cause has received a message with an endpoint reference which is currently not in use on the user-network interface.

Cause Number 91: invalid transit network selection

This cause indicates that a transit network identification was received which is of an incorrect format as defined in Annex D.

Cause Number 92: too many pending add party requests

This cause indicates a temporary condition when the calling party sends an add party message but the network is unable to accept another add party message because its queues are full.

Cause Number 93: AAL parameters can not be supported

This cause indicates that the equipment sending this cause has received a request to establish a call which has ATM adaptation layer parameters which cannot be accommodated.

Protocol Error (e.g., unknown message) class definitions

Cause Number 96: mandatory information element is missing

This cause indicates that the equipment sending this cause has received a message which is missing an information element which must be present in the message before the message can be processed.

Cause Number 97: message type non-existent or not implemented

This cause indicates that the equipment sending this cause has received a message with a message type it does not recognize either because this is a message not defined or defined but not implemented by the equipment sending this cause.

Cause Number 99: information element non-existent or not implemented

This cause indicates that the equipment sending this cause has received a message which includes information element(s) not recognized because the information element identifier(s) are not defined or are defined but not implemented by the equipment sending the cause. This cause indicates that the information element(s) were discarded. However, the information element is not required to be present in the message in order for the equipment sending this cause to process the message.

Cause Number 100: invalid information element contents

This cause indicates that the equipment sending this cause has received an information element which it has implemented; however, one or more of the fields in the information element are coded in such a way which has not been implemented by the equipment ending this cause.

Cause Number 101: message not compatible with call state

This cause indicates that a message has been received which is incompatible with the call state.

Cause Number 102: recovery on timer expiry

This cause indicates that a procedure has been initiated by the expiry of a timer in association with error handling procedures.

Cause Number 104: incorrect message length

This cause is used to report an inconsistent message length.

Cause Number 111: protocol error, unspecified

This cause is used to report a protocol error event only when no other cause in the protocol error class applies.

Annex F

ATM Adaptation Layer Parameters Negotiation

This Annex describes procedures for the use of the ATM adaptation layer parameters information element by endpoint equipment.

F.1 General

The purpose of the ATM adaptation layer parameters information element is to provide a means which may be used for conveying information related to the ATM adaptation layer between endpoints. The ATM adaptation layer parameters information element is transferred transparently between ATM endpoints by the network.

F.2 ATM adaptation layer parameter indication in the SETUP message

When the calling endpoint wishes to indicate to the called endpoint the AAL common part parameters and service specific part to be used during the call, the calling endpoint shall include an ATM adaptation layer parameters information element in the SETUP message. This information element is conveyed by the network and delivered to the called user.

The ATM adaptation layer parameters information element may include the following parameters for different AAL connection types:

a) for AAL Connection type 1:
   - Subtype,
   - CBR Rate,
   - Clock Recovery Type,
   - Error Correction,
   - Structured Data Transfer,
   - Partially Filled Cells Indicator.

b) for AAL Connection type 3/4:
   - Forward and Backward Maximum CPCS-SDU Size (Note),
   - MID Size,
   - Mode,
   - SSCS Type.

c) for AAL Connection type 5:
   - Forward and Backward Maximum CPCS-SDU Size (Note),
   - Mode,
   - SSCS Type.

d) for User defined AAL :
   - User defined AAL information (four octets).

Note - Forward Maximum CPCS-SDU size and Backward Maximum CPCS-SDU Size shall either both be present or both be absent in the ATM adaptation layer parameters information element. For unidirectional (including point-to-multipoint) ATM virtual connections, the Backward Maximum CPCS-SDU size shall be set to 0.

F.3 Maximum CPCS-SDU Size negotiation

When the called user has received an ATM adaptation layer parameters information element in a SETUP message and:

a) the Endpoint reference information element either was not present in the SETUP message or the endpoint reference identifer value was set to 0; and,

b) the AAL type is either AAL 3/4 or AAL5

the ATM adaptation layer parameters information element may be included in the CONNECT message. The ATM adaptation layer parameters information element shall include the Forward Maximum CPCS-SDU Size, indicating the size of the largest CPCS-SDU that the called user is able to receive, and the Backward Maximum CPCS-SDU size, indicating the size of the largest CPCS-SDU that it will transmit. The values of the Forward and Backward Maximum CPCS-SDU Size indicated in the CONNECT message shall not be greater than the values indicated by the calling user in the SETUP message. The ATM adaptation layer parameters information element will be conveyed to the calling user.

Note - For unidirectional ATM virtual connections, the Backward Maximum CPCS-SDU size shall be set to 0.

If the called user does not include the ATM adaptation layer parameters information element in the CONNECT message, the calling user shall assume that the called user accepts the values of the Forward and Backward Maximum CPCS-SDU Size indicated by the calling user in the SETUP message.

If the calling party cannot use the Forward or Backward Maximum CPCS-SDU Size indicated in the CONNECT message (i.e., because the value negotiated by the called party is unacceptably small) then the call shall be cleared with cause #93, *"AAL Parameters can not be supported."*

If the called endpoint includes an ATM adaption layer parameters information element in a CONNECT message and it is a leaf (other than the initial leaf) of a point-to-multipoint call, the network shall follow the procedures of §5.5.6.8.3.

If the calling endpoint receives an ATM adaption layer parameters information element in the CONNECT message which:

a) contains octet groups other than the forward and backward maximum CPCS-SDU size and/or MID or

b) contains a Maximum SDU length which is greater than the Maximum SDU length which was sent in the SETUP message

c) is missing the Forward or Backward Maximum CPCS-SDU Size or both the calling endpoint should clear the call with cause #100, *"invalid information element contents."*

When the called user has received an ATM adaptation layer parameter information element in a SETUP message and the AAL type is User defined AAL, the ATM adaptation layer parameter information may be included in the CONNECT message.

If the calling endpoint receives an ATM adaptation layer parameters information element in the CONNECT message which

a) contains octet groups other than the Forward and Backward Maximum CPCS-SDU Size and/or MID, or

b) contains a MID which is greater than the MID which was sent in the SETUP message,

the calling endpoint should clear the call with cause #100, *"invalid information element contents"*.

F.4 MID Size negotiation

When the called user receives the ATM adaptation layer parameters information element in the SETUP message which indicates AAL type 3/4, the called user shall check the MID Size value. If the called user cannot support the indicated MID Size but it can support a smaller value, the called user includes an ATM adaptation layer parameters information element in the CONNECT message containing the MID Size that it can support.

The calling user will either accept the MID Size contained in the CONNECT message or will clear the call with cause #93, *"AAL Parameters can not be supported."*

F.5 Use of Forward and Backward Maximum CPCS-SDU Size by the AAL entity in the user plane

The values of Forward and Backward Maximum CPCS-SDU Size resulting from AAL parameters negotiation shall be used by the AAL entities in the user plane. The AAL entity in the calling user equipment shall not send a CPCS-SDU size larger than the indicated value specified in the Forward Maximum CPCS-SDU Size parameter, and may allocate its internal resources based on the value indicated in the Backward Maximum CPCS-SDU Size parameter. Similarly, the AAL entity in the called user equipment shall not send a CPCS-SDU size larger than the indicated value specified in the Backward Maximum CPCS-SDU Size parameter, and may allocate its internal resources based on the value indicated in the Forward Maximum CPCS-SDU Size parameter.

Appendix A

Quality of Service Guidelines

A.1 Introduction

A.1.1 Objective

The following quotes from Recommendation I.350 [43] state the objectives of the ATM Bearer Service Quality of Service (QoS).

"... the aspects of Quality of Service that are covered are restricted to the identification of parameters that can be directly observed and measured at the point at which the service is accessed by the user." [1, para. 1.2.1]

".. the definition of QoS parameters should be clearly based on events and states observable at service access points and independent of the network processes and events which support the service." [1, para. 3.1.2]

The defined parameters apply to cell streams in which all cells conform to the negotiated traffic contract. The parameter definitions and measurement methods applicable to cell streams in which some cells do not conform with the traffic contract is for further study. Appendix 1 to I.35B [42] contains material relevant to this problem.

The defined performance parameters are intended to characterize ATM connections in the available state. Availability decision parameters and associated availability parameters and their objectives will be the subject of further study.

A.1.2 Approach

The following outline describes the approach taken to the QoS appendix.

Section A.1 - Introduction
   Covering: Objectives, Approach, Terminology

Section A.2 - QoS Reference Configuration

Section A.3 - ATM Performance Parameters
   Covering: Cell Error Parameters, Cell Loss Ratio, Cell Misinsertion Rate, Cell transfer delay, and QoS provided by the ATM layer

Section A.4 - QoS Classes
   Covering: Specified QoS Classes, Unspecified QoS Class

Section A.5 - Measurement Methods

    Covering: Cell Error Parameters, Cell Loss Ratio, Cell Misinsertion rate, Cell Transfer Delay

Section A.6 - Factors Affecting ATM QoS Performance Parameters

    Covering: Sources of QoS degradation, QoS Performance Parameter guidelines, Principles of allocation

A.1.3 Terminology

A.1.3.1 Cell Event

The following two events are defined based on I.35B [42]. These events will be used in defining the ATM cell transfer performance parameters.

- A "cell exit event" occurs when the first bit of an ATM cell has completed transmission out of an End User Device to a Private ATM network element across the "Private UNI" Measurement Point, or out of a Private ATM network element to a Public ATM network element across the "Public UNI" Measurement Point, or out of an End User Device to a Public ATM network across the "Public UNI" Measurement Point.

- A "cell entry event" occurs when the last bit of an ATM cell has completed transmission into an End User Device from a Private ATM network element across the "Private UNI" Measurement Point, or into a Private ATM network element from a Public ATM network element across the "Public UNI" measurement point or into an End User Device from a Public ATM network element across the "Public UNI" Measurement Point.

A.1.3.2 ATM Cell Transfer Outcome

The following possible cell transfer outcomes between measurement points for transmitted cells are defined based on I.35B.

- Successful Cell Transfer Outcome: The cell is received corresponding to the transmitted cell within a specified time T_{max}. The binary content of the received cell conforms exactly to the corresponding cell payload and the cell is received with a valid header field after header error control procedures are completed.

- Errored Cell Outcome: The cell is received corresponding to the transmitted cell within a specified time T_{max}. The binary content of the received cell payload differs from that of the corresponding transmitted cell or the cell is received with an invalid header field after header error control procedures are completed.

- Lost Cell Outcome: No cell is received corresponding to the transmitted cell within a specified time T_{max}. (Examples include "never showed up" or "late").

- Mis-inserted Cell Outcome: A received cell for which there is no corresponding transmitted cell.

- Severely-Errored Cell Block Outcome: When M or more Lost Cell outcomes, Mis-inserted Cell Outcomes, or Errored Cell outcomes are observed in a received cell block of N cells transmitted consecutively on a given connection.

A.2 QoS Reference Configuration

Recommendation I.350 [Figure 1/I.350] defines Quality of Service (QoS) for Bearer Service and TeleService. The QoS has a direct relationship to the Network Performance (NP) as shown in this figure. The principal difference is that QoS pertains to user oriented performance concerns of an end-to-end service, while NP is concerned with parameters that are of concern to network planning, provisioning and operations activities.

Figure 1-3 of the ATM Forum UNI specification identifies the relationship of the CCITT reference points to the "Private Local Interface" (i.e., R or S reference points) and the "Public Network Interface" (i.e., T or U reference points).

Draft Recommendation I.35E [42] defines Measurement Points (MPs) and Measurement Points at a T interface (MPT). In this ATM UNI specification the Measurement Points are defined to be either at the Private UNI between the End User Device and a Private network element or at the Public UNI between an End User device / Private network element and a Public network element as shown in Figure 1-3 of the ATM UNI specification. Figure A-1 summarizes the Quality of Service (QoS) reference configurations for this ATM UNI specification.

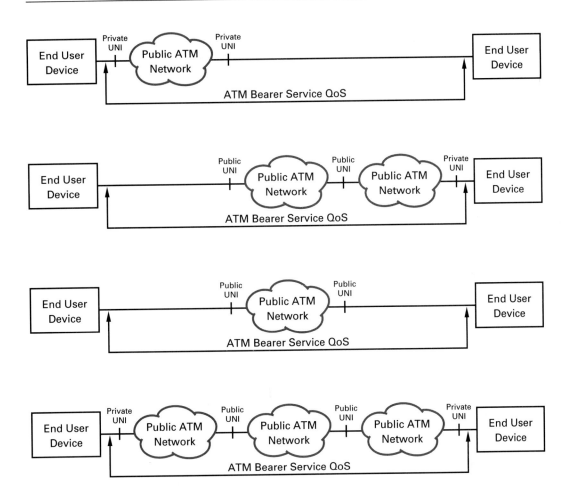

Figure A-1 ATM QoS Reference Configuration

The performance objectives will not be defined in this document. However, alternative means to measure, or estimate the value of performance parameters defined will be described. A Public or Private switch manufacturer should state QoS performance in the terms of the parameters defined in this appendix. A service provider also should state QoS performance objectives in the terms defined in this appendix.

Note, while it is desirable to have the ATM Bearer Service QoS be identical for all of the reference configurations, however, in general, it may be different. Section 6 provides more details on how various factors impact QoS performance parameters.

A.3 ATM Performance Parameters

This section summarizes the set of ATM cell transfer performance parameters defined in I.35B [42]. The cell events and cell transfer outcomes defined in section 1.3 of this appendix are used in defining these performance parameters. This set of ATM cell transfer performance parameters correspond to the generic criteria of the assessment (shown in parentheses) of the QoS (see I.350 [33]), as follows:

Cell Error Ratio	(Accuracy)
Severely-Errored Cell Block Ratio	(Accuracy)
Cell Loss Ratio	(Dependability)
Cell Misinsertion Rate	(Accurarcy)
Cell Transfer Delay	(Speed)
Mean Cell Transfer Delay	(Speed)
Cell Delay Variation	(Speed)

A.3.1 Cell Error Parameters

A.3.1.1 Cell Error Ratio

Cell Error Ratio is defined as follows for an ATM connection:

$$\frac{\text{Errored Cells}}{\text{Successfully Transferred Cells} + \text{Errored Cells}}$$

Successfully Transferred Cells and Errored Cells contained in cell blocks counted as Severely Errored Cell Blocks (see §3.1.2) should be excluded from the population used in calculating Cell Error Ratio.

A.3.1.2 Severely-Errored Cell Block Ratio

The Severely Errored Cell Block Ratio for an ATM connection is defined as:

$$\frac{\text{Severely Errored Cell Blocks}}{\text{Total Transmitted Cell Blocks}}$$

A cell block is a sequence of N cells transmitted consecutively on a given connection. A severely errored cell block outcome occurs when more than M error Cells, Lost Cells, or mis-inserted cell outcomes are observed in a received cell block.

For practical measurement purposes, a Cell Block will normally correspond to the number of user information cells transmitted between successive OAM cells. The size of a Cell Block is to be specified.

A.3.2 Cell Loss Ratio

The Cell Loss Ratio is defined for an ATM connection as:

$$\frac{\text{Lost Cells}}{\text{Total Transmitted Cells}}$$

Lost and transmitted cells counted in severely error cell blocks should be excluded from the cell population in computing cell loss ratio.

A.3.3 Cell Misinsertion Rate

The Cell Misinsertion rate for an ATM connection is defined as:

$$\frac{\text{Misinserted Cells}}{\text{Time Interval}}$$

Severely Errored Cell Blocks should be excluded from the population when calculating the cell misinsertion rate. Cell misinsertion on a particular connection is most often caused by an undetected error in the header of a cell being transmitted on a different connection. This performance parameter is defined as a rate (rather than the ratio) since the mechanism producing mis-inserted cells is independent of the number of transmitted cells received on the corresponding connection.

A.3.4 Cell Transfer Delay

The Cell Transfer Delay is defined as the elapsed time between a cell exit event at the measurement point 1 (e.g. at the source UNI) and the corresponding cell entry event at measurement point 2 (e.g. the destination UNI) for a particular connection. The Cell Transfer Delay between two measurement points is the sum of the total inter-ATM node transmission delay and the total ATM node processing delay between MP_1 and MP_2. The following components of the Cell Transfer Delay are described in more detail in Annex B of I.35B [42].

T3 = Cell Transfer Delay (MPT-MPT)

T31 = Total inter-ATM node transmission delay (e.g. propagation delay)

T32 = Total ATM node processing delay (queuing, switching and routing)

A.3.4.1 Mean Cell Transfer Delay

Mean Cell Transfer Delay is defined as the arithmetic average of a specified number of cell transfer delays for one or more connections.

A.3.4.2 Cell Delay Variation (CDV)

There are two performance parameters associated with cell delay variation: 1-point Cell Delay Variation (1-point CDV) and the 2-point Cell Delay Variation (2-point CDV).

The 1-point CDV describes variability in the pattern of cell arrival events observed at a single measurement point with reference to the negotiated peak rate 1/T as defined in I.371 [41].

The 2-point CDV describes variability in the pattern of cell arrival events observed at the output of a connection portion (MP_2) with reference to the pattern of the corresponding events observed at the input to the connection portion (MP_1).

A.3.4.2.1 1-Point CDV

The 1-point CDV for cell k (y_k) at a measurement point is defined as the difference between the cell's reference arrival time (c_k) and actual arrival time (a_k) at the measurement point: $y_k = c_k - a_k$. The reference arrival time (c_k) is defined as follows:

$$c_0 = a_0 = 0$$

$$c_{k+1} = \begin{cases} c_k + T & \text{if } c_k \geq a_k \\ a_k + T & \text{otherwise} \end{cases}$$

Positive values of the 1-point CDV correspond to cell clumping; negative values of the 1-point CDV correspond to gaps in the cell stream. The reference arrival time defined above eliminates the effect of gaps and provides a measurement of cell clumping.

A.3.4.2.2 2-Point CDV

The 2-point CDV for cell k (v_k) between two measurement points (MP_1 and MP_2) is the difference between the absolute cell transfer delay of cell k (x_k) between the two MPs and a defined reference cell transfer delay ($d_{1,2}$) between MP_1 and MP_2: $v_k = x_k - d_{1,2}$.

The absolute cell transfer delay (x_k) of cell k between MP_1 and MP_2 is the same as Cell Transfer Delay defined in §3.4. The reference cell transfer delay ($d_{1,2}$) between MP_1 and MP_2 is the absolute cell transfer delay experienced by a reference cell between the two MPs.

See I.35B [42] for more details.

A.3.5 Quality of Service provided by the ATM Layer

A user of an ATM connection (a VCC or a VPC) is provided with one of a number of QoS classes supported by the network. It should be noted that a VPC may carry VC links of various QoS classes. The QoS of the VPC must meet the most demanding QoS of the VC links carried as defined in I.150 [40]. The QoS class associated with a given ATM connection is indicated to the network at the time of connection establishment and will not change for the duration of that ATM connection.

A.4 QoS Classes

A Quality of Service (QoS) class can have specified performance parameters (Specified QoS class) or no specified performance parameters (Unspecified QoS class). QoS classes are inherently associated with a connection. A Specified QoS class specifies a set of performance parameters and the objective values for each performance parameter identified. Examples of performance parameters that could be in a QoS class are: cell transfer delay, cell delay variation, and cell loss ratio, as currently mentioned in I.371 [41] section 1.5 and Q.93B [29] section 4.5.15 and 4.5.21.

Within a specified QoS class, at most two cell loss ratio parameters may be specified. If a specified QoS class does contain two cell loss ratio parameters, then one parameter is for all CLP=0 cells and the other parameter is for all CLP=1 cells of the ATM connection. As presently foreseen, other performance parameters besides the cell loss ratio would apply to the aggregate cell flow of the ATM connection. A QoS class could contain, for example, the following performance parameters: mean cell transfer delay, a cell delay variation, a cell loss ratio on CLP=0 cells and a cell loss ratio on CLP=1 cells.

The network may support several QoS classes. At most one (1) unspecified QoS class can be supported. The performance provided by the network should meet (or exceed) performance parameter objectives of the QoS class requested by the ATM end-point. For the purpose of early ATM implementation, both permanent and switched ATM VPCs and VCCs should indicate the requested QoS by a particular class specification. For permanent connections the PVC management can be used by the network to report the QoS classes across the UNI. For a switched connection, signalling protocol's information elements can be used to communicate the QoS class across the UNI.

A.4.1 Specified QoS Classes

A Specified QoS class provides a quality of service to an ATM virtual connection (VCC or VPC) in terms of a subset of the ATM performance parameters defined in Section 3 of this appendix. For each Specified QoS class, there is one specified objective value for each performance parameter identified as defined in section 3 of this appendix.

Initially, each network provider should define objective values for a subset of the ATM performance parameters of section 3 for at least one of the following Service Classes from CCITT recommendation I.362 in a reference configuration that may depend on mileage and other factors:

Service Class A: Circuit Emulation, Constant Bit Rate Video
Service Class B: Variable bit Rate Audio and Video

Service Class C: Connection-Oriented Data Transfer

Service Class D: Connectionless Data Transfer

In the future, more 'QoS Classes' may be defined for a given 'Service Class' described above. The following Specified QoS Classes are currently defined:

Specified QoS Class 1: support a QoS that will meet Service Class A performance requirements

Specified QoS Class 2: support a QoS that will meet Service Class B performance requirements

Specified QoS Class 3: support a QoS that will meet Service Class C performance requirements

Specified QoS Class 4: support a QoS that will meet Service Class D performance requirements

The Specified QoS Class 1 should yield performance comparable to current digital private line performance.

Specified QoS Class 2 is intended for packetized video and audio in teleconferencing and multi-media applications.

Specified QoS Class 3 is intended for interoperation of connection oriented protocols, such as Frame Relay.

Specified QoS Class 4 is intended for interoperation of connectionless protocols, such as IP, or SMDS.

A network operator may provide the same performance for all or a subset of Specified QoS Classes, subject to the constraint that the requirements of the most stringent Service Class are met.

A.4.2 Unspecified QoS Class

In the Unspecified QoS class, no objective is specified for the performance parameters. However, the network provider may determine a set of internal objectives for the performance parameters. In fact, these internal performance parameter objectives need not be constant during the duration of a call. Thus, for the Unspecified QoS class there is no explicitly specified QoS commitment on either the CLP=0 or the CLP=1 cell flow. Services using the Unspecified QoS class may have explicitly specified traffic parameters.

An example application of the Unspecified QoS class is the support of "best effort" service. For this type of service, the user selects the Best-Effort Capability, the Unspecified QoS class and only the traffic parameter for the Peak Cell Rate on CLP=0+1. As indicated in Section 3.6.2.4, this capability can be used to support users that are capable of regulating the traffic flow into the network and to adapt to time-variable available resources.

The Unspecified QoS class is identified by the integer zero (0) in the ILMI MIB or a code point in a signaling message for the requested QoS class.

A.5 Measurement Methods

In this section at least one method to measure each QoS performance parameter in either an in-service or out-of-service mode is defined. Other alternative measurement methods or estimates are possible.

Either in-service or out-of-service methods may be used to estimate values for the ATM cell transfer performance parameters. In-service methods are based on performance monitoring OAM flows which may be introduced into the user cell stream at any VP or VC termination or connecting point, and may then be copied or extracted at any similar point downstream. Details of OAM functions supporting performance measurement are provided in Recommendation I.610. Out-of-service methods consist of establishing a test virtual path or connection at an appropriate measurement point, introducing a cell stream of known content and timing at that point, and then observing the cell stream at a remote measurement point.

A.5.1 Cell Error Parameters

A.5.1.1 Cell Error Ratio

A method using test stream for out-of-service measurement is described in Annex C of I.35B [42]. It basically involves transferring a known data stream into the network at the source measurement point and comparing the received data stream with the known data stream at the destination measurement point.

An in-service measurement is desirable. Annex C of I.35B [42] suggests a BIP-16 indicator to estimate the cell error ratio over a block of N cells.

A.5.1.2 Severely Errored Cell Block Ratio

Severely errored cell block ratio can be estimated in service for a set of S consecutive or non consecutive cell blocks by computing the number of lost cell or mis-inserted cell outcomes in each cell block, identifying cell blocks with more than M lost cell or mis-inserted cell outcomes as severely errored cell blocks and dividing the total number of such severely errored cell blocks by S. This in-service measurement method will undercount severely errored cell blocks to some degree, since it does not include delivered errored cells in the estimation of M. A more accurate estimate of severely errored cell block ratio can be obtained by comparing transmitted and received data in an out-of-service measurement.

A.5.2 Cell Loss Ratio

A method using OAM cells for in-service measurement is described in Annex C of I.35B [42]. The transmitter inserts OAM cells into a transmitted user information cell stream at suitable intervals. Each OAM cell contains a count of the number of user information cells transmitted since the last OAM cell. The receiver keeps a running count of the number of user information cells transmitted (N_t) and received (N_r). Cell loss ratio can then be calculated as $(N_t - N_r) / N_t$ if $N_t - N_r$ is positive. This method will under count cell loss events if misinsertion occurs during the measurement period. It will over count loss if SECB events are not excluded.

A.5.3 Cell Misinsertion Rate

A method using OAM cells for in-service measurement is described in Annex C of I.35B [42]. It is similar to that defined for cell loss ratio measurement. Over a measurement interval, T_m, if $(N_r - N_t)$ is positive, then the cell misinsertion rate is estimated as $(N_r - N_t) / T_m$. Cell misinsertion events will be under counted if cell loss events occur.

An out-of-service measurement method is described in Annex C of I.35B [42]. Basically a VP or VC is maintained for a known period of time, however, no cells are transmitted on it. Any cells received on this VP or VC are mis-inserted cells.

A.5.4 Cell Transfer Delay

A method using OAM cells for in-service measurement is described in Annex C of I.35B [42]. Time stamped OAM cells are transmitted through the network on an established connection. The transmitted OAM cell payload contains the time stamp of cell exit event. The receiver subtracts the received time stamp from the time stamp of the cell entry event to obtain the delay for that cell on that connection. Individual cell transfer delay observations may be combined to calculate statistics of the cell transfer delay distribution. This method requires synchronized clocks at the two MPs, or a suitable reporting mechanism at the receiver, for example a loopback at the receiver.

A.5.5 Measuring Cell Non Conformance Ratio

For the case of a virtual connection described only by Peak Cell Rate and for a single cell flow (such as the aggregate CLP=0+1 cell flow), consider negotiated values for peak emission interval T and CDV Tolerance t. Consider the variable c_k and y_k which are defined as follows:

$$c_0 = a_0$$

$$c_{k+1} = \begin{cases} c_k & \text{if } c_k > a_k + \tau \\ a_k + T & \text{if } c_k \leq a_k \\ c_k + T & \text{otherwise} \end{cases}$$

$$y_k = c_k - a_k$$

where a_k is the observed arrival time of cell k at the measurement point. Figure B-1 of I.35B illustrates a measurement method that calculates, for a cell stream received at a MP, the number of cells that do not comply with a specified peak emission interval and a CDV Tolerance. The virtual scheduling algorithm and continuous-state leaky bucket described in section 3.6.2.4.1 as equivalent versions of the GCRA may be used to implement the cell non conformance ratio. The mapping between the variables of the two equivalent algorithms are summarized in table B-1 of I.35B.

A.5.6 Measuring of Range of Cell Transfer Delay

Buffering procedures to implement AAL1 at the receiving side to compensate for cell delay variation are based on the expected maximum range of cell transfer delay. The actual range of cell transfer delay observed in a set of consecutive cells may be measured using the 1-point CDV parameter y_k which is defined in section 4.4.2 of I.35B. This parameter describes the variability in the pattern of cell arrival events at a MP with reference to the negotiated peak emission interval T. The 1-point CDV y_k for cell k at an MP is the difference between the cell's reference arrival time c_k and the actual arrival time a_k : $y_k = c_k - a_k$. The reference arrival pattern is defined as follows:

$$c_0 = a_0$$

$$c_{k+1} = \begin{cases} a_k + T & \text{if } c_k \leq a_k \\ c_k + T & \text{otherwise} \end{cases}$$

A positive value for y_k corresponds to a cell which experienced a smaller delay than the maximum delay experienced up to cell (k-1). A negative value for y_k corresponds to a cell which experienced the largest delay experienced by cells up to cell k. The following figure provides a method of estimating the range of cell transfer delay for a succession of transferred cells. This method assumes that cells are input uniformly at the Peak Cell Rate.

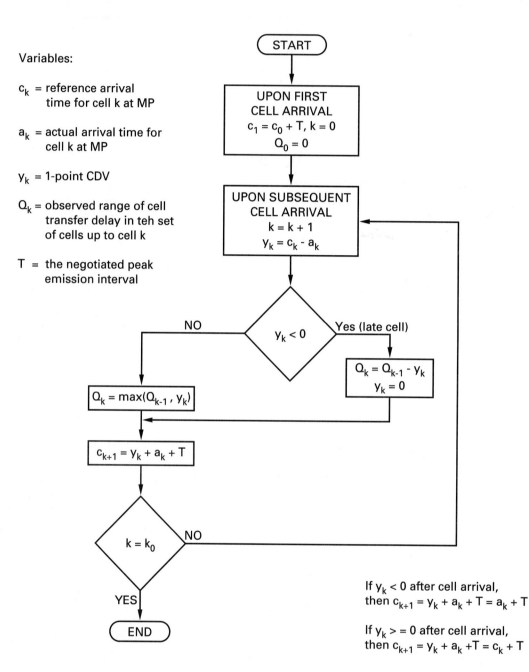

Variables:

c_k = reference arrival time for cell k at MP

a_k = actual arrival time for cell k at MP

y_k = 1-point CDV

Q_k = observed range of cell transfer delay in teh set of cells up to cell k

T = the negotiated peak emission interval

START

UPON FIRST
CELL ARRIVAL
$c_1 = c_0 + T, k = 0$
$Q_0 = 0$

UPON SUBSEQUENT
CELL ARRIVAL
$k = k + 1$
$y_k = c_k - a_k$

$y_k < 0$

NO

Yes (late cell)

$Q_k = Q_{k-1} - y_k$
$y_k = 0$

$Q_k = \max(Q_{k-1}, y_k)$

$c_{k+1} = y_k + a_k + T$

$k = k_0$

NO

YES

END

If $y_k < 0$ after cell arrival, then $c_{k+1} = y_k + a_k + T = a_k + T$

If $y_k >= 0$ after cell arrival, then $c_{k+1} = y_k + a_k + T = c_k + T$

**Figure A-2 Estimation of 2-point CDV from 1-point CDV
for Connections providing CBR service**

A.6 Factors Affecting ATM QoS Performance Parameters

This section provides a list of items to be considered in setting QoS performance parameter objectives dependent upon characteristics that can exist in either private or public networks, or combinations thereof as indicated in Figure A-1. The objective is to have maximum commonalty between public and private networks.

A.6.1 Sources of QoS Degradation

A.6.1.1 Propagation Delay

This is the delay caused by the Physical media which transports the bits comprising ATM cells between UNIs and between ATM switches. This equally impacts public and private networks, dependent upon distance only. Private networks may extend from the desktop to international distances, while public networks generally extend from metropolitan to international distances.

A.6.1.2 Media Error Statistics

This is the random and/or bursty bit errors that are introduced on the physical media.

A.6.1.3 Switch Architecture

The overall architecture of the switch can have significant impacts on performance. Some aspects to consider are the switch matrix design, buffering strategy and the switch characteristics under load. The switch matrix design may range from blocking to non-blocking. The strategy in which the buffer capacity of a port supporting the UNI on an ATM switch is managed may differ significantly across switch architectures. The buffer capacity may be dedicated to a single port, it may be shared between multiple ports, or some combination thereof. The management of this buffer capacity may range from a single First In First Out (FIFO) queue to a more complex, multiple queue system with an algorithmically defined service rule, that could operate based upon priorities. The switch matrix design may introduce some loss under heavy load conditions.

A.6.1.4 Buffer Capacity

This is the actual capacity of the buffer in units of cells at a port supporting the UNI, within an ATM matrix, or in other elements of an ATM switch.

A.6.1.5 Traffic Load

This is the load offered by the set of ATM VPC/VCCs on the same route as the VPC/VCC under consideration.

A.6.1.6 Number of Nodes in Tandem

This is the number of ATM switching nodes that a particular VPC or VCC traverses.

A.6.1.7 Resource Allocation

This is the capacity allocated to a VPC/VCC or to a set of VPC/VCCs, such as the set of VPC/VCCs on a given route that are assigned a given QoS class.

A.6.1.8 Failures

These are events that impact availability, such as port failures, switch failures or link failures. Switch overs between failing equipment or circuits may introduce cell loss.

A.6.2 Impact of QoS Degradation on Performance Parameters

In this section the impact of each of the sources of QoS degradation from section 6.1 on each of the Performance Parameters of section 3 is analyzed in a subjective manner as a guideline for what degradations and factors should be considered in determining a value for the performance parameter. Note that the scope of QoS is from UNI to UNI as defined in section 3. These impacts are summarized in a figure at the end of this section.

A.6.2.1 Cell Error Ratio and Severely Errored Cell Block Ratio

The cell error ratio is expected to be primarily influenced by the error characteristics of the physical media. The severely errored cell block ratio is also expected to be influenced by the error characteristics of the physical media and by buffer overflows.

Error characteristics may also be a function of the physical distance and the characteristics of the media. Operational effects such as transmission protection switching and rearrangements may also introduce errors.

A.6.2.2 Cell Loss Ratio

The Cell Loss Ratio is expected to be influenced by errors in the cell header, buffer overflows, and the non-ideal UPC actions. Loss due to the noncompliance of a connection should be excluded when network caused losses are to be estimated.

Errors detected in the cell header at the physical layer affect the Cell Loss Ratio. Cells may also be lost due to failures, protection switching and path reconfiguration.

Different buffering and resource allocation strategies will cause buffer overflow characteristics to differ.

Queuing implementations in some networks may not provide large buffers, or multiple levels of priority since transmission capacity and resources will be relatively inexpensive. Therefore, cell loss ratios may be higher than in a more complicated network. A lost higher level PDU can be detected in a much shorter period of time in a local area than in a wide area, so that higher layer protocol re-transmissions can be initiated sooner and thus will have less impact on higher layer application throughput in local area networks than in wide area networks.

Buffering strategies in wider area or lower speed networks may be much more complex than that in local, high speed networks. Transmission capacity resources will be relatively more expensive. Multiple levels of delay priority, and possibly relatively large buffers, may be implemented. Within a delay-priority level the CLP bit may also be used to indicate two levels of loss priority. High delay-priority levels will likely have low loss rates, while lower delay-priority levels may have higher loss rates during periods of buffer congestion.

The number of nodes in tandem will also impact the Cell Loss Ratio due to the possibility of overflow in any buffer between the source and destination.

Path reconfiguration from a long to a shorter route is also a possible cause of cell losses, due to the difference in propagation delay. Path reconfiguration is a process at the physical layer used when a path needs to be taken out-of-service to perform maintenance. A possible cause is as follows, after a new path is set up, traffic is transmitted on both paths until it can be verified (at the physical layer) that the new path is operating properly. At this time, a physical layer switch is made at the receiving end of the path. This process is intended to minimize the interruption to the customer service.

A.6.2.3 Cell Misinsertion Rate

The cell misinsertion rate is expected to be primarily influenced by undetected/miscorrected errors in the cell header, which in turn is primarily influenced by the transmission error rate. The likelihood that an undetected/miscorrected cell header error maps into a valid VPI/VCI is also dependent upon the number of VPI/VCI values that are assigned and being actively used.

The cell error ratio will be dependent upon the factors defined in 6.2.1. The number of active ATM sources is likely to be less for a private network than for a public network. This should decrease the likelihood of an undetected/miscorrected cell header error resulting in a cell which is incorrectly mis-inserted into some other VPI/VCI cell stream at the destination UNI.

The number of sources which can be mapped into another cell address will likely be much larger in a public network than in a private network.

A.6.2.4 Cell Transfer Delay

Cell transfer delay is affected by propagation delay, queuing, routing and switching delays, which are likely to differ for local and wide-area networks.

A.6.2.4 1 Mean Cell Transfer Delay

The mean cell transfer delay will likely be dominated by propagation, emission, queuing and routing times in a local private network environment. The propagation delay for local networks will be on the order of 0.1 to 10 microseconds. Queuing delays may likely be very small in high-performance ATM LANs, as long as statistical multiplexing procedures do not induce burst scale congestion. Depending on the media and on distance, the emission time may dominate the propagation time, for example for media operating at the DS-3 rate, the emission time of a cell is roughly 9 microseconds. Additional services, such as ATM cell routing, may introduce additive delay that ranges from insignificant, to something on the order of microseconds. Routing of higher layer protocols will require many microseconds.

In wider area networks the mean cell transfer delay will likely be dominated by propagation delay over longer distances for the highest priority class. Over shorter distances, or for lower priority classes, delay may be significant during periods of high network load. Mean cell transfer delay is expected to be on the order of tens of microseconds for metropolitan areas to tens of milliseconds for national and international areas due to propagation delay.

A.6.2.4.2 Cell Delay Variation (CDV)

Specification of CDV is essential for Constant Bit Rate (CBR) connection performance. Its value is necessary for the dimensioning of the elastic buffer required at the terminating end of the connection for absorbing the accumulated CDV, regardless of whether the network is public or private. Bellcore TA-NWT-001110 issue 1 proposes an objective value of 750 μs delay for absorbing the accumulated CDV (the 10^{-10} quantile) from the ingress public UNI to the egress public UNI for both DS1 and DS3 circuit emulation services.

A common, maximum cell delay variation value for private, public and hybrid private/public networks is essential. As an implementation guideline the receiver CDV tolerance should be designed to handle the case where a connection traverses three networks, each having three switches in tandem.

A.6.2.5 Degradation of QoS Parameters Summary

The following figure summarizes how various sources of degradation can impact the Performance Parameters.

Attribute	CER	CLR	CMR	MCTD	CDV
Propagation Delay				X	
Media Error Statistics	X	X	X		
Switch Architecture		X		X	X
Buffer Capacity		X		X	X
Number of Tandem Nodes	X	X	X	X	X
Traffic Load		X	X	X	X
Failures		X			
Resource Allocation		X		X	X

Figure A-3 Degradation of QoS Parameters

CER = Cell Error Ratio

CLR = Cell Loss Ratio

CMR = Cell Misinsertion Rate

MCTD = Mean Cell Transfer Delay

CDV = Cell Delay Variation

A.6.3 Principles of Allocation

There should be a mapping between the QoS of the bearer service and the network performance of connection elements supporting this service. In hybrid private/public networks the end user sees the combined effects of network performance in the networks that are traversed from end user to end user. One basic principle of performance allocation is that no network provider should bear a disproportionate cost in establishing and operating a service.

Appendix B

Conformance Examples in a Traffic Contract

B.1 Introduction

In the traffic contract, the Cell Delay Variation tolerance specified at the UNI is defined in relation to the PCR by the GCRA (see section 3.6.2.4.1) and the Burst Tolerance specified at the UNI is defined in relation to the SCR also by the GCRA. Additionally, a Conformance Definition that defines the combination of GCRAs in relation to the different cell streams and cell rates of a connection at the UNI is also specified in the Traffic Contract. Depending upon the services provided, different Conformance Definitions could be specified. In this appendix, a few examples are given for information purposes.

For each example described herein, the service needs are summarized and then followed with a Conformance Definition that *could* be used to accommodate the service needs. Specifically, the examples illustrate how one can emulate the traffic definitions of various services by appropriately mapping them into parameters of various GCRAs. The specific Conformance Definition used is for illustrative purposes. Figures are also provided in the form of block diagrams to depict how various GCRAs interact with each other. Two functional blocks are used to represent the high level flowchart of a GCRA(I, L) algorithm and are labeled by C(I) and U(I):

1. Conformance Checking Functional Block:

$$\boxed{\text{C(I)}}$$

2. Update Functional Block:

$$\boxed{\text{U(I)}}$$

The conformance checking functional block represents functions performed in order to determine whether a cell is conforming or not. The update functional block represents the update function performed if a cell is identified as conforming. Note that the only purpose of the block diagrams are to test conformance to the traffic descriptors as defined by the Conformance Definition. The Conformance Definitions indicated in these examples should not be interpreted as the UPC algorithms. Hence, non-conformance does not imply a discard or tagging decision.

B.2 Example 1: Switched Multi-megabit Data Service (SMDS)[44]

SMDS allows customers to send bursts at the full access link rate (e.g. DS3 PLCP). To control the sustainable information rate, an I_{inc}, a N_{inc}, and a C_{max} are specified. I_{inc} is the interval (in number of 53-octet slot times) between increments to the credit. N_{inc} is the number of credits (in user information octets) increase per increment. I_{inc} and N_{inc} together determine a maximum sustainable information rate. C_{max} is the maximum credits that can be accrued. C_{max} is 9188 octets for all access classes. An arriving message will be discarded, if the current accrued credits are less than the estimated user information length.

For an ATM connection supporting the above SMDS application, the following Conformance Definition in relation to a Source Traffic Descriptor that specifies the PCR for the CLP=0 cell stream and SCR for the CLP=0 cell stream *could* be specified in the Traffic Contract *if a proper minimum user information length that the SMDS user could submit is imposed*:

For an ATM connection supporting the above SMDS application, the following Conformance Definition *could* be specified in the Traffic Contract:

1. One $GCRA(T_0, \tau)$ defining the CDV Tolerance in relation to the PCR of the CLP=0 cell stream.

2. One $GCRA(T_{s0}, \tau_{s0}+\tau)$ defining the sum of the Burst Tolerance and CDV Tolerance in relation to the SCR of the CLP=0 cell stream.

   A cell that is conforming to both GCRAs (1) and (2) above is said to be conforming to the Connection Traffic Descriptor. The tagging option is not applicable to this Conformance Definition.

PCR could be chosen to emulate the original SMDS access line rate. The values of PCR and SCR should be chosen to include the extra margin required to accommodate the overhead introduced in transferring the user information via an ATM network in order to deliver an equivalent maximum sustainable information rate to the user. This overhead is closely related to the SMDS message length distribution. The Burst Tolerance τ_{s0} should be set to allow the maximum burst accepted in SMDS to be passed at the PCR.

Figure B-1 depicts this Conformance Definition in terms of the GCRA functional block diagrams. Although traffic conformance at the UNI is defined by this definition, the network provider may use any UPC mechanism as long as the QoS objectives are met for compliant connections.

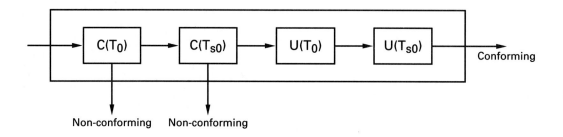

Figure B-1 Example 1

B.3 Example 2a: Frame Relay Service (FRS)[45]

FRS allows customers to send burst at the full access link rate (e.g. DS1). To control the sustainable information rate, a B_c, a B_e, and a CIR are specified. The measurement interval T is derived and is equal to B_c/CIR. The excessive information rate (EIR) is also derived and is equal to B_e/T.

- When a frame with discard eligibility indication not set arrives,

  a. if the current accrued credits for CIR is greater than or equal to the frame length, send the frame;

  b. if the current accrued credits for CIR is less than the frame length, but the current accrued credits for EIR is greater than or equal to the frame length, the frame is sent with discard eligibility indication set;

  c. if the current accrued credits for CIR is less than the frame length and the current accrued credits for EIR is also less than the frame length, the frame is discarded.

- When a frame with discard eligibility indication set arrives and,

  a. if the current accrued credits for EIR is greater than or equal to the frame length, send the frame,

  b. if the current accrued credits for EIR is less than the frame length, discard the frame.

The maximum number of credits that can be accrued for *CIR* is B_c. And, the maximum number of credits that can be accrued for *EIR* is B_e.

This example is intended to emulate the Frame Relay traffic parameters (B_c, B_e and *CIR* and the Frame Relay access line rate. For an ATM connection supporting the above FRS application, the following Conformance Definition in relation to a Source Traffic Descriptor that specifies PCR for the CLP=0+1 cell stream, SCR for the CLP=0 cell stream and SCR for the CLP=1 cell stream *could* be specified in the Traffic Contract *if a proper minimum frame length that the FRS user could submit is imposed*:

1. One GCRA(T_{0+1}, τ) defining the CDV Tolerance in relation to the PCR of the aggregate CLP=0+1 cell stream.

2. One GCRA(T_{s0}, $\tau_{s0}+\tau$) defining the sum of Burst Tolerance and the CDV Tolerance in relation to the SCR of the CLP=0 cell stream.

3. One GCRA(T_{s1}, $\tau_{s1}+\tau$) defining the sum of Burst Tolerance and the CDV Tolerance in relation to the SCR of the CLP=1 cell stream .

A CLP=0 cell that is conforming to both GCRAs (1) and (2) is said to be conforming to the connection Traffic Descriptor. A CLP=1 cell that is conforming to both GCRAs (1) and (3) is said to be conforming to the Connection Traffic Descriptor. A CLP=0 cell that is not conforming to GCRA (2) above but is conforming to GCRAs (1) and (3) above is considered to have the CLP bit changed to 1 and said to be conforming to the Connection Traffic Descriptor.

PCR could be chosen to emulate the original FRS access line rate. The values of PCR and SCR should be chosen to include the extra margin required to accommodate the overhead introduced in transferring the FRS frames via an ATM network in order to deliver an equivalent *CIR* and *EIR* to the user. This overhead is closely related to the FRS message length distribution. The Burst Tolerance (τ_{s0}) should be set to allow the maximum burst accepted in FRS to be passed at the PCR. The Burst Tolerance (τ_{s1}) should be set to allow the maximum excessive burst accepted in FRS to be passed at the PCR.

Figure B-2 depicts this Conformance Definition in terms of the GCRA functional block diagrams. Although traffic conformance at the UNI is defined by this definition, the network provider may use any UPC mechanism as long as the QoS objectives are met for compliant connections.

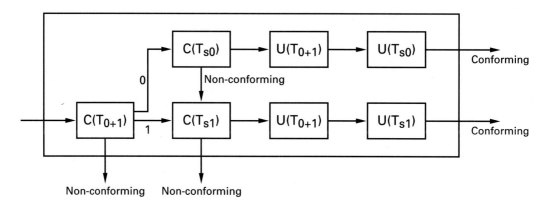

Figure B-2 Example 2a

The Conformance Definition that defines the traffic descriptor can be such that cells that are not conforming with the CLP=0 Sustainable Cell Rate descriptor may or may not be submitted as CLP=1 cells through marking at the source. In this case, the single CLP bit in the ATM header carries two meanings; one for user marked CLP=1 cells and the other for the tagged cells. The network (i.e., the switches) cannot distinguish between the two meanings. Therefore, the same QoS objectives are supported for both the user marked CLP=1 cells and the network tagged CLP=1 cells.

In I.371 it is stated that:

> "If a user requests two levels of priority for an ATM connection, as indicated by the CLP bit value, the intrinsic traffic characteristics of both cell flow components have to be characterized in the Source Traffic Descriptor. This is by means of a set of traffic parameters associated with the CLP=0 component and a set of traffic parameters associated with the CLP=0+1 component."

It should be noted that in this example a Sustainable Cell Rate for the CLP=1 cell stream is specified to model the Frame Relay traffic parameters as described above.

B.4 Example 2b: Frame Relay Service (FRS)

The intent of this section is to provide an example of the interworking of ATM and Frame Relay where the ATM connection is described by only two GCRAs as opposed to three. This restriction to two GCRAs leads to a limitation in matching the ATM parameter to the *EIR* or the Frame Relay access line rate.

For an ATM connection supporting the above FRS application, the following Conformance Definition in relation to a Source Traffic Descriptor that specifies PCR for the CLP=0+1 cell stream, SCR for the CLP=0 cell stream *could* be specified in the Traffic Contract *if a proper minimum frame length that the FRS user could submit is imposed.*

1. One GCRA(T_{0+1}, τ) defining the CDV Tolerance in relation to the PCR of the aggregate CLP=0+1 cell stream.

2. One GCRA(T_{s0}, $\tau_{s0}+\tau$) defining sum of the Burst Tolerance and CDV Tolerance in relation to the SCR of the CLP=0 cell stream.

A CLP=0 cell that is conforming to both GCRAs (1) and (2) above is said to be conforming to the Connection Traffic Descriptor. A CLP=1 cell that is conforming to GCRA (1) above is said to be conforming to the Connection Traffic Descriptor. A CLP=0 cell that is not conforming to GRCA (2) above but is conforming to GCRA (1) above is considered to have the CLP bit changed to 1 and said to be conforming to the Connection Traffic Descriptor.

The values of PCR and SCRs should be chosen to include the extra margin required to accommodate the overhead introduced in transferring the FRS frames via an ATM network. When the PCR is chosen to emulate the FRS access line rate, the *EIR* that is allowed is the difference between the access line rate and the *CIR*. Therefore, the *EIR* that is allowed possibly exceeds the *EIR* negotiated for the FRS. However, using traffic shaping, the PCR may be chosen to be the higher of either the required value to achieve the Transfer Delay objectives, or the required value to achieve the sum of *CIR* and *EIR* to the user. The Burst Tolerance (τ_{s0}) should be set to allow the maximum committed burst accepted in FRS to be passed at the PCR.

Figure B-3 depicts this Conformance Definition in terms of the GCRA functional block diagrams. Although traffic conformance at the UNI is defined by this definition, the network provider may use any UPC mechanism as long as the QoS objectives are met for compliant connections.

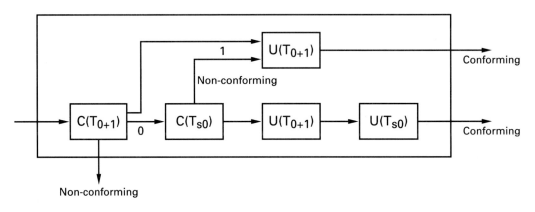

Figure B-3 Example 2b

The Conformance Definition that defines the Traffic Descriptor can be such that cells that are not conforming with the CLP=0 Sustainable Cell Rate parameter set may or may not be submitted as CLP=1 cells through marking at the source. In this case the single CLP bit in the ATM header carries two meanings; one for user marked CLP=1 cells and the other for the tagged cells. The network (i.e., the switches) cannot distinguish between the two meanings. Therefore, the same QoS objectives are supported for both the user marked CLP=1 cells and the network tagged CLP=1 cells.

B.5 Example 3: Constant Bit Rate Services

For an ATM connection supporting a Constant Bit Rate service, the following definition in relation to a Source Traffic Descriptor that specifies PCR for the CLP=0 cell stream *could* be specified in the Traffic Contract:

1. One GCRA(T_0, τ) defining the CDV Tolerance in relation to the PCR of the CLP=0 cell stream.

A cell that is conforming to this GCRA is said to be conforming to the Connection Traffic Descriptor.

PCR is chosen to emulate the constant bit rate of the service.

Figure B-4 depicts this Conformance Definition in terms of the GCRA functional block diagrams. Although traffic conformance at the UNI is defined by this definition, the network provider may use any UPC mechanism as long as the QoS objectives are met for compliant connections.

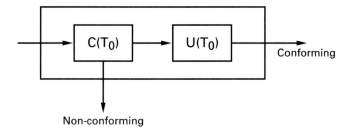

Figure B-4 Example 3

B.6 Example 4: LAN Interconnection

In applications such as LAN interconnection, multiple workstations on a LAN can send data over a public or private ATM WAN to other workstations in other LANs. These LANs can be interconnected through VPs across the ATM backbone. In such applications, the user's packets typically have the same level of importance and therefore are submitted to the ATM network as CLP=0 cells (after being processed at the AAL). Since traffic from multiple workstations are multiplexed on a given VP, there may not be a traffic shaper on the user side of the UNI (this may particularly be the case at the private-UNI). In such applications, it is desirable for the network to tolerate some amount of non-conformance of the CLP=0 stream by tagging these non-conforming cells as CLP=1 cells. This allows the users not to be very pessimistic in their traffic description and therefore may avoid excessive "over-allocation" for bursty data applications.

For an ATM connection supporting the above LAN Interconnection application, a Conformance Definition similar to what is given in Example 2a above *could* be specified in the Traffic Contract.

Appendix C

Point-to-Multipoint Signalling Procedures Using Separate State Machines (Informative)

C.1 Introduction

This Appendix shows the separation of the state machines for the basic point-to-point connections and for the extensions needed for point-to-multipoint communication (ADD PARTY, DROP PARTY, etc); the big advantages of such split being the reuse of the CCITT Q.93B state machine, as adopted in this document for the basic part, and also the possibility to add further extensions with regard to the requirements of the future signalling agreements (e.g. multi-connection calls).

C.2 Description of the Separate State Machines

C.2.1 Control Model

The basic idea of the control model is that the root and leaf terminals, and networks which support the Phase 1 Signalling Protocol is able to maintain two different types of state machines: A point-to-multipoint state machine which maintains states for each party participating in a call; and a link-state machine which maintains the states defined in §5.2.1.

Figure C-1 illustrates the basic control model using this separation of state machines. This model shows the root terminal, a network, and a leaf terminal involved in a call. It is assumed that this leaf terminal will never terminate more than one party of a point-to-multipoint call and therefore only needs to maintain the link-states.

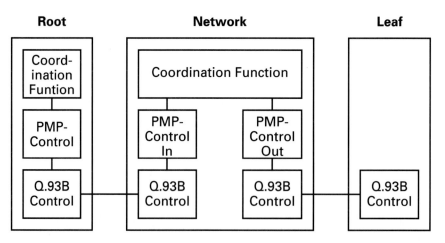

PMP := Point-to-Multipoint

Figure C-1 Control Model with Separated State Machines

Figure C-2 shows that a network involved in a given call uses point-to-multipoint state machines ("In" and "Out"), keeping the PMP-states of each party (identified by an Endpoint Reference, or ER). Further it maintains a link-state machine for the incoming interface where it receives messages related to this call coming from the root, and one link-state machine for each outgoing interface involved in this call. It should be noted that this does not mean that one link-state machine is used for each party of a multipoint call: if several parties of a call are linked to this network via the same outgoing interface, only one link-state machine is maintained for those.

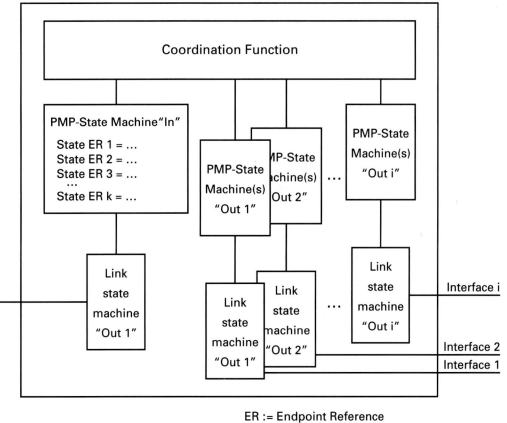

ER := Endpoint Reference
k := Number of Parties
i := Number of different outgoing interfaces involved in this call

Figure C-2 State Machines of a Network involved in a Point-to-Multipoint Call

C.2.2 Party States and Link States

The following Party States and Link States are specified:

- Party States: "Null", "AP-initiated", "AP-received", "DP-initiated", DP-received", "Active".

- Link States: Call / Connection States as defined in §5.2.1.

C.2.3 Primitives between the Multi-Party Control and the Link Control

The two control processes communicate via primitives with each other; the party control sends "requests" to the link control, and receives "indications" from it. The primitives listed below are used for this communication; in the general description below, only "types" of primitives are summarized, i.e., e.g. the primitive "Q.93B-SETUP-Req." is included in the type "Q.93B-<Msg.x>-Req.".

Two types of primitives with the following generic names are used:

- "PMP-<Msg.x>"-primitives, where <Msg.x> may be any message of the Phase 1 signalling protocol which is not used in Q.93B, e.g. "ADD PARTY ACKNOWLEDGE"

- "Q.93B-<Msg.x>"-primitives, where <Msg.x> may be a message of Q.93B (possibly from a subset).

Table C-1 shows which primitives are derived from these generic names:

Generic Name	Request	Indication
PMP-<Msg.x>	X	X
Q.93B-<Msg.x>	X (Note)	X

Note: only for messages with global significance

Table C-1 Primitives Used between Link Control and Point-to-Multipoint Control

C.2.4 Primitives between Point-to-Multipoint Control and Coordination Function

The same primitives are used as between Link Control and Point-to-Multipoint Control.

C.3. Information Flows for Point-to-Multipoint Communication

For illustrative purposes, the model in this section assumes that the UNI 3.0 signalling is used between all nodes within the example network. The UNI 3.0 signalling specification is, of course, normative only at the UNI interface. The model, however, is equally applicable to a concatenation of networks joined by UNI interfaces. For instance, the 'PMP-Node' and 'SP-Node' could represent private ATM LANs, while the 'LC-Node' could represent a Public ATM Network.

C.3.1 Functional Blocks used for the Description of Information Flows

For a given call, the description of the information flows for the establishment and release of point-to-multipoint connections uses the following five functional blocks:

a) Root

This is the functional block which initiates the point-to-multipoint call.

b) PMP-Node (Point-to-multipoint Node)

This is a network node where the information flow uses a connection already established for the information to a party participating in a call.

c) LC-Node (Last Common Node)

This is a network node where the information flow uses a connection already established for the information to another party of a call on the incoming side of the node; on the outgoing side the information flow uses an interface which is not used by any other party of this call.

d) SP-Node (Single Party Node)

This is a network node where the connection is only used for the information flow to/from one single party of a call.

e) B-TE (B-ISDN Terminal Equipment)

This functional block represents the equipment of a user receiving information sent from the root.

Figure C-3 illustrates the description of a point-to-multipoint call using these functional blocks. As usual for functional descriptions, functional blocks only appear once in this figure, although the physical entities which are represented by the functional descriptions may appear more than once for a given call, or may not be present at all. It should also be noted that the functional description is only related to a certain call at a specific point of time: an LC-node may e.g. be an PMP-node for another call or even for the same call at a later point of time.

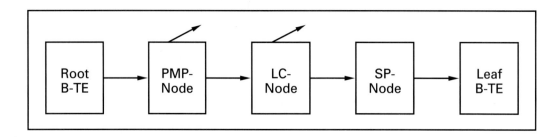

Figure C-3 Functional Blocks of a Point-to-Multipoint Call

C.3.2 Information Flows for the Successful Adding of a Party to an already Existing Call

C.3.2.1 Overall Description of Information Flows

The description of the information flows uses the functional model as specified in section C.3.1, and the separation of the state machines as described in Figures 1 and 2. The information flows summarized in Figure 4 only show the successful adding of a party to an already existing call; a possible rejection of a call attempt and possible error cases are described further below.

The root initiates the addition of a new party by sending an ADD PARTY message which is forwarded by the PMP-Nodes to the LC-Node. The LC-Node sends a SETUP message containing an Endpoint-Reference of the new party to the next SP-Node. The SP-Nodes forward the SETUP message, and the last SP-Node sends the SETUP message to the B-TE. The SETUP message is locally acknowledged by the CALL PROCEEDING message. The B-TE accepts the call by sending a CONNECT message, which is then converted by the LC-Node to become an ADD PARTY ACKNOWLEDGE, sent towards the Root.

To fully show the information flows would require showing three dimensions:
   a) time
   b) horizontal info flow between the link-state machines
   c) vertical info flow between PMP-state machine and link-state machine.

Figure C-4 shows the 2 dimensions a) and b). Additionally, it indicates the local vertical primitives by using primitive numbers (P "n", where "n" is an integer) which are described in detail below, ath the functional entity actions, which are labeled by the number within the functional block.

For reasons of simplicity, the requests and indications from / to the user are not shown in Figure C-4.

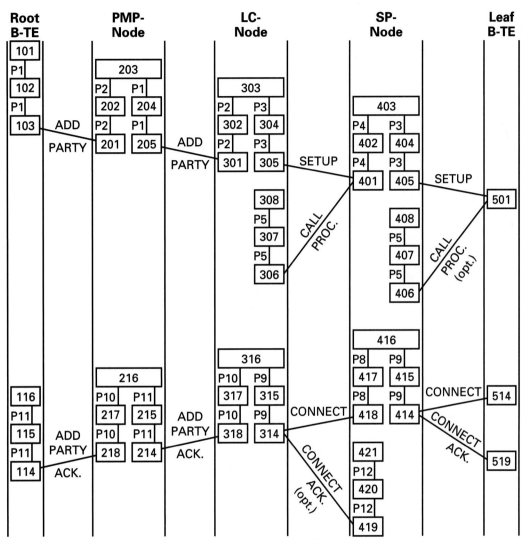

Opt := Optional

**Figure C-4 Information Flows for Successful Adding of a New Party
to a Point-to-Multipoint Call**

C.3.2.2 Primitives between Point-toMultipoint Control and Link Control and between Coordination Function and Point-toMultipoint Control

P1: PMP - ADD PARTY - Req.

P2: PMP - ADD PARTY - Ind.

P3: Q.93B - SETUP - Req.

P4: Q.93B - SETUP - Ind.

P5: Q.93B - CALL PROCEEDING - Ind.

P8: Q.93B - CONNECT - Req.

P9: Q.93B - CONNECT - Ind.

P10: PMP - ADD PARTY ACKNOWLEDGE - Req.

P11: PMP - ADD PARTY ACKNOWLEDGE - Ind.

P12: Q.93B - CONNECT ACKNOWLEDGE - Ind.

C.3.2.3 Functional Entity Actions (FEAs)

Note: Implementations using this description will use timers to control the information flows; however, this is not indicated in this overall description. The acronym "PMP-control" is used in this section for "Point-to-Multipoint Control"

FEA 101:

- Receive and Process Add Party Request from User
- Check: Add Party possible? ("Yes" is assumed here)
- Allocate Endpoint Reference for new party
- Check: Outgoing interface already in use for another party participating in this call? ("Yes" is assumed here.)
- Initiate sending of ADD PARTY message to next node

FEA 102:

- Receive ADD PARTY request from Coordination Function
- Change party state of this party (ER = x) within this call to "AP-initiated"
- Forward P1 to Link control

FEA 103:

- Receive P1 from PMP-Control
- Send ADD PARTY message to next node

FEA 201:

- Receive ADD PARTY message
- Forward this message via P2 to PMP-Control

FEA 202:

- Receive Add Party Indication from incoming Link control
- Change incoming party state to "AP-received"
- Forward this message via P2 to Coordination Function

FEA 203:

- Receive and process ADD PARTY indication
- Select outgoing interface for new party
- Check: Outgoing interface already in use for another party participating in this call?
  (Note: As this is an PMP-node, the assumed answer is "yes"; otherwise, actions as described in FEAs 303 or 403 would be taken)
- Initiate sending of ADD PARTY message to next node

FEA 204:   (as for FEA 102)

FEA 205:   (as for FEA 103)

FEA 301:   (as for FEA 201)

FEA 302:   (as for FEA 202)

FEA 303:

- Receive and process ADD PARTY indication
- Select outgoing interface for new party
- Check: Outgoing interface already in use for another party participating in this call?
  (Note: As this is the LC-node, the assumed answer is "no").
- Initiate sending of SETUP message to next node

FEA 304:

- Receive SETUP request from Coordination Function
- Change outgoing party state of this party within this call to "AP-initiated"
- Forward P3 to Link control

FEA 305:

- Receive P3 from PMP-control
- Send SETUP message (with ER) to next node
- Change link-state to "Call Initiated"

FEA 401:

- Receive and process SETUP message
- Detect trigger for point-to-multipoint call (e.g. presence of an ER)
- Enter "Call Present" state
- Acknowledge the received SETUP message by sending CALL PROCEEDING
- Inform PMP-control using P4
- Enter "Incoming Call Proceeding" state.

FEA 402:

- Receive SETUP indication
- Change incoming party state to "AP-received"
- Inform Coordination Function using P4

FEA 403:

- Receive and process SETUP indication with ER via P4
- Select outgoing interface for new party and check availability of resources
  (Note: As the scope of this section is to describe the successful adding of a new party,
  it is assumed that such an interface with sufficient available resources can be selected).
- Initiate sending of SETUP to next node or to B-TE

FEA 404:   (as for FEA 304)

FEA 405:

- Receive P3 from PMP control
- Send SETUP message to next node or to B-TE
- Change link-state to "Call Initiated".

FEA 501:

- Receive and process SETUP message (as described in Q.93B [29])
- Perform compatibility checking (Note: Assumed result is: "successful")
- Enter "Call Present" state
- Inform user on receipt of SETUP message
- (opt.:) Acknowledge receipt of SETUP by sending back CALL PROCEEDING
- (opt.:) Enter the "Incoming Call Proceeding" state.

FEA 306:

- Receive CALL PROCEEDING message
- (opt.:) Inform PMP-control via P5
- Change link-state to "Outgoing Call Proceeding"

FEA 307 (opt.):

   - Receive and process CALL PROCEEDING message

   - Forward to Coordination Function

FEA 308:

   - (opt.:) Receive information on CALL PROCEEDING via P5

FEA 406 (opt.):

   - Receive CALL PROCEEDING message

   - Inform PMP-control via P5

   - Enter "Incoming Call Proceeding" state

FEA 407 (opt.): (as for FEA 307)

FEA 408 (opt.): (as for FEA 308)

FEA 514:

   - Receive and process indication of call acceptance by the user

   - Send CONNECT message back to last node

   - Change state to "Connect Request"

FEA 414:

   - Receive CONNECT message

   - Acknowledge by sending CONNECT ACKNOWLEDGE

   - Inform PMP-control using P9

   - Enter "Active" state

FEA 519:

   - Receive and process CONNECT ACKNOWLEDGE message

   - Enter "Active" state.

FEA 415:

   - Receive CONNECT message indication

   - Change "outgoing party state" to "active"

   - Forward to Coordination Function

FEA 416:

- Receive and process CONNECT message indication
- Check: Another party within this call active at the interface back towards the root? (Note: As this node is an SP-node, the answer is assumed to be "no")
- Initiate sending of CONNECT back towards the root

FEA 417:

- Receive CONNECT message via P8 from Coordination Function
- change incoming party state of the party to "active"
- Forward this message to Link control

FEA 418:

- Receive P8 from PMP-control
- Send CONNECT back to last node
- Change link-state to "active".

FEA 314:

- Receive CONNECT message
- (opt.) Acknowledge by sending CONNECT ACKNOWLEDGE
- inform PMP-control using P9
- Change link-state to "active".

FEA 315:   (as for FEA 415)

FEA 316:

- Receive and process CONNECT message
- Check: Another party within this call active at the interface back towards the root? (Note: As this node is the LC-node, the answer is assumed to be "yes").
- Initiate sending of ADD PARTY ACKNOWLEDGE towards the root

FEA 317:

- Receive CONNECT message via P10 from Coordination Function
- Change incoming party state to "active"
- Forward this message to Link control via P10

FEA 318:

- Receive P10 from PMP-control
- Send ADD PARTY ACKNOWLEDGE back to last node

FEA 214:
- Receive ADD PARTY ACKNOWLEDGE message
- Forward this message to PMP-control

FEA 215:
- Receive ADD PARTY ACKNOWLEDGE indication from Link control
- Change "outgoing party state" to "active"
- Forward to Coordination Function

FEA 216
- Receive and process ADD PARTY ACKNOWLEDGE indication from PMP-control
- Initiate sending of ADD PARTY ACKNOWLEDGE towards the root

FEA 217:
- Receive ADD PARTY ACKNOWLEDGE via P10 from Coordination Function
- Change incoming party state to "active"
- Forward to Link control

FEA 218:   (as FEA 318).

FEA 114:   (as FEA 214).

FEA 115:
- Receive and process ADD PARTY ACKNOWLEDGE indication from Link control
- Change party state to "active"
- Forward to Coordination Function

FEA 116:
- Receive information on ADD PARTY ACKNOWLEDGE via P11

FEA 419 (opt.):
- Receive CONNECT ACKNOWLEDGE message
- Inform PMP-control via P12

FEA 420 (opt.):
- Receive CONNECT ACKNOWLEDGE indication from Link control
- Forward to Coordination Function

FEA 421 (opt.):
- Receive information on CONNECT ACKNOWLEDGE via P12

C.3.3 Dropping of a Party from an Existing Point-to-Multipoint Call by the Root.

C.3.3.1 Overall Description of Information Flows

The description of the information flows uses the functional model as specified in section C.3.1, and the separation of the state machines as described in Figures C-1 and C-2. The information flows summarized in Figure C-5 only show the dropping of a party from an already existing call initiated by the root.

The root initiates the dropping of a party by sending a DROP PARTY message which is forwarded by the PMP-Nodes to the LC-Node. The PMP-Nodes and the LC-Node locally acknowledged the dropping of the party. The LC-Node sends a RELEASE message containing an Endpoint-Reference of the party to the next SP-Node, which forwards the RELEASE message. The last SP-Node sends the RELEASE message to the B-TE. The RELEASE message is locally acknowledged as specified in Q.93B [29].

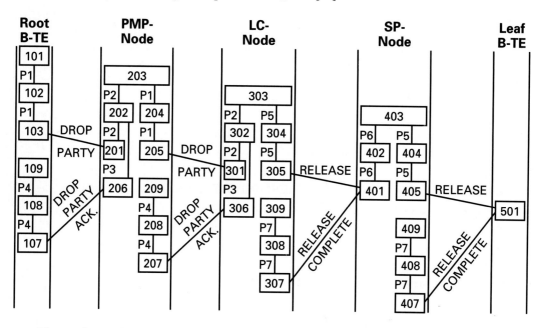

Figure C-5 Information Flows for a Local Acknowledgement of DROP PARTY from an Existing Point-to-Multipoint Call

C.3.3.2 Primitives between Point-to-Multipoint Control and Link Control

P1:   PMP - DROP PARTY - Req.

P2:   PMP - DROP PARTY - Ind.

P3:   PMP - DROP PARTY ACKNOWLEDGE - Req.

P4:   PMP - DROP PARTY ACKNOWLEDGE - Ind.

P5:   Q.93B - RELEASE - Req.

P6:   Q.93B - RELEASE - Ind.

P7:   Q.93B - RELEASE COMPLETE - Ind.

C.3.3.3 Functional Entity Actions (FEAs)

Note: Implementations using this description will use timers to control the information flows; however, this is not indicated in this overall description. The acronym "PMP-control" is used in this section for "Point-to-Multipoint Control".

FEA 101:

- Receive and Process Drop Party Request from User
- Check: Drop Party possible? ("Yes" is assumed here)
- Check: Outgoing interface in use also for another party participating in this call? ("Yes" is assumed here.)
- Initiate sending of DROP PARTY message to next node

FEA 102:

- Receive DROP PARTY request from Coordination Function
- Change party state of this party within this call to "DP-initiated".
- Forward P1 to Link control

FEA 103:

- Receive P1 from PMP-Control
- Send DROP PARTY message to next node

FEA 201:

- Receive DROP PARTY message
- Forward this message via P2 to PMP-Control

FEA 202:

- Receive Drop Party Indication from incoming Link control
- Change incoming party state to "DP-received"
- Initiate sending of DROP PARTY ACKNOWLEDGE to last node
- Change incoming party state to "Null"
- Forward P2 to Coordination Function

FEA 203:

- Receive and process DROP PARTY indication
- Check: Outgoing interface in use also for another party participating in this call?
  (Note: As this is an PMP-node, the assumed answer is "yes"; otherwise, actions as described in FEAs 303 or 403 would be taken)
- Initiate sending of DROP PARTY message to next node

FEA 204:   (as for FEA 102)

FEA 205:   (as for FEA 103)

FEA 206:

- Receive DROP PARTY ACKNOWLEDGE message via P3 from PMP-Control
- Send DROP PARTY ACKNOWLEDGE message to last node

FEA 107:

- Receive DROP PARTY ACKNOWLEDGE message
- Forward this message via P4 to PMP-control

FEA 108:

- Receive and process DROP PARTY ACKNOWLEDGE indication from Link control
- Change party state to "Null"
- Forward P4 to Coordination Function

FEA 109:

- Receive information on DROP PARTY ACKNOWLEDGE via P4

FEA 301:   (as for FEA 201)

FEA 302:   (as for FEA 202)

FEA 303:

- Receive and process DROP PARTY indication
- Check: Outgoing interface in use also for another party participating in this call?
  (Note: As this is the LC-node, the assumed answer is "no").
- Initiate sending of RELEASE message to next node

FEA 304:

- Receive RELEASE request
- Change outgoing party state of this party within this call to "Null".
- Forward to Link control via P5

FEA 305:

- Receive P5 from PMP-control
- Send RELEASE message to next node
- Change link-state to "Release indication"

FEA 306:   (as for FEA 206)

FEA 207:   (as for FEA 107)

FEA 208:   (as for FEA 108)

FEA 209:   (as for FEA 109)

FEA 401:

- Receive RELEASE message
- Acknowledge the received RELEASE message by sending RELEASE COMPLETE to
  last node
- Detect trigger for point-to-multipoint call (e.g. presence of an ER)
- Inform PMP-control using P6
- Enter "Null" state.

FEA 402:

- Receive and process RELEASE indication with ER via P6
- Change incoming party state to "Null"
- Forward this message via P6 to Coordination Function

FEA 403:

- Receive and process RELEASE indication
- Select outgoing interface for the party
- Initiate sending of RELEASE to next node or to B-TE

FEA 404:   (as for FEA 304)

FEA 405:

- Receive P5 from PMP control
- Send RELEASE message to next node or to B-TE
- Change link-state to "Release Indication"

FEA 501:

- Receive and process RELEASE message (as described in Q.93B [29])
- Inform user on receipt of RELEASE message
- Acknowledge the received RELEASE by sending back RELEASE COMPLETE
- Enter the "Null" state.

FEA 307:

- Receive and process RELEASE COMPLETE message
- (optionally) Inform incoming PMP-control using P7
- Change link-state to "Null"

FEA 308: (optionally)

- Receive and process RELEASE COMPLETE Indication from Link control
- Forward P7 to Coordination Function

FEA 309: (optionally)

- Receive information on RELEASE COMPLETE via P7

FEA 407:   (as for FEA 307)

FEA 408:   (as for FEA 308)

FEA 409:   (as for FEA 309)

Appendix D

Example Signalling Codings

This Appendix gives examples of typical codings for information elements. Selection of particular codings to appear in this Appendix is not intended endorse particular applications or higher layer protocols to the exclusion of other applications or higher layer protocols. The values relevant to the examples and their binary codings in the protocol are shown in **boldface** type.

Note - In the event of discrepancies between the text of §5.4 and this Appendix, the text of §5.4 takes precedence.

D.1 ATM Adaptation Layer Parameters

D.1.1 Example of information element coding for AAL1

This example shows how the ATM adaptation layer parameters information element may be coded for a typical video conferencing application.

Bits

8	7	6	5	4	3	2	1	Octet
ATM adaptation layer parameters								1
0	1	0	1	1	0	0	0	
Information element identifier								
1 ext	Coding Standard = **CCITT Specified**		IE Instruction Field = **Not Significant**					2
1	0	0	0	0	0	0	0	
Length of AAL parameter contents								3
Length of AAL parameter contents (continued)								4
= **12** octets								
0	0	0	0	0	0	0	0	
0	0	0	0	1	1	0	0	
AAL Type = **AAL1**								5
0	0	0	0	0	0	0	1	
Subtype Identifier								6
1	0	0	0	0	1	0	1	
Subtype = **Video**								6.1
0	0	0	0	0	1	0	1	
CBR Rate Identifier								7
1	0	0	0	0	1	1	0	
CBR Rate = **n x 64 kbit/s**								7.1
0	1	0	0	0	0	0	0	
Multiplier Identifier								8
1	0	0	0	0	1	1	1	
Multiplier								8.1
Multiplier (continued)								8.2
= **2**								
0	0	0	0	0	0	0	0	
0	0	0	0	0	0	1	0	
Clock recovery type identifier								9
1	0	0	0	1	0	0	0	
Clock Recovery Type = **Adaptive Clock Recovery**								9.1
0	0	0	0	0	0	1	0	
Error correction identifier								10
1	0	0	0	1	0	0	1	
Error Correction Type = **Null**								10.1
0	0	0	0	0	0	0	0	

D.1.2 Example of information element coding for AAL5

This example shows how the ATM adaptation layer parameters information element may be coded for a typical data application using AAL5.

			Bits					
8	7	6	5	4	3	2	1	Octet
ATM adaptation layer parameters								1
0	1	0	1	1	0	0	0	
Information element identifier								
1 ext	Coding Standard = **CCITT Specified**		IE Instruction Field = **Not Significant**					2
1	0	0	0	0	0	0	0	
Length of AAL parameter contents								3
Length of AAL parameter contents (continued)								4
= **11** octets								
0	0	0	0	0	0	0	0	
0	0	0	0	1	0	1	1	
AAL Type = **AAL5**								5
0	0	0	0	0	1	0	1	
Forward Maximum CPCS-SDU Size Identifier								6
1	0	0	0	1	1	0	0	
Forward Maximum CPCS-SDU Size								6.1
Forward Maximum CPCS-SDU Size (continued)								6.2
= **1542 octets**								
0	0	0	0	0	1	1	0	
0	0	0	0	0	1	1	0	
Backward Maximum CPCS-SDU Size identifier								7
1	0	0	0	0	0	0	1	
Backward Maximum CPCS-SDU Size								7.1
Backward Maximum CPCS-SDU Size (continued)								7.2
= **1542 octets**								
0	0	0	0	0	1	1	0	
0	0	0	0	0	1	1	0	
Mode identifier								8
1	0	0	0	0	0	1	1	
Mode = **Message mode**								8.1
0	0	0	0	0	0	0	1	
SSCS-type identifier								9
1	0	0	0	0	1	0	0	
SSCS-type = **NULL**								9.1
0	0	0	0	0	0	0	0	

D.2 Broadband Bearer Capability

D.2.1 Example of information element coding for variable bit rate, connection oriented service with no timing requirements

This example shows how the Broadband bearer capability information element may be coded for a typical variable bit rate data application.

Bits

8	7	6	5	4	3	2	1	Octet
Broadband bearer capability								
0	**1**	**0**	**1**	**1**	**1**	**1**	**0**	1
Information element identifier								
1 ext	Coding Standard = **CCITT Specified**		IE Instruction Field = **Not Significant**					2
1	**0**	**0**	**0**	**0**	**0**	**0**	**0**	
Length of B-BC contents								3
Length of B-BC contents (continued) = **2** octets								4
0	**0**	**0**	**0**	**0**	**0**	**0**	**0**	
0	**0**	**0**	**0**	**0**	**0**	**1**	**0**	
0/1 ext	0 Spare	0	Bearer class = **BCOB-C**					5
1	**0**	**0**	**0**	**0**	**0**	**1**	**1**	
1 ext	Susceptibility to clipping = **Not susceptible**		0	0 Spare	0	User plane connection configuration = **pt-to-pt**		6
1	**0**	**0**	**0**	**0**	**0**	**0**	**0**	

D.3 Broadband Low Layer Information

D.3.1 Example of information element coding for multiprotocol interconnect using the LLC encapsulation

This example shows how the B-LLI information element may be coded when multiprotocol interconnection using the LLC encapsulation is to be used on the VCC (see Internet RFC draft, *Multiprotocol Encapsulation over ATM/AAL5*)

			Bits					
8	7	6	5	4	3	2	1	Octet
Broadband low layer information								1
0	1	0	1	1	1	1	1	
Information element identifier								
1 ext	Coding Standard = CCITT Specified		IE Instruction Field = **Not Significant**					2
1	0	0	0	0	0	0	0	
Length of B-LLI contents								3
Length of B-LLI contents (continued) = 1 octet								4
0	0	0	0	0	0	0	0	
0	0	0	0	0	0	0	1	
0/1 ext	1 Layer 2 id	0	User information layer 2 protocol = **LAN logical link control (ISO 8802/2)**					6
1	1	0	0	1	1	0	0	

D.3.2 Example of information element coding for transport of IP datagrams using the "Null encapsulation" over AAL5

This example shows how the B-LLI information element may be coded when IP datagrams are to be transported within an AAL service data unit without any multiprotocol encapsulation ("Null Encapsulation" — see Internet RFC draft, *Multiprotocol Encapsulation over ATM/AAL5*). Note that no encoding for User Information Layer 3 protocol exists for IP. Therefore, the ISO/IEC TR 9577 Network Layer Protocol Identifier (NLPID) value for IP is used instead.

				Bits				
8	7	6	5	4	3	2	1	Octet
Broadband low layer information								1
0	1	0	1	1	1	1	1	
Information element identifier								
1 ext	Coding Standard = CCITT Specified		IE Instruction Field = **Not Significant**					2
1	0	0	0	0	0	0	0	
Length of B-LLI contents								3
Length of B-LLI contents (continued) = **3** octets								4
0	0	0	0	0	0	0	0	
0	0	0	0	0	0	1	1	
0/1 ext	1 Layer 3 id		User information layer 3 protocol = **ISO/IEC TR 9577**					7
0	1	1	0	1	0	1	1	
0 ext	ISO/IEC TR 9577 Initial Protocol Identification (IPI) (bits 8-2) = **Internet Protocol**							7a
0	1	1	0	0	1	1	0	
1 ext	IPI (bit1)	0	0	Spare	0	0	0	7b
1	1	0	0	0	0	0	0	

3 Example of information element coding for transport of bridged frames using the "Null encapsulation" over AAL5

is example shows how the B-LLI information element may be coded when bridged LAN mes are to be transported within an AAL service data unit without any multiprotocol capsulation ("Null Encapsulation — see Internet RFC draft, *Multiprotocol Encapsulation over TM/AAL5*). Note that no encoding for User Information Layer 3 protocol exists for SNAP lentifier. Therefore, the ISO/IEC TR 9577 Network Layer Protocol Identifier (NLPID) alue for SNAP is used as an escape to include the SNAP identifier in the B-LLI information ement. In this example, the SNAP identifier '00-80-C2-00-0A' indicates bridged FDDI frames without a preserved FCS. Similar coding principles apply for other kinds of bridged MAC frames and for routed frames which can only be identified using the SNAP convention (e.g., Appletalk™, XNS™, and IPX™).

Bits

8	7	6	5	4	3	2	1	Octet
Broadband low layer information								1
0	1	0	1	1	1	1	1	
Information element identifier								
1 ext	Coding Standard = CCITT Specified		IE Instruction Field = Not Significant					2
1	0	0	0	0	0	0	0	
Length of B-LLI contents								3
Length of B-LLI contents (continued) = 9 octets								4
0	0	0	0	0	0	0	0	
0	0	0	0	1	0	0	1	
0/1 ext	1 1 Layer 3 id		User information layer 3 protocol = ISO/IEC TR 9577					7
0	1	1	0	1	0	1	1	
0 ext	ISO/IEC TR 9577 Initial Protocol Identification (IPI) (bits 8-2) = SNAP Identifier							7a
0	1	0	0	0	0	0	0	
1 ext	IPI (bit1)	0	0	0 Spare	0	0	0	7b
1	1	0	0	0	0	0	0	
1 ext	0 0 SNAP ID		0	0	0 Spare	0	0	8
1	0	0	0	0	0	0	0	
SNAP Organization Unique Identifier (octet 1)								8.1
OUI octet 2								8.2
OUI octet 3 = IEEE 802.1								8.3
0	0	0	0	0	0	0	0	
1	0	0	0	0	0	0	0	
1	1	0	0	0	0	1	0	
PID (octet 1)								8.4
PID octet 2 = FDDI without preserved FCS								8.5
0	0	0	0	0	0	0	0	
0	0	0	0	1	0	1	0	

Appendix E

Differences with ITU-TS draft Recommendation Q.93B

The signaling protocol and procedures specified in this UNI Specification are based on ITU-T draft Recommendation Q.93B [29]. The output of the May 1993 ITU-TS Study Group 11 Meeting is used (ITU-TS SG 11 TD 11/2-8R1, TD 11/2-6R1, TD 11/2-63, TD 11/PL-92R1, TD 11/2-43, TD 11/2-18, TD 11/2-51, TD 11/2-62, TD 11/2-19, and TD 11/2-7R1).

Differences exist between this UNI Specification and ITU-T draft Recommendation Q.93B. This Appendix summarizes the differences between this UNI Specification and ITU-T draft Recommendation Q.93B. This Appendix is not represented as complete; implementors cannot assume that the combination of this Appendix and ITU-T draft Recommendation Q.93B will be the same as the main body of this UNI Specification. Not all minor editorial changes made are represented in this Appendix.

Items marked with a "*" are those items for which alignment of ITU-T draft Recommendation Q.93B with this UNI Specification is anticipated.

ITU-T draft Recommendation Q.93B [29] (Output of May 1993 ITU-TS SG 11 Meeting)	ATM Forum User-Network Interface Specification Version 3.0
1. General	5.1 General Introductory section specific to this UNI Specification.
2. Overview of Call/Bearer Control	5.2 Overview of Call Control No differences.
2.1 BISDN Call or Connection States	5.2.1 ATM Call States No differences.
2.1.1 Call States at the User Side of the Interface	5.2.1.1 Call States at the User Side of the Interface No differences.
2.1.1.1 Null (U0)	5.2.1.1.1 Null (U0) No differences.
2.1.1.2 Call Initiated (U1)	5.2.1.1.2 Call Initiated (U1) No differences.
2.1.1.3 Outgoing Call Proceeding (U3)	5.2.1.1.3 Outgoing Call Proceeding (U3) No differences.

2.1.1.4 Call Delivered (U4)	5.2.1.1.4 Call Delivered (U4) Not supported.
2.1.1.5 Call Present (U6)	5.2.1.1.5 Call Present (U6) No differences.
2.1.1.6 Call Received (U7)	5.2.1.1.6 Call Received (U7) Not supported.
2.1.1.7 Connect Request (U8)	5.2.1.1.7 Connect Request (U8) No differences.
2.1.1.8 Incoming Call Proceeding (U9)	5.2.1.1.8 Incoming Call Proceeding (U9) No differences.
2.1.1.9 Active (U10)	5.2.1.1.9 Active (U10) No differences.
2.1.1.10 Release Request (U11)	5.2.1.1.10 Release Request (U11) No differences.
2.1.1.11 Release Indication (U12)	5.2.1.1.11 Release Indication (U12) No differences.
2.1.2 Call States at the Network Side of the Interface	5.2.1.2 Call States at the Network Side of the Interface No differences.
2.1.2.1 Null (N0)	5.2.1.2.1 Null (N0) No differences.
2.1.2.2 Call Initiated (N1)	5.2.1.2.2 Call Initiated (N1) No differences.
2.1.2.3 Outgoing Call Proceeding (N3)	5.2.1.2.3 Outgoing Call Proceeding (N3) No differences.
2.1.2.4 Call Delivered (N4)	5.2.1.2.4 Call Delivered (N4) Not supported.
2.1.2.5 Call Present (N6)	5.2.1.2.5 Call Present (N6) No differences.
2.1.2.6 Call Received (N7)	5.2.1.2.6 Call Received (N7) Not supported.
2.1.2.7 Connect Request (N8)	5.2.1.2.7 Connect Request (N8) No differences.

2.1.2.8 Incoming Call Proceeding (N9)	5.2.1.2.8 Incoming Call Proceeding (N9) No differences.
2.1.2.9 Active (N10)	5.2.1.2.9 Active (N10) No differences.
2.1.2.10 Release Request (N11)	5.2.1.2.10 Release Request (N11) No differences.
2.1.2.11 Release Indication (N12)	5.2.1.2.11 Release Indication (N12) No differences.
2.1.2.12 Call Abort (N22)	5.2.1.2.12 Call Abort (N22) Not supported.
2.2 B-ISDN Call or Connection States Relating to Interworking Requirements	5.2.2 ATM Call States Relating to Interworking Requirements Not supported.
2.3 B-ISDN Call or Connection States for Global Call Reference	5.2.3 States Associated with the Global Call Reference No differences.
2.3.1 Call States at the User Side of the Interface	5.2.3.1 Call States at the User Side of the Interface No differences.
2.3.1.1 Null (Rest 0)	5.2.3.1.1 Null (Rest 0) No differences.
2.3.1.2 Restart Request (Rest 1)	5.2.3.1.2 Restart Request (Rest 1) No differences.
2.3.1.3 Restart (Rest 2)	5.2.3.1.3 Restart (Rest 2) No differences.
2.3.2 Call States at the Network Side of the Interface	5.2.3.2 Call States at the Network Side of the Interface No differences.
2.3.2.1 Null (Rest 0)	5.2.3.2.1 Null (Rest 0) No differences.
2.3.2.2 Restart Request (Rest 1)	5.2.3.2.2 Restart Request (Rest 1) No differences.
2.3.2.3 Restart (Rest 2)	5.2.3.2.3 Restart (Rest 2) No differences.

3 Message Functional Definitions and Contents	5.3 Message Functional Definitions and Contents User-network terminology modified. Information elements from codesets 5, 6, and 7 not supported.
3.1 Messages for B-ISDN Call and Connection Control	5.3.1 Messages for ATM Point-to-Point Call and Connection Control ALERTING message not supported.
3.1.1 ALERTING	5.3.1.1 ALERTING Not supported.
3.1.2 CALL PROCEEDING	5.3.1.2 CALL PROCEEDING Endpoint reference added for the point-to-multipoint procedures.
3.1.3 CONNECT	5.3.1.3 CONNECT AAL parameters maximum length modified. Endpoint reference added for the point-to-multipoint procedures.
3.1.4 CONNECT ACKNOWLEDGE	5.3.1.4 CONNECT ACKNOWLEDGE Sending of CONNECT ACKNOWLEDGE mandatory on the originating UNI.*
3.1.5 RELEASE	5.3.1.5 RELEASE No differences.
3.1.6 RELEASE COMPLETE	5.3.1.6 RELEASE COMPLETE No differences.

3.1.7 SETUP	5.3.1.7 SETUP
	ATM user cell rate minimum and maximum lengths modified.
	Called party number is mandatory in the network-to-user direction.
	Called party number minimum length is increased and maximum length is specified.
	Calling party number maximum length is specified.
	Connection identifier is mandatory in the network-to-user direction.
	End-to-end transit delay not supported.
	Broadband sending complete is optionally included in the user-to-network direction.
	Transit network selection maximum length specified.
	Endpoint reference added for the point-to-multipoint procedures.
3.1.8 STATUS	5.3.1.8 STATUS
	Endpoint reference added for the point-to-multipoint procedures.
	Endpoint state added for the point-to-multipoint procedures.
3.1.9 STATUS ENQUIRY	5.3.1.9 STATUS ENQUIRY
	Endpoint reference added for the point-to-multipoint procedures.
3.2 Messages for the Support of 64 kbit/s based ISDN Circuit Mode Services	5.3.2 Messages for the Support of 64 kbit/s based ISDN Circuit Mode Services
	Not supported.
3.3 Messages Related to Release 1 Supplementary Services	5.3.3 Messages Related to Release 1 Supplementary Services
	Not supported.
3.4 Messages used with the global call reference	5.3.4 Messages used with the global call reference
	No differences.
3.4.1 RESTART	5.3.4.1 RESTART
	Restart of all virtual channels within a virtual path not supported.

3.4.2 RESTART ACKNOWLEDGE	5.3.4.2 RESTART ACKNOWLEDGE Restart of all virtual channels within a virtual path not supported.
	5.3.5 Messages for Multipoint Call and Connection Control New messages added for the point-to-multipoint procedures. This material is not in ITU-T Q.93B.
4 General Message Format and Information Element Coding	5.4 General Message Format and Information Element Coding No differences.
4.1 Overview	5.4.1 Overview CCITT Recommendation Q.931 call reference structure supported.*
4.2 Protocol Discriminator	5.4.2 Protocol Discriminator No differences.
4.3 Call Reference	5.4.3 Call Reference CCITT Recommendation Q.931 call reference structure supported.*
4.4 Message Type and Message Length	5.4.4 Message Type and Message Length No differences.
4.4.1 Message Type	5.4.4.1 Message Type The following message types are not supported: ALERTING PROGRESS SETUP ACKNOWLEDGE RESUME RESUME ACKNOWLEDGE RESUME REJECT SUSPEND SUSPEND ACKNOWLEDGE SUSPEND REJECT INFORMATION NOTIFY Escape to national specific message types is not supported. Explicit indication of message error handling procedures not supported.
4.4.2 Message Length	5.4.4.2 Message Length No differences.

4.5 Variable Length Information Elements	5.4.5 Variable Length Information Elements No differences.
4.5.1 Coding Rules	5.4.5.1 Coding Rules Locking shift repetition rules not supported. Non-locking shift repetition rules not supported. Maximum length and maximum number of occurrences are specified for each supported information element. Coding standard for national standard not supported. Explicit indication of information element error handling procedures not supported.
4.5.2 Extension of Codesets	5.4.5.2 Extension of Codesets Not supported.
4.5.3 Broadband Locking Shift Procedures	5.4.5.3 Broadband Locking Shift Procedures Not supported. Recognition of Broadband locking shift information element is supported.
4.5.4 Broadband Non-Locking Shift Procedures	5.4.5.4 Broadband Non-Locking Shift Procedures Not supported. Recognition of Broadband non-locking shift information element is supported.
4.5.5 ATM Adaptation Layer Parameters	5.4.5.5 ATM Adaptation Layer Parameters AAL type 2 not supported. AAL type is 8 bits.* Renamed Receive Maximum CPCS-SDU size subfield to Backward Maximum CPCS-SDU size.* Added Forward Maximum CPCS-SDU size subfield.*

4.5.6 ATM User Cell Rate	5.4.5.6 ATM User Cell Rate
	
	Traffic descriptor subfields added:
	    Forward Sustainable Cell Rate (CLP=0)
	    Backward Sustainable Cell Rate (CLP=0)
	    Forward Sustainable Cell Rate (CLP=0+1)
	    Backward Sustainable Cell Rate (CLP=0+1)
	    Forward Maximum Burst Size (CLP=0)
	    Backward Maximum Burst Size (CLP=0)
	    Forward Maximum Burst Size (CLP=0+1)
	    Backward Maximum Burst Size (CLP=0+1)
	    Best Effort Indicator
	    Traffic Management Options Identifier
	
	Traffic descriptor identifier is 8 bits in length.*
	
	Forward Peak Cell Rate (CLP=0) is an optional subfield.*
	
	Backward Peak Cell Rate (CLP=0) is an optional subfield.*

4.5.7 Broadband Bearer Capability	5.4.5.7 Broadband Bearer Capability BCOB-D bearer class not supported. BCOB-C bearer class added.* Bits 7-6 of Octet 5a made spare.* Point-to-multipoint user plane connection configuration added.
4.5.8 Broadband High Layer Information	5.4.5.8 Broadband High Layer Information Coding of Vendor-specific application identifier defined.*
4.5.9 Broadband Low Layer Information	5.4.5.9 Broadband Low Layer Information User information layer 1 octet group not supported. Coding of ISO/IEC TR-9577 NLPIDs within the B-LLI defined. Coding for SNAP ID octet group added.
4.5.10 Call State	5.4.5.10 Call State Call states U2, N2, U4, N4, U7, N7, U15, N15, U17, N17, N22, U25, and N25 not supported.

4.5.11 Called Party Number	5.4.5.11 Called Party Number
	
	Only two combinations of Type of Number and Addressing/Numbering Plan Identification are supported:
	    Unknown/ISO NSAP
	    International number/ISDN number plan (E.164)

4.5.12 Called Party Subaddress	5.4.5.12 Called Party Subaddress User-specified subaddress not supported.

4.5.13 Calling Party Number	5.4.5.13 Calling Party Number
	
	Only two combinations of Type of Number and Addressing/Numbering Plan Identification are supported:
	    Unknown/ISO NSAP
	    International number/ISDN number plan (E.164)
	
	Presentation indicator codepoint, "Number not available due to interworking" changed to "Number not available".*

4.5.14 Calling Party Subaddress	5.4.5.14 Calling Party Subaddress User-specified subaddress not supported.
4.5.15 Cause	5.4.5.15 Cause Network-specific cause value 23 added. Cause value 104 changed to 93.* New cause value 104 defined.*
4.5.16 Connection Identifier	5.4.5.16 Connection Identifier VP-associated signaling not supported. Preferred/exclusive indication "Exclusive VPCI/any VCI" not supported. The first octet of the VPCI field is coded to "00000000". The second octet of the VPCI field is numerically equal to the VPI value used. VCI values 16-31 are reserved for present or future use by this UNI Specification.
4.5.17 End-to-End Transit Delay	5.4.5.17 End-to-End Transit Delay Not supported.

4.5.18 Quality of Service Parameter	5.4.5.18 Quality of Service Parameter Network specific coding standard is used. Forward QOS class field is one octet.* Backward QOS class field is one octet.* QOS classes 0-4 are supported.
4.5.19 Broadband Repeat Indicator	5.4.5.19 Broadband Repeat Indicator No differences.
4.5.20 Restart Indicator	5.4.5.20 Restart Indicator Class codepoint "indicated VPC" not supported.
4.5.21 Broadband Sending Complete	5.4.5.21 Broadband Sending Complete No differences.
4.5.22 Transit Network Selection	5.4.5.22 Transit Network Selection Only one combination of Type of Network Identification and Network Identification Plan is supported: National network identification/ Carrier identification code
4.6 Information Elements for the Support of 64kbit/s Based ISDN Circuit Mode Services	5.4.6 Information Elements for Interworking with 64kbit/s Based ISDN Not supported.
4.7 Information Elements for Supplementary Services	5.4.7 Information Elements for Supplementary Services Not supported.
	5.4.8 ATM Forum Specified Information Elements New information elements added for the point-to-multipoint procedures. This material is not in ITU-T Q.93B.
5 B-ISDN Call/Connection Control Procedures	5.5 B-ISDN Call/Connection Control Procedures for ATM Point-to-Point Calls Point-to-multipoint access configurations are not supported. Signaling virtual channel uses VPI=0, VCI=5. Meta-Signaling is not supported. Specification and Description Language (SDL) diagrams are not included.
5.1 Call/Connection Establishment at the Originating Interface	5.5.1 Call/Connection Establishment at the Originating Interface No differences.

5.1.1 Call/Connection Request	5.5.1.1 Call/Connection Request CCITT Recommendation Q.931 call reference structure is supported.* Sending complete is optionally included by the user. Retransmission of SETUP is optional.
5.1.2 Connection Identifier (VPCI/VCI) Allocation/Selection	5.5.1.2 Connection Identifier (VPCI/VCI) Allocation/Selection No differences.
5.1.2.1 Connection Identifier Allocation/ Selection - Origination	5.5.1.2.1 Connection Identifier Allocation/ Selection - Origination VP-associated signaling is not supported. The network side always allocates the VPCI/VCI for the connection. The user does not include the Connection identifier in the SETUP message. Appropriate error handling procedures are defined.
5.1.2.1.1 Associated Signaling	
5.1.2.1.2 Non-Associated Signaling	
5.1.2.2 Use of VPCIs	5.5.1.2.2 Use of VPCIs VPCI values are numerically equal to the VPI value. VP cross connects between the user and the network and non-facility-associated signaling are not supported.
5.1.2.3 VCI Range	5.5.1.2.3 VPCI and VCI Ranges VCI values 16-31 are reserved for present or future use by this UNI Specification. VPCI range added.
5.1.3 QOS and Traffic Parameters Selection Procedures	5.5.1.3 QoS and Traffic Parameters Selection Procedures Error procedure for unsupported combination of traffic parameters added.
5.1.4 Invalid Call/Connection Control Information	5.5.1.4 Invalid Call/Connection Control Information No differences.
5.1.5 Call/Connection Proceeding	5.5.1.5 Call/Connection Proceeding Sending a CALL PROCEEDING message is optional. Consistent with Section 5.1.10 of ITU-T Recommendation Q.93B.

5.1.6 Call/Connection Confirmation Indication	5.5.1.6 Call/Connection Confirmation Indication Not supported.
5.1.7 Call/Connection Acceptance	5.5.1.7 Call/Connection Acceptance Sending a CONNECT ACKNOWLEDGE message is mandatory.*
5.1.8 Call/Connection Rejection	5.5.1.8 Call/Connection Rejection No differences.
5.1.9 Transit Network Selection	5.5.1.9 Transit Network Selection No differences.
5.1.10 Extensions for Symmetric Call Operation	5.5.1.10 Extensions for Symmetric Call Operation Extensions to allow optional sending of the CALL PROCEEDING message is supported in Section 5.5.1.5.
5.2 Call/Connection Establishment at the Destination Interface - Point-to-Point Access Configuration Call Offering	5.5.2 Call/Connection Establishment at the Destination Interface - Point-to-Point Access Configuration Call Offering No differences.
5.2.1 Incoming Call/Connection Request	5.5.2.1 Incoming Call/Connection Request Overlap receiving not supported. Retransmission of SETUP is optional.
5.2.2 Address and Compatibility Check	5.5.2.2 Address and Compatibility Check Compatibility checking is implementation dependent.
5.2.3 Connection Identifier (VPCI/VCI) Allocation/Selection - Destination	5.5.2.3 Connection Identifier (VPCI/VCI) Allocation/Selection - Destination VP-associated signaling is not supported. The network side always allocates the VPCI/VCI for the connection.
5.2.4 QOS and Traffic Parameter Selection Procedures	5.5.2.4 QoS and Traffic Parameter Selection Procedures No differences.
5.2.5 Call/Connection Confirmation	5.5.2.5 Call/Connection Confirmation
5.2.5.1 Response to En-bloc SETUP or Completion of Overlap Receiving	5.5.2.5.1 Response to SETUP Overlap receiving not supported.

	5.5.2.5.1.1 Procedures when the User is an ATM Endpoint
	This section is equivalent to Section 5.2.5.1 of ITU-T Recommendation Q.93B.
	ALERTING message not supported.
	New error procedure using network-specific cause 23, "user rejects all calls with calling line identification restriction (CLIR)", added.
	5.5.2.5.1.2 Procedures when the User is not an ATM Endpoint
5.2.5.2 Receipt of CALL PROCEEDING and ALERTING	5.5.2.5.2 Receipt of CALL PROCEEDING
	ALERTING message not supported.
5.2.5.3 Called User Clearing During Incoming Call Establishment	5.5.2.5.3 Called User Clearing During Incoming Call Establishment
	Timer T301 not supported.
5.2.5.4 Call Failure	5.5.2.5.4 Call Failure
	Retransmission of SETUP is optional.
	ALERTING message not supported.
	Timer T301 not supported.
5.2.6 Call/Connection Acceptance	5.5.2.6 Call/Connection Acceptance
	ALERTING message not supported.
5.2.7 Active Indication	5.5.2.7 Active Indication
	Timer T301 not supported.
5.3 Call/Connection Establishment at the Destination - Point-to-Multipoint Access Arrangement Call Offering	5.5.3 Call/Connection Establishment at the Destination - Point-to-Multipoint Access Arrangement Call Offering
	Not supported.
5.4 Call/Connection Clearing	5.5.4 Call/Connection Clearing
	No differences.
5.4.1 Terminology	5.5.4.1 Terminology
	CCITT Recommendation Q.931 call reference structure is supported.*
5.4.2 Exception Conditions	5.5.4.2 Exception Conditions
	No differences.
5.4.3 Clearing Initiated by the User	5.5.4.3 Clearing Initiated by the User
	CCITT Recommendation Q.931 call reference structure is supported.*

5.4.4 Clearing Initiated by the Network	5.5.4.4 Clearing Initiated by the Network No differences.
5.4.5 Clear Collision	5.5.4.5 Clear Collision No differences.
5.5 Restart Procedures	5.5.5 Restart Procedures Restart of all virtual channels within a virtual path not supported.
5.5.1 Sending RESTART	5.5.5.1 Sending RESTART Restart of all virtual channels within a virtual path not supported.
5.5.2 Receipt of RESTART	5.5.5.2 Receipt of RESTART Restart of all virtual channels within a virtual path not supported.
5.6 Handling of Error Conditions	5.5.6 Handling of Error Conditions No differences.
5.6.1 Protocol Discriminator Error	5.5.6.1 Protocol Discriminator Error No differences.
5.6.2 Message too Short	5.5.6.2 Message too Short No differences.
5.6.3 Call Reference Error	5.5.6.3 Call Reference Error No differences.
	5.5.6.3.1 Invalid Call Reference Format CCITT Recommendation Q.931 call reference structure is supported.*
	5.5.6.3.2 Call Reference Procedural Errors CCITT Recommendation Q.931 call reference structure is supported.*
5.6.4 Message Type or Message Sequence Errors	5.5.6.4 Message Type or Message Sequence Errors Sending of STATUS ENQUIRY for this error not supported. Exception condition for unexpected RELEASE message added.*
5.6.5 Message Length Error	5.5.6.5 Message Length Error Error handling modified.*

5.6.6 General Information Element Errors	5.5.6.6 General Information Element Errors Locking and non-locking shift procedures not supported.
5.6.6.1 Information Element Sequence	5.5.6.6.1 Information Element Sequence No differences.
5.6.6.2 Duplicated Information Elements	5.5.6.6.2 Duplicated Information Elements No differences.
5.6.7 Mandatory Information Element Error	5.5.6.7 Mandatory Information Element Error No differences.
5.6.7.1 Mandatory Information Element Missing	5.5.6.7.1 Mandatory Information Element Missing No differences.
5.6.7.2 Mandatory Information Element Content Error	5.5.6.7.2 Mandatory Information Element Content Error Explicit indication of information element error handling procedure not supported.
5.6.8 Non-Mandatory Information Element Errors	5.5.6.8 Non-Mandatory Information Element Errors Explicit indication of information element error handling procedure not supported.
5.6.8.1 Unrecognized Information Element	5.5.6.8.1 Unrecognized Information Element No differences.
5.6.8.2 Non-Mandatory Information Element Content Error	5.5.6.8.2 Non-Mandatory Information Element Content Error No differences.
5.6.8.3 Unexpected Recognized Information Element	5.5.6.8.3 Unexpected Recognized Information Element No differences.
5.6.9 Signaling AAL Reset	5.5.6.9 Signaling AAL Reset Calls in the establishment phase are cleared. Call states N4, N7, U4, and U7 not supported.
5.6.10 Signaling AAL Failure	5.5.6.10 Signaling AAL Failure User-side procedures when T309 not implemented defined.*
5.6.11 Status Enquiry Procedure	5.5.6.11 Status Enquiry Procedure No differences.

5.6.12 Receiving a STATUS Message	5.5.6.12 Receiving a STATUS Message No differences.
5.7 Forward Compatibility Procedures	5.5.7 Forward Compatibility Procedures Not supported.
6. Provision of 64 kbit/s based Circuit Mode ISDN Services in B-ISDN and Signaling Interworking between N-ISDN and B-ISDN	Not supported.
	5.6 Call/Connection Control for Multipoint Calls This material is not in ITU-T Q.93B.
7 List of Timers	5.7 List of Timers No differences.
7.1 Timers in the Network Side	5.7.1 Timers in the Network Side Timers for the provision of 64 kbit/s based circuit mode ISDN services in B-ISDN and signaling interworking between N-ISDN and B-ISDN not supported. Timer T301 not supported. Retransmission of SETUP is optional. For SAAL disconnection, calls in the Active state are not lost. Timer T398 added for the point-to-multipoint procedures. This material is not in ITU-T Q.93B. Timer T399 added for the point-to-multipoint procedures. This material is not in ITU-T Q.93B.
7.2 Timers in the User Side	5.7.2 Timers in the User Side Timers for the provision of 64 kbit/s based circuit mode ISDN services in B-ISDN and signaling interworking between N-ISDN and B-ISDN not supported. Retransmission of SETUP is optional. For SAAL disconnection, calls in the Active state are not lost. Timer T310 is added.* Timer T398 added for the point-to-multipoint procedures. This material is not in ITU-T Q.93B. Timer T399 added for the point-to-multipoint procedures. This material is not in ITU-T Q.93B.

8 Primitives	Not included.
	5.8 Address Registration This material is not in ITU-T Q.93B.
	References Similar material is in Appendix I of ITU-T Q.93B.
Annex A Specification and Description Language (SDL) Diagrams	Not supported.
	Annex A Guidelines for Use of ATM Address Formats This material is not in ITU-T Q.93B.
Annex B Compatibility Checking	Annex B Compatibility Checking Compatibility checking is implementation dependent.
Annex C Broadband Low Layer Information Negotiation	Annex C B-LLI Negotiation No differences.
C.1 General	C.1 General Text describing the expected implementation of B-LLI negotiation added.
C.2 Low Layer Compatibility Notification to the Called User	C.2 B-LLI Notification to the Called User No differences.
C.3 B-LLI Negotiation Between Users	C.3 B-LLI Negotiation Between Users No differences.
C.4 Alternate Requested Values	C.4 Alternate Requested Values Relationship of B-LLI negotiation procedures to point-to-multipoint procedures defined. Procedure for user incompatibility with B-LLI added.
Annex D Transit Network Selection	Annex D Transit Network Selection Clarifying text based on ANSI T1.607 has been added.
D.1 Selection not Supported	D.1 Selection not Supported No differences.
D.2 Selection Supported	D.2 Selection Supported Specification of more than one transit network is not supported.

Annex E: Mapping Functions to Support 64 kbit/s Based Circuit Mode ISDN Services in B-ISDN and Signaling Interworking between N-ISDN and B-ISDN	Not supported.
	Annex E Cause Definitions This material is not in ITU-T Q.93B.
Annex F ATM Adaptation Layer Parameters Indication and Negotiation	Annex F ATM Adaptation Layer Parameters Indication and Negotiation No differences.
F.1 General	F.1 General No differences.
F.2 ATM Adaptation Layer Parameter Indication in the SETUP Message	F.2 ATM Adaptation Layer Parameter Indication in the SETUP Message User defined AAL indication in the SETUP message added.* Modified Receive Maximum CPCS-SDU size negotiation procedures.*
F.3 ATM Adaptation Layer Indication in the CONNECT Message	F.3 Maximum CPCS-SDU Size Negotiation Relationship of AAL parameters negotiation to point-to-multipoint procedures defined. CPCS-SDU size negotiation procedures modified.* Cause value 104 changed to 93.* User defined AAL indication in the CONNECT message added.*
F.4 ATM Adaptation Layer Negotiation	F.4 MID Size Negotiation Cause value 104 changed to 93.*
	F.5 Use of Forward and Backward Maximum CPCS-SDU Size by the AAL Entity * Additional endpoint procedures for Forward and Backward Maximum CPCS-SDU size defined.
Annex G Signaling for Semi-Permanent Connection Control	Not supported.

Appendix I Definitions, Abbreviations, and References	Similar material is in the References section and Appendix F of the UNI Interface Specification.
	Appendix A Quality of Service Guidelines This material is not in ITU-T Q.93B.
	Appendix B Conformance Examples in a Traffic Contract This material is not in ITU-T Q.93B.
	Appendix C Multipoint State Machines This material is not in ITU-T Q.93B.
	Appendix D Example Signaling Codings This material is not in ITU-T Q.93B.
	Appendix E Differences with ITU-T draft Recommendation Q.93B This material is not in ITU-T Q.93B.
	Appendix F Glossary Similar material is in Appendix I of ITU-T Q.93B.

Appendix F

Glossary

AAL Connection

Association established by the AAL between two or more next higher layer entities.

Assigned cell

Cell that provides a service to an upper layer entity or ATM Layer Management entity (ATMM-entity).

Asynchronous time division multiplexing

A multiplexing technique in which a transmission capability is organized in a priori unassigned time slots. The time slots are assigned to cells upon request of each application's instantaneous real need.

Asynchronous transfer mode (ATM)

A transfer mode in which the information is organized into cells. It is asynchronous in the sense that the recurrence of cells containing information from an individual user is not necessarily periodic.

ATM Peer to Peer Connection

A virtual channel connection (VCC) or a virtual path connection (VPC).

ATM User-User Connection

An association established by the ATM Layer to support communication between two or more ATM service users (i.e., between two or more next higher layer entities or between two or more ATMM-entities). The communication over an ATM Layer connection may be either bidirectional or unidirectional. The same Virtual Channel Identifier (VCI) is used for both directions of a connection at an interface.

ATM Layer link

A section of an ATM Layer connection between two adjacent active ATM Layer entities (ATM-entities).

ATM link

A virtual path link (VPL) or a virtual channel link (VCL).

ATM Traffic Descriptor

A generic list of traffic parameters that can be used to capture the intrinsic traffic characteristics of a requested ATM connection.

Broadband

A service or system requiring transmission channels capable of supporting rates greater than the Integrated Services Digital Network (ISDN) primary rate.

Broadband access

An ISDN access capable of supporting one or more broadband services.

Call

A call is an association between two or more users or between a user and a network entity that is established by the use of network capabilities. This association may have zero or more connections.

Cell

ATM Layer protocol data unit (PDU).

Cell delay variation (CDV)

A quantification of cell clumping for a connection. The cell clumping CDV (y_k), is defined as the difference between a cell's expected reference arrival time (c_k) and its actual arrival time (a_k). The expected reference arrival time (c_k) of cell k of a specific connection is max [$c_{\{k-1\}}$ + T, a_k]. T is the reciprocal of the negotiated peak cell rate.

Cell header

ATM Layer protocol control information.

Cell transfer delay

The transit delay of an ATM cell successfully passed between two designated boundary.

Connection

An ATM connection consists of the concatenation of ATM Layer links in order to provide an end-to-end information transfer capability to access points.

Connection admission control (CAC)

The procedure used to decide if a request for an ATM connection can be accepted based on the attributes of both the requested connection and the existing connections.

Connection endpoint (CE)

A terminator at one end of a layer connection within a SAP.

Connection endpoint identifier (CEI)

Identifier of a CE that can be used to identify the connection at a SAP.

Corresponding entities

Peer entities with a lower layer connection among them.

Demultiplexing

A function performed by a layer entity that identifies and separates SDUs from a single connection to more than one connection.

End system (ES)

A system where an ATM connection is terminated or initiated. An originating end system initiates the ATM connection, and a terminating end system terminates the ATM connection. OAM cells may be generated and received.

Header

Protocol control information located at the beginning of a protocol data unit.

Fairness

As related to Generic Flow Control (GFC), fairness is defined as meeting all the agreed quality of service (QOS) requirements, by controlling the order of service for all active connections.

Interface data

The unit of information transferred to/from the upper layer in a single interaction across the SAP. Each Interface Data Unit (IDU) contains interface control information and may also contain the whole or part of the SDU.

Intermediate system (IS)

A system that provides forwarding functions or relaying functions or both for a specific ATM connection. OAM cells may be generated and received.

Layer entity

An active element within a layer.

Layer function

A part of the activity of the layer entities.

Layer service

A capability of a layer and the layers beneath it that is provided to the upper layer entities at the boundary between that layer and the next higher layer.

Layer user data

Data transferred between corresponding entities on behalf of the upper layer or layer management entities for which they are providing services.

Metasignaling

ATM Layer Management (LM) process that manages different types of signaling and possibly semipermanent virtual channels (VCs), including the assignment, removal and checking of VCs.

Metasignaling VCs

The standardized VCs that convey metasignaling information across a User-Network Interface (UNI).

Multiplexing

A function within a layer that interleaves the information from multiple connections into one connection.

Multipoint access

User access in which more than one terminal equipment (TE) is supported by a single network termination.

Multipoint-to-Point Connection

A Point-to-Multipoint Connection may have zero bandwidth from the Root Node to the Leaf Nodes, and non-zero return bandwidth from the Leaf Nodes to the Root Node. Such a connection is also known as a Multipoint-to-Point Connection.

Multipoint-to-Multipoint Connection

A Multipoint-to-Multipoint Connection is a collection of associated ATM VC or VP links, and their associated endpoint nodes, with the following properties:

1. All N nodes in the connection, called Endpoints, serve as a Root Node in a Point-to-Multipoint connection to all of the (N-1) remaining endpoints.

2. Each of the endpoints on the connection can send information directly to any other endpoint, but the receiving endpoint cannot distinguish which of the endpoints is sending information without additional (e.g., higher layer) information.

Network Node Interface (NNI)

The interface between two network nodes.

Operation and Maintenance (OAM) cell

A cell that contains ATM LM information. It does not form part of the upper layer information transfer.

Peak Cell Rate

At the PHY Layer SAP of a point-to-point VCC, the Peak Cell Rate R_p is the inverse of the minimum inter-arrival time T_0 of the request to send an ATM_SDU.

Peer entities

Entities within the same layer.

Physical Layer (PHY) connection

An association established by the PHY between two or more ATM-entities. A PHY connection consists of the concatenation of PHY links in order to provide an end-to-end transfer capability to PHY SAPs.

Point-to-Multipoint Connection

A Point-to-Multipoint Connection is a collection of associated ATM VC or VP links, with associated endpoint nodes, with the following properties:

1. One ATM link, called the Root Link, serves as the root in a simple tree topology. When the Root node sends information, all of the remaining nodes on the connection, called Leaf Nodes, receive copies of the information.

2. Each of the Leaf Nodes on the connection can send information directly to the Root Node. The Root Node cannot distinguish which Leaf is sending information without additional (higher layer) information. (See note below for Phase 1.)

3. The Leaf Nodes can not communicate directly to each other with this connection type.

Note - Phase 1 signalling does not support traffic sent from a Leaf to the Root.

Point-to-point connection

A connection with only two endpoints.

Primitive

An abstract, implementation independent, interaction between a layer service user and a layer service provider.

Protocol

A set of rules and formats (semantic and syntactic) that determines the communication behavior of layer entities in the performance of the layer functions.

Protocol control information

Information exchanged between corresponding entities, using a lower layer connection, to coordinate their joint operation.

Protocol data unit (PDU)

A unit of data specified in a layer protocol and consisting of protocol control information and layer user data.

Relaying

A function of a layer by means of which a layer entity receives data from a corresponding entity and transmits it to another corresponding entity.

Segment

A single ATM link or group of interconnected ATM links of an ATM connection.

Semipermanent Connection

A connection established via a service order or via network management.

Service access point (SAP)

The point at which an entity of a layer provides services to its LM entity or to an entity of the next higher layer.

Service data unit (SDU)

A unit of interface information whose identity is preserved from one end of a layer connection to the other.

Shaping descriptor

N ordered pairs of GCRA parameters (I,L) used to define the negotiated traffic shape of an APP connection.

Source Traffic Descriptor

A set of traffic parameters belonging to the ATM Traffic Descriptor used during the connection set-up to capture the intrinsic traffic characteristics of the connection requested by the source.

Sublayer

A logical sub-division of a layer.

Switched connection

A connection established via signaling.

Symmetric Connection

A connection with the same bandwidth value specified for both directions.

Traffic parameter

A parameter for specifying a particular traffic aspect of a connection.

Trailer

Protocol control information located at the end of a PDU.

Transit delay

The time difference between the instant at which the first bit of a PDU crosses one designated boundary, and the instant at which the last bit of the same PDU crosses a second designated boundary.

Unassigned cells

A cell identified by a standardized virtual path identifier (VPI) and virtual channel identifier (VCI) value, which has been generated and does not carry information from an application using the ATM Layer service.

Virtual channel (VC)

A communication channel that provides for the sequential unidirectional transport of ATM cells.

Virtual channel connection (VCC)

A concatenation of VCLs that extends between the points where the ATM service users access the ATM Layer. The points at which the ATM cell payload is passed to, or received from, the users of the ATM Layer (i.e., a higher layer or ATMM-entity) for processing signify the endpoints of a VCC. VCCs are unidirectional.

Virtual channel link (VCL)

A means of unidirectional transport of ATM cells between the point where a VCI value is assigned and the point where that value is translated or removed.

Virtual channel switch

A network element that connects VCLs. It terminates VPCs and translates VCI values. It is directed by Control Plane functions and relays the cells of a VC.

Virtual path (VP)

A unidirectional logical association or bundle of VCs.

Virtual path connection (VPC)

A concatenation of VPLs between virtual path Terminators (VPTs). VPCs are unidirectional.

Virtual path link (VPL)

A means of unidirectional transport of ATM cells between the point where a VPI value is assigned and the point where that value is translated or removed.

Virtual path switch

A network element that connects VPLs. It translates VPI (not VCI) values and is directed by Control Plane functions. It relays the cells of the VP.

Virtual path terminator (VPT)

A system that unbundles the VCs of a VP for independent processing of each VC.